THE GREAT CREDIT CRASH

THE GREAT CREDIT CRASH

EDITED BY MARTIJN KONINGS

VERSO
London • New York

First published by Verso 2010
© the collection Verso 2010
© individual contributions the contributors

1 3 5 7 9 10 8 6 4 2

Verso
UK: 6 Meard Street, London W1F 0EG
US: 20 Jay Street, Suite 1010, Brooklyn, NY 11201
www.versobooks.com

Verso is the imprint of New Left Books

ISBN-13: 978-1-84467-433-6 (hbk)
ISBN-13: 978-1-84467-431-2 (pbk)

British Library Cataloguing in Publication Data
A catalogue record for this book is available from the British Library

Library of Congress Cataloging-in-Publication Data
A catalog record for this book is available from the Library of Congress

Typeset in Sabon by Hewer Text UK Ltd, Edinburgh
Printed in the US by Maple Vail

CONTENTS

CONTENTS

Global Dimensions

Politics

ACKNOWLEDGEMENTS

I would like to thank Gavin Fridell for helpful discussions; David Primrose for excellent research assistance; and Bhavani for letting me edit this book as we were relocating halfway across the globe.

Several chapters in this book draw on previously published material: Martijn Konings, "Rethinking Neoliberalism and the Subprime Crisis: Beyond the Re-regulation Agenda," *Competition and Change*, 2009, 13(2) (Maney Publishing); James Livingston, "Their Great Depression and Ours," *Challenge*, 2009, 52(3) (M. E. Sharpe); Peter Gowan, "Crisis in the Heartland," *New Left Review*, 2009, II/55; Thomas Ferguson and Robert Johnson, "Too Big to Bail: The 'Paulson Put,' Presidential Politics, and the Global Financial Meltdown: Part I: From Shadow Financial System to Shadow Bailout," *International Journal of Political Economy*, 2009, 38(1), and "Too Big to Bail: The 'Paulson Put,' Presidential Politics, and the Global Financial Meltdown: Part II: Fatal Reversal—Single Payer and Back," *International Journal of Political Economy*, 2009, 38(2) (M. E. Sharpe); Anastasia Nesvetailova and Ronen Palan, "A Very North Atlantic Credit Crunch: Geopolitical Implications of the Crisis," *International Affairs*, 2008, 62(1); William Greider, "Dismantling the Temple," *The Nation*, 15 July 2009; Leo Panitch and Sam Gindin, "The Current Crisis: A Socialist Perspective," *Socialist Project e-bulletin*, No. 142, and *Studies in Political Economy*, 2009, 83 (Spring).

Permission is gratefully acknowledged in all these cases.

Sadly, as this volume was being prepared, Peter Gowan passed away. Peter was a Professor of International Relations at London Metropolitan University and a longtime contributor to as well as editorial board member of *New Left Review*. His book *The Global Gamble*, which appeared in 1999, stands as one of the most profound analyses of American power that we have. But Peter was known for being more than just an incisive political observer. In the words of his close friend Tariq Ali, he was "the most generous and steadfast of comrades. Peter was a socialist intellectual of the highest calibre, combining enormous energy and independence of mind with a truly collective spirit." The piece that is printed in this volume presents a uniquely penetrating analysis of the financial crisis and demonstrates how much Peter's insight will be missed in the years to come.

INTRODUCTION

The Great Credit Crash will go into history as the most serious crisis of global capitalism since the Crash of 1929 and the Great Depression of the 1930s. Even if the crisis has bottomed out—which at the time of writing is far from clear—it has already fundamentally changed the contours of American and global capitalism. Moreover, it will continue to wreak havoc on the lives of people around the globe long after the pundits declare the world economy to have emerged from its protracted slump. They have lost houses, jobs and pension savings; they have seen their opportunities for advancement dwindle and their children's life chances reduced to levels unknown for more than half a century.

It took some time for the full dimensions of the Credit Crash to become apparent. For the first six months, most observers were not quite sure what they were dealing with. While there was widespread agreement that a particularly profitable phase of financial growth had come to an end, most comparisons were with the stock market crash of 1987 and the dot-com meltdown at the turn of the century—events whose effects, while dramatic, did not reverberate so far as to cause a wholesale freezing of the financial system. Metaphors used to portray the situation were mostly pitched at the psychological level, emphasizing the lack of confidence and collective anxiety that had gripped markets as the major obstacles to recovery.

During the first half of 2008, the crisis began to take on entirely new dimensions. It gradually appeared that, rather than merely having to weather a period of illiquid markets, some of the world's most venerable financial institutions were heading for full-blown insolvency. Many commentators began to consider the possibility that we were witnessing not a relatively localized financial meltdown, but the onset of a drawn-out economic depression that could well end up threatening the very foundations of capitalist order. Financial journalists increasingly resorted to the language of natural catastrophe (with "perfect storm," "tsunami" and "hurricane" featuring prominently), as if to suggest that the forces of disintegration had begun to overpower society's control over economic life.

The Great Credit Crash—a.k.a. the Credit Crunch, the Subprime Crisis or the Global Financial Crisis—was now born, and the search for answers and solutions began. Comparisons with the Great Depression of the 1930s became commonplace. Indeed, the experience of early twentieth-century capitalism has emerged as a key point of reference in public debate, serving not only as a source of causal analogies but equally as a mirror in which to examine and diagnose the moral and social warts of our age. But if public debate was now forced to go beyond the technicalities of financial markets to encompass the social, political and moral aspects of what had gone wrong, the dominant assessments of our subprime predicament have remained rather superficial.

At the heart of these discourses is the notion that an era of political irresponsibility has come to an end: the Crisis is widely viewed as representing the breakdown of an economic model characterized by the abdication of public control over financial life—i.e. the regulatory indifference that allowed brokers to foist expensive mortgages on underprivileged Americans and investment managers to recklessly pour massive amounts of "other people's money" into markets for lemons. We are all Keynesians again, aware of the need for government to regulate the unruly dynamics of free markets—so is the message. After three decades in which the mantra of "less state, more market" reigned supreme, advocating for the proper regulation of economic activities has become respectable again.

The shallowness of this new Keynesian discourse should have been apparent from the very ease with which an ideological climate shaped so profoundly by decades of neoliberal hegemony gave way to a new common sense concerning the benefits of prudent regulation. Almost overnight, heterodox economists such as Joseph Stiglitz and Paul Krugman, who for years had been portrayed as brilliant theoreticians who should be kept out of the real-world business of policymaking, sounded quite conventional in their concerns about deregulation and their calls for re-regulation.

The change in political climate was already well underway during the last days of the Bush administration but has by now consolidated to give rise to high hopes for a "new New Deal." While announcing his administration's proposal for the reform of the American financial system, President Obama put the need for a rebalancing of government and market front and centre: "It is an indisputable fact that one of the most significant contributors to our economic downturn was an unraveling of major financial institutions and the lack of adequate regulatory structures to prevent abuse and excess."[1] This diagnosis of America's economic malaise corresponded to the remedies proposed by his administration in the Treasury's report on "Financial Regulatory Reform," which outlined several ways to enhance the ability of regulators to supervise the financial services industry. If Obama was at pains to stress that his mission was "not to stifle the market, but to strengthen its ability to unleash . . . creativity and innovation," to those who saw his re-regulation program as a perilous exercise in governmental overreach, he pointed out that the consequences of a failure to ensure transparency, fairness and prudence had been nothing short of catastrophic.[2] If the market cannot be expected to work its magic while being stifled by regulation, the Great Credit Crash had made abundantly clear that government needs to define and police the rules of the game in order to ensure that market participants direct their efforts to the creation of wealth rather than the construction of "Ponzi-schemes" and other parasitical practices.

Such themes and interpretations have by no means remained confined to the event-driven spheres of journalism and policy-making, but have penetrated deeply into realms of public debate that should offer more opportunity for analysis and contemplation. The recent period has seen a veritable torrent of publications dealing with the causes, consequences and significance of the Credit Crunch. For all their differences, these contributions have converged on a common theme: the lack of regulation and the resulting acceleration of irresponsible speculation. Scholarly

---

1   "President Obama's Speech on Financial Regulatory Overhaul," http://www.bloomberg.com.
2   Ibid.

books tend to argue that lax and misguided policies allowed financial innovation to proceed unchecked, while the more anecdotal literature details the ways in which the unscrupulous lenders and traders who were thus given free rein exploited this lack of regulatory supervision. But neither branch of literature has offered readers much beyond the kind of information that can be gleaned from the headlines of newspapers, magazines and talk shows: ineffective regulation, out-of-control markets and greedy bankers.

Such aspects are no doubt important, but only as part of a much broader story of socio-economic change. This book examines the Crisis and its aftermath not just as a result of misguided policies but, more fundamentally, as a product of the social dynamics and economic institutions constructed over the course of many decades and consolidated during the neoliberal era. These include the dramatic rise in levels of inequality and the increasingly intense financial constraints on working people; the ways in which financial elites imposed a regime of austerity and discipline on corporations and their employees, as well as the rich world of opportunities that such growing indebtedness provided them with; and the ways in which such practices and power inequalities were consistently promoted and facilitated by political decisions to enlarge the room within which elite actors could maneuver while using public funds to socialize the risks they took in doing so. Viewing the Crisis against this background, this volume hopes to present a more complete and convincing account of its origins and development than is currently available.

The willingness to question the established version of what happened also allows the authors to critically assess current events and the political responses to the Crisis. Suspicious of the role of government and regulation not just before but also after the summer of 2007, they point out that the Keynesian understanding of the Crisis suggests a communal interest in re-regulation that is hardly reflective of existing levels of inequality. Owing to the ease with which it can be invoked in calls to refrain from pointing fingers (at least once the bad apples have been dealt with), this apparently progressive discourse has been complicit in the legitimation of some of the most inegalitarian uses to which state power has ever been put. Public rescue efforts have overwhelmingly benefited those who already did very well for themselves during the preceding years of frantic financial growth, while the process whereby those benefits are supposed to trickle down to the rest of society remains fraught with uncertainty. The future of the American and global financial order does not just involve a debate over better policies guided by a common interest but rather a confrontation of political projects and forces.

As Naomi Klein has recently reminded us, the effects of a Crisis are often quite paradoxical and by no means necessarily progressive.[3] The impact of shock and trauma tends to be highly uneven, often further debilitating the political capacities of already marginalized actors while opening up new opportunities for elites. It is especially important to remember this when analyzing the particular brand of socio-economic life that has been constructed in the US over the course of the twentieth century and has gone global over the past decades. Critically, its highly financialized nature means that participation in relations of credit and debt has come to be seen as the royal road to personal autonomy, and this in turn means that the maintenance or restoration of these relations has come to appear as an indisputable necessity.

This logic was evident in the aftermath of the Dot-com Crash at the start of the twenty-first century. When companies such as Enron and WorldCom were revealed to have engaged in elaborate fraud schemes, the public outcry in the US was enormous. Yet the resulting legislation (the Sarbanes-Oxley Act) did little more than provide the American public with a minimal degree of protection from the most flagrant abuses of corporate privilege, while reinvigorating the ability of financial elites to tap into new sources of profit and accumulation. What connected in much more visceral ways with the anger of the American people was the public beheading of several "bad apples." While none of this did much to help those people who had seen their pensions evaporate, it was highly effective in dissipating the flurry of popular anger, thereby opening the door to a new episode of rapid financial expansion. Indeed, while the gap between rich and poor had been widening for decades, the astronomic fees that financiers were able to reap from private equity funds and securitization (which came on top of steadily growing basic compensation packages, the sum of which was taxed at lower rates than before) meant that inequality accelerated like never before.

The vilification of financiers since the onset of the Great Credit Crash has been swift and merciless, at times reminiscent of the days when ordinary people mistrusted banks and credit.

---

3 Naomi Klein, *The Shock Doctrine*, New York: Metropolitan, 2007.

Such sentiments were greatly intensified by the use of massive public funds for bailing out the very financial institutions whose irresponsible behavior had produced the Crisis in the first place. But for all the widespread popular resentment these bailouts provoked, they have throughout been able to count on an appearance of dire necessity: the fortunes of ordinary Americans, so intricately bound up with a functioning financial infrastructure, were effectively held hostage by the bankers. In the absence of meaningful choice when it came to the political course of action, intense feelings of hostility have found their way into a highly moralistic discourse in which bloated bankers, once again wearing monocles and top hats, feature as villains. For all their unpleasantness, the prospect of redemption is central to such morality plays: their message is invariably that Wall Street can expect to be bailed out if it promises to change its errant ways and to ensure that henceforth financial intermediation will once again operate in the service of the public interest at large.

It is here—namely in the belief in the possibility of using existing structures of political authority and regulation to effect reforms that will make the financial system more responsive to the public interest—that such incendiary populist narratives intersect with the Keynesian interpretation of the Crisis that has been so widely espoused by scholars and commentators. The notion that, once upon a time, finance operated in the public interest has in the past often been a useful myth, allowing critics of capitalism to argue from a position that enjoys some degree of socially recognized validity and enabling the Left to command a higher price for the renewal of its allegiance to capitalist order. But at a time when our daily lives and personal ambitions have become so profoundly dependent on credit relations and their management by financial elites, it has become harder than ever for such ideologies of progressive reform to exact significant material concessions.

All too often, progressive commentators and scholars allow their political commitments to be shaped by willful optimism, by appraisals of power that take their cues from its rationalizations and idealized self-representations. The current celebration of the return of the state in the wake of the Crisis is one such moment: public intervention has been so flagrantly slanted in favor of the very actors and practices that had dominated the neoliberal era that progressive commentators' willingness to read into this an actual departure from the power structures of the neoliberal era has often been nothing short of belief-begging. Indeed, the continuity in underlying practices and interests quickly made itself felt in very material ways. When bankers began to distribute their bail-out funds as bonuses among their managerial ranks, popular furor ensued yet again. Progressive commentators expressed shock that such things could still happen in the new era of Keynesian intervention and regulatory prudence; and thus their intellectual capital became instrumental in channeling popular anger into the highly manageable format of new morality plays and the empty threats they pose.

Those given to more cynical appraisals of the world have had a keener sense of what was really going on. As progressive commentators and critical scholars were falling over each other to express their hopes for a second New Deal, the satirical newspaper *The Onion* reported aspects of the Crisis in ways that better captured the spirit of actual practices: "$700 Billion Bailout Celebrated With Lavish $800 Billion Executive Party"[4] ran one of its headlines. *The Daily Show*, in a news item entitled "American Grandstand," had similarly sarcastic commentary to emphasize the rather symbolic nature of politicians' indignation: "When our nation is faced with catastrophic problems . . . there are two actions that Congress can take. One: common-sense interventions that prevent the catastrophe. Or two: post-catastrophe histrionics." It then went on to highlight the discrepancy between political rhetoric and practice by reporting on how "eight bank CEOs who took federal bail-out money head to Washington to answer questions from Congressmen, who have received between five hundred and two hundred thousand dollars from said CEOs' companies. There the CEOs will answer questions as to why they have not complied with the conditions Congress never actually attached to the bailout money in the first place."[5]

If *The Daily Show* was primarily concerned to satirize journalists' reporting (or absence thereof) on the close connections, both before and after the Crisis, between politicians, regulators and Wall Street, the point applies no less to the narratives of American and global financial life constructed by much of mainstream social science. At a time when massive public assistance for the world's wealthiest people is legitimated through appeals to the common good, we should not be too quick to celebrate the return of Keynesianism or too eager to participate in the construction of

4   http://www.theonion.com.
5   http://www.thedailyshow.com.

a new consensus regarding the potential virtues of government. While it is crucial that we develop political responses based on a clear perspective on the meaning of the Crisis, we should not be too eager to seize on every dim prospect for progressive change promised by states presiding over a capitalist system in disarray. All too often, progressive political projects have been tempted into assuming responsibility for the restoration of capitalist order, thereby undermining their long-term transformative capacities in the process. Now more than ever, they will need to go beyond appeals to a common interest in prudent regulation to challenge the vast inequalities of power and wealth that have been built up over the past decades.

ORIGINS AND CAUSES

RETHINKING NEOLIBERALISM AND THE CRISIS

Beyond the Re-regulation Agenda

Martijn Konings

One of the most spectacular consequences of the Financial Crisis has been Alan Greenspan's willingness to contemplate the possibility that the free-market model of the world—which he had done nothing but praise throughout his career—may contain flaws. Greenspan's cautious but seemingly sincere doubts about the virtues of unbridled markets will provide ammunition for progressives and liberals who view the Crisis as an opportunity to move away from the neoliberal dogma that has governed public discourse for almost three decades and to bring such things as public regulation and social protection back into the realm of the possible. If even the former high priest of neoliberal capitalism has come to believe that more rules and constraints might have helped to prevent the American financial system from spinning out of control, then surely the task of convincing more pragmatically inclined policy-makers of the benefits of prudent regulation has become a great deal easier and we may reasonably hope for the emergence of a consensus that will allow for the implementation of a new New Deal, both at home (through a return to Keynesian regulation) and abroad (through the construction of a new regime of multilateral governance).

In other words, the time might well be ripe for public authority to push back against the hegemony of the market. Many years of deregulation, which allowed financial markets to impose their logic on social life, have generated such deep problems

4 MARTIJN KONINGS

that the prescriptions of neoliberal theory have lost much of
their credibility and legitimacy and this is seen as opening up
a space for re-regulation. In Polanyian terms, we are possibly
witnessing a new phase of "re-embedding" after several decades
of market "disembedding." In his *New York Times* columns,
Paul Krugman has argued that the excesses of neoliberal
deregulation are directly responsible for the instability that has
terrorized financial markets since the summer of 2007. Joseph
Stiglitz, until recently portrayed as a brilliant economist who
could win a Nobel prize but had little awareness of what works
in the real world, no longer sounds out of step with current
political realities when he asserts that "government regulation
and oversight are an essential part of a functioning market
economy" or that the world needs a "new global regulatory
agency" other than the American government.[1] Suddenly these
maverick economists were part of the new consensus. Wade
has stated the implications of the progressive analysis of the
roots of the Crisis well. "Governmental responses to the crisis
. . . suggest that we have entered the second leg of Polanyi's
'double movement,' the recurrent pattern in capitalism whereby
(to oversimplify) a regime of free markets and increasing
commodification generates such suffering and displacement as
to prompt attempts to impose closer regulation of markets and
de-commodification."[2]

   This chapter suggests that such assessments of the possibilities
created by the current Crisis rest on a misappraisal of its nature
and, more broadly, the nature of the neoliberal era. As a result,
they do not offer very helpful precepts for political action,
and unintentionally increase the possibility that we might be
squandering the opportunities for progressive change that
are presented to us by the situation. In particular, this essay
criticizes the idea that the financial expansion of the neoliberal
era can be adequately understood as propelled by the state's
failure to regulate financial markets and the permissive attitude
of its agencies towards innovation. The financial growth of
the past few decades does not represent a subordination of
public authority and political capacity to the expansionary
forces of global financial markets, but has rather been a
process whereby new organizational linkages were forged and

---

1 J. Stiglitz, "How to get out of the financial crisis," *Time*, October 17, 2008.
2 R. Wade, "Financial Regime Change?", *New Left Review*, II/53, 2008 p. 6.

particular relations of institutional control were constructed and consolidated. Fundamentally, financial expansion is a process of institutionalization whereby the web of capitalist power is cast over a wider set of social relations and becomes more, rather than less, rooted and organically embedded in the fabric of social life. The institutional capacities of the American state, sitting on top of these cross-cutting and complex networks of institutional linkages, have not been reduced but *enhanced* by the reconfigurations of the neoliberal era, as have the leverage and power resources available to those who enjoy privileged access to the state's organizational mechanisms of control.

RETHINKING NEOLIBERALISM

The idea that the neoliberal era is about deregulation and the growth of market discipline is one of the central myths of that era. It is a myth that is part of contemporary capitalism's common sense: the association of neoliberalism with a shift from government to markets is no longer a theoretical assumption but rests on deeply rooted, intuitive convictions about the way economic life works. In order to point out some of the problems with the idea of market disembedding, it is useful to consider what it means exactly to analyze neoliberalism as an ideology. Constructivist approaches in political economy often emphasize that neoliberal discourse does not represent neutral or objective knowledge. Wary of Marxist theories of ideology, which often understand ideology as veiling or distorting an objective economic reality, they stress the role of neoliberal ideas in the actual construction of economic life.[3] However, what gets lost in this way is a crucial sense in which neoliberal discourse is ideological in nature—namely, that it does not actually correspond to neoliberal practices. This is not to return to a reductionist Marxist understanding of ideology. Rather, it is to suggest that the very fact that ideas are not mere effects of an already existing socio-economic structure but key

---

3 E. Helleiner, *States and the Reemergence of Global Finance: From Bretton Woods to the 1990s*, Ithaca, NY: Cornell University Press, 1994; L. Seabrooke *The Social Sources of Financial Power: Domestic Legitimacy and International Financial Orders*, Ithaca: Cornell University Press, 2006; M. Blyth, *Great Transformations: Economic Ideas and Political Change in the Twentieth Century*, Cambridge: Cambridge University Press, 2002; T. J. Sinclair, *The New Masters of Capital: American Bond Rating Agencies and the Politics of Creditworthiness*, Ithaca/London: Cornell University Press, 2005.

factors in its very construction means that we can no longer
assume that reflecting or matching reality is what they do, or that
the emergence of a hegemonic neoliberal discourse means that
the world is becoming more like a free market. Critical political
economists tend to assume that neoliberalism has been reshaping
the world in its own image, that it has replaced public decision
making with economic logics, and social bonds with a formalistic
and individualist market rationality. But it is important to be
critical of such strong constructivism: beliefs and ideas shape the
world, but they do not do so by producing a reality that resembles
or approximates their idealized version. To be sure, it is often
recognized that the implementation of neoliberal policies has
not involved a straightforward retreat of the state but is rather a
complex process of re-regulation; but what persists is the notion
that the significance of the neoliberal era resides in the decline of
political capacities vis-à-vis the expansion of markets.

It is the claim of this essay that financial life does not correspond
to the model of neoliberal economics any more than it did several
decades ago. It is only on an *ideological* level that neoliberalism
has been about market disembedding or the subordination
of politics to the market. Neoliberal *practices* have never been
about institutional retreat or diminishing political capacities but,
instead, about the construction of new institutional mechanisms
of control. Taken by itself, this might just sound like a different
way of phrasing things. But it is intended as a new starting point
rather than a conclusion: it is meant to effect a shift of focus,
to suggest that we start looking for different things in order to
understand the neoliberal age. Thus, this essay suggests that we
might get a much better sense of what the neoliberal era really
has been about when we abandon our indignation-driven concern
with the supposed tendency of markets to dissolve their social and
cultural context, escape from their institutional environment and
impose an abstract regime of anonymous discipline (that is, when
we no longer treat capitalist markets as essentially negative and
destructive forces that tend to atomize social life and drain it of
substance) and instead try to understand the dramatic capitalist
expansion of the neoliberal era as a process of institutional
construction and consolidation that has involved not the
destruction but precisely the *creation* of new social connections,
cultural affinities and political capacities.

Such institutionalization could be seen on different levels.
Over the past decades, financial relations have penetrated more

deeply into everyday life than ever before. From a historical point of view, there is something extraordinary about the fact that when Americans are faced with financial difficulty, the first thing they do is try to get credit. This is a phenomenon that would have been unthinkable a century ago, and it is sustained by a wide variety of cultural symbols and facilitated by the central operational rules of American finance. Turning to the more traditional level of high finance: while it is easy to lose sight of it in the midst of the current situation, for most of the neoliberal era financial elites have been able to innovate without running into or generating the same kind of contradictions as during the 1960s and 1970s. The greater systemic coherence assumed by these strategies has meant that American finance has been capable of absorbing a much higher degree of economic activity and so of sustaining higher rates of financialization. At the same time, regulators created new policy channels that gave them more grip on the direction of financial flows and their rate of expansion, and the state has been much more consistently capable of using capital markets to finance deficits.

Thus, in some crucial ways, the neoliberal era has not seen the *reduction* but precisely the *growth* of institutional control. Critical social scientists tend to focus primarily on the former aspect, seeking to demonstrate how the disciplinary effects of neoliberal policies do not represent benevolent incentives but rather a more pernicious straitjacketing. But they tend to pay much less attention to the flipside of this trend, the fact that such intensified discipline translates into increased strategic flexibility for financial elites and their enhanced capacity to control and steer the dynamics of social life. That is, the effects of neoliberal discipline are often seen to be more or less universal, applying to government and financial intermediaries as well as to ordinary people. But this is, again, to buy into the neoliberal portrayal of market power. As Savage and Williams have pointed out, over the last decades social scientists have not paid nearly as much attention to the specific capacities and powers of elites as is warranted.[4] This neglect was itself born of a progressive impulse: from the 1960s critical social scientists and historians began to dedicate themselves to uncovering and writing the stories of ordinary people whose everyday lives were not adequately covered in the traditional focus on great men, major events and large structures. But this shift in focus had one odd side

---

4 M. Savage and K. Williams, "Elites: Remebered in Capitalism and Forgotten by Social Sciences," *Sociological Review*, 2008, 56 (51).

effect: it lent credence to the notion that the lives and capacities of elites in fact *were* adequately covered in official history, as if their lives resembled their self-rendered versions. But, of course, hegemonic narratives obscure as much about their heroes and their authors as about the downtrodden, the grey masses or the altogether unacknowledged.

Thus, this essay explores the possibility that we might be misreading the present Crisis if we consider it as an outcome of unleashed markets and as an opportunity for the re-regulation of financial life. While the Crisis does represent a major kink in some of the cables anchoring American capitalism, it is only on an ideological level that this rupture is about the relationship between states and markets. On a deeper level, this is a crisis of institutionalization, a breakdown of particular relations of power supported by particular ideas, routines and political subjectivities. It is not the result of a clash between different logics, but the result of contradictions internal to a particular way of organizing social control. This opens up political opportunities, but if we look primarily to regulators, politicians and policy-makers for its realization and put our hopes on a re-regulation of the market, we are likely to end up supporting attempts to restore and expand the very patterns of power and control that we were criticizing when they still went under the banner of neoliberalism.

FORDIST FINANCE

Perspectives that take the idea of neoliberalism as a return to free-market liberalism too seriously tend to be associated with a historical narrative that takes the breakdown of liberal world order during the early twentieth century as a key point of reference. Economic and political collapse during the interwar period is seen as a result of America's unwillingness to provide the global market economy with stabilizing institutional foundations.[5] After the New Deal and the Second World War, the US took a different approach and committed itself to the construction of an order of "embedded liberalism," based on multilateralism abroad and a New Deal sustained by Keynesian policies at home.[6] This

5 R. Gilpin, *The Political Economy of International Relations*, Princeton: Princeton University Press, 1987.
6 J. G. Ruggie, "International regimes, transactions and change: embedded liberalism in the post-war economic order," *International Organization*, 36 (2), 1982.

order came under pressure with the onset of post-war financial globalization. The rise of neoliberalism was seen as the American polity's decision to submit its priorities to the disciplinary effects of global finance—a measure that itself further unleashed those markets.[7] Since the 1980s, political economists have pointed out that the neoliberal era has seen not just the imposition of constraints but a more complex reconfiguration of financial relations that has involved the continued ability of the American state and citizens to fund debts and deficits.[8] Yet this is still often seen as speculative, short-term indulgence that is accompanied by a reduction of the structural coherence of American finance.[9] Neoliberal market fundamentalism is still seen as having eroded the long-term solidity of the American financial infrastructure and the Subprime Crisis is viewed as a manifestation of that fact.[10]

This narrative does not accurately characterize the key moments and turning points of twentieth-century capitalism. The image of a Polanyian pendulum, swinging back and forth between the market and society, suggests a cyclicality that is very misleading, not merely as a means to understand the past but also when it comes to our assessment of the nature of neoliberalism and the present conjuncture. When we adopt a more open and less conceptually preoccupied perspective, the reforms of the mid-twentieth century appear not so much as a movement whereby forces emerged to secure the integrity of the social fabric by pushing back the frontiers of the market but rather as a moment in a much longer process whereby the lower classes were integrated into the capitalist order through the extension of citizenship rights—civic, political and later social rights.[11] During the era of embedded liberalism, the reach of exchange and commodity relations was not limited but extended, in a manner that was much more stable than during the early part of the twentieth century.[12] Of course, the nature of this

---

7   Helleiner, *States and the Reemergence of Global Finance*.

8   L. Seabrooke, *US Power in International Finance. The Victory of Dividends*, New York: Palgrave, 2001.

9   G. Arrighi, *The Long Twentieth Century: Money, Power, and the Origins of Our Times*, London/New York: Verso, 1994.

10   Wade, "Financial regime change?"

11   T. Marshall, *Citizenship and Social Class*, Cambridge: Cambridge University Press, 1950; R. Bendix, *Nation-Building and Citizenship: Studies of Our Changing Global Order*, New York: Transaction Publishers, 1996.

12   H. Lacher, "Embedded liberalism, disembedded markets: reconceptualising the Pax Americana," *New Political Economy*, 1999, 4 (3); M. Konings, "The Construction of US Financial Power," *Review of International Studies*, 2009, 35 (1).

process as one of *capitalist* integration and expansion was more evident in the US than in Europe: whereas in European countries legitimacy was built through public institutions that provided citizens with some degree of protection from the mechanisms of capital accumulation and the vagaries of the labor market,[13] America's New Deal reforms expanded citizenship rights in ways that served to integrate citizens further into the modalities of capitalist growth and connected their identities and interests more firmly to financial and exchange relations.[14]

The New Deal was rooted in the tradition of Progressive reform, which rose to prominence as a conception of public life in the early years of the twentieth century. Although more radical programs for a republic of independent yeoman producers had been defeated at the end of the nineteenth century,[15] social unrest and protest retained a strongly populist character that extolled independence and self-sufficiency.[16] This made the American working classes very receptive to the promises of freedom and even advancement held out by consumer and mortgage credit, and the efforts of reformers were not just, as in Europe, oriented towards the construction of public schemes for social protection and income replacement, but rather towards the integration of American workers into the institutions of corporate capitalism through advocacy of broader access to the mechanisms of finance and credit.[17] The gradual transformation of the American Dream from a potentially disruptive impulse into an ethos of responsible consumption laid the basis for a steady expansion of mortgage and consumer credit that was a significant factor in the expansionary financial dynamics before the Crash and the Depression.

The New Deal found considerable support among business interests that had grown deeply hostile to the way the Republican

13 G. Esping-Andersen, *The Three Worlds of Welfare Capitalism*, Princeton: Princeton University Press, 1990.

14 M. Konings, "American finance and empire in historical perspective," in L. Panitch and M. Konings, eds, *American Empire and the Political Economy of Global Finance*, New York: Palgrave, 2009, second end.

15 G. Kolko, *The Triumph of Conservatism: A Reinterpretation of American History, 1900–1916*, Chicago: Quadrangle Books, 1963.

16 T. Goebel, "The political economy of American populism from Jackson to the New Deal," *Studies in American Political Development*, 11 (Spring), 1997.

17 M. Jacobs, "'Democracy's third estate': New Deal politics and the construction of a 'consuming public'," *International Labor and Working-Class History 55*, April 1999; L. Cohen, *A Consumers' Republic: The Politics of Mass Consumption in Postwar America*, New York: Alfred A. Knopf, 2003.

administrations of the 1920s had mishandled not only the international situation of the 1920s (when they let narrow self-interest prevail and threw Europe into crisis by demanding full repayment of the war debts) but also developments at home.[18] Their domestic economic policies had been passive, except in the area of industrial relations, where they had resorted to increasingly repressive measures. The business interests that stood at the basis of Roosevelt's presidential victory were acutely aware of the potential benefits of reforms that would not merely seek to pacify American workers but would further integrate them into the mechanisms of capitalist expansion as active consumers.[19] They realized that consumer and mortgage credit, far from accommodating idleness, locked working people into a schedule of repayments that served to intensify rather than loosen the disciplinary pressures on them. Hence, unlike the more reactionary interests that had supported Hoover's onslaught on workers' civic and political rights, they discerned opportunities for making an expansion of social rights serviceable to American business. This political project unfolded against the background of an emerging awareness that the hands-off approach to economic management had done more harm than good, and that the growing connectivity of financial life had created opportunities for manipulating its institutional parameters in more creative and flexible ways than had been imagined possible during the era of nineteenth-century British liberalism, making available new policy levers that would provide a means to guide and stabilize such expansion (a development of which the rise of Keynesian ideas was the clearest manifestation).[20]

The decommodifying effects of the New Deal reforms were very minimal. Their overall thrust was not to shield the lower classes from market discipline but to lay the basis for their deeper integration into the financial mechanisms of capitalist society. Central to the reconstruction of the financial system was the establishment of agencies charged with creating secondary markets for loans and so reducing borrowing costs and increasing the supply of household credit. The so-called Government-Sponsored

---

18 T. Ferguson, "From Normalcy to New Deal: Industrial Structure, Party Competition, and American Public Policy in the Great Depression," *International Organization* 38(1), 1984.

19 M. Aglietta, *A Theory of Capitalist Regulation*, London: NLB, 1979.

20 T. Mitchell, "Economists and the Economy in the Twentieth Century," in George Steinmetz, ed., *The Politics of Method in the Human Sciences: Positivism and its Epistemological Others*, Durham: Duke University Press, 2005.

Enterprises seized on a particular feature of the American financial system – the highly securitized nature of credit relations – and gave it public backing. The most prominent among these was Fannie Mae, which laid the foundation for the modern American mortgage market. By buying, pooling and standardizing mortgage loans, they enhanced the liquidity of banks' asset portfolios, increasing not only their ability to extend new mortgages but their credit-creating capacities at large.

While European financiers were enlisted in post-war reconstruction efforts, American bankers were experiencing a wealth of profitable lending opportunities generated by Fordist patterns of work and consumption, and their ability to take advantage of these was greatly facilitated by the American state's commitment to providing banks with liquidity. In the US, finance was anything but embedded in the sense of suppressed or constrained: financial relations penetrated into new areas of life and the financial entanglements and connections of the average American multiplied rapidly.[21] This process of financial expansion was overseen by more effective public institutions such as a revamped Federal Reserve System which could avail itself of a much wider range of policy instruments, a Securities and Exchange Commission which permitted the securities industry to regulate itself, and a Treasury keen on monetizing the public debts incurred during the New Deal and the war.[22] Total private debt between 1949 and 1954 increased nearly three times as fast as during the five-year period preceding the Crash.[23]

But the social integration of American workers and the improvement of their material conditions did not by any means come at the expense of financial elites, who had a firm grip on the conditions and parameters of financial growth and reaped the bulk of the benefits. Indeed, "the years from 1949 through the late 1960s became the twentieth century's second great wealth explosion,"[24] a development that compensated sufficiently for steadily rising manufacturing wages as to considerably blunt the egalitarian impact of the post-war order, particularly when compared to the

---

21 M. Konings and L. Panitch, "The Politics of Imperial Finance," in L. Panitch and M. Konings, eds, *American Empire and the Political Economy of Global Finance*, New York: Palgrave, 2009.

22 R. A. Degen, *The American Monetary System: A Concise Survey of its Evolution Since 1896*, Massachusetts/Toronto: D. C. Heath and Company, 1987.

23 J. Grant, *Money of the Mind: Borrowing and Lending in America from the Civil War to Michael Milken*, New York: Noonday Press, 1992, p. 265.

24 K. Phillips, *Wealth and Democracy*, New York: Broadway, 2002, p. 82.

considerable leveling of socio-economic conditions in the social-democratic welfare states of Northern Europe.

POST-FORDIST RECONFIGURATIONS

From the late 1950s, various developments combined to put a great deal of pressure on the New Deal order. The economic revival of Europe intensified competition in the manufacturing sector and put a squeeze on profitability,[25] while the growth of cross-border financial flows added to the deterioration of America's payments position. Employers' initiatives to drive down wages met with considerable resistance. Such confrontations seemed to have a galvanizing effect on industrial militancy and the willingness of unions to go on strike for wage increases.[26] Their integration into capitalist order had constituted workers as more competent social and political actors who were increasingly aware of how to effectively exercise their agency. Indeed, just as the rate at which the economic pie grew was slowing down, sections of the Democratic Party woke up to the limits of the New Deal's achievements and began to push for more serious government initiatives to redress the still dramatic inequalities of American society. Such radicalization resulted in what many perceived (and either lamented or celebrated) as a crisis of governability. The result was "political and economic disarray" and a "stalling of wealth formation."[27]

However, the radicalism of the sixties did little to slow down the growth in demand for privatized consumption and suburban homeownership. Those who had grown up in the heyday of Fordist capitalism were not only capable of exercising their political rights to criticize the order of things, but had also become steeped in a culture of middle-class entitlement that led them to count on steadily growing access to the conveniences, opportunities and technologies of modern capitalism. In other words, the unrest of the sixties was produced primarily by the system's growing inability to guarantee the resources for the continued integration of the American middle and working classes and to make available

---

25 R. Brenner, "Uneven Development and the Long Downturn: The Advanced Capitalist Economies from Boom to Stagnation," *New Left Review*, 1998, I, 229.
26 T. E. Dark, *The Unions and the Democrats: An Enduring Alliance*, Ithaca: Cornell University Press, 2001.
27 Phillips, *Wealth and Democracy*, p. 82.

to the new generation the same prospects of socio-economic advancement. As Fordist means to guarantee widespread access to the benefits of a consumer society (i.e. wage rises) became increasingly contested, the readily available alternative means to the same end (i.e. household debt) gained in popularity. In this context, the growth of the financial system accelerated further. While social unrest and industrial militancy remained intense throughout the 1970s, they gradually lost their political edge, remaining relatively fragmented and uncoordinated and producing disorder rather than a viable counterhegemonic politics.

The baby-boomer generation borrowed money for homes, cars, college and consumption.[28] Even though this occurred at the same time as the international institutions of the Bretton Woods system began to crumble, there is little point in subsuming the growth of Americans' indebtedness under the broader heading of global market disembedding. In recent years, many authors have argued that we cannot fruitfully understand financialization in terms of the supposedly autonomous tendency of markets to impose their logic on social life when given a chance, and that we need to conceptualize the operation of such expansionary financial logics as produced through specific discursive forms and cultural norms, situated both at the level of financial intermediation and at the level of everyday life.[29] These new theories tend to rely on an understanding of social construction that is subtly different from its conceptualization in the constructivist political-economy literature. Emphasizing the complexities of the process of social construction, they rely on the notion that the institutional and discursive forms of financial life are "performed." Actors sometimes play their roles with a knowing chuckle and at other times are fully absorbed in their parts without much awareness of the play's larger dynamics; there is always already a social script, yet it never operates autonomously.

However, what this conceptual scheme still cannot easily

28 C. R. Geisst, *Visionary Capitalism: Financial Markets and the American Dream in the Twentieth Century*, New York: Praeger, 1990.
29 R. Aitken, *Performing Capital: Toward a Cultural Economy of Popular and Global Finance*, New York: Palgrave, 2007; D. Mackenzie, *An Engine, Not a Camera: How Financial Models Shape Markets*, Cambridge, Mass.: MIT Press, 2006; J. Froud, J. Sukhdev, A. Leaver and K. Williams *Financialization and Strategy: Narrative and Numbers*, London: Routledge, 2006; P. Langley, *The Everyday Life of Global Finance: Saving and Borrowing in Anglo-America*, Oxford: Oxford University Press, 2008.

accommodate are the strategic elements of human agency. On the side of financial elites, the idea that financial innovation can primarily be understood in terms of the enactment of concepts and theories fails to fully acknowledge the considerable strategic latitude with which financial elites operated as they entered into and propelled accelerating financial expansion, as well as the additional opportunities and room for maneuver that they created for themselves in the course of this process. On the other hand, to explain the growing financial role of ordinary Americans in terms of the cultural discourses that extol independence and ownership does not tell us much about what exactly pushed and lured people into financial mechanisms that served to confine their agency to the disciplinary mechanisms of borrowing and repayment. The "performance" metaphor is not particularly helpful when it comes to understanding the differential construction of strategic capacities or the sources from which discursive-institutional forms derive their authority. To explain people's participation in a culture of debt with reference to their cultural disposition is to divert attention from the process through which people become invested in these cultural codes. While we owe our existence as recognizable, socially competent actors to our insertion into particular institutional, discursive and cultural structures, we need to recognize that such roles and constructions never fully eradicate our distinctively subjective points of view, our negative and antagonistic relationships to social life.[30] In other words, if we are to conceive of social construction as a process involving power and domination, we need to realize that such construction is never exhaustive or fully coherent. As Fromm emphasized long ago, the submission to authority is a contradictory process: even in eras where much agency is performative and routine-driven, the internalization of power still requires its ongoing compensations.[31]

The psychological correlates of post-Fordist governmentality that fueled consumption and indebtedness were perhaps most powerfully described in Lasch's analysis of cultural narcissism.[32] If modern life had always fostered a certain degree of vainglorious

30 S. Žižek, *The Sublime Object of Ideology*, New York/London: Verso, 1989; Žižek, *Tarrying with the Negative: Kant, Hegel and the Critique of Ideology*, Durham, NC: Duke University Press, 1993.

31 E. Fromm, *Escape from Freedom*, New York: Holt, Rinehart & Winston, 1941.

32 C. Lasch, *The Culture of Narcissism: American Life in an Age of Diminishing Expectations*, New York: Norton, 1979.

self-preoccupation, and if the Fordist era had brought the means for such external self-validation within the reach of ordinary Americans, according to Lasch the defeat of 1960s radicalism and the retreat from political ambitions and solidaristic projects were accompanied by new heights of narcissism, the artificial self-love that individuals resort to in order to compensate for the anxiety produced by inauthentic living. The growing preoccupation with identity, authenticity and self-realization served to divert American citizens' energies from political issues and public life towards the quality of their personal lives. But Lasch emphasized that the content of these processes was radically at odds with the discourses through which they were produced and rationalized. An age that comprehended itself in terms of invidualization and growing self-reliance in fact represented an erosion of "everyday competence" and a growing dependence on external sources of validation and social structures of authority.[33] The newly emerging selves, far from solid and self-sufficient, were intensely dependent on the menu of lifestyle accessories made available by Fordist capitalism and even more by the post-Fordist cultural industries and the service sector. If modern consumer culture is based on the internalization of, and personal identification with, what had hitherto been seen as external devices and objects, consumer credit epitomizes the way in which such processes temporarily alleviate the pressures of modern life yet at the same time draw people further into their disciplinary regimes.

Lasch stressed that, although these processes of com-mercialization and hegemonic integration had not been set in motion through the intentional machinations of American elites, they were nevertheless the ones who benefited from them and often promoted them. But, while these trends were instrumental in neutralizing the more serious challenges to American capitalism, they generated their own contradictions. For Lasch, these were bound up precisely with the rapidly declining ability of people to help themselves, the societal pathologies this produced, and the way in which this threatened to undermine the very illusion of individual self-sufficiency. This assessment corresponded to a wider sense of national malaise that also had more concrete economic coordinates. As the growth of Americans' indebtedness accelerated and banks created credit accordingly, financialization began to strain against the institutional parameters of the New

---

33 Ibid., p. 10.

Deal. When American banks found their ability to take full advantage of the growing demand for credit constrained by the New Deal regulations, they responded by pursuing new strategies and instruments to enhance their liquidity-creating capacities. The Federal Reserve was torn. Doing nothing was not an option, but its attempts to tighten money were largely ineffective, as banks would quickly find new ways to access and produce liquidity. When, in the second half of the 1960s, the banks began to apply such techniques in the Eurodollar markets (offshore pools of American dollars that were the result of American capital outflows during the previous decades), virtually all checks on their ability to create and extend credit were gone.[34] What all this meant was a huge inflationary pressure on the American economy, which in turn fuelled wage demands and industrial militancy. It also produced considerable pressure on the dollar. By the end of the decade, it was clear that the New Deal institutional order was no longer adequate to the task of securing social cohesion and integration.

NEOLIBERAL FINANCE

It was in this context that the turn to neoliberalism occurred. Due to growing anti–New Deal sentiments, the administrations of the 1970s had enjoyed considerable leeway for reform of the financial system. The main problem was that policy-makers just did not really know how they would regulate a liberalized system of financial markets. Reagan did not know this either, but his commitment to a retreat of the government from economic life was sufficiently strong that his administration embarked on a program of ambitious liberalization without much delay. The way this worked out was deeply affected by the policy turn that the new Federal Reserve Chairman Volcker had implemented just the year before.[35] Monetarism was hardly the work of concerting financial elites: the Federal Reserve's primary objective was to clamp down on inflation and regain control over the gyrations of financial markets. Volcker decided that the Federal Reserve would no longer do anything to accommodate banks' lending practices

34 M. Mayer, *The Bankers*, New York: Weybright & Talley, 1974; W. Greider, *Secrets of the Temple: How the Federal Reserve Runs the Country*, New York: Simon & Schuster, 1987.
35 C. Rude, "The Volcker Monetary Policy Shocks: A Political-Economic Analysis," unpublished paper, Department of Economics, New School University, 2004.

and would allow interest rates to rise as much as the demand for credit dictated. While inflation came down, monetarism did not work the way it was supposed to, namely by restricting the creation of money and credit. Given the socio-economic configuration that had already evolved over the course of the 1970s, financial elites had access to a range of means and instruments that allowed them to escape the Volcker shock's disciplinary effects. Indeed, the creation of liquidity accelerated dramatically.[36] The Fed initially viewed these developments with considerable concern, but pretty soon it noticed that, in contrast with the 1970s, the expansion of liquidity and credit no longer resulted in inflation. The high interest rates meant that, rather than finding its way into the real economy and causing price inflation, credit now remained in the financial sector, where it drove up asset prices and accelerated processes of financialization. They also drew in large flows of foreign capital, which pushed up the exchange rate and so reinforced the economic recession while fueling financial growth.[37] The Fed's turn to monetarism did not eliminate but *redirected* inflationary pressures.[38]

This dynamic of financialization was much more manageable than the price inflation of the 1970s. The neoliberal shift reconfigured the institutional connections between financial expansion and public authority in a way that largely eliminated the contradictions of the 1970s and so *enhanced* rather than reduced state capacity.[39] This was, of course, not the assessment that emerged in the 1980s themselves. The instability that followed the financial explosion (the debt crisis, the failure of several major banks, the Savings and Loan Crisis, and ultimately the stock market crash of 1987) all served to instill widespread doubt concerning the fundamental health of the American economy.[40] It seemed as if the US had been able to buy some

---

36 Greider, *Secrets of the Temple*.

37 G. Arrighi, "The Social and Political Economy of Global Turbulence," *New Left Review* II/20, 2003.

38 M. Konings, "The institutional foundations of US structural power in international finance: from the re-emergence of global finance to the monetarist turn," *Review of International Political Economy* 15(1), 2008.

39 L. Panitch and S. Gindin, "Finance and American Empire," in L. Panitch and M. Konings, eds, *American Empire and the Political Economy of Global Finance*, New York: Palgrave, 2009.

40 P. M. Kennedy, *The Rise and Fall of the Great Powers: Economic Change and Military Conflict from 1500 to 2000*, New York: Random House, 1987; Gilpin, *Political Economy of International Relations*.

short-term relief but that economic constraints were now coming back to haunt it with a vengeance: neoliberalism had unleashed a monster that the US state did not know how to control. The theme of imperial decline echoed Lasch's assessment that the culture of narcissism, the passive consumerism it sustained, and the cynical politics it permitted were on their last legs.[41] However, just as progressive political economists have consistently underestimated Americans' capacity to sustain ever higher levels of indebtedness and the state's ability to finance its deficits, so Lasch underestimated Americans' capacity to sustain higher levels of cultural narcissism.

While Lasch associated the new cultural constellation primarily with the tragic turn taken by East-coast liberals' political ambitions and affinities, not all Americans were liberal intellectuals sublimating their alienation through self-deprecation and psychoanalysis. Elsewhere, in other strata and areas, the culture that would come to shape the neoliberal era was formed not through the subtle evaporation of progressive ideals but rather through the aggressive assertion of conservative ones. The foundations for this shift in American political culture had been laid during the New Deal era itself. Whereas the postbellum and Progressive eras had been characterized by the hegemony of Northern elites, the New Deal era was based on a geographically much more diverse coalition. Its policies were more conducive to the economic development of the American South, and the relocation of many American businesses seeking to take advantage of weak labor laws gave the region a further economic boost. The 1960s saw the rise of a set of Southern elites who enjoyed access to a very different kind of cultural capital than their Northern brethren,[42] based on a mixture of "Birchite conspiracism, traditionalist Protestant morality, and cultural nationalism."[43] The conservative discourse that this produced was more exclusionary and outwardly sadistic in nature; it was not about the relatively thoughtful exploration or reconstruction of the individual personality, but rather about a resolute refusal to interrogate the socially constructed self.

---

41 Lasch, *Culture of Narcissism*, p.11.
42 Phillips, *Wealth and Democracy*, p. 87.
43 M. N. Lyons, "Business Conflict and Right-Wing Movements," in A. E. Ansell, ed., *Unraveling the Right. The New Conservatism in American Thought and Politics*, Boulder/Oxford: Westview, 1998, p. 86.

Based on the collective affirmation of the authenticity and purity of such identities against external elements and otherness, it drew on and fostered strong nationalist, racist and religious sentiments. Interestingly, this discourse viewed progressive liberalism much the same way Lasch did, associating it with self-absorbed do-goodery that brought ordinary working people little material benefit and added insult to injury through its condescending attitude towards their values and sentiments. In this way it managed to align large sections of the working class with an anti-government discourse and produced the new electoral constellation that ensured a period of Republican hegemony that, interrupted only by Carter, stretched from 1968 to 1992.

What predictions of decline failed to recognize was that the American state and financial capital derived very significant capacities from processes of financialization and the new cultural configuration with which it existed in intricate relationships of interdependence. What neoliberalism meant was not an across-the-board internalization of financial discipline but a *redistribution* of discipline: it gave the US state a lot more policy room and financial capital much more leverage, and the flipside of this was the intensification of economic discipline on the lower strata of the American population. Banks innovated like never before, and their strategic room for maneuver was considerably enlarged in the new regime of financialization: because their strategies no longer resulted in price inflation they had much greater leeway. The Fed was no longer so concerned with slowing down credit creation but rather with channeling it. It no longer felt the need to get in the way of intermediaries' innovative strategies but rather supported them by granting regulatory exemptions and opening up loopholes. The Reagan administration spent enormous amounts on tax cuts and the military, and the Treasury had no difficulty financing the huge deficits that resulted. At the same time as the economic recession resulted in mass layoffs, the Reagan administration dismantled social programs and initiated an assault on labor unions, often undermining basic civic and political rights and freedoms that had long been considered consolidated gains. These events had a devastating impact on the income of the lower strata of the American population, and the result was a huge growth in the household demand for credit, which partly compensated for declining incomes but also drew them into the discipline of repayment and refinancing against historically unfavorable rates.[44]

The dramatic growth in household credit would become the most reliable and consistent mainstay of financial expansion during the neoliberal era, and the innovations produced by elites in financial markets were the very means through which working people could gain access to credit. The increased room for maneuver for the state and the growing leverage of financial intermediaries thus evolved hand-in-hand with tightening pecuniary constraints on the American working class. The turn to neoliberalism hardly served to lift the market out of its social context, but, on the contrary, was able to last for more than a few years precisely because its key organizing rules became organically anchored in the most everyday habits and cultural norms of American citizens. It represented a deepening of social connectedness rather than the abstraction of social life. Capitalist integration now advanced through a more cultural dimension: if, until the late 1970s, cultural dimensions had primarily supplemented the other dimensions of capitalist legitimation, from the early 1980s they were tested for their capacity to support part of the burden that had previously been borne by those other pillars.

The growth of political capacities and the amplification of their asymmetrical and differential effects was perhaps most visible in the emergence of a "too-big-to-fail" regime. This policy is often portrayed as a very recent development and a sign of how incoherent neoliberal policies have become. But it has actually been a very consistent feature of American financial policy since the early 1980s. The bail-outs during the debt crisis, the Continental Illinois Crisis and the Savings and Loans Crisis all created expectations for the way in which authorities would deal with the imminent failure of large financial intermediaries in the future.[45] "Too-big-to-fail" is inherently asymmetrical in nature, as access to its benefits is conditional on a participant's degree of market power and the likelihood that its bankruptcy could throw a wrench into the operation of the financial system's key mechanisms. The risks that are guaranteed through this policy are only those that have already effectively been externalized,

---

44 J. Montgomerie, "Giving Credit Where It's Due: public policy and household indebtedness in the United States, the United Kingdom and Canada," *Policy and Society* 25(3), 2007.

45 M. de Cecco, "The Lender of Last Resort," CIDEI Working Paper no. 49, n.d.

and involve the exposure of a wider range of social interests. "Too-big-to-fail" has definitely entailed a major element of moral hazard, but it is crucial to see that it has never just been a problem, and has been a key factor in the creation of an infrastructure of incentives that continuously generates new products and services. This makes it comprehensible that since the Savings and Loans Crisis, policy-makers and legislators have hardly been concerned with finding ways to reduce moral hazard but much more with increasing the public resources available for bail-out interventions.

Over the course of the 1990s things began to look quite different than they had in the late 1980s. Of course, a key theme in recent work in political economy has been that the "new economy" of the 1990s was little more than a huge bubble,[46] and the "roaring nineties" have often been compared to the "roaring twenties."[47] The latter comparison is appropriate in some respects: banks, often assisted by financial authorities who granted exemptions and opened up loopholes, undermined the last New Deal barriers, and constructed a pattern of rapid financial expansion that was based on a very dense network of linkages between high and low finance. The formation of Citigroup in 1998 meant the birth of a new kind of institution that incorporated virtually all financial functions. But the key difference with the 1920s was that this pattern of financial expansion possessed much greater internal coherence, as it was embedded in a wide range of cultural, social and economic norms and rules and was connected to regulatory authority in much more functional ways.

Financial norms and principles penetrated further into everyday life and were sustained by the deepening of a financialized culture that shaped the American psyche in new ways. Although regional divisions remain central to American politics to this very day, the cultural shift that had produced a political configuration dominated by the Republican Party had of course never remained confined to the American South. But it was especially during the 1990s that it began to blend in subtle ways with the trends described by Lasch to produce a particularly powerful and cohesive cultural configuration, based on the dialectical mixture of affirmatively therapeutic ("You're

---

46 R. Brenner, "Towards the precipice," *London Review of Books*, 6 February 2003; R. Duncan, *The Dollar Crisis*, New York: Wiley, 2005.
47 J. Stiglitz, *The Roaring Nineties: A New History of the World's Most Prosperous Decade*, New York: W. W. Norton, 2003.

worth it!") and sadistic ("Earn it!") sensibilities that is so central to debt-based consumption. The culture of self-help that is crucial to neoliberal governmentality involves a dialectic of continuous affirmation and rejection, seduction and denial. The interplay of these elements is very visible in the financial discourses employed on America's most influential major talk shows. One day's broadcast will feature an emotional celebration of a particular individual who is living the American Dream and enjoying all the social recognition and human appreciation that comes with material abundance; the next day will see a financial adviser lecturing a young couple who "let themselves go" and ended up with a crushing mortgage and credit card debt, berating them for their profligacy and their inability to behave responsibly and spend only what they earn.

The public put-down, and the announcement of the financial pain that will be part of their rescue package, are a key part of the narcissistic deal. The self-love involved in the narcissistic personality structure is a fragile one. Except for the most self-absorbed among us, it cannot merely be sustained by empty affirmations of entitlement. If we were only ever told that being wealthy is really just a matter of overcoming our fear of owning what is rightfully ours (as suggested in the title of financial self-help guru Suze Orman's book *The Courage To Be Rich*, which resembles the title of theologian Paul Tillich's spiritual treatise *The Courage To Be*),[48] we would soon become incredulous. Instead, the dynamics of narcissism must involve an active *externalization* of our insecurity: the opportunity to see others falter and to disapprove of their lives.[49] Dr Phil–style entertainment affords us an extraordinary degree of intimacy, familiarizing us with issues in others' lives that we do not confront in our own, while at the same time allowing us to put a distance between our own lives and those on public display. It is not just that, as Lasch tended to emphasize, the difficulty of living an authentic life under prevailing social conditions produces an artificial self-love that feeds our consumption habits. The fact that narcissism only *appears* as an inwardly directed emotion

---

48 S. Orman, *The Courage to Be Rich: Creating a Life of Material and Spiritual Abundance*, New York: Riverhead Books; P. Tillich, *The Courage to Be*, New Haven: Yale University Press, 2000 [1952].
49 L. S. Chancer, *Sadomasochism in Everyday Life: The Dynamics of Power and Powerlessness*, Rutgers University Press, 1992.

and more fundamentally represents a problematic relationship to others means that it is anchored in the institutional mechanisms available to us for externalizing our insecurity. Neoliberal governmentality involves the creation of chains of disciplinary pressures, networks composed of acts of everyday sadism, and expressions of judgment that serve to distract us from the resentment provoked by our submission to authority structures that we do not fully understand and experience as oppressive and constraining. This redirection of our anger and discontent serves to consolidate the very disciplinary mechanisms that wreak so much havoc on our lives and contort our notions of self-realization and responsible living in such a way that we end up ascribing a spiritual dimension to balancing the household budget.

It was through mechanisms constructed along these lines that three decades of growing inequality and stagnant wages came to exist in a relationship of mutually reinforcing interaction with neoliberal governmentality. Neoliberalism represents a shift in the modalities and instruments through which the integration of the American middle and working classes into the financial system was effected. This provided financial elites with a world of opportunities. The internet-driven stock market was the most visible element of the 1990s, but it was only part of the picture. After the Savings and Loans Crisis, the government had viewed securitization as the best way to ensure that mortgage credit would be widely available, and Fannie Mae and Freddie Mac produced a steadily growing volume of securitized mortgages that enjoyed implicit government guarantees. The Clinton administration did little to reverse the Republican cutbacks on public schemes for income provision and instead promoted wider access to financial products and services, giving intermediaries incentives to increase their lending to lower-income Americans. Maximum rates were abolished, so now households that in the past had been seen as not creditworthy became very attractive as customers because they could be charged high rates and fees.[50]

The growth of US state power was especially apparent in the capacities that the Federal Reserve developed over the course of

---

50 G. A. Dymski, "From Financial Exploitation to Global Banking Instability: Two Overlooked Roots of the Subprime Crisis," this volume.

the decade.[51] What during the 1970s had been such a source of complications (namely, the dense web of connections between different parts of the financial system and the strategic options that this gave to financial actors) now became a point of great leverage for the Fed: the high degree of connectivity of the financial system came to serve as a very effective transmission channel for monetary policy[52] that allowed the Fed to promote and manage financial expansion.[53] So while the Fed was still not able to limit, on a structural basis, the overall quantity of credit created, it had acquired a definite capacity when it came to keeping financialization going. This was allied to a labor-market regime that, until the very end of the decade, prevented any significant wage growth (itself, in turn, partly facilitated by the growing reliance on cheap imports from developing countries) and so prevented price inflation from resurfacing.[54]

When the internet bubble unwound around the turn of the century, political economists viewed this as proof of the fundamentally unsustainable nature of neoliberal growth. But what really stands out about the dot-com meltdown, as well as the financial shock after 9/11, was the ease with which the Fed's liquidity infusions were capable of containing the effects of events that might easily have proved disastrous had they occurred in a less well institutionalized system. Unlike the crash of 1929, the dot-com meltdown did not trigger a system-wide credit crunch, and was contained and managed within the modalities of neoliberal governance. Banks quite quickly embarked on a new set of profitable strategies such as mergers and acquisitions and private equity, but the real driving force behind financial growth was securitized mortgage and consumer debt.[55]

---

51 E. Newstadt, "Neoliberalism and the Federal Reserve," in L. Panitch and M. Konings. eds, *American Empire and the Political Economy of Global Finance*, New York: Palgrave, 2009.

52 S. M. Phillips, "The Place of Securitization in the Financial System: Implications for Banking and Monetary Policy," in L. T. Kendall and M. J. Fishman, eds, *A Primer on Securitization*, Cambridge, MA/London: MIT Press, 1996.

53 G. Krippner, "The Making of US Monetary Policy: Central bank transparency and the neoliberal dilemma," *Theory & Society* 36(6), 2007.

54 J. Montgomerie, *Re(politicizing) Inflation Policy: A Global Political Economy Perspective*, CRESC Working Paper 53, 2008.

55 R. Blackburn, "The Subprime Crisis," *New Left Review*, II/50, 2008, p. 81.

Subprime Finance and Beyond

Many lenders expanded their activities into the poorest neighborhoods and their practices took on increasingly predatory qualities. The real boom in subprime lending came in 2004–6, and by 2006 one of out every five new mortgages was subprime.[56] Although the last years of the roaring nineties had seen a resumption of wage growth, the Dot-Com crisis had put an end to this and returned the bulk of the American population to a regime of stagnant wages. The growing debt burden of the American lower classes was not accompanied by growing earning capacity, and the Bush administration's bankruptcy law reforms did much to tighten the screws on debtors. But this intensification of discipline did not produce the steady income streams that might have kept the system going. In the summer of 2007, large numbers of Americans turned out to be less creditworthy than lenders had assumed or hoped, and large amounts of securitized debt (especially mortgage-backed securities) turned out to be "bad debt." This time, the Fed's attempts to restore confidence by cutting rates and supplying liquidity were not very effective. The following year can be understood as a period in which financial authorities tried one thing after another, finding each time that what they tried did not do enough, and addressing the Crisis in ever more rigorous ways. By September of 2008 several key institutions of American capitalism had been taken over, bailed out by the government, or gone bankrupt, and even after all that the danger had not disappeared. In this context the "too-big-to-fail" policy assumed new dimensions. The infamous $700 billion bail-out package was part of a series of programs and initiatives through which the government made its resources available to private parties.

We should be very cautious when it comes to depicting the highly visible role of the state in the present situation as a break with the neoliberal era. If we bear in mind the constituted disparity between neoliberal practices and neoliberal ideology, then the government's response appears not so much as the breakdown but rather as the provisional *culmination* of the neoliberal era. The American state has been wielding capacities constructed over the course of the neoliberal era, and it is precisely the expansion of state capacities during those decades that has made it less

---

56 Ibid., pp. 72–3.

justifiable than ever to think of the American state as external to the mechanisms of financial expansion.

The idea that we need to re-embed financial markets suggests that at present economic life is characterized by an absence of institutional control. This chapter has argued that the whole of financial life, right down to its very core, is made up of relations of control supported by very complex institutional mechanisms. Financial expansion does not proceed by dissolving social bonds, destroying human conventions and reducing us to one-dimensional calculative beings; it operates precisely through the creation of new connections, rules and practices, as well as the construction of new identities with complex, thoroughly interlinked motivational and emotional households.[57] What that means for the present is that, given the fact that twentieth-century financial development has constituted financial actors in particular ways, and given the widespread dependence on the financial system, any reform project will necessarily need to aim at improving it, not at cutting Americans off from financial relations. So promoting state control over financial life, re-embedding and re-regulating the financial system, would come down to supporting a restoration and fortification of the infrastructure of financial power. The room for managing the network of social power relations in a progressive way has contracted greatly, and the present Crisis does not make a genuinely social-democratic politics any more viable than it has been over the past three decades. Reform strategies that fail to penetrate beneath the ideological representations that have dominated the neoliberal era will be refracted by so many unseen mediations as to increasingly blunt their progressive potential. For many decades, an intricate web of institutional mechanisms has grown under the cover provided by an ideology of institutional retreat; if we rely on conceptualizations that reproduce this ideological obfuscation, our consciously held concepts and the intentional strategies based on them will give us an ever weaker grip on the world.

A useful way to highlight some of the issues at stake here is to look at the proposals put forward by Robert Shiller in his book *The Subprime Solution*.[58] His proposal for a democratization

---

57 For a similar argument made in a different context, see G. Fridell, "Fair-Trade Coffee and Commodity Fetishism: The Limits of Market-Driven Social Justice," *Historical Materialism*, 2007, 15 (4).

58 R. J. Shiller, *The Subprime Solution*, Princeton: Princeton University Press, 2008.

of the financial system gives a very good sense of what political strategies aiming at the re-embedding or re-regulation of the financial system would amount to. Some of his recommendations are as follows: "good-quality, comprehensive financial advice, delivered ... one-on-one, Suze Orman-style"; "standardized default-option financial plans that operate well when people are inattentive and fail to act"; "the authoritative assertion of new standard boilerplate for common contracts such as mortgages. Most individuals will accept a standard contract if it is put forward by those whom they consider experts, and they will not try to judge the issue for themselves"; large information databases which "would permit, for example, the construction of an array of up-to-date and specific personal income indices by occupation, demographics, or health status."[59] Clearly this would be a nightmare of Foucauldian discipline. Shiller is not just addressing issues of institutional reform in the political-economy sense of the word: his recommendations go much deeper, and what he is outlining seems to be a full-scale capitalist conquest of the American psyche, a thoroughgoing financialization of the self.[60]

This is not a project that progressive political economists should support. The argument made here is intended as a new starting-point—one that may close off some political possibilities but will open up many more. Precisely the fact that Shiller's recommendations seem so extreme is an indication that the present situation is not just a regular crisis. In many past crises, legitimacy—as a key ingredient of the integrity of the American financial infrastructure and the institutional linkages that are at the root of the state's control over socio-economic life— remained intact or was restored relatively easily, and the main problem was the more or less technical problem-solving. The relatively predictable susceptibility of the American middle and working classes to the temptations of consumer and mortgage credit allowed the state and financial elites considerable room for maneuver. Even the radicalism of the 1960s never prevented the steady growth of suburban homeownership, consumption and household debt. But, clearly, the present Crisis does involve some significant legitimacy problems—not produced by conscious, purposeful resistance, but rather by people simply buckling under the pressure of financial discipline.

---

59 Ibid., p. 126, p. 130, p. 133, p.138, respectively.
60 I would like to thank Victoria Hattam for suggesting this term.

The Crisis has shown us that there are some limits to how much hegemonic forces can disempower people and still expect them to be competent actors in a capitalist economy. In this sense, the current situation is a vivid illustration of Hegel's understanding of power as set out in his narrative of the master/slave dialectic.[61] Power always has constraining effects, but it can never fully eradicate the subjective powers and agency of the oppressed. When it does end up crippling people's capacities to be more or less competent actors, the result is an erosion of social bonds that includes the master's own socially constructed status. So the current Crisis is not a product of politics and regulation having let the market spin out of control, but precisely a product of contradictions internal to the operation of power and control, of financial power having gone beyond its own conditions of possibility. And this is where the real moment of political possibility lies, in the lived experience of the contradictory effects of power: there is an openness here that we will never find in the organizational structures of the state taken by themselves. Of course, our experience of power is profoundly shaped by everything the state does, but the point is precisely that the state presents power in its coherent, ideal and formal aspects and not its contradictory aspects. The state aims to make power work, not to expose its contradictions. And this means that, as long as we do not question the way the state presents itself and its relationships to economic life, there will be strict limits to the range and variety of sources of oppression that we can address.

The objective of this chapter has not, of course, been to offer a political program. But having more precise understandings of how the edifice of financial power is constructed tells us more about where we should look to find spaces for political intervention. Yet this does not mean that we can replace existing arguments for re-regulation with alternative, less state-centered political programs. We should begin to entertain the possibility that there is something problematic about the desire to offer a political program in the way that has been traditionally conceived. The idea that intellectuals only behave responsibly if they not only offer criticism but also prescribe alternatives is bound to be either presumptuous and pointless (because the political agencies that we would like to carry our programs are difficult to find) or conservative (because, after many calls in the desert, we learn to ratchet down our ambitions to a level where they can easily

---

61   G. W. F. Hegel, *Phenomenology of Spirit*, Oxford: Clarendon, 1977.

be taken up by existing political agencies). The leverage of the institutional mechanisms offered by society as it is presently constituted is not available to any and all political projects. Whereas dominant interests can access organizational mechanisms that at least potentially permit the effective implementation of political projects, the experience of oppression that motivates subordinate agency is likely to get lost through the engagement of such complex, ideology-ridden and intricately constructed institutional chains. Genuinely transformative projects will have to dig much deeper, deconstructing social meanings that we have come to rely on intuitively, denaturalizing identities and connections that we are deeply attached to, disarticulating institutional linkages that seem like basic preconditions for any kind of coherent social order, and exposing the operation of power and dependency in areas where we tend to experience little more than objective pressures and personal inadequacy.

2

THEIR GREAT DEPRESSION AND OURS

James Livingston

I

Now that everybody is accustomed to citing the precedent of the Great Depression in diagnosing the recent economic turmoil—and now that a severe recession is unfolding—it may be useful to treat these episodes as historical events rather than theoretical puzzles. The key question that frames all others is simple: Are these comparable moments in the development of American capitalism? To answer it is to explain their causes and consequences.[1]

Contemporary economists seem to have reached an unlikely consensus in explaining the Great Depression—they blame government policy for complicating and exacerbating what was just another business cycle. This explanation is still gaining intellectual ground, and it deeply informed opposition to the plans for bailing out US financial institutions. The founding father here is Milton Friedman, the monetarist who argued that the Fed unknowingly raised real interest rates between 1930 and 1932 (nominal interest rates remained more or less stable, but as price deflation accelerated across the board, real rates went

---

[1] Figures and arguments on the Great Depression can be consulted and tested in James Livingston, *Pragmatism and the Political Economy of Cultural Revolution, 1850–1940*, Chapel Hill, NC: University of North Carolina Press, 1994, Chapters 1 and 4; all other figures are from contemporary periodicals and recent government publications.

up), thus freezing the credit markets and destroying investor confidence.

But the argument that government was the problem, not the solution, has no predictable political valence. David Leonhardt has presented the liberal version of the same argument—that if government does its minimal duty and restores liquidity to the credit markets, this crisis will not devolve into the debacle that was the Great Depression.[2] Niall Ferguson's essay on "The End of Prosperity" takes a similar line: "the underlying cause of the Great Depression—as Milton Friedman and Anna Jacobson Schwartz argued in their seminal book *A Monetary History of the United States 1867–1960*, published in 1963—was not the stock market crash but a 'great contraction' of credit due to an epidemic of bank failures."[3] Ben Bernanke's argument for the buyouts and the bail-outs derives, of course, from the same intellectual source. At Friedman's ninetieth birthday party in 2002, Bernanke, then a member of the Fed's board, said, "I would like to say to Milton and Anna: Regarding the Great Depression. You're right, we did it. We're very sorry. But thanks to you, we won't do it again."[4]

The assumption that regulates the argument, whether conservative or liberal, is that these two crises are like any other, and can be managed by a kind of financial triage, by treating the immediate symptoms and hoping the patient's otherwise healthy body will bring him back to a normal, steady state. Certain fragile, flamboyant or fraudulent institutions will be liquidated in the normal course of this standard-issue business cycle, and that is a good thing—otherwise the "moral hazard" of validating the "corrupt and incompetent practices on Wall Street and in Washington," as John McCain put it, will prevail.[5]

Crisis management, by this accounting, is an occasional activity that always addresses the same problems of liquidity and "moral hazard." By the same accounting, the long-term causes of crisis must go unnoticed and untreated because they are temporary deviations from the norm of market-determined equilibrium,

2 D. Leonhardt, "Lesson From a Crisis: When Trust Vanishes, Worry," *New York Times*, October 1, 2008.
3 N. Ferguson, "The End of Prosperity?", *Time Magazine*, October 6, 2008.
4 Remarks by Governor Ben S. Bernanke at the Conference to Honor Milton Friedman, University of Chicago, Chicago, Illinois, November 8, 2002. http://www.federalreserve.gov.
5 "McCain Takes A Little Credit for Bailout Passage", *CBS News.com*, October 3, 2008, http://www.cbsnews.com.

and because the system appears to be the sum of its parts: if the central bank steps in with "ready lending" when investor confidence falters, these parts will realign themselves properly and equilibrium will be restored.

From this standpoint, the Great Depression and today's economic crisis are comparable not because they resulted from similar macroeconomic causes but because the severity of the credit freeze in both moments is equally great, and the scope of the financial solution must therefore be equally far-reaching. Then and now, as Anna Schwartz explained in an interview with the *Wall Street Journal*, a "credit tightening" accounts for the collapse of the boom.[6]

There is another way to explain the Great Depression, of course. It requires looking at the changing structure or "long waves" of economic growth and development, digging all the while for the "real" rather than the merely monetary factors. This explanatory procedure focuses on "the fundamentals" and typically treats the financial system as a tertiary sector that merely registers the value of goods on offer—except when it becomes the repository of surplus capital generated elsewhere, that is, when personal savings and corporate profits cannot find productive outlets and flow instead into speculative channels.

The "long wave" approach has fallen out of favor, as more mainstream economists have adopted the assumptions enabled by the Friedman-Schwartz rendering of monetary history. This structural approach does, however, make room for crisis management at the moment of truth; here, too, the assumption is that financial triage will suffice during the economic emergency. When things settle down, when normal market conditions return, the question of long-term trends will remain.

The problem with the "long wave" approach—the reason it has less traction than the tidy alternative offered by Friedman and Schwartz—is that it cannot specify any connection between macroeconomic realities and conditions in the financial markets. Michael Bernstein's brilliant book on the origins of the Great Depression, for example, treats the Stock Market Crash of 1929 as a "random event" that complicated and amplified events happening elsewhere in the economy.[7]

---

6 "Bernanke Is Fighting the Last War," *Wall Street Journal*, October 18, 2008. http://online.wsj.com.
7 M. A. Bernstein, *The Great Depression: Delayed Recovery and Economic Change in America, 1929–1939*, New York: Cambridge University Press, 1987.

This theoretical stand-off has crippled our ability to provide a comprehensive explanation for the Great Depression, and thus to offer a convincing comparison between it and the current crisis. So let's start over—let's ask the kind of questions that are already foreclosed by the competing models. Was the Great Depression just another business cycle that the Fed messed up because it didn't understand the money supply? Or was it a watershed event that registered and caused momentous structural changes in the sources of economic growth? Or would more astute crisis management have saved the day?

Does the current crisis bear any resemblance to the Great Depression? Or is it just another generic business cycle that requires an unprecedented level of government intervention because the staggering amount of bad debt has compromised the entire financial system? The short answers, in order, are No, Yes, No, Yes, No. The long answers are as follows.

The underlying cause of the Great Depression was not a short-term credit contraction engineered by central bankers who, unlike Ferguson and Bernanke, hadn't yet had the privilege of reading Friedman. The underlying cause of that economic disaster was a fundamental shift of income shares away from wages and consumption to corporate profits that produced a tidal wave of surplus capital that could not be profitably invested in goods production. According to classical, neoclassical, and supply-side theory this shift of income shares should have produced more investment and more jobs, but it failed to do so. Why?

Let's first look at the new trends of the 1920s. This was the first decade in which the new consumer durables—autos, radios, refrigerators, etc.—became the driving force of economic growth. This was the first decade in which a measurable decline of net investment coincided with spectacular increases in non-farm labor productivity and industrial output (roughly 60 percent for both). This was the first decade in which a relative decline of trade unions gave capital the leverage it needed to enlarge its share of revenue and national income at the expense of labor.

These three trends were the key ingredients in a recipe for disaster. At the very moment that higher private-sector wages and thus increased consumer expenditures became the only available means to enforce the new pattern of economic growth, income shares shifted decisively away from wages, toward profits. For example, 90 percent of taxpayers had less disposable income in 1929 than in 1922; meanwhile corporate profits rose 62 percent, dividends doubled, and the top 1 percent of taxpayers increased their disposable income by 63 percent. At the very moment *that net investment became unnecessary to enforce increased productivity and output*, income shares shifted decisively away from wages, toward profits. For example, the value of fixed capital declined at the cutting edge of manufacturing—in steel and automobiles— even as productivity and output soared, because capital-saving innovations reduced both capital/output ratios and the industrial labor force.

What could be done with the resulting surpluses piling up in corporate coffers? If you can increase labor productivity and industrial output without making net additions to the capital stock, what do you do with your rising profits? In other words, if you can't invest those profits in goods production, where do you place them in the hope of a reasonable return? The answer is simple: in the most promising markets in securities listed on the stock exchange. You also establish time deposits in commercial banks and start issuing paper in the call-loan market that feeds speculative trading in securities. That is what corporate CEOs *outside the financial sector* did between 1926 and 1929, to the tune of $6.6 billion. They could not, and they did not, invest these profits in expanded productive capacity, because merely maintaining and replacing the existing capital stock was enough to enlarge capacity, productivity and output.

Those inflows of funds explain why a speculative bubble developed in the stock market. It was the single most important receptacle of the surplus capital generated by a decisive shift of income shares away from wages, toward profits—and that surplus drove demand for new issues of securities even after 1926. By 1929 about 70 percent of the proceeds from such IPOs were spent unproductively (that is, they were not used to invest in plant and equipment or to hire labor), according to Moody's Investors Service.

The stock market crashed in October 1929 because the non-financial firms abruptly pulled their $6.6 billion out of the call-loan market. They had experienced the relative decline in demand for consumer durables, particularly autos, since 1926, and knew better than the banks that the outer limit of consumer demand had already been reached. Demand for stocks, whether new issues or old, disappeared accordingly, and the banks were left holding the bag of "distressed assets." That is why they failed so spectacularly in the early 1930s—again, not because of a "credit contraction" engineered by a clueless Fed, but because the assets they were banking on and loaning against were suddenly worthless.

The financial shock of the Crash froze credit, including the novel instrument of installment credit for consumers, and thus amplified the income effects of the shift to profits that dominated the 1920s. Consumer durables, the new driving force of economic growth, suffered most in the first four years after the Crash. By 1932, demand for and output of automobiles was half the level of 1929; industrial output and national income were similarly halved, while unemployment reached almost 20 percent.

And yet, recovery was on the way, even though increased capital investment was not (by 1934 non-financial corporations could borrow from Herbert Hoover's Reconstruction Finance Corporation at almost interest-free rates). By 1937, industrial output and national income had regained the levels of 1929, and the volume of new auto sales exceeded that of 1929. Meanwhile, however, net investment out of profits continued to decline, so that by 1939 the capital stock per worker was lower than in 1929.

How did this unprecedented recovery happen? According to classical, neoclassical, and supply-side theory, it *couldn't have happened*—in their terms, investment out of profits must lead the way to growth by creating new jobs, thereby increasing consumer expenditures and causing feedback effects on profits and future investment. But as H. W. Arndt explained long ago, "Whereas in the past cyclical recoveries had generally been initiated by a rising demand for capital goods in response to renewed business confidence and new investment opportunities, and had only consequentially led to increased consumers' income and demand for consumption goods, the recovery of 1933–7 seems to have been based and fed on rising demand for consumers' goods."[8]

That rising demand was above all a result of net contributions to consumers' expenditures out of federal deficits and of new collective bargaining agreements. In this sense, the shift of income shares away from profits, toward wages, which permitted recovery was determined by government spending and enforced by labor movements.

So the "underlying cause" of the Great Depression was a distribution of income that, on the one hand, choked off growth in consumer durables—the industries that were the new sources

---

8 H. W. Arndt, *The Economic Lessons of the Nineteen-Thirties*, London: Oxford University Press, 1944.

of economic growth—and, on the other hand, produced the tidal wave of surplus capital which fuelled the stock market bubble of the late 1920s. By the same token, recovery from this economic disaster registered, and caused, a momentous structural change by making demand for consumer durables the leading edge of growth.

II

So far I have asked five questions that would allow us to answer this one: Does the recent and recurring economic turmoil bear the comparisons to the Great Depression we hear every day, every hour? On my way to these questions, I noticed that mainstream economists' explanations of the Great Depression converge on the idea that a "credit contraction" engineered by the hapless Fed was the "underlying cause" of that debacle. They converge, that is, on the explanation offered by Friedman and Schwartz. In this sense, the presiding spirit of contemporary thinking about our current economic plight—from Niall Ferguson to Henry Paulson and Ben Bernanke—is Friedman's passionate faith in free markets.

I am not suggesting that there is some great irony or paradox lurking in the simple fact that a new regulatory regime resides in the programs proposed by Paulson and Bernanke. Saving the financial system is a complicated business that will produce innumerable unintended consequences. Instead, my point is that rigorous regulation, even government ownership of the commanding heights, is perfectly consistent with the development of capitalism.

Here, then, are the remainder of those five questions— questions that are foreclosed by the theoretical consensus gathered around Friedman's assumptions about business cycles and crisis management. Would more astute crisis management have prevented the economic disaster of the 1930s? Does the current crisis bear any resemblance to the Great Depression? Or is it just another generic business cycle that requires an unprecedented level of government intervention because the staggering amount of bad debt has compromised the entire financial system?

More astute crisis management could not have saved the day in the early 1930s, no matter how well schooled the Fed's governors might have been. The economic crisis was caused by long-term structural trends that, in turn, devastated financial markets (particularly the stock market) and created a credit freeze—that is, a situation in which banks were refusing to lend and businesses were afraid to borrow. The financial meltdown was, to this extent, a function of a larger economic debacle caused by a significant shift of income shares away from wages and consumption toward profits, at the very moment that increased consumer expenditures had become the fulcrum of economic growth.

So, even when the federal government offered all manner of unprecedented assistance to the banking system, including the Reconstruction Finance Corporation of 1932, nothing moved. It took a bank holiday and the Glass-Steagall Act—which barred commercial banks from loaning against collateral whose value was determined by the stock market—to resuscitate the banks, but by then they were mere spectators to the economic recovery created by net contributions to consumer expenditures out of federal deficits.

A glance at the relevant reports of the Comptroller of the Currency demonstrates conclusively that a "financial fix" was not the proximate cause of a recovery that featured growth rates unsurpassed in twentieth-century economic history. Between 1933 and 1937, according to the Comptroller's *Report* of 1937,[9] total bank deposits increased 52 percent, bank holdings of government securities increased 57 percent, idle reserves held in Federal Reserve banks increased 140 percent, but loans and discounts increased only 8 percent.

So the current crisis does bear a strong resemblance to the Great Depression, if only because its "underlying cause" is a recent redistribution of income toward profits, away from wages and consumption, and because all the unprecedented assistance offered to the banking system since the sale of Bear Stearns and the bankruptcy of Lehman Brothers in September 2008—AIG, Washington Mutual, Fannie Mae, Freddie Mac, the bail-out package, the equity stake initiative, etc.—has not thawed the credit freeze. The markets have responded accordingly, with extraordinary volatility.

The liquidation of "distressed assets" after the Crash of 1929 was registered in the massive deflation that halved wholesale and retail prices by 1932. This outcome is precisely what Bernanke and Paulson have been trying desperately to prevent since August 2007—and before them, it is precisely what Alan Greenspan was

---

9 The report was published in 1938.

trying to prevent by skirting the issue of the housing bubble and placing his faith in the new credit instruments fashioned out of securitized assets. Their great fear, at the outset of the crisis, was not another Great Depression, but the deflationary spiral that Japan experienced in the 1990s, after its central bank pricked a similar housing bubble by raising interest rates and disciplining the mortgage dealers.

On the one hand, these men feared deflation because they knew it would cramp the equity-loan market, drive down housing prices, slow residential construction, erode consumer confidence, disrupt consumer borrowing and reduce consumer demand across the board. Meanwhile, the market value of the assets undergirding the new credit instruments—securitized mortgages—would have to fall, and the larger edifice of the financial system would have to shrink as the banks recalculated the "normal" ratio between assets and liabilities. In sum, Greenspan, Bernanke, and Paulson understood that economic growth driven by increasing consumer expenditures—in this instance, increasing consumer debt "secured" by home mortgages—would grind to a halt if they did not reinflate the bubble.

On the other hand, they feared deflation because they knew its effects on the world economy could prove disastrous. To be sure, with deflation would come a dollar with greater purchasing power and thus lower trade and current-account deficits, perhaps even a more manageable national debt. But so, too, would come lower US demand for exports from China, India, and developing nations, and thus the real prospect of "decoupling"—that is, a world economy no longer held together by American demand for commodities, capital, and credit. The centrifugal forces unleashed by globalization would then have free rein; American economic leverage against the rising powers of the East would be accordingly diminished.

So Greenspan is not to be blamed for our current conditions, as every Congressman and all the CNBC talking heads seem to think. Under the circumstances, which included the available intellectual and theoretical alternatives, he did pretty much what he had to, hoping, all the while, that the inevitable market correction would not be too severe. Have Bernanke and Paulson then done their duty? There may well be corruption, fraud, stupidity, and chicanery at work in this mess, but they are much less important than the systemic forces that have brought us to the brink of another Great Depression.

The real difficulty in measuring the odds of another such disaster, and thus averting it, is that those available intellectual alternatives are now bunched on an extremely narrow spectrum of opinion—a spectrum that lights up a lot of trees but does not illuminate the surrounding forest. Again, everyone, including Bernanke, now seems to think, along with Friedman, that the "underlying cause" of the Great Depression was a "credit contraction" that froze the financial system between 1930 and 1932.

M. Gregory Mankiw recently joined this monetarist chorus: "The 1920s were a boom decade, and as it came to a close the Federal Reserve tried to rein in what might have been called the irrational exuberance of the era. In 1928, the Fed maneuvered to drive up interest rates. So interest-sensitive sectors like construction slowed." Then the Crash came, and "banking panics" followed— the "money supply collapsed" and credit froze as fear gripped the "hearts of depositors." So the recovery after 1933 was a function of "monetary expansion" eased by the end of the gold standard; the "various market interventions" we know as the New Deal "weakened the recovery by impeding market forces."[10]

By this accounting, pouring more money into the financial system will fix it, allowing the larger economy to find a new equilibrium at a reflated price level. The goal is to recapitalize the banks so that they can resume lending to businesses at a volume that sustains demand for labor and to consumers at a volume that sustains demand for finished goods. By the terms of the $700 billion bail-out package and according to new (and unprecedented) initiatives by the Fed, this recapitalization will take three forms.

First, the Treasury will buy equity stakes in banks deemed crucial to reanimating the lifeless body of the financial system— to make this move is *not to nationalize these banks* by installing government as their owner, but rather to provide "start-up" capital free and clear, as if Paulson were backing an Initial Public Offering. Second, the Fed can buy short-term commercial paper from firms who need money to maintain inventory, pay vendors and hire labor. This move opens the central bank's discount window to mutual funds as well as non-financial firms, presumably small businesses that have neither cash reserves nor credibility with local bankers. Third, and most important, the Treasury will conduct an auction through which the mortgage-related "distressed assets"

---

10 Mankiw, "But Have We Learned Enough?", *New York Times*, October 26, 2008.

now held by lenders are liquidated—that is, are bought by the government for more than their market value, but less than their nominal value. Once those assets are "off the books," banks will have sufficient unencumbered capital to resume lending at volumes and rates conducive to renewed growth and equilibrium. Investor confidence will return as investment opportunities appear, so the logic runs, and new borrowing will soon follow.

Let us suppose, then, that Ferguson, Paulson, and Bernanke are right to assume that monetary policy is both the necessary and the sufficient condition of crisis management under present circumstances. Let us suppose, in other words, that the recapitalization of the banks proceeds exactly according to plan, and that interest rates keep falling because the Fed wants to encourage borrowing. Does the reflation and recovery of the larger economy naturally follow?

If Friedman was right to specify a "credit contraction" as the "underlying cause" of the Great Depression, then a "credit expansion" on the scale accomplished and proposed by Paulson and Bernanke should restore investor confidence and promote renewed economic growth; it should at least abort an economic disaster. But if a "credit contraction" was not the "underlying cause" of the Great Depression and its sequel in our own time, then no amount of "credit expansion" will restore investor confidence and promote renewed economic growth.

The historical record of the 1930s and the slow-motion crash of the stock market since 2007 would suggest that Friedman's theoretical answer to our question lacks explanatory adequacy— and that Paulson and Bernanke's practical program, *which follows the Friedman line*, has not restored, and cannot restore, investor confidence. The effective freeze of interbank lending which, contrary to recent news reports, was already an alarming index as early as September 2007, would suggest the same conclusion. ("The system has just completely frozen up—everyone is hoarding," said one bank treasurer back then: "The published LIBOR rates are a fiction."[11])

Moreover, a severe recession now waits on the other side of recapitalization, mainly because consumer confidence, spending and borrowing have been compromised or diminished, if not destroyed, by the credit freeze and the stock market crash:

---

11 Quoted in G. Tett, "Sense of Crisis Growing over Interbank Deals", *Financial Times*, September 5, 2007, p. 23.

"Discretionary spending is drying up as Americans grapple with higher food and energy prices, depressed home values and diminished retirement accounts."[12] Every indicator, from unemployment claims to retail sales, now points toward an economic crisis on a scale that has no postwar parallel.

Monetary policy, no matter how imaginative and ambitious, cannot address this crisis. For, just as a "credit contraction" was not the "underlying cause" of the Great Depression, so the reflation and recovery of the larger economy were not, and are not, the natural consequences of a financial fix. Our questions must then become, what *was* the "underlying cause" of the Great Depression, and how does the current crisis recapitulate the historical sequence that produced the earlier economic disaster? And finally, if monetary policy cannot solve the real economic problems that now face us, what more is to be done?

As I argued in the first part of this chapter, the Great Depression was the consequence of a massive shift of income shares to profits, away from wages and thus consumption, at the very moment— the Roaring Twenties—that expanded production of consumer durables became the crucial condition of economic growth as such. This shift produced a tidal wave of surplus capital that, *in the absence of any need for increased investment in productive capacity* (net investment declined steadily throughout the 1920s even as industrial productivity and output increased spectacularly), flowed inevitably into speculative channels, particularly the stock market bubble of the late twenties; when the bubble burst—by my calculation, when non-financial firms abruptly pulled out of the call-loan market—demand for securities listed on the stock exchange evaporated, and the banks were left holding billions of dollars in "distressed assets." The credit freeze and the extraordinary deflation of the 1930s followed; not even the Reconstruction Finance Corporation could restore investor confidence and reflate the larger economy.

So, recovery between 1933 and 1937 was *not* the result of renewed confidence and increased net investment determined by newly enlightened *monetary* policy (replacement and maintenance expenditures as a percentage of total private investment actually grew in the 1930s). It was, instead, the result of net contributions

---

12 M. Bustillo and A. Zimmerman, "Retailers Brace for Lean Holidays—Wal-Mart Sales Rise Just 2.4%, Other Chains Post Declines as Economic Outlook Spooks Consumers," *Wall Street Journal*, October 9, 2008, p. 1.

to consumer expenditures out of federal budget deficits. In other words, it was *fiscal policy under the New Deal that reanimated the new growth pattern that had first appeared in the 1920s*. It validated the consumer-led pattern that had been disrupted by the shift of income during the years before 1929.

That consumer-led pattern of economic growth was the hallmark of the postwar boom—the heyday of consumer culture. It lasted until 1973, when steady gains in median family income and non-farm real wages slowed and then ended. Since then, this stagnation has persisted, even though increases in labor productivity should have allowed considerable wage gains. Thus a measurable shift of income shares away from wages and consumption, toward profits, has characterized the pattern of economic growth and development over the last thirty-five years.

We hardly need Paul Krugman or Robert Reich to verify the result—that is, the widening gap between rich and poor, or rather between capital and labor, profits and wages. Two arch-defenders of free markets, Martin Wolf of the *Financial Times* and Alan Greenspan, have repeatedly emphasized the same trend. For example, last September Greenspan complained that "real compensation tends to parallel real productivity, and we have seen that for generations, but not now. It has veered off course for reasons I am not clear about."[13] A year earlier, Wolf similarly complained that "the normal link between productivity and real earnings is broken," and that the "distribution of US earnings has, as a result, become significantly more unequal."[14]

The partial offset to this shift of income shares came in the form of increasing transfer payments (i.e. government spending on "entitlements" and social programs); from 1959 to 1999 these payments were the fastest-growing component of labor income (10 percent per annum). The moment of truth was accordingly postponed. But then George Bush's tax cuts produced a new tidal wave of surplus capital with no place to go except into real estate, where the boom in lending against assets that kept appreciating allowed the "securitization" of mortgages—that is, the conversion of consumer debt into promising investment vehicles.

---

13 Quoted in K. Guha, "A Global Outlook," *Financial Times*, September 16, 2007, p. 8.
14 M. Wolf, "The Rich Rewards and Poor Prospects of a New Gilded Age," *Financial Times*, April 26, 2006, p. 13.

No place to go except into real estate? Why not into the stock market, or, better yet, directly into productive investment by purchasing new plant and equipment and creating new jobs? Here is how Wolf answered this question back in August 2007, when trying to explain why the global "savings glut"—as Ben Bernanke named his special concern before he became the chair of the Fed—was flowing to the US:

> If foreigners are net providers of funds, some groups in the US must be net users: they must be spending more than their incomes and financing the difference by selling financial claims to others. . . . This required spending is in excess of potential gross domestic product by the size of the current account deficit [the difference between spending and income]. At its peak that difference was close to 7 percent of GDP. . . . Who did the offsetting spending since the stock market bubble burst in 2000? The short-term answer was "the US government." The longer-term one was "US households."[15]

Wolf argues that once the dot-com bubble burst, the Bush tax cuts and the resulting federal deficit became the fiscal boost that forestalled a deep recession. Then he turns to the different but similarly effective deficit created by *consumer* debt:

> Now look at US households. They moved ever further into financial deficit (defined as household savings, less residential investment). Household spending grew considerably faster than incomes from the early 1990s to 2006. By then they ran an aggregate financial deficit of close to 4 percent of GDP. *Nothing comparable has happened since the Second World War, if ever.* Indeed, on average households have run small financial surpluses over the past six decades.[16]

And while consumers were going deeper into debt to service the current account deficit and finance economic growth, corporations were abstaining from investment: "The recent household deficit more than offset the persistent financial surplus in the business sector. For a period of six years—the longest since the Second World War—US business invested less than its retained earnings."[17]

Greenspan concurred: "intended investment in the United States has been lagging in recent years, judging from the larger

---

15 M. Wolf, "Why the Federal Reserve has to Keep the Party Going," *Financial Times*, August 22, 2007, p.13.
16 Ibid.
17 Ibid.

share of internal cash flow that has been returned to shareholders, presumably for lack of new investment opportunities."[18]

So the Bush tax cuts merely fueled the housing bubble—they could not and did not lead to increased productive investment. And that is the consistent lesson to be drawn from fiscal policy that corroborates the larger shift to profits, away from wages and consumption. A fiscal policy that cuts taxes on the wealthy and lowers the capital gains levy cannot work to restore growth because increased investment does not automatically flow from increased savings created by tax cuts—and, more importantly, *because the conversion of increased savings to increased private investment is simply unnecessary to fuel growth.*

In its lead editorial of October 23, 2008, called "An Obamanomics Preview," the *Wall Street Journal* offered the following account of America's pattern of economic growth since the start of the new millennium:

> After the dot-com bust, President Bush compromised with Senate Democrats and delayed his marginal-rate income tax cuts in return for immediate tax rebates. The rebates goosed spending for a while, but provided no increase in incentives to invest. Only after 2003, when the marginal-rate cuts took effect immediately, combined with cuts in dividend and capital gains rates, did robust growth return. The expansion was healthy until it was overtaken by the housing bust and even resisted recession into this year.

What is implied here is that robust growth after 2003 was a function of increased incentives to invest provided by reductions in tax rates on dividends and capital gains. But, as Wolf and Greenspan emphasize, rising profits precisely did not flow into productive investment. Growth occurred in the absence of increased investment.

This last simple fact—which could never be acknowledged by existing economic theory—is the sticking point. *There is no clear correlation between lower taxes on corporate or personal income, increased net investment, and economic growth.*

For example, the fifty corporations with the largest benefits from Reagan's tax cuts of 1981 reduced their investments over the next two years. Meanwhile, the share of national income from wages and salaries declined 5 percent between 1978 and 1986, while the share from investment (profits, dividends, rent) rose 27 percent, as per the demands of supply-side theory—but net investment

---

18 Alan Greenspan, *The Age of Turbulence*, New York: Penguin, 2007, p. 387.

kept falling through the 1980s. In 1987, Peter G. Peterson, the
Blackstone founder who was then chairman of the Council on
Foreign Relations, called this performance "by far the weakest net
investment effort in our postwar history." Yet economic growth
resumed in the aftermath of recession, in 1982, and continued
steadily until the sharp but brief downturn of 1992.

The responsible fiscal policy for the foreseeable future is, then,
to raise taxes on the wealthy and to make net contributions to
consumer expenditures out of federal deficits if necessary. When
asked why he wants to make these moves, Barack Obama doesn't
have to retreat to the "fairness" line of defense Joe Biden used
when pressed by Sarah Palin in debate, or, for that matter, by
the leader of the liberal media, the *New York Times* itself, which
admonished the then Democratic candidate as follows: "Mr.
Obama has said that he would raise taxes on the wealthy, starting
next year, to help restore fairness to the tax code and to pay for his
spending plans. With the economy tanking, however, it's hard to
imagine how he could prudently do that."[19] In fact, if our current
crisis is comparable to the early stages of the Great Depression, it's
hard to imagine a more prudent and more productive program.

19 Editorial, "The Crisis Agenda," *New York Times*, October 6, 2008.

3

THE CRISIS IN THE HEARTLAND

Peter Gowan

The long Credit Crunch that began in the Atlantic world in August 2007 is strange in its extraordinary scope and intensity. Mainstream discourse, referring to a "Subprime" Crisis, implies that the Credit Crunch has been caused, rather than triggered, by a bubble in the real economy. This is at best naïve: after all, the bursting of an equally large bubble in the Spanish housing market led to no such blow-out in the domestic banking system.[1] The notion that falling house prices could shut down half of all lending in the US economy within a matter of months—and not just mortgages, but car loans, credit-card receivables, commercial paper, commercial property and corporate debt—makes no sense. In quantitative terms this amounted to a credit shrinkage of about $24 trillion, nearly double US GDP.[2] Erstwhile lenders were soon running not just from subprime securities but from the supposedly safest debt of all, the "super senior" category, whose price by the end of 2007 was a tenth of what it had been just a year before.[3]

An understanding of the Credit Crunch requires us to transcend the commonsense idea that changes in the so-called real economy drive outcomes in a supposed financial superstructure. Making this

1 Leslie Crawford and Gillian Tett, "Spain spared because it learnt lesson the hard way," *Financial Times*, February 5, 2008.
2 The total debt owed by financial and non-financial private sectors in the US in 2008 has been calculated at $48 trillion. George Magnus, "Important to curb destructive power of deleveraging," *Financial Times*, September 30, 2008.
3 David Patterson, "Central banks must find or become buyers of system risk," *Financial Times,* February 5, 2008.

"epistemological break" is not easy. One reason so few economists saw a crisis coming, or failed to grasp its scale even after it had hit, was that their models had assumed both that financial systems "work," in the sense of efficiently aiding the operations of the real economy, and that financial trends themselves are of secondary significance.[4] Thus the assumption that the massive bubble in oil prices between the autumn of 2007 and the summer of 2008 was caused by supply-and-demand factors, rather than by financial operators who, reeling from the onset of the crisis, blew the price from $70 a barrel to over $140 in less than a year, before letting the bubble burst in June 2008; a cycle with hugely negative "real economy" effects. Similar explanations were tendered for soaring commodity prices over the same period; yet these were largely caused by institutional investors, money-market and pension funds, fleeing from lending to the Wall Street banks, who poured hundreds of billions of dollars into commodities indices, while hedge funds with their backs against the wall pumped up bubbles in coffee and cocoa.[5]

Breaking with the orthodoxy that it was "real economy" actors that caused the crisis carries a political price: it means that blame can no longer be pinned on mortgage borrowers for the Credit Crunch, on the Chinese for the commodities bubble, or on restrictive Arab producers for the sudden soaring of oil. Yet it may allow us to understand otherwise inexplicable features of the crisis; not least, as we shall see, the extraordinary growth of subprime itself. We will thus take as our starting point the need to explore the structural transformation of the American financial system over the past twenty-five years. I will argue that a New Wall Street System has emerged in the US during this period, producing new actors, new practices and new dynamics. The

---

4 For a useful survey of why most economists were completely incapable of grasping the crisis, see Chris Giles, "The Vision Thing," *Financial Times*, November 26, 2008.
5 Javier Blas, "Commodities have proved a saving grace for investors," *Financial Times*, March 6, 2008; Chris Flood, "Speculators give a stir to coffee and cocoa prices" *Financial Times*, February 5, 2008. That these financial operators were able to build and burst such bubbles derived, of course, from the fact that the markets for oil and commodities are organized in London, New York and Chicago, with rules made to match the interests of American and British capital. As Jeff Sprecher, CEO of Intercontinental Exchange (ICE), the London-based market whose rules enabled the blowing of the oil bubble, explained to the *Financial Times*, the market's organizers could not understand why members of Congress should want to give up control over this sector by closing ICE down. "View from the Top," *Financial Times*, August 6, 2008.

resulting financial structure-cum-agents have been the driving force behind the present crisis. En route, it proved spectacularly successful for the richest groups in the US: the financial sector constituted by far the most profitable component of the American and British economies and their most important "export" earner. In 2006, no less than 40 percent of American corporate profits accrued to the financial sector.[6] But the new structure necessarily produced the dynamics that led towards blow-out.

This analysis is not offered as a monocausal explanation of the Crisis. A fundamental condition, creating the soil in which the New Wall Street System could grow and flourish, was the project of the "fiat" dollar system, the privatization of exchange-rate risk and the sweeping away of exchange controls—all euphemized as "financial globalization." Furthermore, the system could not have risen and flourished if it had not offered answers—however ultimately pathological—to a range of deep-seated problems within American capitalism overall. There is thus a rational, dialectical kernel in the superficial distinction between financial superstructure and the "real" US economy. In what follows, I will first sketch the main elements of the New Wall Street System, and briefly show how its crisis took such spectacular forms. I will then argue that, to understand the deeper roots of the malaise, we do indeed need to probe into the overall socio-economic and socio-political characteristics of American capitalism as it has evolved over the past twenty-five years. I will raise the possibility of systemic alternatives, including that of a public-utility credit and banking model. Finally, I will consider the international dynamics unleashed by the present crisis and their implications for what I have elsewhere described as the Dollar–Wall Street Regime.[7]

THE NEW WALL STREET SYSTEM

The structure and dynamics of Wall Street banking changed dramatically in the quarter of a century after the mid-1980s. The main features of the New System include: (i) the rise of the lender-

---

6 Lawrence Summers, "The pendulum swings towards regulation," *Financial Times*, October 27, 2008. The figure of 40 percent actually understates the share of profits accruing to the financial sector, since these are in part concealed by being transformed into huge employee bonuses, to reduce headline profits data; one reason for the bonus system that is often overlooked.

7 For an earlier exploration of these issues see my *Global Gamble*, New York and London: Verso, 1999.

trader model; (ii) speculative arbitrage and asset-price bubble-blowing; (iii) the drive for maximizing leverage and balance-sheet expansion; (iv) the rise of the shadow banking system, with its London arm, and associated "financial innovations"; (v) the salience of the money markets and their transformation into funders of speculative trading in asset bubbles; (vi) the new centrality of credit derivatives. These changes mutually reinforced each other, forming an integrated and complex whole, which then disintegrated in the course of 2008. We will briefly examine each of them in turn.

Trading models

For most of the post-war period, Wall Street investment banks engaged in very little securities trading on their own account, as opposed to trading on behalf of clients; while the big depository commercial banks shunned such activity. But from the mid-1980s on, proprietary trading in financial and other assets became an increasingly central activity for the investment banks, and for many commercial banks, too. This turn was connected, firstly, to the new volatility in foreign-exchange markets after the dismantling of Bretton Woods; and then to the opportunities created by domestic financial liberalization, above all the scrapping of capital controls and the opening of other national financial systems to American operators. These changes offered opportunities for a massive expansion of Wall Street trading activity, which would become a crucial source of profits for the investment banks.[8] The turn toward speculative proprietary trading was pioneered by Salomon Brothers, whose Arbitrage Group was established in 1977 and acquired extraordinary profitability under John Meriwether during the 1980s.[9]

---

8 The bread-and-butter of Wall Street investment bank income had been fixed (cartelized) fees for trading securities on behalf of clients until 1975, when a change in the law limited such fees. At the start of the 1980s, this fee income was still greater for the investment banks than profits from trading on their own account. But from the mid-1980s, these banks plunged seriously into proprietary trading. By the end of the 1990s, trading income was a third bigger than income from commissions for trading on behalf of others. And some of the biggest banks earned over half their profits from such trading. See John Gapper, "After 73 years: The last gasp of the Broker-Dealer," *Financial Times*, September 16, 2008.
9 On Salomon Brothers and the subsequent career of John Meriwether's team in the 1990s, when they constructed ITCM under the sponsorship of Merrill Lynch, see Roger Lowenstein, *When Genius Failed*, New York: Random House, 2001.

As well as trading on their own account, the Wall Street banks became increasingly involved in lending funds for other bodies to use in their trading activities: hedge funds, so-called private equity groups (trading in companies), or special investment vehicles (SIVs) and conduits, created by the investment banks themselves.[10] Such lending, known in the jargon as prime brokerage, was also an extremely profitable activity for the Wall Street banks: for many, their single greatest earner.[11] This turn to the lender-trader model did not mean that the investment banks ceased their traditional activities in investment banking, broking, fund management, etc. But these activities acquired a new significance in that they provided the banks with vast amounts of real-time market information of great value for their trading activity.[12]

Trading activity here does not mean long-term investment, Warren Buffett–style, in this or that security, but buying and selling financial and real assets to exploit—not least by *generating*—price differences and price shifts. This type of "speculative arbitrage" became a central focus, not only for the investment banks but for commercial banks as well.[13] So, too, did the related effort to generate asset-price bubbles. Time and time again, Wall Street could enter a particular market, generate a price bubble within it, make big speculative profits, then withdraw, bursting the bubble. Such activity was very easy in so-called emerging market economies with small stock or bond markets. The Wall Street banks gained a wealth of experience in blowing such bubbles in the Polish, Czech or Russian stock markets in the 1990s and then bursting them to great profit. The dot-com bubble in the US then showed how the same operation could be carried through in the heartland without any significant loss to the Wall Street banks (as opposed to some European operators, notably insurance companies, eager to profit from the bubble but hit by the burst).

---

10 After the Enron scandal, SIVs and conduits were initially not allowed to engage in active trading on their own account, but this restriction was soon lifted.
11 James Mackintosh, "Collapse of Lehman leaves prime broker model in question," *Financial Times*, September 25, 2008.
12 Philip Augar gives a vivid account of how key such informational centralization from all the main markets was in giving the investment banks a decisive competitive edge over their smaller or non-investment banking rivals. See his *The Greed Merchants: How the Investment Banks Played the Free Market Game*, London: Penguin, 2006.
13 See Nasser Saber, *Speculative Capital: The Invisible Hand of Global Finance*, London: FT Prentice Hall 1999.

Both the Washington regulators and Wall Street evidently believed that together they could manage bursts.[14] This meant there was no need to prevent such bubbles from occurring: on the contrary, it is patently obvious that both regulators and operators actively generated them, no doubt believing that one of the ways of managing bursts was to blow another dynamic bubble in another sector: after dot-com, the housing bubble; after that, an energy-price or emerging-market bubble, and so on. This may seem to imply a formidably centralized financial power operating at the heart of these markets. Indeed, the New Wall Street System was dominated by just five investment banks, holding over $4 trillion of assets, and able to call upon or move literally trillions more dollars from the institutions behind them, such as the commercial banks, the money-market funds, pension funds, and so on. The system was a far cry from the decentralized market with thousands of players, all slavish price-takers, depicted by neoclassical economics. Indeed, the operational belief systems of what might be called the Greenspan-Rubin-Paulson milieu seems to have been post-Minskian. They understood Minsky's theory of bubbles and blow-outs, but believed that they could use it strategically for blowing bubbles, bursting them, and managing the fallout by blowing some more.

Maximizing leverage

The process of arbitrage and bubble-blowing requires more of financial operators than simply bringing together the maximum amount of information about conditions across all markets; it also demands the capacity to mobilize huge funds to throw into any particular arbitrage play, in order to shift market dynamics in the speculator's favor.

A striking feature of the New Wall Street System business model was its relentless drive to expand balance sheets, maximizing the assets and liabilities sides. The investment banks used their leverage ratio as the target to be achieved at all times rather than as an outer limit of risk to be reduced where possible by holding surplus capital. A recent New York Federal Reserve report demonstrates how this approach proved powerfully pro-cyclical in an asset-market bubble, driving the banks to expand their borrowing

---

14 Alan Greenspan, "We will never have a perfect model of risk," *Financial Times*, March 17, 2008.

as asset prices rose.[15] In their illustration, the report's authors, Tobias Adrian and Hyun Song Shin, assume that the bank actively manages its balance sheet to maintain a constant leverage ratio of 10. Suppose the initial balance sheet is as follows: the bank holds 100 worth of securities, and has funded this holding with an equity of 10, plus debt worth 90.

Assets	Liabilities	
Securities 100	Equity	10
	Debt	90

The bank's leverage ratio of security to equity is therefore 100/10=10.

Suppose the price of the securities then increases by 1 per cent, to 101. The proportions will then be: securities 101, equity 11, debt 90. So its leverage is now down to $101/11 = 9.2$. If the bank still targets leverage of 10, then it must take on additional debt ("d"), to purchase d worth of securities on the asset side, so that the ratio of assets/equity is: $101/11 + d = 10$, i.e. $d = 9$.

The bank thus takes on additional debt worth 9, and with this money purchases securities worth 9. After the purchase, leverage is back up to 10. Thus, an increase in the price of the security of 1 leads to an increased holding worth 9: the demand curve is upward-sloping.

Assets	Liabilities	
Securities 110	Equity	11
	Debt	99

The mechanism works in reverse, too. Suppose there is shock to the securities price, so that the value of security holdings now falls to 109. On the liabilities side, it is equity that bears the

---

15 Tobias Adrian and Hyun Song Shin, "Liquidity and Leverage," Staff Report no. 328, Federal Reserve Bank of New York, May 2008. The term "leverage" refers to the relationship between a bank's "equity" or "capital" and its assets—the sum that it has lent out. It is usually expressed as a ratio, so that if we say that Lehman's leverage at the time of its collapse was 25, this means that for every one dollar of capital the bank had 25 dollars of assets. But this figure of 25 also means that for every one dollar of capital, Lehman had 24 dollars worth of borrowings—i.e. liabilities.

burden of adjustment, since the value of debt stays approximately constant.

Assets	Liabilities
Securities 109	Equity 10
	Debt 99

But with securities at 109, equity at 10, debt at 99, leverage is now too high: 109/10 = 10.9 .

The bank can adjust down its leverage by selling securities worth 9, and paying down 9 worth of debt. Thus, a fall in the price of securities leads to sales of securities: the supply curve is downward-sloping.

A central mechanism through which the investment banks could respond to asset-price rises was borrowing in the "repurchase agreement"—or "repo"—market. Typically, the investment bank wishes to buy a security, but needs to borrow funds to do so. On the settlement day, the bank receives the security, and then uses it as collateral for the loan needed to pay for it. At the same time, it promises the lender that it will repurchase the security at a given future date. In that way, the bank will repay the loan and receive the security. But typically, the funds for repurchasing the security from the lender are acquired by selling the security to someone else. Thus, on the settlement day, the original lender to the investment bank is paid off and hands over the security, which is immediately passed on to the new buyer in exchange for cash. This kind of repo funding operation presupposes an asset-price boom. It has accounted for 43 percent of leverage growth amongst Wall Street banks, according to the same New York Fed report. Repos have also been the largest form of debt on investment banks' balance sheets in 2007–08.[16]

The question arises as to why the Wall Street banks (followed by others) pushed their borrowing to the leverage limit in such a systematic way. One explanation is that they were doing this in line with the wishes of their shareholders (once they had turned themselves into limited liability companies). "Shareholder value" capitalism allegedly requires the ratio of assets to capital to be maximized. Surplus capital reduces the return on shareholder

---

16 Ibid.

equity and acts as a drag on earnings per share.[17] But there is also another possible explanation for borrowing to the leverage limit: the struggle for market share and for maximum pricing power in trading activities. If you are a speculative arbitrageur or an asset-bubble blower, financial operational scale is essential to moving markets, by shifting prices in the direction you want them to go. In assessing which of these pressures—shareholder power or pricing power—drove the process, we should note how ready the Treasury, Fed and Wall Street executives have been to crush shareholder interests during the Credit Crunch, yet how resolutely they sought to protect the levels of leverage of the bulge-bracket banks during the bubble. By all accounts, Citigroup's turn to maximum balance-sheet and leverage expansion for trading activities derived not from shareholder pressure, but from the arrival there of Robert Rubin after his stint as US Treasury Secretary.[18]

Shadow banking

The drive for scale and for increasing leverage leads on to another basic feature of the New Wall Street System: the drive to create and expand a shadow-banking sector. Its most obvious features were the new, entirely unregulated banks, above all the hedge funds. These have had no specific functional role—they have simply been trader-banks free of any regulatory control or transparency in their speculative arbitrage. Private equity groups have also been, in essence, shadow trading banks, specializing in the buying and selling of companies. Special Investment Vehicles (SIVs) and conduits are similarly part of this system. In the words of the director of regulation at Spain's central bank, these SIVs and conduits "were like banks but without capital or supervision." Yet, as a *Financial Times* report noted: "In the past two decades, most regulators have encouraged banks to shift assets off their balance sheets into SIVs and conduits."[19]

The shadow banking system was not in competition with the regulated system; it was an outgrowth of it. The regulated

---

17 The rewards of senior bank executives were often linked to changing earnings per share. See John Kay, "Surplus capital is not for wimps after all," *Finacial Times*, October 22, 2008.
18 See, among others, "Singing the Blues," *The Economist*, November 27, 2008.
19 Leslie Crawford and Tett, "Spain spared because it learnt lesson the hard way," *Financial Times*, February 5, 2008.

commercial and investment banks acted as the prime brokers of the shadow banking operators, thereby gaining very large profits from their activities. This increasingly central feature of official bank activity was, in reality, a way of massively expanding their balance sheets and leverage. To tap the Wall Street banks for funding, the hedge funds had to hand over collateral; but through a practice known as rehypothecation, a proportion of these collateral assets could then be used by the prime broker as *its own* collateral for raising *its own funds*. The result was the self-financing of hugely profitable prime brokerage activities by the Wall Street banks, on a vast scale, without any extra commitment of their own capital: an ingenious way of greatly enlarging their leverage ratios.[20] The debate about whether deregulation or re-regulation in the financial sector has been occurring since the 1980s seems to miss the point that there has been a combination of a regulated and an unregulated shadow system, working dynamically together.

Shadow banking refers not only to institutional agents, like hedge funds, but also to the practices and products which allowed the investment banks to expand their leverage. Since the late 1990s an increasingly important part of this side of shadow banking has been the "over-the-counter" credit derivatives market, notably collateralized debt obligations (CDOs) and credit default swaps (CDSs). The most obvious attraction of these lay in the regulatory arbitrage they offered, enabling banks to expand leverage.[21] Traditionally banks had to insure their credit operations, and such insurance entailed supplying collateral. The beauty of CDSs lay in the fact that, as shadowy "over-the-counter" products, they did not require the commitment of appropriate tranches of capital as collateral, and thus facilitated more leverage. CDS expansion began on a major scale after derivatives specialists from JP Morgan Chase persuaded AIG to start writing them on CDOs in 1998.[22]

CDOs were also a clever solution to leverage problems. By acquiring large quantities of securitized loans and thus greatly expanding their balance sheets, banks should have expanded

20 Mackintosh, "Collapse of Lehman leaves prime broker model in question."
21 Christina Bannier and Dennis Hänsel, "Determinants of European Banks' Engagement in Loan Securitization," Deutsche Bundesbank Discussion Paper Series 2: Banking and Financial Studies no. 10/2008.
22 Gretchen Morgenson, "Behind crisis at AIG, a fragile web of risks," *International Herald Tribune*, September 29, 2008.

their equity base. But CDOs famously bundled together dozens or hundreds of such loans, of very varied quality, enabling the banks to increase their leverage. The CDOs were typically written by the rating agencies, for a fee, and then given a Triple A rating by the same agency, for a second fee. Such ratings allowed the banks' equity commitments to be minimized. These securitized loans—mainly from the housing market, but also from credit-card debt and car loans—offered investors far higher rates of return than they could get in the money markets. The crucial point about these so-called "structured securities" was not that they were securitized loans: these could in principle be perfectly safe; after all, a bond is, in reality, nothing but a securitized loan. But bonds have a clearly identifiable source, in an economic operator whose creditworthiness and cash-flow capacities can be assessed; they also have clear prices in the secondary bond markets. The products bundled in CDOs, however, came from hundreds of thousands of unidentifiable sources, whose creditworthiness and cash-flow capacity was not known; they were sold "over the counter," without any secondary market to determine prices, far less an organized market to minimize counterparty risk. In short, they were at best extremely risky because more or less totally opaque to those who bought them. At worst they proved a scam, so that within a few months of late 2007 the supposedly super-safe super-senior debt tranches within such CDOs were being downgraded to junk status.

Leverage restrictions were also removed through public policy. Hank Paulson achieved a notable success in this area in 2004 when, as head of Goldman Sachs, he led the Wall Street campaign to get the Securities and Exchange Commission to agree to relax the so-called net capital rule, restricting leverage for large investment banks. Henceforth, firms were effectively allowed to decide their own leverage on the basis of their risk models. The result was a rapid rise in the big banks' leverage ratios.[23] Importantly it enabled them to transfer their capital base to new activities, such

---

23 Stephen Labaton, "How SEC opened path for storm in 55 minutes," *International Herald Tribune*, October 4/5, 2008. In a classic maneuver, this was dressed up as a turn by the SEC towards *more* regulation of the investment banks. From a formal point of view this was right: the SEC acquired regulatory jurisdiction over them; but it simultaneously removed basic capital-base restrictions. Furthermore, from 2004 onwards the SEC had seven staff to supervise the big five investment banks, which had combined assets of over $4 trillion by 2007.

as collateralized debt obligations, which subsequently became such a significant element in their trading activities.

London's role

All these shifts are grouped under the euphemistic heading of "financial innovation"—changes in institutional arrangements, products, oversight structures, enabling Wall Street banks to escape regulatory restrictions and expand their activities and profits. Dozens of shifts of this sort could be documented. But one of the most fundamental was the construction of a large, new shadow banking system in London, alongside the "official" regulated sector. By the early 1990s the American investment banks had wiped out their London counterparts and dominated the Square Mile's asset markets, with the City acquiring an increasingly "wimbledonized" role within the New Wall Street System.[24] Gordon Brown institutionalized the new relationship in 1997 by creating the unified Financial Services Authority, which claimed to operate according to "principles" rather than binding rules: one central principle was that the Wall Street banks could regulate themselves. London thus became for New York something akin to what Guantánamo Bay would become for Washington: the place where you could do abroad what you could not do back home; in this instance, a location for regulatory arbitrage.

The term "Wall Street" should therefore be understood to include London, as a satellite for these American operators.[25] Together London and New York dominate the issue of new shares and bonds. They are the center of the foreign-exchange markets. Most significantly they have dominated the sale of over-the-counter derivatives, which make up the overwhelming bulk of derivatives sales.[26] In 2007, the UK had a global share of 42.5

---

24 The annual tennis tournament in Wimbledon is widely considered, at least in the UK, to be the greatest in the world; yet for decades there has been no British finalist.

25 There are some very large British commercial banks, but these should be distinguished from the City of London because, while some have participated heavily in the New Wall Street System, others such as the Hongkong and Shanghai Banking Corporation (HSBC), by some measures the largest bank in the world, and the Standard Chartered Bank, have been heavily focused on activities in East Asia.

26 The Chicago Mercantile Exchange, however, dominates sales of exchange-traded derivatives.

percent of derivatives based on interest rates and currencies, with the US handling 24 percent. In terms of credit-derivatives trading, the US handled 40 percent in 2006, while London handled 37 percent (down from 51 percent in 2002).

Funding speculation

The enormous expansion in the activities of the Wall Street banks and their shadow system required ever larger amounts of funding. Such funding was classically supplied by the recycling of retail savings sitting in deposit accounts and, even more importantly, by the commercial banks creating large supplies of credit money. But in post-1980s America such retail savings were minuscule—a point to which we will return—and credit money from the commercial banks, though significant, was soon hopelessly inadequate. In these circumstances the trader banks turned to the wholesale money markets. At the heart of such markets were the interbank markets, with interest rates on, or just a few basis points above, the Fed's policy rates. Historically these markets were used to ensure that the banks were able to clear smoothly on a daily basis, rather than as a source of new, large-scale funding, let alone funding of a speculative nature. There was also the commercial-paper market, typically used by the big corporations for short-term funding, again principally to smooth their operations.

But in the New Wall Street System, these money markets were transformed. They remained centers of short-term lending, but they were increasingly funding speculative trading activity. On the supply side, the funds available for lending to Wall Street were expanding rapidly, especially through the expansion of pension funds during the 1980s and 1990s. In rather typical American style, a small change in the tax code through amendment 401(k) in 1980 opened the door to this development. This amendment gave a tax break to employees and employers if they put money into pension plans; the result was a massive flow of employee income into these plans, totaling nearly $400 billion by the end of the 1980s. By the late 1990s it had climbed to almost $2 trillion.[27]

---

27 Roger Lowenstein, *Origins of the Crash*, New York: Penguin, 2004, pp. 24–5. This expansion of bank funding for speculative trading through the transformation of the "wholesale" markets intersected, of course, with the ending of capital controls, enabling the growth of international wholesale borrowing by banks and the rise of "carry trade" operations, such as that based on the yen: banks borrowing in yen, at 0.5 percent or less, and taking the funds into

At the same time as becoming key sources for the liabilities of the investment banks through short-term lending to them, the mutual funds, pension funds and so forth also became increasingly important targets for Wall Street's efforts to sell asset-backed securities, and in particular collateralized debt obligations. Thus the New Wall Street System attempted to draw the fund managers into speculative bubble activity on both the funding (liability) side and on the asset side, enabling ever larger balance-sheet expansion.

The Causes of the Crisis

It might, in principle, have been the case that the cluster of mutually reinforcing innovations which we have called the New Wall Street System were *responses* to the emergence of a housing-market bubble in the US from 2001. If so, we would have had a classic Minskian crisis linked to housing. In fact, all the key innovations were set in place before the onset of the bubble. Indeed there is ample evidence that the Wall Street banks quite deliberately planned a house-price bubble, and spent billions of dollars on advertising campaigns to persuade Americans to increase their mortgage-related debt. Citigroup ran a billion-dollar campaign with the theme "Live Richly" in the 1990s, designed to get home owners to take out second mortgages to spend on whatever they liked. Other Wall Street banks acted in a similar fashion, with a great deal of success: debt in second mortgages climbed to over $1 trillion in a decade.

But the bubble that generated the Credit Crunch of 2007 lay not only—or even mainly—in the housing market, but in the financial system itself. The crisis was triggered not only by the scale of the debt bubble, but by its forms. In a normal over-lending crisis, when banks have ended up with non-performing loans (as in Japan in the 1990s), both the location and scale of the problems can be identified without much difficulty. But in 2007 the debt bubble within the financial system was concentrated in over-the-counter derivatives, in the form of individual CDOs that had no market price or pricing mechanism—beyond the say-so of the ratings agencies—and which were distributed in their tens of thousands between the institutions at the summit of the financial

---

the Icelandic krona, at 18 percent. The funding of British commercial banks, overwhelmingly domestic at the start of the 1990s, had become largely based on overseas wholesale lending, to the tune of about £650 billion, by 2007.

system, as well as their satellite bodies such as SIVs. Once this set
of debt-accumulation arrangements was shown to be junk, in the
two Paribas cases in August 2007, the suppliers of credit funding,
such as money-market and pension funds, grasped that they had
no way of knowing how much of the rest of the CDO mountain
was also worthless. So they fled. Their refusal to keep supplying
the handful of opaque Wall Street investment banks and their
spin-offs with the necessary funds to keep the CDO market afloat
was what produced the Credit Crunch.

The investment banks had initially spread the word that the
effect of their securitization of debt had been to disperse risk widely
across a multitude of bodies. But this seems to have been false: the
Wall Street summit institutions themselves had been holding on to
the so-called super-senior debt tranches, in tens of thousands of
CDOs.[28] They had been borrowing billions in the money markets
to buy these instruments, gaining an interest rate on them some
10 basis points above their money-market borrowing costs. To
continue to turn that profit they had to keep going back to the
money markets to roll over their debts. Yet now the money markets
were shutting down.[29] When investors in the money markets fled
the recycling of short-term borrowing in the summer of 2007, the
entire pyramid centered on the CDOs began to crumble. When the
Wall Street banks tried to off-load their CDOs, they found there
was no market for them. The insurance companies that had insured
the CDOs with CDSs found their market collapsing, too.

Much remains obscure about the precise mechanisms through
which the Credit Crunch acquired its scope and depth in 2007–
08, principally because the main Wall Street operators themselves
sought to obfuscate both the nature of their plight and their
survival tactics. But it is possible to trace a number of phases
through which the crisis has passed. First, the attempt by the
Fed and Treasury to defend the investment-bank model as the
summit of the system, by acting as its lender of last resort. Second,
with the fall of Lehman Brothers, the collapse of this effort and
disappearance of the investment-bank model, producing a drive to
consolidate a universal-bank model in which the trading activities

---

28 Gillian Tett, "Misplaced bets on the carry trade," *Financial Times*, April 17,
2008.
29 For a useful mainstream (and apologetic) account of the risks involved in
CDOs and over-the-counter derivatives like CDSs, see the IMF publication by
Garry Schinasi, *Safeguarding Financial Stability: Theory and Practice*, Washington
DC: International Monetary Fund, 2005.

of the investment banks would occur within, and be protected by, the depository universal bank. In this phase, the Fed essentially substituted itself for the creditor institutions of the credit system, supplying loans, "money-market" and "commercial-paper market" funding for the banks. Between April and October 2008 this massive Central Bank funding operation involved about $5 trillion of credit from the Fed, the ECB and the Bank of England—equivalent to about 14 percent of global GDP. Insofar as this state funding can continue without raising serious sovereign creditworthiness problems, the most difficult and dangerous phase of the response to the crisis can get under way in a serious fashion. This will involve the deleveraging of the biggest banks, now in the context of negative feedback loops from deepening recessions. How and when this is achieved will give us a sense of the overall contours of the Credit Crunch.

Prevailing theories

Much of the mainstream debate on the causes of the crisis takes the form of an "accidents" theory, explaining the debacle as the result of contingent actions by, say, Greenspan's Federal Reserve, the banks, the regulators or the rating agencies. We have argued against this, proposing rather that a relatively coherent structure which we have called the New Wall Street System should be understood as having generated the crisis. But in addition to the argument above, we should note another striking feature of the last twenty years: the extraordinary harmony between Wall Street operators and Washington regulators. Typically in American history there have been phases of great tension, not only between Wall Street and Congress but also between Wall Street and the executive branch. This was true, for example, in much of the 1970s and early 1980s. Yet there has been a clear convergence over the last quarter of a century, the sign of a rather well integrated project.[30]

An alternative explanation, much favored in social-democratic circles, argues that both Wall Street and Washington were gripped by a false "neoliberal" or "free-market" ideology, which led them astray. An ingenious right-wing twist on this suggests that the problematic ideology was "laissez-faire"—that is, no regulation—

---

30 There were tensions between Wall Street and New York state regulator Eliot Spitzer after the dot-com bubble burst, but this simply highlighted how strong was the consensus at a higher level.

while what is needed is "free-market thinking," which implies some regulation. The consequence of either version is usually a rather rudderless discussion of "how much" and "what kind" of regulation would set matters straight.[31] The problem with this explanation is that, while the New Wall Street System was *legitimated* by free-market, laissez-faire or neoliberal outlooks, these do not seem to have been *operative* ideologies for its practitioners, whether in Wall Street or in Washington. Philip Augar's detailed study of the Wall Street investment banks, *The Greed Merchants*, cited above, argues that they have actually operated in large part as a conscious cartel—the opposite of a free market. It is evident that neither Greenspan nor the bank chiefs believed in the serious version of this creed: neoclassical financial economics. Greenspan has not argued that financial markets are efficient or transparent; he has fully accepted that they can tend towards bubbles and blow-outs. He and his colleagues have been well aware of the risk of serious financial crisis, in which the American state would have to throw huge amounts of tax-payers' money into saving the system. They also grasped that all the various risk models used by the Wall Street banks were flawed, and were bound to be, since they presupposed a general context of financial market stability, within which one bank, in one market sector, might face a sudden threat; their solutions were in essence about diversification of risk across markets. The models therefore assumed away the systemic threat that Greenspan and others were well aware of: namely, a sudden negative turn across all markets.[32]

Greenspan's two main claims were rather different. The first was that, between blow-outs, the best way for the financial sector to make large amounts of money is to sweep away restrictions on what private actors get up to; a heavily regulated sector will make far less. This claim is surely true. His second claim has been that, when bubbles burst and blow-outs occur, the banks, strongly aided by the actions of the state authorities, can cope with the consequences. As William White of the BIS has pointed out, this was also an article of faith for Bernanke.[33]

---

31 References to these kinds of debates can be found in Andrew Baker et al., *Governing Financial Globalization*, London: Routledge, 2005.
32 See Greenspan, "We will never have a perfect model of risk"; Alan Beattie and James Politi, "Greenspan admits he made a mistake," *Financial Times*, October 24, 2008.
33 Cited in John Cassidy, "Anatomy of a Meltdown: Ben Bernanke and the Financial Crisis," *New Yorker*, December 1, 2008.

Systemic Options

The real debate over the organization of financial systems in capitalist economies is not about methods and modes of regulation. It is a debate between systemic options, at two levels.

- A public-utility credit and banking system, geared to capital accumulation in the productive sector *versus* a capitalist credit and banking system, subordinating all other economic activities to its own profit drives.
- An international financial and monetary system under national-multilateral co-operative control *versus* a system of imperial character, dominated by the Atlantic banks and states working in tandem.

We can briefly look at each of these in turn.

A public-utility model?

All modern economic systems, capitalist or not, need credit institutions to smooth exchanges and transactions; they need banks to produce credit money and clearance systems to smooth the payment of debts. These are vital public services, like a health service. They are also inherently unstable: the essence of a bank, after all, is that it does not hold enough funds to cover all the claims of its depositors at any one time. Ensuring the safety of the system requires that competition between banks should be suppressed. Furthermore, policy questions as to where credit should be channeled are issues of great economic, social and political moment. Thus public ownership of the credit and banking system is rational and, indeed, necessary, along with democratic control. A public-utility model along these lines can, in principle, operate within capitalism. Even now the bulk of the German banking system remains in public hands, through savings banks and *Landesbanken*. The Chinese financial system is overwhelmingly centered on a handful of huge, publicly owned banks and the Chinese government does indeed steer the credit strategies of these banks. It is possible to envisage such a public-utility model operating with privatized banks. The post-war Japanese banking system could be held to have had this character, with all its banks strictly subordinated to the Bank of Japan's policy control via the "window-guidance system." The post-war British commercial bank cartel could also be viewed as broadly operating within that framework, albeit raking off excessive profits from its customers.

But a private capitalist credit system, centered on banks, would operate under the logic of money capital—in Marx's formula, M–M′: advancing money to others to make more money. Once this principle is accepted as the alpha and omega of the banking system, the functional logic points toward the Greenspan apotheosis. This has been the model adopted in the US and the UK since the 1980s: making money-capital king. It entails the total subordination of the credit system's public functions to the self-expansion of money capital. Indeed, the entire spectrum of capitalist activity is drawn under the sway of money capital, in that the latter absorbs an expanding share of the profits generated across all other sectors. This has been the model that has risen to dominance as what we have called the New Wall Street System. It has been a generator of extraordinary wealth within the financial system and has actually transformed the process of class formation in the Anglo-Saxon economies. This model is now in deep crisis.

The second debate centers on the underwriting of financial systems. Whether public or private, banking and credit systems are inherently unstable in any system where output is validated after production, in the market-place.[34] In such circumstances, these systems must be underwritten and controlled by public authorities with tax-raising capacities and currency-printing presses. Insofar as they are minimally public bodies—not utterly captured by the private interests of money capital—these authorities will aim to prevent crises by trying to bring the behavior of the financial system roughly into line with broad (micro as well as macro) economic goals. At present, only states have the capacity to play this role. Rule books like Basel I or II cannot do it; neither can the EU Commission or the ECB.

Intriguingly, the Atlantic projects grouped under the name of "economic globalization"—the fiat dollar system, ending of capital controls, free entry and exit of big Atlantic operators in other financial systems—have ensured that most states have been deprived of the capacity to underwrite and control their own financial systems: hence the endless financial blow-outs in the South over the last thirty years. Atlantic business interests benefited from these crises, not only because their losses were fully covered by IMF insurance—paid for later by poor people in the countries hit—but also because they were used as occasions to sweep open

---

34 Though this does not mean that they are all *equally* unstable.

the product and labor markets of these countries to Atlantic
penetration. But now the blow-outs have hit the metropolitan
heartland itself. Obviously the Atlantic economies will want
to keep this system going: the practices covered by "financial
globalization" constitute their most profitable export sector. But
it is not so clear that the rest of the world will buy a formula
for more of the same. The alternative would be some return to
public control, along with public underwriting. This could only be
achieved by individual national states regaining effective control,
via new multilateral co-operative systems comparable to those
that existed before 1971, implemented on a regional if not fully
international scale.

Here, however, we will focus on the question of why the
financial model centered on the New Wall Street System has
achieved such complete hegemony within American capitalism
over the past few decades. This takes us, finally, back out of
the financial sphere into the wider field of socio-economic and
socio-political relations in the US since the 1970s. Within this
broader context, we can begin to understand how the New Wall
Street System's rise to dominance within the US could have been
seen as a strategic idea for tackling the problems of the American
economy.

Financial dominance as national strategy

From the 1970s through to the early 1980s, the American
state waged a vigorous battle to revive the industrial economy,
partly through a mercantilist turn in external trade policy,
but above all through a domestic confrontation with labor to
reduce its share of national income. This was the vision of such
leaders as Paul Volcker; it was assumed that these measures
would return American industry to world dominance. Yet the
hoped-for broad-based industrial revival did not take place.
By the mid-1980s, non-financial corporate America was falling
under the sway of short-term financial engineering tactics,
geared toward the goal of enhancing immediate "shareholder
value." What followed was wave after wave of mergers and
acquisitions and buyouts by financial operators, encouraged
by Wall Street investment banks who profited handsomely
from such operations. The legitimating argument that this was
"enhancing industrial efficiency" seems scarcely credible. A
more convincing case would be that these trends were driven

by the new centrality of the financial sector within the structure of American capitalism.[35]

A full explanation of this development is, I think, not yet available. But the trend produced some structural features of American capitalism that have been present ever since. On the one hand, a protected military-industrial sector remains intact, funded from federal and state budgets. Some high-tech sectors, especially in ICT, were also strongly supported by state subsidies in the 1980s and 1990s, and have involved real new industrial investment, without as yet playing a transformative role in the overall economy: the main impact of ICT has been in the financial sector and retail. But the bulk of the American economy, on which growth depends, has been marked by stagnant or even declining incomes amongst the mass of the population and no growth motor from new investment, whether public or private. With the partial exception of ICT investment in the late 1990s, GDP growth in the US has not been driven by new investment at all. As is widely recognized, it has come to depend upon the stimulus of consumer demand; yet such household consumption was itself inhibited by stagnant mass incomes.

This circle was famously squared in two ways. First and most important, the problem of stimulating consumer demand was tackled through the sustained supply of credit from the financial system. Second, cheap commodities could be bought on an endless basis from abroad—especially from China—since dollar dominance enabled the US to run up huge current-account deficits, as other countries allowed their exports to the US to be paid for in dollars. The supply of credit from the financial system to the mass of consumers through the usual mechanisms of credit card, car debt and other loans and mortgages was, however, supplemented by the distinctive mechanism of asset-price bubbles, which generated so-called wealth effects among a relatively broad layer. The stock-market bubble of the 1990s raised the paper value of the private pensions of the mass of Americans, thus giving them a sense that they were becoming richer and could spend (and indebt themselves) more. The housing bubble had a double effect: it not only made American consumers feel confident that the value of their house was rising, enabling them to spend more; it was

---

35 This is not to say that American industrial production disappeared: it remained large, notably in the defense-budget related sector, as well as in cars, aerospace, ICT and pharmaceuticals.

reinforced by a strong campaign from the banks, as we have seen, urging them to take out second mortgages and use the new money for consumption spending.

Thus the New Wall Street System directly fuelled the 1995–2008 consumer-led American boom, which ensured that the US continued to be the major driver of the world economy. This was backed by a global campaign to the effect that the US boom was not the result of debt-fed growth aided by highly destructive trends in the financial system, but of American free-market institutions. Here, then, was the basis in the broader social relations of American capitalism for the rise to dominance of the New Wall Street System: it played the central role in ensuring debt-fed growth. This Anglo-Saxon model was based upon the accumulation of consumer debt: it was growth today, paid for by hoped-for growth tomorrow. It was not based upon strengthening the means of value-generation in the economies concerned. In short, it was a bluff, buttressed by some creative national accounting practices which exaggerated the extent of the American boom and productivity gains in the US economy.[36]

The role of China and other Asian exporting economies in this growth model extended beyond their large export surpluses of consumer goods to the US. These export surpluses were recycled back into the American financial system via the purchasing of US financial assets, thus cheapening the costs of debt by massively expanding "liquidity" within the financial system. The results of these trends can be summarized in the following figures. Aggregate US debt as a percentage of GDP rose from 163 percent in 1980 to 346 percent in 2007. The two sectors which account for this rise were household debt and internal financial-sector debt. Household debt rose from 50 percent of GDP in 1980 to 100 percent of GDP in 2007. But the really dramatic rise in indebtedness occurred within the financial sector itself: from 21 percent of GDP in 1980 to 83 percent in 2000 and 116 percent in 2007.[37]

---

36 A series of changes in US national accounting rules from 1995 onwards exaggerated both growth and productivity figures. Notable here was the use of so-called hedonic indicators.

37 Martin Wolf, "Why Paulson's plan was not a true solution to the crisis," *Financial Times*, September 24, 2008.

IMPLICATIONS

The ideological effects of the crisis will be significant, though of course far less significant than imagined by those who believe financial regimes are the product of intellectual paradigms rather than power relations. Yet the cant dished out in the past by the US Treasury and IMF is over. American-style financial-system models are now grasped as being dangerous. No less risky is the EU banking and financial-system framework, which the crisis has shown to be a house of cards, even if still standing at the time of writing. The EU's guiding notion is that banking systems are secured by good rules rather than by authoritative states with tax-raising powers. This has been shown to be a dangerous joke. The whole EU-EMU project has encouraged banks to grow too big for their national states to save them, while offering no alternative at EU or even Eurozone level. Absurdly, the Single Market and Competition rules in the financial sector insist on free competition between banks at all costs, and proscribe any state aid for them; while if the stability criteria were respected, any full-blown credit crisis would necessarily be transformed into a 1930s-style depression. Obviously these rules are for the birds, yet they are simultaneously the principal planks of the EU political economy.[38]

This crisis of the American and European set-ups will no doubt have two intellectual effects. First, to raise the credibility of the Chinese model of a state-owned, bank-centered financial system. This is the serious alternative to the credit models of the Atlantic world. The maintenance of capital controls and a non-convertible currency—which China has—are essential for the security of this system. Second, as the crisis unfolds, broader discussion of the public-utility model seems likely to return to political life, reopening a debate that has been silenced since 1991.

Some predict much more sweeping short-term changes, such as the replacement of the dollar as the global currency or the collapse of Western leadership institutions within the world economy. A complete debauching of the dollar by the Obama administration could, perhaps, lead to a stampede to dump it globally, along with

---

38 In addition, Western EU states made an unstated but real precondition for Eastern enlargement that the new entrants hand over the bulk of their commercial banks to their Western counterparts; a remarkable imperial move. These Western banks will now wish to starve the Eastern EU members of credit, as they seek every trick to deleverage and survive. Will the EU political authorities intervene in the market to block this? If so, how?

a retreat into regional or narrow imperial trading blocs.[39] But no less likely could be a temporary strengthening of the use of the dollar over the next decade: a long stagnation in the US may well be combined with very low interest rates and a low dollar. This could produce a new dollar carry trade, in which everybody borrows in dollars to take them across the exchanges into higher-value assets. This would produce a strong trend toward a decoupling of other exchange rates from the dollar, but it would not necessarily undermine the central element in dollar dominance: the readiness of other states to accept payments for their goods and credits in greenbacks.

We are also likely to see the intensification of the two basic structural trends in long-term credit-debt relations in the world economy. First, the creditor relations between the Atlantic world and its traditional South in Latin America, Africa and elsewhere, historically policed by the IMF. This relationship weakened over the last decade but is likely to be reinforced in the present crisis. Second, the contrary debtor relations between the United States and the East Asian New Growth Centre economies, which are also likely to deepen and tighten, particularly between China and the US. This is a power relationship in which China (and other creditors) can exercise real political leverage over Washington. We have seen this operating in both the timing and the form of the renationalization of Fannie Mae and Freddie Mac.[40] We will see it again as the US Treasury seeks buyers for its large new tranches of debt in 2009. The East Asian economies, above all China, will likely become ever more critical to global macro-economic trends, while the centrality of the US will weaken during its long stagnation. The strengthened financial clout of China and other East Asian states could impinge upon the old imperial credit-debt relationships between the Atlantic world and the South, by offering the latter alternative sources

---

39 A trend in this direction is evident in the US decision to give special treatment to Mexico, Brazil, Singapore and South Korea in terms of dollar-funding support.
40 The *Financial Times* reported that US Treasury Secretary Paulson confronted the fact that "the Bank of China had cut its exposure to agency debt over the summer" and thus: "found himself with a *fait accompli*. The federal government had to give reassurance to foreign investors in agency debt if it wanted to avoid chaos in financial markets and a run on the dollar. It smacks of debt crises past in Latin American countries, where the ultimate pressure for a bail-out came from foreign investors." John Gapper, "A US government bail-out of foreign investors," *Financial Times*, September 8, 2008.

of financial support. This threat is already prompting warnings in the Atlantic world for Washington to soften the predatory conditions it has traditionally imposed on Africa, Latin America and elsewhere.[41]

But whether this will mean that East Asia will start to build new market institutional arrangements for the world economy, challenging those of the Anglo-American world, remains unclear, for two reasons: first, the internal divisions within East Asia; and second, the question of China's strategic priorities at the present time. Thus, East Asia has an obvious rational collective interest in building its own, centralized commodity and oil markets and promoting them to world leadership, ending the dominance of London and Chicago. Such new market frameworks have sprung up, but they are divided: one in Hong Kong, one in Japan, and one in Singapore. As for China, it is currently overwhelmingly concentrated on maintaining domestic growth and carrying through the leap of dynamic capital accumulation from the coast to the interior. At present, it is showing not the slightest interest in challenging the Americans for leadership in shaping the institutions of the world economy. Thus the US has some breathing space. But such is the social and political strength of Wall Street, and the weakness of social forces that might push for an industrial revival there, that it would seem most likely that the American capitalist class will squander its chance. If so, it will enjoy another round of debt-fed GDP growth funded by China and others while the US becomes ever less central to the world economy, ever less able to shape its rules, and increasingly caught in long-term debt subordination to the East Asian credit matrix.

---

41 David Rothkopf, "The Fund Faces up to Competition," *Financial Times*, October 22, 2008.

FROM FINANCIAL EXPLOITATION TO GLOBAL BANKING INSTABILITY

Two Overlooked Roots of the Subprime Crisis

Gary A. Dymski

The proximate cause of the Subprime Lending Crisis was the end of the US housing bubble, which precipitated a rapid increase in mortgage delinquencies, especially among subprime mortgages issued in overheated markets. These mortgages were held as securities in portfolios across the globe; so payment difficulties at the base of the financial food chain led to seismic financial-market eruptions at the top.

Many analysts have dissected the macro and micro sources of the collapse of mortgage- and asset-backed finance, and of the subsequent global economic plunge. At the macro level, attention has concentrated on persistent current-account and savings imbalances; at the micro level, on flaws in regulatory mechanisms, which enabled the explosion of risk-amplifying behavior by borrowers and lenders alike. This chapter focuses attention on two factors that have been largely overlooked: the strategic transformation of banking at the onset of the neoliberal era; and long-established patterns of racial exclusion in the US markets for housing credit.

The strategic transformation of banking in the neoliberal age led step-by-step to the current crisis. The behavioral shifts that banks—and especially megabanks—made at the onset of the neoliberal age in the 1980s enabled them, through lending, to generate financial risks without absorbing them. In the 1990s, this permitted the transformation of racial and social exclusion in US credit markets. Financial exclusion and loan denial were transformed into financial exploitation: households previously denied mortgage credit were now awarded high-cost, high-risk loans. In the early 2000s, these predatory loan-making practices were adapted and brought into the broader housing market. This led, on the one hand, to the explosion of prices in the US housing market and, on the other, to pressure on market liquidity—the combination of which proved to be unsustainable. In sum, the perverse interaction between America's legacy of racial discrimination and social inequality and its hyper-competitive, world-straddling financial sector were among the triggers of the Subprime Crisis.

Discussions of policy responses to the Subprime Crisis have the same blind spot as debates on its causes. Attention centers on addressing global macro-structural imbalances and fixing the gaps and perverse incentives in financial regulations. But implications of the crisis for banking strategy, especially vis-à-vis racial inequality in lending markets, have received little attention. This chapter argues that these implications are hugely significant. Post-crisis policy responses will profoundly—and, if nothing changes, adversely—affect both the landscape of racial exclusion in credit markets and the economic functionality of banks.

Banking Risks and the Transformation of US Banking and Mortgage Markets

By definition, banks are financial firms that emit liquid deposits and create credit. The performance of these two functions for the economy entails risks: default risk, the possibility that borrowers may not meet their repayment obligations in a timely manner; and liquidity risk, which is assumed by any economic entity that finances a longer-term asset position with liabilities of shorter duration.

Banks experience tension between their liquidity-provision and credit-creation functions because these functions give rise to interlinked risks. In downturns or periods of heightened uncertainty, being liquid commands a premium: holding assets that are readily convertible into money is preferable to holding non-monetary assets that may be impossible to sell readily except at a steep discount. Non-bank economic units will be better able to survive such periods if banks provide them with fresh infusions of credit; but to do so banks must sacrifice their own liquidity.[1]

When banks generate default risks and liquidity risks through loan-making and absorb those risks on their balance sheets, there are built-in brakes on tendencies toward speculative and overly risky lending. For example, banks can lend more if they are willing to borrow more funds in short-term money markets. In the latter stages of an expansion, banks must then consider both that default risk will worsen on marginal loans, and that the liquidity risks on funds borrowed to make those loans will rise as well. This curbs the expansion of bank credit and slows economic growth.

This self-braking feature would be lost if banks no longer absorbed default and liquidity risk when lending. If banks could make loans without being in any way accountable for the resulting default risk, then a slowdown in credit growth would have to originate with whatever entity was underwriting banks' growing default risk. Even in this case, banks might slow lending over the cycle if the cost of the funds they borrowed to support lending climbed systematically. If this liquidity risk too was eliminated (in this extreme case), banks could make as many loans as they wished without any risk. The potential for disjunctures between systemic and individual dimensions of default- and liquidity-risk generation is clear.

Banking and mortgage market turbulence since 1980

Prior to the 1980s, US banks kept the loans they made on their own balance sheets, and absorbed the risks their lending generated. Operating with long-standing geographic and product-line restrictions, banks focused primarily on local depositors and borrowers. Housing credit was provided primarily by savings and loan companies and savings banks ("thrifts"), which attracted longer-term consumer savings.

This structure proved unsustainable in the macroeconomic turmoil of the late 1970s. In this context, stagflation and interest rates well above banks' regulatory maxima (stipulated in Regulation Q) led to systematic disintermediation, i.e. the loss of depositors to innovative savings outlets such as money-market money instruments. Their credit supply threatened, large

---

1 G. A. Dymski, "A Keynesian Theory of Bank Behavior," *Journal of Post Keynesian Economics*, 1988, 10(4).

non-financial firms created the modern commercial paper market and vastly expanded the scope of corporate bond markets. The combination of disintermediation and an inverted yield-curve, however, also decimated the thrift industry, which had originated and held most US mortgage debt.

This led to the passage, in 1980 and 1982, of legislation designed to modernize the regulation of commercial banking and the thrift sector. A period of competitive deregulation between the federal and state regulators of thrifts followed, leading some states' thrifts to undertake ill-advised speculative investments in the mid-1980s. This triggered many defaults and helped to transform the problem of thrift illiquidity into a crisis of thrift insolvency. A number of spectacular crashes of savings and loan institutions followed, as did 1989 legislation that permitted a federal industry bail-out. The thrift industry shrank dramatically. The 1980s were no less troubled for commercial banks: the Latin American debt crisis, loan problems in oil-patch states and other troubles generated widespread industry losses and a surge in bank failures.

Banks reacted to this period of tumult differently, depending on their size, activities, and strategies. We focus attention here on megabanks—the very large, globally active banking firms that operate via bank holding companies in numerous retail and wholesale markets. For these banks, the next several years brought mergers and institutional innovations that reshaped the competitive and institutional terrain of US banking and mortgage markets as a whole.

Banks shifted their strategic focus from earnings based on interest margin to earnings based on the fees they could earn from providing services. Some of these services were supplied to the retail market. In the 1980s, the focus was on creating a complete menu of financial products for upscale (asset-owning, income-secure) customers. Other services involved wholesale markets. There, banks began to bundle and sell off some of the credit contracts they had made with their commercial customers. Banks also accounted for an ever larger share of mortgage originations.

Indeed, banks' need to find new revenue sources corresponded with thrifts' reduced capacity to provide mortgage loans. It also corresponded with the transformation of housing finance from an intermediary-based to a securities-market-based system. Previously, lenders held mortgages to maturity and consequently bore substantial default and liquidity risk. In the new system, lenders made mortgages to sell them. This enhanced the importance of high-volume, fee-based operations: the process of originating, servicing and holding mortgages was split into its constituent parts, with each part priced and performed separately.

Establishing a mass securities-based system of housing finance required the commodification of risky mortgage assets. The first step in this process was the standardization of the instruments being bundled and sold. In the 1980s, this required the adoption of standardized mortgage eligibility criteria. These criteria made "relationship" lending unnecessary, making it possible for a new array of non-local, non-thrift lenders to originate mortgage debt. A second step was to generate a demand for these claims. Financial funds and intermediaries were induced to take on securitized mortgage debt because of the ready availability of government and private underwriting of mortgage debt. Two federally chartered agencies, FNMA (the Federal National Mortgage Association, or Fannie Mae) and FHLMC (the Federal Home Loan Mortgage Corporation, or Freddie Mac) provided a secondary market for qualifying mort-gages. A third agency, GNMA (Government National Mortgage Association, or Ginnie Mae), provided a secondary market for federally supported mortgages. These agencies insured market-wide homogeneity in terms and conditions by establishing balance-sheet and contractual thresholds which "conforming" mortgages must meet. The "plain vanilla" loans that met these standards were relatively safe: first, because substantial down payments were mandatory; second, because homeowners had to satisfy mortgage-payment-to-income criteria. FNMA and FHLMC set dollar limits on the mortgages they would underwrite; underwriting for larger, "jumbo" (non-conforming but otherwise "plain vanilla") mortgages was provided by several private mortgage insurers

This shift toward securitization radically changed the landscape of financial risks in the mortgage system. Default risk, monitored increasingly via riskiness criteria established centrally rather than by individual lenders, appeared to decline. Further, financial market participants widely held the view that FNMA underwriting implied government insurance against mortgage defaults. Liquidity risk, which was shifted from mortgage originators to mortgage holders, appeared to decline as well. Another factor keeping mortgage flows resilient was the United States' unique position within the global neoliberal regime, which could be traced to the fact that the US was both a supplier of global reserve currency and a safe haven in this period.[2]

From the mid-1980s to the mid-1990s, most mortgages were conforming conventional loans, underwritten by these agencies and then either held in agency portfolios or sold off. These agencies accommodated the larger flow of demand for securitized mortgages by increasing their proportion of pass-through securities (securities whose owners have claims on the underlying mortgage cash-flows). Accompanying this new epoch of securitization was ambiguity about the extent and locus of risk-bearing. Banks appeared to have shed much risk; but it wasn't clear to what extent risks had actually been lowered and to what extent they had merely been shifted.

So the "risk-absorption" function of banks as lenders became ever more remote, even as the competition to be risk originators grew ever more intense. Facing banks on this new competitive field were mortgage companies, which were far more lightly regulated.

THE EVOLUTION OF FINANCIAL EXPLOITATION

Since its founding in the 1930s, the Federal Housing Administration had adopted guidelines that precluded homes in neighborhoods with significant minority populations from participation, leading to stagnating housing values and lower rates of homeownership in minority areas. This began to change in the 1960s. The 1968 Fair Housing Act and 1974 Equal Credit Opportunity Act extended the anti-discrimination principles of Civil Rights law to housing and credit markets, respectively. The Home Mortgage Disclosure Act (HMDA) of 1975 and the Community Reinvestment Act (CRA) of 1977 provided the means for monitoring bank loan-making and outlawed "redlining"—the implicit or explicit refusal of lenders to make mortgage credit available to neighborhoods with large minority populations. HMDA reporting requirements were strengthened in the 1989 thrift bail-out bill.

This legislative environment provided support for demands by community advocates that banks meet credit and banking needs in their entire market areas. The advocates for minority and lower-income ("inner city") communities were pushing banks and thrifts to make "mainstream" loans to households seeking to own homes

---

2   G. A. Dymski, "Racial Exclusion and the Political Economy of the Subprime Crisis," *Historical Materialism*, 2009, 17(2).

and businesses in need of working capital. Depository institutions objected to these demands, using an evolving set of rationales. They first argued that there was a lack of home-purchase demand in minority-dominated (inner-city) areas. When this was disproven, banks pointed out the excessive riskiness of inner-city lending. This claim too was challenged. From banks' viewpoint, externalities and coordination problems justified their less than full participation in inner-city credit markets; from another angle, banks' reluctance to lend entailed a prisoners' dilemma, wherein all banks' unwillingness to lend robustly in the inner city justified every individual bank's reluctance.[3]

From the 1970s to the mid-1990s, community reinvestment struggles focused, first, on whether all bank customers were provided with equal access to credit, and second, on whether banking services were available uniformly throughout banks' market areas. In effect, racial inequality encompassed households who qualified for "plain vanilla" loans but were denied access to credit, as well as households with a more marginal existence.

For years, financial services were provided to minorities and low-income households by a plethora of check-cashing stores, finance companies and pawnbrokers; these were usually poorly capitalized and locally run. But with the increasing number of lower-income households and the growing market for cross-border remittances, these financial-service markets attracted the attention of major financial companies, including megabanks. Underbanked and unbanked households generated huge fees. In the early 2000s, these averaged $200 annually per household, and $6.2 billion in total;[4] but banks had only 3 percent of the remittance market.[5]

In the mid-1990s, banks began increasing their activities in lower-income markets. They acquired subsidiaries and designed special instruments aimed at the lower-income and minority customers they had previously overlooked. Prominent among these new products were "predatory" loans. These new instruments grew at a frenetic pace in neighborhoods historically subject to financial exclusion. Such loans often led to excessive rates of non-payment,

3   G. A. Dymski, "The Theory of Bank Redlining and Discrimination: An Exploration," *Review of Black Political Economy*, 1995, 23(3).

4   N. Katkov, *ATMs: Self-Service for the Unbanked*, Tokyo: Celent Communications, 2002.

5   M. Orozco, *The Remittance Marketplace: Prices, Policy, and Financial Institutions*, Washington, DC: Pew Hispanic Center, 2004.

and to foreclosures and personal financial distress—well *before* the 2007 mortgage-market meltdown. There are two principle categories of these loans: payday loans and housing-based loans.

Payday loans

Payday loans advance workers a portion of the money they will be due from their next paycheck. The average fee for a $100 check is $18. Financing for these loans has often been provided by megabanks. The customers for these loans are not the unbanked: to receive a payday loan requires a checking account. At the same time, these are lower-income bank customers: some 29 percent earn less than $25,000 per year, and 52 percent earn between $25,000 and $50,000 per year.[6] African Americans and military families are overrepresented. Some 41 percent are homeowners. Most customers use payday loans seven to twelve times per year.[7]

Unheard of fifteen years ago, this form of credit spread very fast. While in 2001 there were 15,000 stores that generated $2.6 billion in fees, by 2005 22,000 store locations offered payday loans, with a market volume of $40 billion and fees of $4.4 billion.[8] The payday loan industry grew so rapidly for several reasons. First, banks have steadily raised the fees they impose on a customer account when it lacks sufficient funds to pay all checks written against it. Second, late fees for rent, credit-card and utility payments have also been rising dramatically. Some $22 billion in NSF fees and $57 billion in late fees were collected in 2003.[9] Third, lower-income US households have much more volatile incomes than do other households, and hence need credit to close income-expenditure gaps more frequently.[10] Also, since many such households lack the financial track record that could qualify them for credit cards or bank loans, they turn to payday loans instead.

---

6   S. Bair, *Low-Cost Payday Loans: Obstacles and Opportunities*, Amherst, MA: Isenberg School of Management, University of Massachusetts, Amherst, 2005.
7   Ibid.
8   Ibid.
9   Ibid.
10   P. Gosselin, "The Poor Have More Things Today—Including Wild Income Swings," *Los Angeles Times*, December 12, 2004.

Subprime mortgage lending

Subprime lending began when mortgage brokers and other lenders began to combine aggressive marketing and sale of second mortgages with demographic targeting. Predatory mortgages—with excessive fees, high penalties and high interest rates—were sold to households that had traditionally been denied access to credit.[11] Initially, these were primarily second mortgages. While costly, they permitted owners of modest homes to gain access to money for whatever financial contingencies they faced.

Soon, loans with these characteristics were being marketed to those seeking to acquire homes. A controversy has accompanied them from the very beginning: Are these high costs and penalties predatory, or do they represent legitimate responses to some homeseekers' (or homeowners') special risk characteristics?

From the beginning, subprime loan practices have heavily impacted the elderly, people of color, and minority neighborhoods. Many low-income and minority borrowers obtained loans at high interest rates and with very unfavorable terms from housing-related and payday lenders. For example, in 1998, subprime and manufactured housing lenders accounted for 34 percent of all home-purchase mortgage applications and 14 percent of originations. These lenders' impact on low-income and minority individuals is even more pronounced: in that same year, subprime and manufactured housing lenders made a fifth of all mortgages extended to lower-income and Latino borrowers, and a third of all those made to African-American borrowers.[12] Subprime lending grew 900 percent in the period 1993–99, even while other mortgage lending activity declined.[13] A nationwide study of 2000 HMDA data found that African Americans were, on average, more than twice as likely as whites to receive subprime loans, and Latinos between 40 and 220 percent more likely.[14]

---

11   California Reinvestment Coalition, *Inequities in California's Subprime Mortgage Market*, San Francisco: CRC, 2001.
12   G. B. Canner, W. Passmore, and E. Laderman. "The Role of Specialized Lenders in Extending Mortgages to Lower-Income and Minority homebuyers," *Federal Reserve Bulletin*, November 1999.
13   *Unequal Burden: Income and Racial Disparities in Subprime Lending in America*, Washington, DC: Department of Housing and Urban Development, April 2000.
14   C. Bradford, *Risk or Race? Racial Disparities and the Subprime Refinance Market*, Washington, DC: Center for Community Change, 2002.

While community-reinvestment advocates and consumers challenge business practices that victimize borrowers, lower-income and minority borrowers are effectively targeted by these specialized—and often predatory—lenders. As evidence of the aggressive business practices pursued in this market, Ameriquest Mortgage Company of Orange, California was forced to settle a consumer protection lawsuit for $325 million in January 2006. Tellingly, this was second in dollar value, in US history, only to Household Finance Corporation's $484 million settlement in 2002 (after its sale to HSBC). The *Washington Post* story summarizing the agreement indicates some of this industry's perverse practices:

> Ameriquest loan officers will be required to tell borrowers such things as what a loan's interest rate will be, how much it could rise and whether the loan includes a prepayment penalty. Loan officers who do not make that disclosure will be subject to discipline. The company would also be forbidden from giving sales agents financial incentives for pushing consumers into higher-interest loans or prepayment penalties.[15]

Why lower-income credit markets grew

Acquisitions and changing practices in consumer finance have led to ever higher degrees of interpenetration between major banking corporations, finance companies and subprime lenders. Already in the 1990s, subprime mortgage loans and payday loans had common structural features: (1) they were based on some collateral (homes and paychecks), which had value no matter the cash-flows of the borrower units; (2) they represented higher-risk assets, whose holders could anticipate higher returns in compensation for these risks; (3) the lenders originating these loans needed to move this paper systematically off their balance sheets.

To take off, these markets required a conveyor belt that could convert credit originated by banks and other lenders into instruments that wealth-holding households seeking above-market returns (and thus higher-risk assets) would readily accept. The links required for this chain were established via new technologies of securitization and risk-pooling. Wall Street investment banks channeled ever more funds to subprime lenders; indeed, these securitizations already averaged $80 billion annually by 1998

---

15 K. Downey, "Mortgage Lender Settles Lawsuit: Ameriquest Will Pay $325 Million," *Washington Post*, January 24, 2006, p. D01.

and 1999. Further, Wall Street insurers underwrote the mortgage-backed securities that subprime lenders sold on to the markets.[16]

Not content to generate fees from securitizing non-prime loans, some bank holding companies purchased subprime lenders. Citicorp acquired Associates First Capital Corporation, which was then under investigation by the Federal Trade Commission and the Justice Department. First Union Bancorp bought the Money Store in June 1998 while HSBC bought Household International, parent of Household Finance Company, in 2003, after settling charges that it had engaged in predatory lending.

Linked to these forces was a new consumer-banking business model for lower-income households: riskier customers were provided access to credit in exchange either for fees paid upfront or for loans made on the basis of attachable assets. Since homes are most households' primary asset, especially if mortgage loans have been paid down, the growth of the subprime mortgage lending market is readily grasped. The logic of the payday-loan industry is very similar: next month's paycheck serves as a guarantee against loss. Data for the period 1989–2004 from the Survey of Consumer Finances shows that households in the two lowest-income quintiles have experienced surging levels of debt, not paralleled by proportionate increases in asset levels.

Megabanks had different degrees of success in their forays into subprime lending. Just two years after acquiring the Money Store, Union Bancorp closed this unit in mid-2000 due to massive losses.[17] By contrast, Associates First stabilized Citi's cash flow during a period in which most megabanks' earnings slumped.[18] Fair-lending advocates protested this strategic turn; for example, Martin Eakes, founder of the non-profit Self-Help Credit Union in Durham, NC, asserted, "Associates is a rogue company and may alone account for 20 percent of all abusive home loans in the nation."[19] Nonetheless, this consumer-lending

---

16 D. B. Henriques, and L. Bergman, "Profiting from Fine Print with Wall Street's Help," *Wall Street Journal*, March 15, 2000.

17 D. K. Berman, C. Mollenkamp, and V. Bauerlein, "Wachovia Strikes $26 Billion Deal for Golden West," *Wall Street Journal*, May 8, 2006, p. A1.

18 J. Sapsford, L. Cohen, M. Langley, and R. Sidel, "JPMorgan Chase to Buy Bank One," *Wall Street Journal*, January 14, 2001; *Business Week*, "The Besieged Banker: Bill Harrison Must Prove JPMorgan Chase Wasn't a Star-Crossed Merger," April 22, 2002.

19 R. A. Oppel, Jr, "Citigroup to pay up to $20 Million in Deceptive-Lending Case," *New York Times*, September 7, 2001.

subsidiary represented a step toward Citi's goal of establishing its CitiFinancial subsidiary as the nation's largest consumer finance company.[20]

In sum, the growth of predatory credit markets inverted the previous prisoners' dilemma regarding bank lending in inner-city areas. Previously, banks would have been reluctant to make any loans in inner-city areas. Now, banks—and their proxies and subsidiaries—rushed to make and securitize such subprime and payday loans. Both prime-heavy and subprime-heavy areas were awash with credit. The difference was that much of the debt in subprime-heavy areas was contracted at terms and conditions that threatened borrowers' future financial sustainability. Indeed, banks and markets learned to regard aggressive and even expectationally unsustainable terms and conditions on borrowers as normal business practices. These practices soon migrated from inner-city areas to the broader markets.

FROM THE MARGINS OF THE CITY TO THE CORE OF GLOBAL FINANCE

The initial premise of securitization was the homogenization of risks: bundling involved loans to borrowers who were expected to pay, and whose risks were both readily calculable and implicitly backed by the federal government through Government-Sponsored Enterprises.

The emergence of subprime and predatory loan markets systematically punctured these premises, for several reasons: heightened competition in financial markets; more relaxed attitudes about risk-taking; and increases in computability. Consequently, lenders increasingly originated and sold off heterogeneous loans, which sometimes were made to borrowers whose longer-term viability as payers was doubtful. To compensate for these risks, fees, penalties and margins were made sufficiently high that these loans would turn a profit even if the relationship between lender and borrower broke down.

Figure 4.1 illustrates relationships in the emerging system for originating and distributing risk. A subprime lender makes mortgage loans and sells them to banks that securitize them. This lender is most likely funded by money-market borrowing and by

20   R. A. Oppel, Jr, and P. McGeehan, "Citigroup Announces Changes to Guard Against Abusive Loan Practices," *New York Times*, November 8, 2000.

investors holding shares in its enterprise. Note that no bank or thrift appears: in effect, banks simply connect originators with investors. A bank can be a mortgage originator; but mortgage originators need not be banks.

Figure 4.1:   Subprime Lenders and Structured Investment Vehicles

Subprime mortgage originator		Structured investment vehicle	
Reserves	Short-term money market	Collateralized debt obligations (including mortgages) with diverse risk, maturity characteristics	Short-term money market borrowing
Mortgage loans	Borrowing		Private-equity or hedge-fund investors
	Shares		

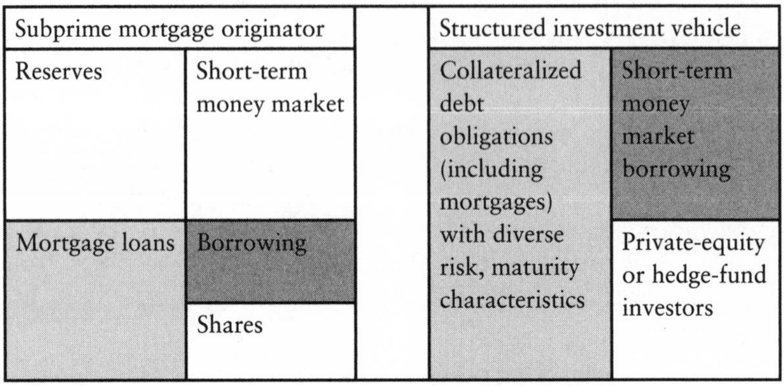

Note: Light-grey shading indicates default risk, while dark-grey shading indicates liquidity risk.

Increasingly, the buyers of the loans thus originated were structured investment vehicles (SIVs). The first SIVs were created for Citigroup in 1988 and 1989.[21] Whereas "plain vanilla" mortgages had formerly permitted the bundling of homogeneous risks in securitization processes, now many different forms of collateralized debt could be combined on the asset side of SIVs. This permitted diverse forms of paper to be moved off lenders' balance sheets. The liabilities used to support SIVs also became more complex. Funds might be obtained from private-equity funds, from hedge funds, or from money markets (especially the commercial paper markets). SIVs, unlike pass-through securities, were opaque. And it was unclear if investors in SIVs were taking on the default and other risks implicit in such financial instruments. Credit-risk derivatives were used in many cases to shift these risks onto third parties.[22] The largest such third party was, of course, AIG. In any case, SIVs quickly became a $400 billion industry. As

21   C. Mollenkamp, D. Solomon, R. Sidel and V. Bauerlein, "How London Created a Snarl in Global Markets," *Wall Street Journal*, October 18, 2007, p. A1.
22   *The Economist*, "At the Risky End of Finance," August 21, 2007, pp. 80–2.

the *Wall Street Journal* put it, SIVs "boomed because they allowed banks to reap profits from investments in newfangled securities, but without setting aside capital to mitigate the risk."[23]

Once securitization markets learned to accept asset heterogeneity not backed by iron-clad underwriting, the door was open for the further evolution of both mortgages and securities.

The financial markets were no strangers to non-homogeneous risks in securitized mortgage debt: since the 1970s, real-estate investment trusts (REITs) had been marketed and sold off to investors. Indeed, REIT investments by the Franklin National Bank led to its 1974 failure.[24] In many cities, residential real estate began to take off in value in the late 1990s. An asset-boom mania began to emerge among homeowners and potential homeowners. Those who had homes wanted bigger ones; those who did not wanted to get into the housing market. While there had been periods of sustained housing-price increases before in the US, and while the US market's appreciation was actually less than that experienced in several other countries, euphoric sentiments abounded.

The fact that many potential buyers had neither the income nor the savings to support "plain vanilla" mortgages within prescribed parameters (no more than 30 percent of income spent on housing, and 20 percent down on any mortgage loan) created a special challenge. Lenders' and brokers' successful experience in creating loans for borrowers with very risky parameters suggested the required solution: to create loans tailored to the special risks of those whose income and down-payment profiles had not kept pace with many cities' white-hot housing markets. Since housing prices were rocketing upward, buyers could be given loans for more than 80 percent of their homes' prices; or they could be given two loans, one for this 80 percent—making the loan potentially sellable to FNMA—and another for the other 20 percent of the sales price.

Previously, subprime loans had gone only to borrowers whose terms and conditions were less than optimal. But, from the early 2000s onward, subprime loans were made to homeowners who were unable to support "plain vanilla" mortgage packages. To get potential buyers "into" a home, a loan could be made at a below-

---

23 Mollenkamp et al., "How London Created a Snarl in Global Markets."
24 J. F. Sinkey, Jr, *Problem and Failed Institutions in the Commercial Banking Industry*, Greenwich, Connecticut: JAI Press, Inc., 1981.

market "teaser" rate for the first year or two of the mortgage. Any gap between market and "teaser" rates could be amortized, and the entire mortgage refinanced at a risk-adjusted market rate after the "teaser" rate expired. Housing-price appreciation would eventually negate the risks of a 100-percent-financed home purchase; and anticipated income and/or housing-price growth could, in turn, offset overly burdensome home payments. Fees and penalty clauses could be attached as warranted for such paper.

As euphoria about housing-price increases intensified, especially in some regional hot-spots, buyers were more and more forced into "teaser" rates, hybrid ARMs, and so on.[25] But housing-price appreciation so dominated market consciousness that anything (including high fees and payments) seemed acceptable if that meant being able to move in while the window of opportunity was still open. The idea was that home-price appreciation would allow the renegotiation of non-viable terms and conditions in two years, when that 2/28 mortgage loan would "flip" from a "teaser" to a fixed market rate.

In any case, while housing-market euphoria explains part of the growing demand for subprime mortgage loans, it does not explain all of it. Mortgage brokers manufactured some of it themselves. A survey of those acquiring subprime mortgages in 2005 and 2006 found that 55 percent and 61 percent of these mortgagees, respectively, had credit scores high enough to obtain conventional loans.[26] The fees earned by the mortgage brokers on these subprime loans were substantially higher than they would otherwise have been.

And if demand for funds was robust, on the supply side of the housing-finance market such funds were plentiful. For one thing, macro-circumstances remained favorable—the US's current account remained strongly negative, so that funds continued to funnel into the US through its capital accounts. Foreign fund-holders were familiar with US mortgage-backed securities, which had been the largest global securities market for over a decade. Many European banks rushed into subprime paper.[27]

---

25 L R. Wray, "Lessons from the Subprime Meltdown," Working paper no. 522, Levy Economics Institute of Bard College, December 2007, p. 9.
26 R. Brooks and R. Simon, "As Housing Boomed, Industry Pushed Loans to a Broader Market," *Wall Street Journal*, December 3, 2007, p. A1.
27 C. Mollenkamp, E. Taylor and I. McDonald, "How Subprime Mess Ensnared German Bank; IKB Gets a Bailout," *Wall Street Journal*, August 10, 2007, p. A1.

East Asian sovereign wealth funds bought fewer subprime mortgages;[28] nonetheless, their marginal demand for more Treasuries kept US interest rates low and so sustained the subprime market.

Micro-circumstances also favored a ready supply of subprime loans. Megabanks, as discussed above, were shifting toward the offloading of risk and fee-based income. Further, hyper-competition broke out amongst lenders. An analysis of the "once-lucrative partnership" between Wall Street and subprime lenders quotes a Wall Street insider, Ronald Greenspan, as follows: "There was fierce competition for these loans. . . . They were a major source of revenues and perceived profits for both the investors and the investment banks."[29] Some banks slowed their involvement as the market heated to its peak in mid-2005: for example, Credit Suisse reduced its underwriting 22 percent in 2006 compared with 2004. But others surged ahead: Morgan Stanley increased its subprime underwriting by 25 percent between 2004 and 2006, developing a special relationship with New Century Financial, a large subprime lender. Morgan paid above-market in order to lock in a monthly flow of $2 billion from this firm alone. New Century, whose subprime loans' delinquency rate is twice that of other lenders such as Wells Fargo, filed for bankruptcy in March 2007. Jeffrey Kirch, president of a firm that buys home loans, stated, "The easiest way to grab market share was by paying more than your competitors." These arrangements were lucrative, with total 2006 compensation for managing directors in investment banks averaging $2.5 million.[30]

Subprime loan volumes exploded in 2004–06, even as the housing boom peaked. In the 2001–03 period, mortgage originations totaled $9.04 trillion, of which 8.4 percent were subprime loans, while 55 percent of subprime originations, or $418 billion, were securitized. In the 2004–06 period, total mortgage originations were the same in nominal terms, $9.02 trillion. However, 19.6 percent of all originations consisted of

28 Reuters New Service, "China exposure to U.S. subprime ills limited," August 28, 2007. Available at http://www.reuters.com/article/gc06/idUSPEK26110220070828; accessed on December 10, 2007.
29 J. Anderson and V. Bajaj, "Wary of Risk, Bankers Sold Shaky Debt," *New York Times*, December 6, 2007, p. A1.
30 Ibid. The quote from Kirsch appears in this article.

subprime loans, of which 78.8 percent—some $1,391 billion—were securitized.[31]

The inherently flexible and non-transparent nature of SIVs soon opened the door for more types of credit.[32] For example, private-equity funds required a huge volume of bridge loans to support their efforts to undertake leveraged buyouts of ever larger target firms; many such loans were incorporated into SIVs. So too were other categories of firm and household loan.

THE UNCERTAIN CONCEPTUAL BASIS FOR STRUCTURED FINANCE

In the heady atmosphere of the subprime explosion, participants and analysts imagined that they were reinventing banking. In one account, structured finance overcomes "adverse selection and segmentation."[33] Jobst asserted that collateralized loan obligations (CLOs, one form of structured finance) reduce risk for investors and make investment less costly: "As the origination of loans and portfolio investment is unbundled, the *risk-oriented determination of credit conditions and increased efficiency in the lending process through standardized credit terms are essential components* of a new organizational model of bank lending."[34]

The conceptual basis for this new model of bank lending received little attention. This was unfortunate, for troubling questions might have been raised. In any conceptual model of banking, banks must have a *raison d'etre*. Diamond's model of banks as "delegated monitors," for example, posits that there are economies of scale in information acquisition about borrowers (agents). So banks emerge as centralized lenders because, as information specialists, they can make appropriate allocations of available credit more efficiently than could wealth-owning units operating independently.[35]

---

31 L. R. Wray, "Lessons from the subprime meltdown," p. 30, Table 1.
32 As Hyman Minsky put it in a 1987 memo on securitization that Randy Wray unearthed at the Levy Institute, "That which can be securitized will be securitized."
33 I. Fender and J. Mitchell, "Risk, Complexity, and the Use of Ratings in Structured Finance," working paper, Bank for International Settlements and National Bank of Belgium, March 2005, p. 2.
34 A. A. Jobst, "Collateralized Loan Obligations: A Primer," *The Securitization Conduit*, 6(1–4), 2003, pp.79-80. Italics in original.
35 D. W. Diamond, "Financial Intermediation and Delegated Monitoring," *Review of Economic Studies*, 1984, 51 (July).

This explanation seems to deny the need for SIVs or CLOs. This would be correct—unless banks were not the most efficient evaluators of credit risk. Suppose credit-rating agencies can evaluate risk more efficiently than banks; banks would then offload their credit-evaluation function, instead acquiring and distributing packages of securities.

Another conceptual basis for structured finance emerges in the complete-information world of efficient markets theory. Oldfield provides the clue when he writes that "an underwriter must defeat arbitrage between pass-throughs and derivatives." If information were complete, transactions costless, assets infinitely scaleable, and a complete set of contingent (derivatives) markets existed, then no structured finance could arise. Any agent seeking the particular combination of risk-return characteristics available through the acquisition of a given set of securities could efficiently acquire those securities him/herself—no intermediary (that is, no seller of a structured investment vehicle) would be needed by any wealth-owning agent. The SIV can efficiently exist only if it embodies a set of contingent and underlying claims that a wealth-owner cannot access directly. The efficiency of the SIV can thus be due either to transaction costs, the imperfect scaleability of assets, or both. In effect, in this approach, structured finance vehicles help to make markets more complete. Oldfield goes on:

> A structured finance transaction transforms a pool of more or less similar loans into a set of derivative instruments collateralized by the pool. An underwriter who structures a transaction has a simple purpose: to sell the set of derivatives for more money than a direct sale of the pool or a pass-through instrument alone would fetch. The underwriter accomplishes a transaction by establishing an independent entity, usually a trust, which becomes the mechanism for structuring the derivatives. This entity represents a passive financial intermediary.[36]

Partnoy and Skeel describe this as using "financial engineering" to complete markets.[37]

Both approaches carry implicit warnings about subprime lending. In the Diamond model, why do banks exist if they are not delegated risk-monitors? Moreover, if credit-rating agencies

---

36 G. S. Oldfield, "Making Markets for Structured Mortgage Derivatives," *Journal of Financial Economics*, 2000, 57, p. 445.
37 F. Partnoy and D. A. Skeel, Jr, "The Promise and Perils of Credit Derivatives," *University of Cincinnati Law Review*, 2007, 75(2), p. 1027.

were introduced into the Diamond world, efficiency requires that risk assessment be subject to competition, and that risk assessors be hired by the savers, not by the lenders. Neither condition— competition in credit assessment and payment by buyers, not sellers, of assets—was met in the real world. So rating agencies were "particularly significant in situations where investors face relatively high costs in assessing the structure and risk profile of a given instrument—that is, in structured finance."[38] But no student of mechanism design could be surprised when rating agencies' underassessment of risk emerged as a problem.[39]

Turning to Oldfield, completing financial markets through offering hitherto-unavailable risk-return combinations requires Oldfield's "passive intermediary" to assemble a dizzying array of derivative and stripped assets. In his argument, the only way that an SIV can offer unique risk-return combinations to the market is by creating opaque combinations of the risk-return characteristics of the underlying securities. Doing this in a well-informed manner that permits the bundler/lender to make normal profits, in real time, would be a herculean task. Again, real-world passive intermediaries were not up to it.

The slim analytical literature on the emerging synthetic credit instruments reflects this ambivalence: on one hand, faith that rational behavior will ultimately generate efficient-market outcomes; on the other, skepticism about the plausibility of what rational agents are being asked to do. An example is a 2005 paper on risks in structured finance by Fender and Mitchell, which includes these passages:

> This paper . . . argues that certain structural features of structured finance products raise special governance issues and create important risks that are not directly related to the default risk of the assets comprising the underlying portfolios, but which may ultimately be as important to the performance of structured finance products as are the default properties of the asset pool . . . structured finance instruments also transform risk in unique ways via the tranching

---

38 Committee on the Global Financial System, "The role of ratings in structured finance: issues and implications," Bank for International Settlements, Basel, Switzerland, January 2005, p. 3.
39 M. Pittman, "Moody's, S&P Understate Subprime Risk, Study Says (Update2)," Bloomberg News Service, May 3, 2007. This finding is verified by the US Securities and Exchange Commission, Summary Report of Issues Identified in the Commission Staff's Examinations of Select Credit Rating Agencies. Washington, DC: US Securities and Exchange Commission, July 2008.

of claims, generating exposures to different, transaction-specific "slices" of the underlying asset pool's loss distribution. As a result of this "slicing" and the contractual structures needed to achieve it, tranche risk-return characteristics can be quite difficult to assess.[40]

Ratings, though important, are argued to be inappropriate for gauging the risk of structured securities, despite the fact that the complexity of structured finance transactions gives investors incentives to rely more heavily on ratings than for other types of rated securities.[41]

When this paper was published in the June 2005 issue of the *BIS Quarterly Review*, these passages were no longer included.[42] Needless to say, Minsky's relevance to the unfolding crisis was not appreciated until market forces had been extended much too far. Even when it was recognized, most commentators referred only to a "Minsky moment."[43] Fewer analysts have brought to bear other relevant elements of Minsky's financial-fragility framework: the uncertainty that surrounds time-intensive processes in and out of the financial markets; the problem of developing and sustaining confidence; the boom-bust tendencies rooted in the interaction between varying balance-sheet exposures and varying lender/borrower motivations.

The notion that banks have strategies and can sometimes perform very different roles in the economy is itself, of course, rather different from the information-theoretic approaches just discussed. So is the notion that outcomes like exploitation or exclusion are possible not only because of transaction or information costs, but because of historical legacies of inequality and racial oppression. Also unexplored in analyses rooted in efficient markets is the possibility that lenders may make contracts that maximize short-term profits but create longer-term default and foreclosure risk. These possibilities arise very naturally when Minskyian and institutionalist perspectives are used to explore economic dynamics. [44] Yet, they are all but invisible when the

---

40 Fender and Mitchell, "Risk, Complexity, and the Use of Ratings in Structured Finance," pp. 1–2.

41 Ibid. p. 8.

42 I. Fender and J. Mitchell, "Structured Finance: Complexity, Risk and the Use of Ratings," June 2005.

43 For example, see C. W. Calomiris, "Not (yet) a 'Minsky moment'," BIS Quarterly Review, http://www.aei.org, December 11, 2007.

44 See, for example, Wray, "Lessons from the subprime meltdown"; A. Pollock, "Subprime Bust Expands," *The American—a magazine of ideas*, http://american. com, December 11, 2007; and G. A. Dymski, "Why the Subprime Crisis is Different: A Minskyian approach," *Cambridge Journal of Economics*, July, 2009.

more rigid lenses of efficient-market or information-theoretic economic theory are used.

SOLVING THE CRISIS WITHOUT DISTURBING ITS OVERLOOKED ROOTS?

This brings us to the Subprime Crisis period per se. This crisis, of course, obeyed no limits: it became both a generalized financial crisis and a global economic crisis, whose manifestations have continued to emerge with full force the world over. This chapter does not trace out all the post-crisis dynamics; it instead outlines megabank and financial-market responses, and relates these to the two overlooked roots of the crisis that are emphasized here.

The crisis broke out when the asset-backed commercial paper market melted down in September 2007. This meltdown meant that SIVs could no longer be financed and had to be brought back onto the balance sheets of the banks that had emitted them. HSBC made the first move, in November 2007.[45] By the first quarter of 2008, most other megabanks had followed suit. Admitting that they were responsible for the off-balance-sheet paper they had issued forced banks to declare huge losses on their balance sheets. This in turn led banks to seek out capital injections. By November 2007, Citibank got a $7.5 billion capital injection from the Abu Dhabi government, while UBS sold an 11 percent stake to Singapore.[46] Other injections followed through mid-2008. Banks also tried creating off-shore funds that could sell shares to investors willing to absorb risk-laden assets. This approach, proposed in mid-October 2007, attracted little industry or political support.[47]

Soon different proposals for government intervention were put forward. In 2007, these focused on the provision of relief to distressed homeowners. The Bush administration's initial plan attempted to restrict relief implicitly to those who might be termed "meritorious" homeowners—those who were current on payments but threatened by the "kicking in" of higher rates. In principle, keeping people in their homes would reduce supply in depressed housing markets. But a problem that has continued to

45 S. Goldstein, "HSBC Restructures Two SIVs," *Wall Street Journal*, November 26, 2007.
46 V. Bauerlein and A. Edwards, "WaMu to Cut Dividend, Slash Jobs," *Wall Street Journal*, December 11, 2007.
47 E. Dash, "Big Banks Scale Back Plan to Aid in Debt Crisis," *New York Times*, December 10, 2007.

plague efforts at helping distressed homeowners soon emerged. As the *Los Angeles Times'* Tom Petruno put it in a prescient article:

> The success of the Bush administration's plan to stem home foreclosures will hinge in large part on whether the investors who own sub-prime mortgages will play along and accept lower interest payments to keep people in their houses. That may be asking a lot—and not just because of many investors' visceral negative reaction to government strong-arming on the issue of home-loan modifications. . . . Thanks to the alchemy of modern finance, investors who put up funds for the same "pool" of thousands of sub-prime mortgages can face very different levels of risk, depending on the section of the pool they own. Those whose sections would be well-protected from loss, even if loan defaults soared, may have little incentive to agree to changes in the terms of the underlying mortgages. That could invite a torrent of investor lawsuits challenging moves to ease loan terms.[48]

The pressure-point for relief soon turned, however, from distressed homeowners to megabanks and financial markets. In September and October 2008, the roof fell in: Lehman Brothers failed; the interbank market seized up; FNMA and FHLMC went into receivership; Washington Mutual failed, as did Wachovia; and AIG collapsed. These events necessitated a dramatic response by the outgoing Bush administration: Treasury Secretary Paulson proposed, and Congress agreed, to a $700 billion fund, the Troubled Asset Relief Program (TARP), which could stabilize troubled banks and financial markets.

TARP funds were soon committed to the two primary strategies that banks had already begun to deploy: they were used to support financial firms' balance sheets and to provide a means of offloading bad debts. No clearly successful strategy for the use of TARP funds emerged. One problem was that while the government held a controlling interest in several banks (including Citibank), it was unwilling to take managerial control of bank operations. Second, the unloading of toxic assets would assist banks only if these were sold at cut-rate prices that imposed losses on taxpayers. This was sensitive politically, as a non-trivial number of taxpayers found themselves in foreclosure. The one clear pattern in TARP fund allocation was that megabanks and large financial firms received the lion's share of the money.

---

48 T. Petruno, "Loan Fix Requires Investors to Yield," *Los Angeles Times*, December 8, 2007.

Meanwhile, a third dimension of the financial-rescue efforts soon came to the fore: the need to restore "normal" banking activity. The collapse of confidence and capacity was so total and so swift that the Federal Reserve brought much of the money market onto its balance sheet (this practice, also engaged in by the UK and European central banks, was termed "quantitative easing"). But the question then was how to reignite lending and borrowing, so that finance-linked economic activity could resume and recovery begin. The Bush administration unveiled its answer to this question, the Term Asset-Backed Securities Loan Facility (TALF) on November 25, 2008.

These three strands of post-crisis action—relief for homeowners, relief for banks and key financial market institutions, and restoration of credit-market activity—have been fine-tuned and re-geared more than once. With no clear strategic impetus, a range of initiatives has been unleashed, none completely successful. What is striking from the perspective of this essay is that none of the public-policy or market responses have addressed the two overlooked roots of the Subprime Crisis highlighted here.

Banking strategy

We observed above that banks shifted their strategic focus in the 1980s in several ways: in particular, they began to derive profits more from fee-based income than from interest income. Megabanks led the way here, deriving revenue from many aspects of the securitization process. Another shift in banking—again, in which megabanks were especially implicated—was the separation of risk-generation from risk-bearing.

It might have been imagined that the dramatic failures of so many large financial firms would lead to a rethinking of the systemic rationality of the originate-distribute-and-underwrite, securitization-based model of banking. This rethinking would seem needed in light of the excessive costs of subprime-asset securitization. For not only was the too-big-to-fail principle invoked, but several large non-bank financial companies—to name most of those among the largest in asset size, Goldman Sachs, Morgan Stanley, Metlife, Barclays Group, American Express, the CIT Group, and GMAC—were permitted to qualify as bank holding companies. This extension of the umbrella of public bank holding-company (BHC) protection to firms whose prior activity footprint was not remotely linked to banking illustrates both the level of fear that has pervaded Wall Street and the willingness of policy-makers to set precedents when necessity dictated in this climate. Whatever the need, no rethinking has occurred.

Instead, the strategic thrust that led to the Subprime Crisis has not been abandoned. As noted, relief for banks has focused largely on megabanks. TARP money has disproportionately supported the small number of megabanks and mega financial firms that fueled the shift of banking from lend-and-hold to originate-distribute-and-underwrite. As the crisis has deepened, small banks have felt financial stress, leading them too to a need for additional capital.[49] No sense of urgency accompanies this need; on the contrary, attention in the financial pages centered on which megabanks have emerged triumphant from Wall Street's "ruins."[50]

The TALF program, designed to jump-start consumer and small-business lending, is also biased toward the new banking model. Under the terms of this program, the US Treasury provides credit protection for newly issued consumer-credit and SBA-guaranteed small business loans, for an amount originally pegged at $200 billion (and later increased to $1 trillion). Specifically, these loans would be bundled into asset-backed securities and sold onto the markets. Despite the 20-to-1 leverage available under this program, investors were wary and sought out additional concessions.[51] Subsequently, the scope of the program was broadened to permit more types of credit to qualify, in part to help loan-servicers participate in "work-outs" with insolvent homeowners.[52]

Another indication that post-crisis policy preserves the strategic thrust associated with megabanking is provided by the US Treasury's program for removing toxic assets from banks' balance sheets. The Public-Private Investment Program (P-PIP), announced on March 23, 2009, provides loan guarantees for up to 85 percent of the purchase price of existing (legacy) loans, with the private sector and US Treasury providing the remaining assets,

49 See C. Piller, "Small Banks Start Feeling Financial Stress," *Sacramento Bee*, July 5, 2009; and S. Scholtes, J. MacIntosh and F. Guerrera, "Small Banks Need Additional $24 Billion," *Financial Times*, May 19, 2009.
50 G. Bowley, "Two Giants Emerge from Wall Street's Ruins," *New York Times*, July 17, 2009.
51 P. Eavis, "TALF Investors Wary of Collateral Damage," *Wall Street Journal*, March 11, 2009.
52 M. Thiruvengadam, "Fed Expands TALF Collateral," *Wall Street Journal*, March 19, 2009.

and the FDIC providing loan guarantees (without recourse). While this plan has been criticized for subsidizing asset managers and bank shareholders, it has not succeeded.[53] Indeed, the FDIC and Treasury delayed the sale of assets under the P-PIP. Banks, especially megabanks, have not participated due both to their reluctance to declare toxic-asset losses and their belief that private markets will be able to provide the capital they need.[54]

Racial exclusion and the Subprime Crisis

The second overlooked root of the Subprime Crisis is racial exclusion in the credit market, especially the mortgage market. As noted above, subprime loans began life as one of several forms of predatory loans pioneered in minority neighborhoods. This legacy—the fact that subprime loans were developed as a means of lending profitably to those excluded from the mortgage market—has been forgotten or reduced to a secondary factor in most contemporary writing and debate.

The subprime meltdown and subsequent financial crisis have generated a large flow of books. Virtually all of these books make no mention of "discrimination," "redlining," or "racial inequality."[55] Some books do acknowledge that predatory lending aimed at lower-income households is amongst the roots of the current crisis.[56] Only a few acknowledge both the racial-inequality and predatory dimensions of the crisis.[57]

Instead, debate has increasingly centered on whether misconceived government policies pushed banks into making inherently risky loans in lower-income or minority areas. This

---

53   One critic has been P. Krugman, "Geithner plan arithmetic," The Conscience of a Liberal, *New York Times* blog, http://krugman.blogs.nytimes.com/2009/03/23/geithner-plan-arithmetic/, March 23, 2009.
54   T. Braithwaite and F. Guerrera, "FDIC stalls sale of toxic loans," *Financial Times*, June 4, 2009.
55   For example, R. J. Shiller, *The Subprime Solution*, Princeton: Princeton University Press, 2008; and A. Felton and C. Reinhart, *The First Global Financial Crisis of the 21st Century*, A VoxEU.org Publication, London: Center for Economic Policy Research, June 2008.
56   See, for example, C. Morris, *Trillion-Dollar Meltdown*, Jackson, TN: PublicAffairs, 2008; and M. Zandi, *Financial Shock: A 360° Look at the Subprime Mortgage Implosion, and How to Avoid the Next Financial Crisis*, Upper Saddle River, NJ: FT Press, 2008.
57   G. Soros, *The New Paradigm for Financial Markets: The Credit Crisis of 2008 and What It Means*, PublicAffairs, 2008.

debate is sometimes carried out at high decibels.[58] The factual history is, in turn, sometimes twisted. For example, one 2008 book asserts:

> Two things happened as a result of the Community Reinvestment Act. First, banks closed branches in those areas so they wouldn't have to loan money in those areas. . . . Second, they needed to find a way to charge higher rates and fees for loans to low and moderate income earners [and after deregulations were passed in 1980 and 1982] the subprime market was born. What's ironic is that some of the same congressional leaders who insisted that our financial institutions lend to low-income people are now charging our financial institutions with "predatory lending."[59]

On other occasions, the tone is more measured. For example, Hoover Institution economist Michael Boskin warned in early 2009 of the deleterious effects of "the government's meddling in the housing market to bring homeownership to low-income families, which became a prime cause of the current economic and financial disaster."[60]

The link between the Community Reinvestment Act and the subprime meltdown has been refuted definitively. Randall Krozner, a member of the Board of Governors of the Federal Reserve, observed in a December 2008 speech,

> Some critics of the CRA contend that by encouraging banking institutions to help meet the credit needs of lower-income borrowers and areas, the law pushed banking institutions to undertake high-risk mortgage lending. We have not yet seen empirical evidence to support these claims, nor . . . over the past 30 years [has] the CRA . . . contributed to the erosion of safe and sound lending practices.
>
> Our analysis of the loan data found that about 60 percent of higher-priced loan originations went to middle- or higher-income borrowers or neighborhoods. Such borrowers are not the populations targeted by the CRA. In addition, more than 20 percent of the higher-priced loans were extended to lower-income

---

58 See T. J. DiLorenzo, "The CRA scam and its defenders," Mises daily (blog), posted on the Ludwig von Mises Institute website at http://mises.org/story/2963, April 30, 2008, and R. Roberts, "The House that Government Built," *Wall Street Journal*, October 3, 2008, on one side, and R. Gordon, "Did Liberals Cause the Subprime Crisis?" *The American Prospect*, http://www.prospect.org, April 7, 2008.

59 C. Brownell, *Subprime Meltdown: From U.S. Liquidity Crisis to Global Recession*, Scotts Valley: CreateSpace, 2008, p. 17.

60 M. J. Boskin, "Obama's radicalism is killing the Dow," *Wall Street Journal*, March 6, 2009.

borrowers or borrowers in lower-income areas by . . . institutions
not covered by the CRA.[61]

While Federal Reserve Governor Krozner's defense of the
CRA is laudable, the erasure from historical memory of the
exploitative origins of subprime lending—and its replacement
by a quasi-myth that bears overturning—is a remarkable
testament to some banks' undying resistance to this 1977
legislation. This is especially the case because of the racially
non-neutral impact of the Subprime Crisis itself. Given that
subprime and alt-A loans were made disproportionately to
minority borrowers, and that borrowers with loans of this type
are disproportionately likely to experience foreclosure, clearly
one impact of the Subprime Crisis will be to substantially
worsen the wealth gap between minorities and non-minorities
in the US. The prospect of more than 2 million foreclosures
by the end of 2009 and more coming in 2010 and 2011 only
deepens this devastation.[62]

Business as Usual

Post-Crisis reactions to the two overlooked roots of the Subprime
Crisis identified in this chapter have amounted to little or nothing.
The strategic thrust of banking that created the Subprime Crisis
has been affirmed. Promises of tighter regulation, with lessons
learned from the thrift crisis, have given way to the notion that
a light regulatory touch is appropriate.[63] Even market-friendly
analysts anticipate relapses in the near future.[64] The recent push to
"bail out" CIT Group—a non-bank lender to non-financial firms
that was newly installed as a BHC—and the audacious bonuses
paid in mid-2009 by Morgan Stanley, another newly installed

---

61   R. Kroszner, "The Community Reinvestment Act and the Recent Mortgage
Crisis," Speech before the Confronting Concentrated Poverty Policy Forum,
Board of Governors of the Federal Reserve System, Washington, DC, December
3, 2008.
62   See J. H. Carr, "Responding to the Foreclosure Crisis," *Housing Policy
Debate*, 2007, 18(4), and J. Crump, K. Newman, E.S. Belsky, P. Ashton, D. H.
Kaplan, D. J. Hammel, and E. Wyly, "Cities Destroyed (Again) for Cash: Forum
on the U.S. Foreclosure Crisis," Special Issue of *Urban Geography*, 2008, 29(8).
63   M. Wolf, "The end of lightly regulated finance has come far closer," *Financial
Times*, September 16, 2008.
64   M. Wolf, "After the storm comes a hard climb," *Financial Times*, July 14,
2009.

BHC, speak volumes about both regulatory support for financial megafirms and power relations on Wall Street.[65]

The consensus among many banking analysts that the CRA forced banks' hands may well justify the launching of a new era of racial exclusion in financial markets. This will result in part from forgetful attitudes towards the history of social and political struggles against redlining and discrimination, and in part from the great priority now being given to the need to just let bankers do banking—with light regulation that doesn't push them into taking undue risks. For example, Robert Rubin asserted, in an early symposium on the emerging crisis, "My own view is that liquidity is not primarily a monetary phenomenon, but rather a psychological phenomenon. . . . Thus, when the psychology changes, creditors and investors withdraw from riskier assets, reduce leverage, reduce exposure, and then as the prices fall and credit tightens . . . commentators say the liquidity has shrunk."[66] That is, providing bankers and financial investors with the confidence that they can conduct megabanking business as usual is itself part of any healing process.

CONCLUSION

The separation of risk-origination from risk-bearing led to the transformation of banks from prudential stewards of systemic risk to turnstiles for ever higher levels of credit, whether those levels are sustainable for borrowers or not. Before 1980, US housing finance involved a relationship between a homeowner and a bank or thrift. The household took on foreclosure risk, while the lender absorbed default and liquidity risk. This system broke down in the savings and loan crisis; lenders unburdened themselves of excessive risk by offloading mortgage loans they had originated onto offshore investors and onto insurance and pension funds.

The two roots of the crisis identified here played their part in creating the conditions for the subprime meltdown. Banks, having shed their traditional roles as risk absorbers, were seeking out ever more ways to generate net income. They created products

---

65 See, respectively, D. Paletta and S. Ng, "US in Talks to Rescue CIT," *Wall Street Journal*, July 14, 2009, and G. Farrell and S. O'Connor, "Goldman Sachs staff set for record pay," *Financial Times*, July 14, 2009.

66 R.E. Rubin, "Introductory Remarks," *Recent Financial Market Disruptions: Implications For the Economy and American Families*, Washington, DC: The Brookings Institution, September 26, 2007.

designed to provide services to different segments of their customer base in different ways, generating substantial fee-based income along the way. Their successful direct and indirect forays into higher-risk loan products for lower-income and minority markets, together with the emergence (and in some cases, creation) of new outlets for higher-risk debt, opened up the subprime mortgage markets. The boom market in housing in some US regions then created opportunities to structure subprime instruments for new homeowners, not just retirees in inner-city neighborhoods. SIVs emerged as means of using leverage (with lax oversight) to generate off-balance-sheet net interest income. An apparently endless supply of liquidity provided the fuel for this fire.

In effect, banks' legacy of unequal access to credit led them to create new instruments of financial exploitation that, once transported into a raging housing market, led the banking system and the US economy off a cliff. This scenario entailed an historical irony. One Achilles heel in the market for SIVs was overly optimistic assumptions about housing price appreciation (HPA). Alex Pollock remembered an investment manager that asked a rating agency, "What if HPA were to [be a negative] 1 percent to 2 percent for an extended period of time? They responded that their models would break down completely."[67] The irony here is that in the era that wanted to believe housing prices can only go up, much of the housing on which subprime loans were made was located in or near areas that had historically been subject to mortgage redlining.

Blaming victims or interrogating history?

One essential step in the process of resolving any financial crisis rooted in bad debt is to find the sector responsible and reform it—whether through tighter regulation, through eliminating or selling off especially weak institutions, or through offering banks some support while asset prices recover. All these steps were taken in the savings and loan crisis of the 1980s. In that context, a debate ensued about whether to punish wrongdoers, and whether to rescue losers or to let them suffer—thus discouraging future breakdowns in market discipline.

The same debate arose regarding the Subprime Crisis. Early in the crisis, Alex Pollock pointed out that since the Subprime

---

67 Pollock, "Subprime Bust Expands."

Crisis is a case of history repeating itself, it is useless and even counterproductive to intervene to offset losses.[68] Allen Meltzer expressed this view clearly in the *Wall Street Journal*: "Capitalism without failure is like religion without sin. The answer to excessive risk-taking is 'let 'em fail'. . . . Bailouts encourage excessive risk-taking; failures encourage prudent risk taking."[69]

On the other side of this debate, liberals such as *New York Times* columnist Bob Herbert pointed out the special circumstances of the Subprime Crisis—its roots in racial exclusion and in unjust, largely unregulated lending practices.[70] A December 2007 essay by the *Times*' Paul Krugman pointed out the daunting challenge posed by the Subprime Crisis:

> There are, in fact, three distinct concerns associated with the rising tide of foreclosures in America. One is financial stability: as banks and other institutions take huge losses on their mortgage-related investments, the financial system as a whole is getting wobbly. Another is human suffering: hundreds of thousands, and probably millions, of American families will lose their homes. Finally, there's injustice: the subprime boom involved predatory lending—high-interest loans foisted on borrowers who qualified for lower rates—on an epic scale.[71]

Policy response has not met Krugman's triple challenge. The anticipated showdown between "let 'em fail" and "address the injustice" views never came to a head. Financial stability was prioritized, and other challenges set aside. In effect, US officials have done all in their power to revitalize a too-little-regulated, too-big-to-fail, socially unresponsive and economically dysfunctional system of megabanks and mega financial firms, whose de-facto insolvency cannot be publicly admitted by a leadership playing a game of make-believe.

So, policy responses to the Subprime Crisis have yet to acknowledge that it was born in the perverse interaction between historical patterns of credit-market redlining and discrimination, on the one hand, and banks' strategic transformation in the neoliberal era, on the other. This history has not been erased; it requires further interrogation. And while the destruction of billions of dollars' worth of bank equity may be some kind of

---

68 Ibid.
69 A. Meltzer, "Let 'em fail," *Wall Street Journal*, July 21, 2007, p. A6.
70 B. Herbert, "A Swarm of Swindlers," *New York Times*, November 20, 2007.
71 P. Krugman, "Henry Paulson's Priorities," *New York Times*, December 10, 2007.

retribution for banks' historical patterns of exclusion and injustice, the destruction of billions of dollars of homeowner wealth sours the taste of such rough justice. For only the former devastation has attracted aggressive interventions and public subsidies. This makes more urgent the remaining question: How can banks again play a productive economic role in a world in which all people can find sustainably affordable housing?

5

NEOLIBERALISM AND THE MAKING OF SUBPRIME BORROWERS

Johnna Montgomerie

"Subprime" lending represented a relatively small but increasingly important part of the credit-driven economic expansion that America experienced prior to the Credit Crash. Its development has been shaped by specific national and global institutions. For instance, subprime lending could not have occurred without the debt relations between the US and Asian, particularly Chinese, investors over the past decade or so.[1] Domestically, specific macroeconomic conditions—from the "Roaring Nineties" to the "Goldilocks" economy in the 2000s—characterized by sustained expansion and low inflation rates, created a protracted period of financialized growth.[2] While there can be little doubt that these structural conditions facilitated the subprime lending boom, they pertain primarily to the supply side of credit growth. We must also consider what generated the demand for credit extended on "subprime" terms: the long-term consequences of neoliberalism—such as insecure employment, slow income growth, dwindling state income support and rising living costs—were key factors shaping why vulnerable households borrowed in the first place.

---

1 Herman Schwartz, "Housing, Global Finance, and American Hegemony: Building Conservative Politics One Brick at a Time," *Comparative European Politics*, 2008, 6(2).
2 Andrew Glyn, *Capitalism Unleashed: Finance, Globalization, and Welfare*, Oxford: Oxford University Press, 2006; J. Stiglitz, *The Roaring Nineties*, London: Penguin, 2004.

This chapter frames the subprime boom as a product of the interaction between longer-term processes of neoliberal restructuring and the more recent financialization trends. I focus on three specific socio-economic groups likely to be "subprime" borrowers by virtue of their risk characteristics and/or uptake of higher-cost loans: low-income households, young adults and senior citizens.[3] Using the triennial Survey of Consumer Finances (SCF) we can see a dramatic change in levels of indebtedness for these three groups from the 1990s to the 2000s, indicating that indebtedness is the product of prolonged financial distress. The growth of subprime borrowing should be related to processes of neoliberal restructuring whereby the business community retreated from its traditional obligations to workers and the government abandoned responsibility for those at the margins of economic life.

Low-income households, young adults and senior citizens have been profoundly affected by economic and social transformations over the past two decades and have experienced declining state support. The cumulative effects of labor market deregulation and welfare reform, in combination with corporate campaigns to shed jobs, keep wages low and reduce "legacy" and non-wage labor costs (especially pensions and health-care benefits), not only deepened inequality but also ushered in a previously unfathomable trend of indebtedness among America's most socially and economically marginalized groups.[4] Access to mortgage credit, in particular, became a key fix to temporarily stave off the political and economic consequences of deepening financial inequality, while conveniently serving to fuel the credit boom. Initially, subprime lending was politically justifiable because it "democratized finance" by giving previously excluded groups access to the financial market boom. Indeed, homeownership was seen as a political panacea to address a wide range of issues—including neighborhood renewal, wealth creation, and even child development.[5]

This chapter outlines three significant downsides to promoting

---

3 These three groups are categorized in the SCF as households earning less than $20,000 per year, households whose head is under thirty-five, and households whose head is over sixty-five.

4 W. Lazonick and M. O'Sullivan, "Maximizing Shareholder Value: A New Ideology for Corporate Governance," *Economy and Society*, 2000, 29(1).

5 M. Carliner, "Development of Federal Homeownership 'Policy'," *Housing Policy Debate*, 1998, 9(2); G. Wright, *Building the Dream: A Social History of Housing in America*, Cambridge, MA:, MIT Press, 1983.

homeownership through subprime loans. First, the minor gains in homeownership rates created massive increases in debt levels for those households that participated in the recent credit boom. In part this trend reflects the overall credit expansion and property boom of the previous seven years, but subprime borrowers were more adversely affected because they were the "last-in" and "first-out" in the credit-property bubble, compounding their losses. Second, rising consumer debt levels suggest mortgages are not the only problem facing economically marginalized groups. For many American households, but especially for subprime borrowers, the lack of social support created conditions where consumer debt is used as a "plastic safety net" to finance daily living costs.[6] Third, minimal income growth is a significant, yet underemphasized, aspect of indebtedness. Consumer debt is often used to plug the gap between (stagnant) income and household expenditures, and the fact that mortgages represented ever higher multiples of income reflected that income growth did not keep pace with rising property values. For all three groups, debt-servicing costs amount to more than half of their pre-tax income levels in 2007. Without adequate income growth and social support, subprime borrowers will continue to default on outstanding loans, extending the current Crisis from financial markets to the household sector more generally.

THE POLITICS OF ABANDONMENT

The term "subprime" applies to individuals with various credit and life-cycle characteristics seen to fall below a standard (or prime) benchmark.[7] The creation of the subprime credit status is the product of decades of development in credit-scoring practices evolving from simple "accept" or "reject" criteria to more refined risk profiles based on an individual's probability of default. The most pertinent example is the FICO model (developed by the Fair Isaac Company), which produced standard risk scorecards for the entire US population. FICO scores are based on a number of employment, income and credit-history characteristics, with those

---

6 J. Wheary and T. Draut, *The Plastic Safety Net: The Reality Behind Debt in America*, Demos The Center for Responsible Lending, 2005.
7 T. Jacobson and K. Roszbach, "Bank Lending Policy, Credit Scoring and Value-at-Risk'," *Journal of Banking and Finance*, 2003, 27(4); W. F. Treacy and M. Carey, "Credit and Risk Rating Systems at Large US Banks'," *Journal of Banking and Finance*, 2000, p. 24.

scoring below 600 considered to fall into the "subprime" category. This credit-score definition of a "subprime" borrower has come to shape the terms of inquiry into the practices of subprime lending. For some, the practices of credit scoring and risk-based pricing are "performed" through the calculative technologies that constitute modern subjectivities.[8] Others have placed more emphasis on the way in which credit scoring determines who can access mainstream financial products.[9]

Alternatively, the term "subprime" applies to an array of consumer loans including mortgages, refinancing, home equity lines of credit, credit cards, home improvement loans, payday loans and automobile title loans. For example, "subprime" and "high-cost subprime" mortgages are classified by the Home Mortgage Disclosure Act (HMDA) as mortgages with a 3 percent and 5 percent spread, respectively, between the annual percentage rate (APR) of designated loans and the yield on a US Treasury security of comparable maturity. Using this framework, the Federal Reserve found that subprime lending grew from 4 percent of mortgage lending in 1994 to 26 percent of all loans (both purchase and refinancing) in 2005, meaning that about one in four home loan originations in 2005 were higher-rate loans.[10] This definition of subprime provides an empirical basis to reveal important systemic and special inequalities, such as gender and race discrimination and neighborhood redlining.[11]

However, these definitions of subprime often do not go far enough in relating the subprime experience to the neoliberal transformation of American capitalism. This chapter considers the subprime experience as the product of a convergence of chronic financial distress among subprime groups with the

---

8 P. Langley, *The Everyday Life of Global Finance: Saving and Borrowing in Anglo-America*, Oxford: Oxford University Press, 2008; D. Marron, "'Lending by Numbers': Credit Scoring and the Constitution of Risk within American Consumer Credit'," *Economy and Society*, 2007, 36(1).

9 A. Leyshon and N. Thrift, "Geographies of Financial Exclusion: Financial Abandonment in Britain and the United States'," *Transactions of the Institute of British Geographers* 1995, 20 (3); E. K. Wyly, M. Atia and D. J. Hammel, "Has Mortgage Capital Found an Inner-City Spatial Fix?'," *Housing Policy Debate*, 2004, 15(3).

10 R. B. Avery, K. P. Brevort, et al. "Higher-Priced Home Lending and the 2005 HMDA Data'," *Federal Reserve Bulletin*, 2006, Summer, vol. A125.

11 A. Leyshon and N. Thrift, "Lists Come Alive: Electronic Systems of Knowledge and the Rise of Credit-Scoring in Retail Banking'," *Economy and Society*, 1999, 28(3).

financial sector's eagerness to expand its business into the world of subprime mortgages. As such, financial abandonment involves much more than just the terms of access to mainstream finance. Tracing patterns for low-income, under-thirty-five and over-sixty-five households over the past two decades, we can see a marked difference between the 1990s and 2000s. The shift can be interpreted as the result of a meeting of two trends: processes of neoliberal restructuring on the one hand, and the emergence of a financialized culture which made credit amply available to these households on the other.

The reduction of government support and a virtual abdication of social responsibility by the business community combined to shape a neoliberal "politics of abandonment." Over the past two decades, corporate America has abandoned its social responsibility to employees. Imperatives of global competitiveness and profitability now come before obligations to the workforce. This is manifested in the growing difficulty of finding and keeping a job. Health-care and pension plans have been restructured to reduce costs. At the same time, the government allowed imperatives of fiscal restraint to redefine its obligations to its citizens, hitting subprime groups hardest. Capped funding for health-care and higher education dramatically increased the costs of these services, while already low levels of social security fell further. The "politics of abandonment" made subprime borrowers increasingly dependent on an ever expanding and aggressive financial services industry.

LOW-INCOME HOUSEHOLDS

Low-income households are, by all accounts, the archetypal subprime borrower. Ample empirical evidence shows that subprime lending was disproportionately concentrated in low-income urban communities and among low-income women and minority groups.[12] Throughout the neoliberal era, de-industrialization meant that relatively well-paid manufacturing

---

12 HUD, *Unequal Burden: Income and Racial Disparities in Subprime Lending in America*. US Department of Housing and Urban Development, 2000; US Treasury Department and Department of Housing and Urban Development, "Joint Report on Recommendations to Curb Predatory Home Mortgage Lending'," *Housing and Urban Development (HUD) Reports* no. 36, June 20, 2000; C. E. Weller, "Have Differences in Credit Access Diminished in an Era of Financial Market Deregulation?'," *PERI Working Paper Series*, 2007, no. 144.

jobs were replaced with low-skilled and low-paid service work in offices and retail sales outlets. This economic process intensified as political support for labor-market deregulation and anti-union legislation significantly decreased the number of workers able to collectively bargain for higher wages.[13] The result has been wage stagnation for most workers, even when US productivity rates recovered from the late 1990s onward. In addition, the federal government virtually froze the minimum-wage rate, while state governments engaged in successive rounds of liberalization (often competing against one another to attract investment). The adoption of active labor-market policies was accompanied by wholesale welfare reforms that particularly affected low-skill workers. Many workers have become ineligible for benefits, especially low-wage, low-skill workers and "nonstandard" workers such as temporary or part-time employees. The combined effects of flexible labor markets and waning state support for the unemployed translated into a re-emergence of the working poor in America.–

Until recently many believed that the effects of neoliberalism were offset by the "democratization" of finance. The credit boom and asset-price bubble gave many households access to retail investments packages and credit sources. The US government enthusiastically embraced the idea that improved access to credit for homeownership would dramatically improve the wealth holdings of low-income families and communities.[14] However, it turns out that participating in the recent credit and property-market boom by having a mortgage or refinancing loan has created significant liabilities and risks for low-income households. The rather modest 2 percentage-point increase in homeownership rates from 1992 to 2007 (from 39 percent to 41 percent, as measured by the SCF), was achieved through an enormous growth in private debt holdings—compounding the financial insecurity of low-income households.

The following figures provide a broad-based illustration of the composition of liabilities for subprime households. "Mortgage debt" is the total value of outstanding mortgages, home equity loans and home equity lines of credit secured by primary residence,

---

13 Glyn, *Capitalism Unleashed*, Chapter 5.
14 H. Karger and A. Gluckman, "The Home Ownership Myth'," *Dollars & Sense*, 2007, no. 270.

Figure 5.1: Average debt levels for all families earning less than $20,000

Source: Survey of Consumer Finances, 1992–2007

while "consumer debt" is the total value of all outstanding loans on credit cards, installment loans, other lines of credit, vehicle and education loans. Combining these loan categories allows us to capture the fluidity between households' different borrowing instruments. Loans secured against property and "unsecured" consumer loans are conventionally considered distinctly different types of borrowing. This perspective, however, overlooks how many households use mortgage loans (refinancing, cash-out and home equity lines of credit) to finance consumer purchases or pay off outstanding consumer debts. By combining these categories we can see how the overall composition of liabilities has changed and grown over time.

Figure 5.1 illustrates the outstanding mortgage and consumer-debt liabilities for all households earning less than $20,000 a year in pre-tax income (which includes wages, returns on investments and government income transfers). These figures include both renters and homeowners; therefore, the levels of mortgage debt and consumer debt are fairly evenly matched. We see that from 1992 to 2007 the average low-income household's debt holdings increased by over 200 percent, reaching nearly $18,000 in 2007.

The impact of homeownership for low-income households, through the uptake of often-higher-cost (subprime) mortgage

loans, is shown in Figure 5.2, which filters out renters
and other households that do not have mortgages or loans
against their property. We see that mortgage debt holdings
become a much larger proportion of household debt
holdings, but also that average mortgage debt levels more
than double from approximately $27,000 in 1992 to $67,000
in 2007. Yet this large expansion in mortgage debt did
not translate into any meaningful gains in homeownership
rates.

The politics of abandonment translates into the use of
consumer debt to provide short-term solutions for immediate
and pressing living expenses. Unforeseen events such as job
loss, medical expenses or car breakdowns force households
to borrow in order to pay for temporary expenses or loss of
income. A Demos survey showed that 70 percent of low-income
households used consumer credit as a "plastic safety net" to
pay for one-off misfortunes.[15] One third of households reported
using credit cards to cover basic living expenses, on average in
four out of the last twelve months.[16]

Other economic factors also contribute to the reliance on
consumer debt to fund regular expenses or to cover temporary
income shortfalls. Limited access to unemployment benefits
compounds the effect of job loss on low-income families. In
addition, low-income families are particularly vulnerable to
rising health-care costs. Health insurance is no longer a standard
employee benefit, especially among low-skilled service workers.
Moreover, government subsidies have steadily eroded, leaving
low-income families to meet rising health-care costs through
whatever means necessary, or not at all.[17] Seventy-five percent of
households *lacking* medical coverage carried debt on a credit card,
compared to 55 percent of families that had medical coverage.[18]

15 The survey asked households whether they had used credit cards in the past
year to pay for basic living expenses, such as rent, mortgage payments, groceries,
utilities or insurance, because they did not have money in their checking or savings
account. See J. Garcia, "Borrowing to Make Ends Meet: The Rapid Growth of
Credit Card Debt in America," Demos: A Network for Ideas and Action, 2006.
16 Wheary and Draut, *Plastic Safety Net*, p.11.
17 C. DeNavas-Walt, B. D. Proctor and R. J. Mills, *Income, Poverty, and Health
Insurance Coverage in the United States*, Washington DC: US Census Bureau,
2003.
18 C. Zeldin and M. Rukavina, *Borrowing to Stay Healthy: How Credit Card
Debt Is Related to Medical Expenses*, New York: Demos: A network of ideas and
action, and The Access Project, 2007.

Figure 5.2: Average debt levels for all families earning less than $20,000 with holdings

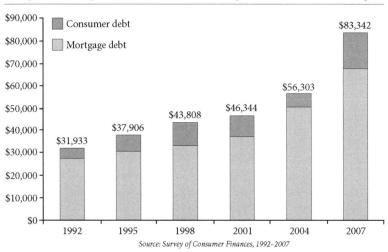

Source: Survey of Consumer Finances, 1992–2007

Therefore, we must consider rising unsecured debt levels in conjunction with dwindling state support for low-income families when they lose a job or have a medical emergency. Often, low-income families are using consumer credit as a way to fund a drop in income or unexpected expenses.

Therefore, over the past decade, low-income households have been amassing huge amounts of debt not only to participate in homeownership but also to supplement their meager incomes to pay for daily living expenses, or as a "plastic safety net." Servicing these debts also creates new claims on income; according to the SCF, in 2007 households earning less than $20,000 had $9,845 in annual debt repayment obligations. This makes debt repayment the largest category of expenditure for low-income households and demonstrates the degree to which indebtedness has created a new level of financial insecurity among America's working poor. In addition, low-income households are also the most vulnerable to temporary income losses and the most likely to lack savings or wealth to draw on during unemployment, compounding their financial insecurity.

"GENERATION DEBT"

In the same way the rhetoric of financial inclusion was galvanized to legitimate subprime lending, so the logic of the wealth life-cycle (or life-cycle permanent income hypothesis) was used to justify the growing financial insecurity of the young and old during the recent credit boom. Rising debt levels among the under-thirty-fives and over-sixty-fives was considered a predicable outcome of life-cycle models which presume a balance between income, assets, savings and debt changes across an adult's lifetime. According to this rationale, young adults will have low income, limited savings and assets, and will borrow relatively more. As individuals acquire longer employment histories with related increases in income and savings levels, wealth is assumed to increase. Upon retirement, individuals are assumed to go into a phase of dis-saving in which assets and savings are depleted to replace employment income. These assumptions limited the scope for criticism of the potential social costs of rising indebtedness and growing financial insecurity for the young and old in American society. That is, the life-cycle rhetoric sanitized the political implications of abandoning these socially marginalized groups to the whims of the free market.

Young adults, or those households whose head is under-thirty-five, are unique because almost their entire working life has been in the era of financialization. For them, credit has become one of the most important factors shaping their participation in American society. They rely on credit to gain access to education, to buy a home, to pay for daily living costs or to start a family: this is "generation debt."[19] Ever higher debt levels are needed to access what were previously considered standard middle-class entitlements such as a college education and homeownership. Moreover, high levels of borrowing early on in life serve to intensify financial insecurity as indebtedness can become a lifelong condition, especially if income, savings and assets never exceed cumulative debt levels or servicing costs create a sustained drain on income. Dwindling government subsidies for education and health-care have meant that households just starting out have less public support than previous generations. Youth unemployment and growing employment flexibility has

---

19 T. Draut, *Strapped: Why America's 20- and 30-Somethings Can't Get Ahead*, New York: Doubleday, 2006.

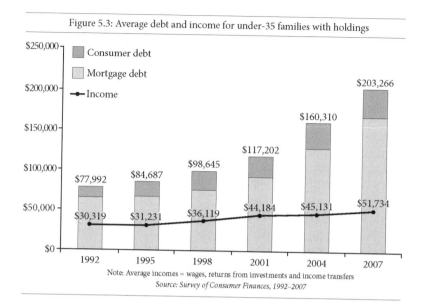

Figure 5.3: Average debt and income for under-35 families with holdings

Note: Average incomes = wages, returns from investments and income transfers
Source: Survey of Consumer Finances, 1992–2007

hampered wage growth for young adults. As they get on the housing ladder in the midst of an asset-price bubble and are more likely to be affected by job losses, the current economic downturn and falling property prices will undoubtedly affect the young disproportionately.

Figure 5.3 shows debt holdings overlaid by income levels. It is clear that under-thirty-fives have experienced an astronomical growth in debt relative to income from the 1990s to the 2000s. While income levels for under-thirty-fives are higher than those of low-income households, they are dwarfed by the rapid escalation of overall debt levels from 2001 to 2007. Average income increased by 70 percent from approximately $30,000 in 1992 to $50,000 in 2007; yet their debt holdings grew at almost twice that rate over the same period.

These figures include only those households that have mortgages or a foot on the property ladder. Rising indebtedness only amounted to a 4 percentage-point increase in homeownership rates in the SCF from 1992 to 2007 (i.e. from 37 percent to 41 percent). Moreover, many young people unwittingly bought into the housing market when the asset-bubble was inflating, which means that their overall wealth gains are likely to be much less than those of households that already owned property prior to the housing bubble. Compared to previous generations, most young people, especially those living in major metropolitan areas, do not have access to affordable housing. Also, young adults typically have higher-cost loans because of their comparatively short credit and employment histories and, in the case of mortgages, because they typically have no existing equity holdings and/or minimal down payments.

As Figure 5.3 demonstrates, unsecured lending is as important to young households as mortgages. Over the past two decades unsecured debt levels increased from $14,500 to $36,700, which represents over half of average pre-tax income levels. Young workers have been particularly hard hit by employer efforts to curtail non-wage benefits coverage as they are most often new, temporary, or contract-based workers. Especially when it comes to the medical costs for young families, the lack of benefits coverage and rising health-care costs are a problem not experienced to the same extent by older generations. Slow income growth means that wages are often not enough to cover housing costs, living expenses and health-care costs. Moreover, the annual cost of servicing this stock of debt in 2007 was $22,700, almost half of average income levels.

SENIOR CITIZENS

Senior citizens' experience of financial abandonment is particularly acute, and they are increasingly using debt to maintain a steadily eroding standard of living. Over-sixty-fives have the highest rates of homeownership of all age groups; the key factor in determining financial security is therefore whether or not senior citizens own their home outright or have outstanding loans against the equity in their home. For the total group of households over sixty-five, the picture of liabilities compared to income looks relatively healthy. However, the group with debt holdings has experienced a tripling of debt relative to income since 2001, typically the result of the withdrawal of existing equity rather than a new home purchase. Senior citizens are converting home equity into cash in order to finance their living costs. The result is a new form of financial insecurity in old age.

Most over-sixty-fives have limited sources of income and have increasingly used debt simply to get by. The low nominal interest rates that fuelled the credit boom significantly undercut interest income from private savings. Many followed the general trend of transferring traditional savings accounts into investment vehicles, such as 401(k), market-indexed and mutual funds. Multiple downturns in stock markets (in 1997, 2001 and 2007) significantly reduced investment returns, especially for those households unfortunate enough to retire in the immediate aftermath of each of these events. Low interest rates and spotty returns on private investment left senior citizens with lower incomes, "turning what should have been comfortable retirements into hand-to-mouth existences."[20] Similarly, many retired households have borne the brunt of successive rounds of corporate restructuring of "legacy costs" such as company-sponsored medical coverage and pension plans. Many corporations have drastically curtailed or eliminated health insurance for their retirees, leaving seniors to shoulder soaring medical expenses at a time when they are encountering more frequent and serious health problems. In 2003, only 38 percent of large employers, offered medical coverage to retired employees compared with 66 percent in 1988.[21] Many businesses have changed pension schemes from Defined-Benefit to Defined-Contribution in order to reduce legacy costs, making more households dependent on poorly performing stock-market-linked investments.[22]

With private-sector benefits declining, most seniors have become increasingly reliant on state support such as social security and welfare benefits to sustain basic living costs. However, 84 percent of households aged sixty-five and over receive social security benefits, while 40 percent claim social security is their largest source of income.[23] Government efforts to cap expenditure on social security under the rubric of fiscal austerity meant that benefits have steadily declined. Faced with an aging population and a declining tax base, successive US administrations since the 1990s have attempted to "plug the fiscal gap" by reducing benefit pay-outs. The cumulative effects of corporate and government restructuring of pensions and benefit programs has been escalating indebtedness for retired households.

20 L. Punch, "Subprime Cards," *Credit Card Management*, 2003, 16(9).
21 H. C. McGhee and T. Draut, *Retiring in the Red: The Growth of Debt among Older Americans*, New York: Demos, 2006, p. 3
22 T. Cutler and B. Waine, "Social Insecurity and the Retreat from Social Democracy: Occupational Welfare in the Long Boom and Financialization," *Review of International Political Economy*, 2001, 8(1).
23 AARP Policy Research Institute, *Fact Sheet: Sources of Income for Older Persons*, Washinton DC: American Association for Retired Persons (AARP), 2006.

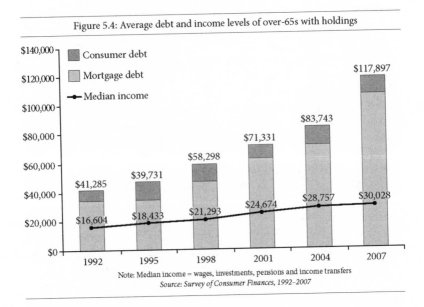

Figure 5.4: Average debt and income levels of over-65s with holdings

Note: Median income = wages, investments, pensions and income transfers
Source: Survey of Consumer Finances, 1992–2007

Figure 5.4 illustrates how debt holdings have increased from relatively high levels in the 1990s to an astronomical four times income levels by 2007. Here, secured debt holdings increase mostly from new loans against existing home equity. By and large, this increase in debt levels is related to rising costs of health-care, prescription drugs, housing, fuel and food. For low-income seniors, dwindling state subsidies for Medicaid mean that those without medical insurance must still contribute up to a third of their income to health-care-related expenses.[24] Most often these expenses are for prescription drugs, which average $860 a year in out-of-pocket expenses for those covered under Medicaid.[25]

The overall effect of rising living costs, stagnating private sources of income and declining state support has been a growing reliance on debt to bridge the gap between income and the cost of essential goods and services. The sheer scale of indebtedness can be seen in the fact that the average annual cost of servicing this debt is $16,000. As with low-income households and under-thirty-fives,

---

24 *The 2008 Retirement Confidence Survey*, Washington DC: Employment Benefit Research Institute: 2008; *Out-of-Pocket Spending on Health Care by Medicare Beneficiaries Aged 65 and Older*, Washington DC: Public Policy Institute: 2003.
25 Zeldin and Rukavina, *Borrowing to Stay Healthy*.

debt-servicing costs are the single largest drain on net income; but unlike working households, senior citizens' reliance on fixed incomes makes this debt burden even more acute. Pressures to make repayments on outstanding debts have led to new markets (and marketing campaigns) for senior-citizen equity-release loans and viaticles—which involve the selling of life insurance to third parties for one-off or monthly payments.[26]

CONCLUSION

This chapter has sought to challenge perceptions of subprime mortgage lending as an acute period of financial overextension by emphasizing that chronic over-indebtedness prevailed among low-income households, young adults and senior citizens well before the frenzy in mortgage lending gathered pace. While the years of feverish and speculative expansion that preceded the Credit Crash did a great deal to bring the tensions of financialization to the fore, those tensions themselves are very much the result of decades of neoliberal policies and deepening inequality.

Few analyses of the current Financial Crisis have connected it to the long-term growth in inequality under neoliberalism. Typically, labor-market and welfare reform, liberalized finance and macroeconomic policies are considered separate economic spheres. Yet when we examine the contours of the Crisis from the household's perspective, we see the cumulative effects of these transformations. It was not just rising asset prices and skyrocketing profitability that blinded many to the cracks already present in the edifice of financialized expansion. Neoliberal ideologies did their part too: free-market logics presented subprime lending as a step toward greater financial inclusion for groups previously excluded from mainstream financial services. Credit scoring was heralded as proof of the efficiency and expertise of financial markets to adequately price risk. Policy-makers dismissed concerns about escalating debt levels, claiming that they were part of the wealth-effect. For those groups with limited asset holdings, such as under-thirty-fives and over-sixty-fives, life-cycle assumptions blinded policy-makers to the systemic threats of driving already financially fragile groups further into debt. However, as this chapter has

---

26 L. Punch, "Older Debtors, New Problems," *Credit Card Management*, 2004, 17 (5); C. Vincentini and P. Jacques, "Seniors Get Ready To 'Charge'," *MarketFacts Quarterly*, 2004, 23(1).

argued, access to credit is no replacement for real wage growth
and adequate social protection. Any political attempts to stem the
current economic downturn are likely have only limited success
unless they address the financial hardship and instability facing
American households.

6

TOO BIG TO BAIL

The "Paulson Put,"
US Presidential Politics,
and the Global Financial Meltdown

Thomas Ferguson and Robert Johnson

In March 2008 the Death's Head suddenly appeared over the offices of Bear Stearns, the giant brokerage house, in lower Manhattan. To the astonishment of the world, US Treasury Secretary Henry Paulson and Federal Reserve Chair Ben Bernanke—both Republicans nominated to their positions by President George W. Bush—and then New York Federal Reserve Bank President Timothy Geithner responded by introducing a visionary single-payer government insurance scheme—not for sick Americans, but for ailing financial houses. Stretching both law and precedent, they threw open the Federal Reserve's discount window not only to commercial banks, but also to investment banks that were primary dealers in government securities. By special agreement with the Treasury, the New York Fed also took on to its books $30 billion dollars of Bear Stearns' bad assets so that JPMorgan Chase could take over what remained of the Bear.[1]

---

1 This paper draws liberally on our "Too Big To Bail: The 'Paulson Put,' Presidential Politics, and the Global Financial Meltdown, Part I: From Shadow Banking System To Shadow Bailout," *International Journal of Political Economy* 2009, 38 (spring), pp. 3–34; and "Too Big To Bail: The 'Paulson Put,' Presidential Politics, and the Global Financial Meltdown Part II: Fatal Reversal— Single Payer and Back," *International Journal of Political Economy*, 2009, 38(Summer), pp. 5–45. These essays are extensively documented; given their ready availability, this paper trims references to a minimum. Unless specifically noted, citations to newspapers and magazines are normally to their internet sites, not the printed

On September 7, Paulson and Bernanke dramatically confirmed the new collectivist course by taking over Fannie Mae and Freddie Mac, the two gigantic government-sponsored enterprises (GSEs) that support mortgage markets. At a stroke the government acquired new gross liabilities equal to 40 percent of US Gross Domestic Product.[2]

But on September 15—a date that will be forever emblazoned in the financial history of the world, alongside that fatal June 5, 1931, when German Chancellor Heinrich Brüning repudiated reparations and precipitated chain-bankruptcy in Western Europe—the reluctant revolutionaries suddenly had second thoughts.[3] They decided to cross up markets and do what free-market conservatives had been demanding since the beginning of the Crisis: let a giant financial house—Lehman Brothers—go bankrupt.

The result was catastrophic. Gigantic runs began on money-market funds, commercial paper and many banks. Stock markets everywhere went into free fall as panicky investors drove yields on safer government securities down practically to zero—in effect signaling a preference for government bonds to all other assets in the world. As interbank markets ground to a terrifying halt, Paulson, Bernanke, and Geithner borrowed another page from Lenin (or, more accurately, Mussolini, for their clear intention was to support, not replace, private markets) and effectively nationalized AIG, the giant insurer. Then Paulson

edition. We cite specific URLs only if confusion seems likely. Note that many daily papers post articles late on the night before the print edition appears.

We thank Jane D'Arista, William Black, Jan Kregel, Gerald O'Driscoll, Mario Seccareccia, Peter Temin, and the editor of this book for comments and assistance. We owe special debts to Joseph Stiglitz and Walker Todd for very extensive comments and discussions. Our study started out as a chapter in a projected book on the economic crisis being put together by Stiglitz with José Antonio Ocampo and Stephany Griffith-Jones for Oxford University Press. The chapter we submitted was lavishly praised, but we were later asked to shorten the essay and specifically to remove the names of a series of predominantly Democratic Party politicians now in power. We were agreeable to shortening, but not to airbrushing the names and withdrew the chapter.
2   Formally the Federal Housing Finance Authority took them into conservatorship. For the gross liabilities, see Martin Wolf, "No Alternative to Nationalization," *Financial Times*, September 8, 2008.
3   Cf. T. Ferguson and P. Temin, "Made in German: The German Currency Crisis of July 1931," in A. J. Field, ed., *Research in Economic History* 21, Oxford: JAI Press, 2003; and Ferguson and Temin, "Comment on 'The German Twin Crises of 1931'," *Journal of Economic History*, 2004, 64 (September).

and Bernanke raced to Congress to confront it with a stunning choice: pass at once a gigantic, ill-defined $700 billion asset-buying program that the Treasury would administer with no review or accountability, or else bear responsibility for a real-life financial Armageddon.

With the public seething and elites bitterly divided, the American political system itself seemed for a few vertiginous days on the verge of melting down. In the end an amended bail-out bill passed, larded up with more pork than a runaway Oscar Mayer refrigeration car.

Shockingly, however, world markets just shrugged and continued melting down. Eventually British Prime Minister Gordon Brown stepped in. Openly deriding Paulson's vague asset-buying proposal as a clueless giveaway of taxpayer money, Brown focused on recapitalizing British banks at a relatively stiff price. The amount injected was too small to solve the problem, and the government did not take the bad assets off the banks' books or force the banks to write them down; but next to the pathetic US effort, Brown's plan almost glowed. Along with the Irish government's decision to guarantee all deposits, it set off a competitive scramble among the G7 countries to ring-fence their financial systems from total collapse via partial nationalizations, state loan guarantees and extended insurance on bank deposits.

The swift creation of relative safe havens in the core capitalist countries triggered an enormous inflow of capital from developing countries into First World financial centers. Many investors dumped assets indiscriminately in their haste for safety. Financial systems in the developing world, including Eastern Europe, teetered on the brink of collapse. The US Federal Reserve, which had already opened unlimited swap lines with several First World central banks, brushed aside concerns about multilateralism and opened new $30 billion swap lines for central banks in Mexico, Korea, Brazil, and Singapore.

As this book goes to press, the usual suspects—finance ministers, heads of state, leading bankers—are, like Humpty Dumpty's men, struggling to put all the pieces back together again. But a jumble of discordant viewpoints and the changeover of the American presidency in the midst of the Crisis have made it hard to come to grips with what has happened and why.

Some key points are obvious. The widely touted American investment banking–led model of global finance has plainly collapsed. All major American investment houses have either gone bankrupt or defensively transformed themselves into commercial bank holding companies. Out of the debris a new, universal bank-based financial system appears to be taking shape, one in which preferential access to government aid and the Federal Reserve's discount window is likely to be pivotal.[4] The place of money-market funds, hedge funds and non-banks in this new system is murky. What is clear is that a new round of "corporatism" in which the state moves more deeply into the day-to-day functioning of markets is taking shape.

But the giant tide of bail-outs has done little more than stave off complete collapse. While officials and business leaders celebrate the "green shoots" of recovery (principally rises in share prices and declines in risk premia on the yields of some financial instruments), unemployment rates around the world remain stubbornly high. Mortgage defaults and bankruptcies are still running at high levels, while private consumption in the US and elsewhere stagnates. Financial markets have still not returned to "normalcy." Banks are not lending—though many are paying bonuses, lobbying and making political-campaign contributions—and most private credit markets remain at least semi-frozen. The so-called shadow banking system of so-called non-banks that formerly lent prodigiously, almost literally to all comers, has collapsed, while the rest of American business is engrossed in "deleveraging" (paying down debt). The US Treasury is plainly "picking winners" in finance as other sectors of the economy queue up for bail-outs of their own. The Federal Reserve continues not only to support the banking system but in many instances to replace it via the myriad "special lending facilities" that it set up earlier in the Crisis.

Clearly, the long-running debates about the future of the International Monetary System badly missed the mark. These all focused on the likelihood that foreign dollar-holders—possibly China, or Japan, or major Arab oil exporters—might some day bring down the curtain on the system by dumping their holdings in response to unsustainable current-account deficits.[5] This Crisis,

---

4 Universal banks should not be confused with financial supermarkets, as the recent split up of Citigroup suggests; see P. T. Larsen, "Death call on universal banking premature," *Financial Times*, January 14, 2009.

5 See for example the gigantic literature on the "New Bretton Woods System" spawned by such papers as M. P. Dooley, D. Folkerts-Landau, and P. Garber, "The Revived Bretton Woods System: The Effects of Periphery Intervention and

however, has "Made in America" stamped all over it; a complete breakdown of financial regulation lies at its heart.

Yet not only the public, but many participants in financial markets continue to shake their heads about precisely what happened and why nothing seems to be working very well, even though the Federal Reserve's balance sheet more than doubled in size between the start of the Crisis and spring of 2009.

This chapter analyzes the World Financial Meltdown from its origins to Election Day 2008. We suggest that the serial disasters had little to do with conventional "policy errors" or, as many have increasingly wondered, sheer incompetence, though both were plentifully in evidence. Instead, what we term the "Paulson Put" (on par with the fabled "Greenspan Put" that implicitly promised Fed action in cases of steep stock-market declines) is key to understanding what happened.[6]

The original idea of the Paulson Put was to stave off high-profile public financial bail-outs until after the election, when they were less likely to trigger a political firestorm that could threaten existing wealth-holders by opening up a Pandora's Box of reform demands. The key expression here is "high profile," for the Paulson Put had two distinct policy faces. One, already alluded to, embraced the highly visible adoption of "single payer" government insurance for banks, investment houses and GSEs (Fannie and Freddie). The second was a much less heralded "shadow bail-out" designed to prop up the financial system in ways that would attract as little attention as possible. This latter effort knit together another emergency safety net for banks in

---

Reserve Management on Interest Rates and Exchange Rates," Cambridge, MA: National Bureau of Economic Research, 2004, Working Paper 10332.

6 When someone buys a "put" he or she purchases the right to sell an asset at a specified price. In effect, one is buying insurance against price declines. By extension, the "Greenspan Put" referred to the market's belief that the Fed Chair would steer the Fed to counteract large declines in the market. The existence of a "Greenspan Put" was widely acknowledged within financial markets for excellent reasons: Greenspan, in speeches, left no doubt about his intentions. See the discussion in G. O'Driscoll, "Money and the Present Crisis," manuscript, 2008. But various scholars have questioned the evidence about the Fed's actual behavior. A good review is W. Buiter, "Central Banks and Financial Crises," a paper presented at the Federal Reserve Bank of Kansas City Symposium on "Maintaining Stability in A Changing Financial System" (Jackson Hole, Wyoming, August 21–23, 2008). As O'Driscoll observes, the put was entailed by Greenspan's (and Bernanke's) insistence that the Fed could clean up asset bubbles after they burst.

trouble out of separate threads that were individually all but imperceptible: assistance on a gigantic scale to banks and thrifts from the obscure Federal Home Loan Bank System; a concerted effort to play down eventual taxpayer liabilities for Federal Deposit Insurance pay-outs; emergency purchases by the GSEs, especially Fannie Mae, of home mortgages and mortgage bonds to stem declines in those markets; and unconventional expansions of the Federal Reserve's balance sheet.

Unfortunately, bursting asset bubbles nourished on high leverage are reverse Cinderella stories on steroids. At midnight the transit is not from a beautiful dream to drab reality, but to the very gates of Hell itself, as whole economies and credit systems crash for years.[7] By striving to put off a reckoning as long as possible, the Paulson Put guaranteed that the final clean-up bill would rise astronomically. In a political system in which "no new taxes" is an axiom of political life for both political parties, it also set off a desperate search for short cuts that would not work, such as turning the Federal Reserve's balance sheet inside out, to avoid going to Congress.

Eventually the Paulson Put collapsed under the weight of all these contradictions. As Bear Stearns vividly illustrated, there was no unobtrusive way to stretch the Put to cover investment banks. That could only happen during a cataclysm. No less fatefully, involving the GSEs in the shadow bail-out was quixotic. Already compromised by political pressures and past accounting scandals, the GSEs were too financially fragile to be used as safety valves. The efforts of Paulson & Co. to use them for this purpose pushed them over the edge, leading anxious foreign investors to dump their bonds and forcing their de facto nationalization.

The reaction to the takeover of Fannie and Freddie in turn threw the switch on the doomsday machine—the disastrous series of actions and reactions that destroyed the (first) Paulson Put as well as all chances Republican Senator John McCain had of winning the presidency. First, there were the unpopular GSE bail-outs in the midst of the election campaign. Then, in convulsive reaction to furious critics in and out of the Republican Party, the decision to let Lehman Brothers go

---

7 The best discussion of the macroeconomics of bursting bubbles is R. Koo, *The Holy Grail of Macroeconomics: Lessons From Japan's Great Recession*, revised edition, Singapore, 2009.

bankrupt—in effect, the definitive expiration of the original Paulson Put. The latter then morphed into a newer, chastened version fixated on protecting existing shareholders in America's leading financial firms from dilution—a preoccupation that led directly to the meltdown of the world financial system, since it fatally compromised any chance of a serious bail-out. As a result, the banking system remains under pressure. With the Federal Reserve continuing to make markets for many classes of assets, the serious work of reconstructing the financial system has barely begun.

THE PAULSON PUT IS BORN

The "Paulson Put" was a response to the problems growing out of the more famous "Greenspan Put" and the deregulatory bacchanal that it supported. But that story, along with its relation to global imbalances, is too complex to trace here. We have presented that discussion elsewhere.[8] Here we begin with the situation in early August, 2007, when the Fed was still acting as though inflation was the biggest threat to the American economy.

Market reaction to the Fed's refusal to cut rates on August 7 was brutal. The stock market swooned; the dollar fell. A broken trail of evidence suggests that neither Bernanke nor Paulson fully appreciated the danger to the economy as a whole, but they quickly got the message that Wall Street and America's greatest banks were in peril. Both the Fed and the Treasury abruptly switched gears. Still cautioning against proposals from the Democratic Congress to bail out homeowners, Bernanke and Paulson now began improvising a strategy for getting help to the banks that would not attract attention.

The Treasury Secretary and the Fed Chair knew, like everyone else in the markets, that chances for success hinged on cooperating with each other. If markets sensed that their two institutions were working at cross-purposes, the response would be swift and disastrous. But their positions were not institutionally equivalent.

---

8 Ferguson and Johnson, "'Paulson Put' Part I"; the campaign mounted by the Fed under Greenspan to shuck its traditional responsibility for regulating primary dealers in government securities has still not received the attention it deserves. This striking case of a government agency lobbying to shrink its mission should be a yellow flag in the face of the current push to make the Fed responsible for monitoring the stability of the US financial system.

The Secretary of the Treasury was part of the president's team, formally partisan and by design responsive to direct political pressures. By contrast, the Fed had a more restricted range of action and was formally nonpartisan. Indeed, in political mythology, it was nonpolitical. Although the president could fire Paulson at any time, he could not dismiss Bernanke once he had appointed him. Traditional banking-crisis doctrine assigned to the Treasury Chief the responsibility for bailing out banks, on the excellent grounds that back-door bail-outs by central banks were hard to police and even harder to stop before they started inflating the currency. The traditional view thus insisted that Congress and the president, acting through the budget process, shoulder responsibility for bail-outs.[9]

This defined the problem that the Paulson Put was designed to overcome. For the president and Congress to assume responsibility for bail-outs was fine in theory. But the Republicans had only recently been mauled in the 2006 midterm Congressional elections. Having lost control of both Houses of Congress, they now faced a housing crisis of their own: losing the White House. The Republican Right was on a tear about spending. Even more seriously, income distribution had at last emerged as a public issue. In the face of years of propaganda about the "magic of the marketplace," the spectacle of the US government pouring in large sums of money to rescue institutions controlled by America's most affluent citizens promised to be toxic. Neither party's leaders were likely to be enthusiastic; but because Republicans would be making the key decisions in the White House and Treasury, the brunt of the blame would fall on them.

---

9   See for example W. Todd, "Lessons of the Past and Prospects for the Future of Lender of Last Resort Theory," Federal Reserve Bank of Cleveland, 1988, Working Paper No. 8805; and Todd, "History of and Rationales For the Reconstruction Finance Corporation," *Federal Reserve Bank of Cleveland Economic Review*, 1992, IV. Our own approach would stress more strongly public-goods aspects of the problem. The Reconstruction Finance Corporation, it is important to note, was in fact the creation first of all of the largest US banks. See the detailed account, based on extensive archival research, in G. Epstein and T. Ferguson, "Monetary Policy, Loan Liquidation, and Industrial Conflict: The Federal Reserve and the Open Market Operations of 1932," *Journal of Economic History*, 1984, 44. We regard the Swedish bail-out as superior to the RFC, which looks good mostly by comparison to the approach of the Bush and Obama administrations.

The Shadow Bail-Out: Federal Home Loan Banks

Paulson and Bernanke, accordingly, evolved a two-track strategy for getting out of the Crisis or, to be precise, for rescuing Wall Street and the banks. The Fed, whose every move in money markets was closely scrutinized, at once took measures that were customary for central banks, or at least the US Central Bank, in these situations. It cut rates sharply—once even by a startling three-quarters of a point—and talked up cooperation with other central banks, which were now discovering that many financial houses in their own countries had also been drinking the Kool-Aid of "riskless" collateralized debt obligations (CDOs).

Paulson's moves, by contrast, were much more circumspect. Indeed, at times he virtually disappeared from public view. Behind the scenes, however, he was very much engaged. Formally or informally, the Treasury Department was the dominant force in a network of lesser-known financial agencies that collectively commanded massive financial and regulatory resources that could help distressed financial houses. Paulson, as head of Treasury and—in this case perhaps more importantly—informal chief of the administration's economic-policy-making apparatus, could thus preside over a gigantic shadow bail-out of the shadow banking system with public money that almost no-one tracked. With most of the media and even the markets fixated on the Fed, his first move was simple: sit back and watch quietly while regional Federal Home Loan Banks shoveled billions and billions of dollars out to banks and mortgage companies, including many of America's largest.[10]

Figure 6.1, with its associated table, tells the story. In the late summer of 2007, as the Housing Crisis snowballed into the Credit Crunch, the balance sheet of the Federal Home Loan Bank System exploded. As Figure 6.1 indicates, lending in the form of advances and other purchases of mortgage-related securities increased sharply. The aid went not only to the small banks or thrifts that were traditionally regarded as the system's clients but also—as Table 6.1 shows—to many of the very largest financial institutions in the United States.

---

10 The Treasury Secretary's formal authority over the various agencies we discuss here varies; his real influence is also subject to informal pressures and suasion. In practice, however, we agree with Barton Gellman (*Angler*, New York, 2008) that Paulson had taken over the reins of economic policy from Vice President Cheney.

Table 6.1: Advances to Seven Large Banks

Year	Total	Subtotal Large	Large %
2005	619880	127096	20.50
2006	640681	178874	27.92
2007Q1	624418	190724	30.54
2007Q2	640035	191630	29.94
2007Q3	824000	263545	31.98
2007Q4	875061	261753	29.91
2008Q1	913104	265922	29.12
2008Q2	913897	256424	28.06

Source: FHLB and FDIC

Figure 6.1

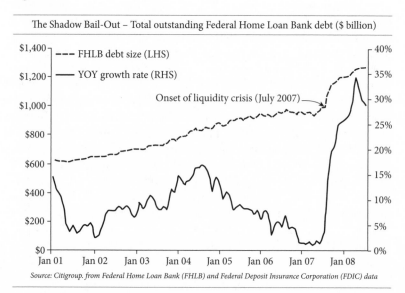

The Shadow Bail-Out – Total outstanding Federal Home Loan Bank debt ($ billion)

Source: Citigroup. from Federal Home Loan Bank (FHLB) and Federal Deposit Insurance Corporation (FDIC) data

The colossal dimensions of this shadow bail-out, which drew little notice in the national press (and no discussion in presidential campaign coverage), are tellingly illustrated by a single comparison. In March 2008, the Fed rocked the world by advancing $30 billion to subsidize JPMorgan Chase's takeover of Bear Stearns. By contrast, in the third quarter of 2007, Countrywide Credit, the nation's largest mortgage institution, borrowed $22.3 billion from the Federal Home Loan Bank of Atlanta. This was on top of $28.8 billion that it already owed the Atlanta Regional Bank.[11]

Most American banks are members of the Federal Deposit Insurance Corporation (FDIC), which insures their deposits. Funds for paying out on that insurance come from charges on banks that the FDIC sets. Amounts vary by need, rising when bank failures proliferate. It is thus the banks themselves that are first on the hook for bank failures.

Since the 1990s, bank failure rates have generally been low. But as housing markets tanked in 2007, it became obvious that they were going to rise. This quickly raised concerns about the adequacy of the FDIC's "insurance fund." The obvious answer— raise assessments on banks—was not politically appealing. They are, after all, massive contributors to political campaigns at all levels.[12] On the other hand, if they did not pay, someone else eventually would have to. It was obvious who—the public, just as it had after the last election in which waves of banks failed, in 1988. Public discussion of this eventuality was precisely what the shadow bail-out was designed to avoid.

Paulson & Co.'s solution was to try to slide through the campaign on the audacity of hope and let the FDIC spend down its reserves, while letting current and former FDIC officials explain that the "insurance fund" was backed by the Treasury, which would provide whatever sums were needed. Lost in the shuffle was the potential shift in the burden of payment, from banks to

---

11 See Ferguson and Johnson, "'Paulson Put': Part I," p. 29, note 33.
12   See for example T. Ferguson, *Golden Rule: The Investment Theory of Party Competition and the Logic Of Money-Driven Political Systems*, Chicago, 1995; Ferguson, "Blowing Smoke: Impeachment, the Clinton Presidency, and the Political Economy," in W. Crotty, ed., *The State of Democracy in America*, Washington, DC: Georgetown University Press, 2001. Some scholars who should know better have recently argued that the political influence of banks is uniquely a result of financial deregulation in the 1970s and after. But this is plainly false; see for example Ferguson, "Beyond Their Means? The Costs of Democracy from Jefferson to Lincoln," *Journal of the Historical Society*, 2006, 6(4).

taxpayers. As everyone's attention focused on the GSE bailout, discussed later in this chapter, the Treasury quietly inserted language into the bill removing penalties on Fed loans to failed banks. This was widely regarded as "a backdoor way to shore up the FDIC" by making it easier to tap the Fed for support.[13]

Eventually, snowballing bank failures (some very large) forced the FDIC to raise charges on the banks. In the bail-out legislation, however, the Treasury included not only a much-ballyhooed provision raising limits on deposit insurance from $100,000 to $250,000, but also a proviso permitting unlimited loans from the Treasury to the FDIC. The American public, which knew nothing of the "Ricardian Equivalence" beloved by conservative economists—according to which people immediately start saving to pay taxes they know are coming—was left in blissful ignorance, even as bank stock prices fell off a cliff.

By tapping the Federal Home Loan Bank Boards and blurring who would pay when the FDIC ran through its funds, the shadow bail-out seemed for a time to be succeeding spectacularly. The press, scholars and the Washington community let down their guard. Instead of following the money, they focused on the pageantry and drama of the presidential campaign. But, even as the Republican candidates cut each other up and Barack Obama started to whittle down Hillary Clinton's seemingly insurmountable lead, Paulson made a fatal miscalculation: he decided to press Fannie Mae and Freddie Mac into the shadow bail-out.

THE SHADOW BAIL-OUT: FREDDIE AND FANNIE

In January 2008, the Republican administration and the Democrat-controlled Congress agreed that modest fiscal stimulus through tax rebates would be good public policy in an election year. Some Democrats, mostly in the House, appear to have favored a larger stimulus. Most Democratic leaders, however, were at best lukewarm to this, whereas Republican Congressional leaders were actively hostile. Proposals for mortgage relief provoked additional discord. Representative Barney Frank (D–MA), chair of the House Financial Services Committee, talked up a plan to let bankruptcy judges modify mortgage terms—normal American legal practice for everything but mortgages.

---

13 Y. Smith, "Housing Bailout Bill Also Eased Having Fed Rescue Banks," *Naked Capitalism*, July 31, 2008.

Other Democratic leaders in both houses shied away from forcing the issue in the face of intense opposition from banks and the mortgage industry. In the end, the Democrats settled on a plan for mortgage relief originally promoted by Credit Suisse, Bank of America and other financial institutions. Although decidedly more aggressive than the administration's, it did not include the bankruptcy language. The Democrats also embraced a proposal supported by the Mortgage Bankers Association that expanded the size of mortgages Fannie Mae and Freddie Mac could purchase. Both choices limited mortgage relief because few banks saw any reason to make concessions while the jumbo provision aided primarily affluent neighborhoods.[14]

Because the GSEs were, along with the Home Loan Banks, the instruments most perfectly adapted for use in a bail-out intended to stay below the radar scan, they were swept up in the shadow bail-out. Bending them to this purpose, however, was fraught with political peril and economic risk. Because of the clouds of sometimes partisan misinformation that now swirl around the GSEs, some clarification is necessary about exactly what they were and how they figured in the debacle that unfolded.

The Federal National Mortgage Association ("Fannie Mae") was founded during the high tide of the New Deal. For decades, it was the only game in town when it came to secondary mortgage markets; because of defaults and prepayments, making markets in secondary mortgages was just too risky for private lenders. In 1968, President Lyndon Johnson wanted to get as much debt as possible off the government's books, so Fannie Mae was privatized. In 1971, Congress chartered a similarly structured competitor: the Federal Home Loan Mortgage Corporation ("Freddie Mac").

14 For Frank and the mortgage provisions, see J. Politi and K. Guha, "Bush Attacks Democrats Housing Crisis Plan," *Financial Times,* February 29, 2008; for Credit Suisse, Bank of America, and the Democrats, see Reuters, "Mortgage Bailout Plan Gains Traction in Congress," *Reuters,* March 13, 2008. Compare this last with A. Mian, A. Sufi and F. Trebbi, "The Political Economy of the US Mortgage Default Crisis," National Bureau of Economic Research, Working Paper 14468, Cambridge, 2008, a paper we otherwise much admire. For the jumbos, see K. Guha and J. Grant, "Analysts Predict Wave of Home Refinancing," *Financial Times,* January 25, 2008. For the Mortgage Bankers Association support, see L. R. Mayer, "Update: Fannie Mae and Freddie Mac Invest in Lawmakers," in *Center for Responsive Politics,* 2008. The jumbo provision and a small provision for expanding Federal Housing Administration lending made it into the economic stimulus bill. Wider mortgage relief without the bankruptcy provision came later in the year.

Various administrations kept repeating the mantra that the GSEs were private corporations without full government backing. Markets, however, mostly did not believe this. Possibly, in the end, widespread confidence that the GSEs would be bailed out stemmed as much from their sheer size as from any putative moral obligation. In any case, once foreign central banks began buying large amounts of their bonds, perhaps on assurances of government guarantees offered by individuals who may not have had authority to make such commitments, Fannie and Freddie evolved into American originals: semi-public institutions too big and complicated to fail without international ramifications.

The spectacular growth of mortgage lending in the 1980s fundamentally altered the GSEs' environment. They were allowed to buy only medium-size ("conforming") mortgages from high-grade credit risks. Unlike the much smaller Government National Mortgage Association ("Ginny Mae"), whose obligations were carried on the books of the Treasury and were therefore backed by the "full faith and credit" of the US government, Fannie Mae and Freddie Mac remained privately run and owned. But the presumption that they could count on a government bail-out allowed them to raise money more cheaply than private firms. The latter thus had little prospect of competing in market segments the GSEs dominated.

As mortgage companies proliferated and secondary mortgage markets boomed in the 1980s, increasing numbers of banks and other potential competitors began to lobby Congress and successive administrations to prune back or even eliminate Fannie Mae and Freddie Mac. Wells Fargo Bank, General Electric (GE) Finance, Household Finance, and other large firms all became players in one or another of these efforts. GE even tried to persuade a group of Wall Street firms to form a direct competitor to the GSEs.[15] Prominent business-supported think tanks on the political Right took up the cause of abolishing the GSEs; the notion became a staple of media commentators who wanted to appear sophisticated and curry favor.

The GSEs defended themselves by spending more and more money on political contributions and lobbying. A conservative analysis, limited to GSE contributions flowing only to sitting members of Congress in 2008, reported total donations of just under $5 million since 1989. Another 2008 study that included

---

15 P. Muolo and M. Padilla, *Chain of Blame*, Hoboken: Wiley, 2008.

lobbying totals as well as contributions suggested that "over the past decade" the two GSEs had spent almost $200 million "to buy influence." Through foundations they controlled, Fannie Mae and Freddie Mac also distributed millions of dollars more in grants, which, reporters have suggested, were sometimes awarded as favors to influential political figures.[16]

The subtlety of the GSEs' maneuvering has been insufficiently appreciated by their myriad critics, in part because of the serpentine ways political money flows in the American political system. The New Deal legacy ensured that the two GSEs had a natural elective affinity with Democrats. Their political contributions reflect this: between 1989 and 2008, they channeled 57 percent of their political funds to Democrats, with the three biggest recipients being Senate Banking Committee Chair Chris Dodd (D–CT) ($165,400) and Senators Barack Obama (D–IL) ($126,349) and John Kerry (D–MA) ($111,000). But they also maintained strong ties with a succession of "moderate" Republicans and lobbyists linked to the highest levels of the GOP, including Kenneth Duberstein, Frederick V. Malek, and Robert Zoellick.[17]

In the meantime, Fannie Mae and Freddie Mac mirrored with special force the Democratic Party's broad "right turn" after 1980.[18] Many "New Democrats" gravitated naturally to the GSEs, which were, after all, exactly what New Democrats professed to admire: big, highly profitable businesses. Gradually, the GSEs began to function as a kind of political machine for this wing of the Party. As Bill Clinton left office as president, for example, he appointed several top staffers to the boards of the GSEs, including Rahm Emmanuel and Harold Ickes. In the 1990s, long-time Democratic operative Jim Johnson ran Fannie Mae before moving on to the compensation committee of Goldman Sachs, where he helped set the remuneration of Hank Paulson, then head

16 For the contributions, see L. R. Mayer, "Seeking Stimulation," *Center for Responsive Politics*, January 31, 2008; and "Update: Fannie Mae and Freddie Mac Invest in Lawmakers," Center for Responsive Politics, September 11, 2008; for the lobbying, see L. Lerer, "Fannie, Freddie Spent $200 Million To Buy Influence," *Yahoo.com*, July 16, 2008; for the foundations, see "Fannie Mae's Political Immunity," *Wall Street Journal*, July 29, 2008.

17 For the contributions, see Mayer, "Update," and the discussion in Ferguson and Johnson, "'Paulson Put', Part II"; for the Republicans, see Jack Shaffer, "Fannie Mae and the Vast Bipartisan Conspiracy," *Slate*, September 16, 2008.

18 T. Ferguson and J. Rogers, *Right Turn: The Decline of The Democrats and The Future of American Politics*, New York: Hill and Wang, 1986.

of the firm. (In 2008, Democratic presidential nominee Barack Obama picked Johnson to vet possible running mates; he was forced to step aside when it came out that he, along with many other political figures, including Senate Banking Committee Chair Dodd, received a sweetheart loan from Countrywide Credit, long a staunch GSE ally.)[19]

The GSEs' political evolution affected their business strategies as the housing boom took off in the new millennium. By then they ranked amongst the largest enterprises in the United States. Like the rest of corporate America, remuneration of their top officers and advisers had spiraled upward, despite all the talk about their public-service mission. An indulgent Congress also permitted the concerns to behave like most private companies and conceal or camouflage much of that compensation. Individual members of Congress who inquired about these arrangements were sometimes bluntly threatened.

Developments in mortgage markets after 2001, however, made traditional GSE rhetoric about their unique role in promoting homeownership ring hollow. Nothing Fannie Mae or Freddie Mac had to offer could top privately offered NINJA (no income, no job, no assets) mortgages that—as long as they lasted—funneled home loans to people who would otherwise not qualify. In the meantime Franklin Raines, who left the job as budget director in the Clinton administration to take over as Johnson's successor at Fannie Mae, and other GSE executives continued steering the two giants in what was sometimes described as more "business-like" directions—or, in other words, on a trajectory embracing many of the shenanigans other financial houses engaged in to inflate reported profits. This was not because of any "dual mandate" Fannie Mae had to serve the public interest and also make profits, but because the top management would then become fabulously rich and share the wealth with friendly members of Congress and allied community groups.

---

19 For Johnson, Paulson, and Obama, see B. Mclean, "Fannie Mae's Last Stand," *Vanity Fair*, February 2009, which records Johnson's denial when he left the Obama campaign that he had received favors from Countrywide. But see Z. Goldfarb, "House GOP Report Details Countrywide's Efforts to Benefit VIPs," *Washington Post*, March 19, 2009, on the House Republican investigative study on Countrywide's "special loans." Note that a number of prominent McCain backers also had ties to the GSEs, though links to the Democrats generally ran somewhat tighter. See for example, for the Republicans, J. Weisman, "Figures in Both Campaigns Have Deep Ties to Mortgage Giants," *Washington Post*, July 17, 2008.

Soon after he took the helm of Fannie Mae in 1998, Raines explicitly set a target of doubling earnings per share. William Black has shown that suborning the audit department's internal controls through high pressure and a munificent new bonus scheme appear to have been critical to his success.[20]

The explosive boom in collateralized debt obligations (CDOs) gave the GSEs a new, crucial, and hugely remunerative role: they provided guarantees that helped secure AAA ratings for the top tranches of the CDOs rolling off the assembly lines of Wall Street. Eventually, however, the GSEs' emulation of Wall Street's business models caught up with them. To increase earnings, the firms took on more leverage. Along with the additional risk, they also tried smoothing earnings, just as many American businesses did during the stock-market boom. They were caught and eventually forced to restate earnings.

Raines, an African American who was by then co-Chair of the Business Roundtable, lashed back at his critics in a stormy congressional hearing. The hearing transcript reveals that he

---

20   This point is worth emphasizing, considering studies such as P. J. Wallison and C. Calomaris, "The Last Trillion Dollar Commitment: The Destruction of Fannie Mae and Freddie Mac," in *Financial Services Outlook*, American Enterprise Institute, Washington, DC, 2008. As Black shows, it was the bonus and executive compensation systems modeled on those that were then proliferating in the private sector that created the incentive structures that led to the accounting debacles:

Raines learned that the unit that should have been most resistant to this "overwhelming" financial incentive, Internal Audit, had succumbed to the perverse incentive. Mr. Rajappa, Senior Vice President for Operations Risk and Internal Audit, instructed his internal auditors in a formal address in 2000 (and provided the text of the speech to Raines): "By now every one of you must have 6.46 [the earnings per share target] branded in your brains. You must be able to say it in your sleep, you must be able to recite it forwards and backwards, you must have a raging fire in your belly that burns away all doubts, you must live, breathe and dream 6.46, you must be obsessed on 6.46. . . . After all, thanks to Frank [Raines], we all have a lot of money riding on it. . . . We must do this with a fiery determination, not on some days, not on most days but day in and day out, give it your best, not 50 percent, not 75 percent, not 100 percent, but 150 percent. Remember, Frank has given us an opportunity to earn not *just* our salaries, benefits, raises, ESPP, but substantially over and above if we make 6.46. So it is our *moral obligation* to give well above our 100 percent and if we do this, we would have made tangible contributions to Frank's goals." (William Black, "Expert Witness Statement William K. Black in the Matter of Raines, Howard, and Spencer—Notice No. 2006-1," *Office of Federal Housing Enterprise Oversight*, 2008, emphasis in original.)

was vigorously assisted by several members of the Congressional Black Caucus who had supported Raines and the GSEs for years. They sought to deflect criticism by drawing attention to the campaign business interests that had been mounting against the GSEs. One, Representative William Clay (D–MO), compared the attacks to a "witch hunt" and a "lynching." Eventually, however, mounting evidence of accounting irregularities and disclosures of bonuses and pension benefits of almost Medician proportions to Raines and other executives soured the mood. Representative Barney Frank labeled Raines's compensation and pension benefits "inappropriate," and members of Congress started demanding the money be returned.[21]

Although there was talk of indictments, no-one was charged, though the Securities and Exchange Commission (SEC) sued Raines and two others. The case was settled after Raines departed Fannie Mae in December 2004 amid a chorus of promises of sweeping reforms by politicians in both parties.

At the time, the GSEs' prospects looked dire. But, in fact, their position was not as bleak as it seemed. With the housing boom cresting, homeownership as a political goal was irresistibly attractive, even to Republicans, who might normally be sympathetic to the idea of cutting the GSEs down to size. In addition, the administration, like the Fed, warmly approved of subprime or any other kind of lending "free markets" threw up.

In a speech in Arizona in 2004, for example, President George W. Bush proclaimed, "We want more people owning their own homes." Yet, the president lamented, "Not enough minorities own their own homes. And it seems like to me it makes sense to encourage all to own homes. And so we've done some interesting things. . . . we passed down payment assistance programs that will help low-income folks buy their own home. . . . I proposed

---

21 For Raines, Clay, Democrats, and bonuses, see L. Bebchuck and J. Fried, "Executive Compensation at Fannie Mae: A Case Study of Perverse Incentives, Nonperformance Pay, and Camouflage," *Journal of Corporation Law*, 2005, 30; S. Lebaton, "Chief Says Fannie Mae Did Nothing Wrong," *New York Times*, October 7, 2004; for the reaction, see S. Lebaton, "Shakeup at Fannie Mae: The Overview Assessing What Will Now Happen To Fannie Mae," *New York Times*, December 17, 2004. For the transcript, see US Congress, House (2004), "The OFEHO Report: Allegations of Accounting and Management Failure at Fannie Mae," *Subcommittee on Capital Markets, Insurance, and Government Sponsored Enterprises, Committee on Financial Services,* available at http://commdocs.house.gov.

that mortgages that have FHA [Federal Housing Administration]-backed insurance pay no down payment." Just in case that was not enough, however, the housing-boom Cheerleader-in-Chief also averred that "I've called on private sector mortgage banks and banks to be more aggressive about lending money to first-time home buyers. And the response has been really good."[22]

Almost simultaneously, the CEO of the most aggressive mortgage bank in the United States—who, not coincidentally, happened to be a prominent financial supporter of the president's re-election bid—was cranking up a broad national campaign in favor of the president's proposal of "homeownership for all." But Angelo Mozilo, Countrywide Credit's visionary founder, was also a long-time supporter of Fannie Mae and Freddie Mac. He and his now gigantic concern were also anything but doctrinaire: although he supported Bush for re-election, along with many other Republicans, Mozilo and his firm had also maintained close relations with many Democrats in Congress and the GSEs. The mortgage giant quickly reached across the aisle to Democrats for help with its homeownership campaign—and to shield Fannie Mae and Freddie Mac in their moment of maximum vulnerability.[23]

The campaign to save the GSEs enjoyed a singular advantage: it could tap a broad, pre-existing network of allies for help. For many years, a network of community organizations including parts of ACORN (the Association of Community Organizations for Reform Now) and small, local businesses had functioned as a loose, decentralized, and pluralistic support network for the GSEs. The original inspiration for many participants appears to have been the cause of low-income housing. But as the neoliberal Democratic tilt in the GSEs increased, the network's uses for

---

22 F. Norris, "Who's To Blame," *New York Times Floyd Norris Blog*, October 18, 2008.
23 Mozilo himself donated at least $5,500 to the 2004 Bush campaign, narrowly defined to exclude donations to the Republican National Committee. He was not the only executive from the firm who personally contributed. Countrywide's political action committee also donated $5,000. Note that total political contributions by the firm and its executives ran substantially larger, and some Party contributions should perhaps be reckoned in. But the subject is too complicated for this paper. It is enough to say that Countrywide's donations in 2004 definitely tilted toward Republicans, though, as discussed below, the firm had important Democratic allies even that year, making smaller contributions even to John Kerry's campaign. The campaign finance data comes from the Federal Election Commission, as presented by Political Money Line.

broader campaigns that benefited the GSEs and allied mortgage bankers became apparent.[24]

The result was a political movement and ideological syncretism that has not received the attention it deserves. The mostly neoliberal business executives and their friends in Congress reached out to community activists who were hungry for funds and meaningful roles in a social system that increasingly exalted business as the *speculum mentis,* the highest activity of the human mind. As they became comfortable with casual references to "working-class housing," mortgage bankers often joined the GSEs in picking up the tab for community "housing campaigns."

Countrywide's drive for "home ownership for all" brought this impeccably politically correct movement to a new level of refinement. Fannie Mae, Freddie Mac, Countrywide, Washington Mutual, Ameriquest, New Century Financial, HSBC, and other mortgage firms joined leaders from non-profit organizations and the Hispanic Political Caucus to support an organization to promote homeownership called Hogar (Spanish for "home"). Mozilo himself actively preached the gospel, and his activities were widely appreciated.

---

24 The *Wall Street Journal,* in its editorial and op-ed pages, along with many analysts from think tanks in Washington, DC, have encouraged notions that the Subprime Crisis was somehow integrally related to earlier battles over the Community Reinvestment Act (CRA). See Robert Gordon, "Did Liberals Cause the Subprime Crisis?" in *American Prospect,* September 16, 2008; this viewpoint was also represented at the 2008 Jackson Hole Conference sponsored by the Kansas City Federal Reserve Bank; see G. Gorton, "The Panic of 2007," Paper Presented at the Federal Reserve Bank of Kansas City Symposium on "Maintaining Stability in a Changing Financial System," Jackson Hole, Wyoming, August 21–23, 2008. But the evidence is overwhelmingly against this claim: most lenders that were enthusiastic users of mortgage bonds in the 1980s strongly supported Reagan-administration efforts to trim back the CRA. It is true that in the mid-1990s, the Clinton administration sought to link fulfillment of CRA requirements by banks to purchases of GSE bonds, but that effort was watered down by the Bush administration after 2001, just as subprime lending exploded. Even more to the point, though, most subprime loans were made by finance companies and mortgage banks that were not subject to the CRA, or by banks that only partially were (Gordon, "Did Liberals"). It is also clear that institutions not subject to the CRA afforded notably worse loan terms to their clients; cf. J. Yellen, "Opening Remarks to the 2008 National Interagency Community Reinvestment Conference," Federal Reserve Bank of San Francisco, March 31, 2008, http://www.frbsf.org. Analyses such as that of Wallison and Calomaris neglect the context of private-sector interests that are the real roots of the GSE's wreck. The story is really another variation on Epstein and Ferguson, "Monetary Policy." Such accounts also omit all mention of the shadow bail-out, which, as described below, was directly responsible for pushing Fannie and Freddie over the edge.

In 2004, the National Housing Conference declared him "Person of the Year" for his efforts to advance homeownership among minority and low-income families. As the Bush administration moved to cut the GSEs down to size in the wake of the scandals, Mozilo and like-minded private-sector supporters closed ranks with the network to beat back attacks on the GSEs.[25]

Democratic congressional leaders were willing to consider certain reforms, but they wanted safeguards on subprime mortgages. They also drew a line at eliminating GSE support for programs promoting public and low-income housing that nourished the activist network. The administration, the financial industry, and the Federal Reserve all strongly opposed restrictions on subprime mortgages. Indeed, though the point vanished in the heat of the 2008 presidential campaign, at the time the administration wanted even more subprime lending. Eventually, Bush and Greenspan concluded that the game of reforming the GSEs was not worth the candle. With mortgage markets booming, they left House Republican leader Michael Oxley of Ohio in the lurch after he had promoted reforms at their urgings.

Ironically, given what the private mortgage firms were up to, in the short run the failure to rein in the GSEs came with a silver

---

25 For the campaign, see for example *Mortgage Banking*, "Countrywide Announces $1 Trillion Commitment," *Mortgage Banking*, February 5, 2005; or Jeffrey Lubell, "Homes For Working Families: Increasing the Availability of Affordable Homes," Center for Housing Policy, Washington, DC, 2006. One vehicle for the effort was an organization called Homes for Working Families. Mozilo chaired its board, on which sat the CEOs of both Fannie and Freddie. Lubell's 2006 report was issued for this group by the Center for Housing Policy, which described itself as "the research affiliate" of the National Housing Conference. For Hogar, see S. Schmidt and M. Tamman, "Housing Push for Hispanics Spawns Wave of Foreclosures," *Wall Street Journal*, January 5, 2009. *LatinoPoliticsBlog.com*, "The Great American Mortgage Scam and the Latino Community," March 15, 2009, notes how, since the mortgage bubble burst, the Hispanic Congressional Caucus has distanced itself from even the memory of the effort. For Fannie and Freddie's support of ACORN and the Citizenship Education Fund, which grew out of the Reverend Jesse Jackson's Operation PUSH (People United to Save Humanity), see *Wall Street Journal*, "Fannie." For Mozilo's award, see "National Housing Conference to Honor Angelo Mozilo for Lowering Homeownership Barriers," *Nation's Building News*, May 17, 2004, available at http://www.nbnnews.com (accessed on October 10, 2008). This is the newspaper of the National Homebuilders Association; it was sponsored by Countrywide. The attack on Freddie and Fannie is the real context of the story related in Charles Duhigg, "Pressured To Take More Risk, Fannie Hit A Tipping Point," *New York Times*, October 4, 2008 and explains why Daniel Mudd was so eager to please Mozilo.

lining. Although they, too, eventually started playing with lower-grade mortgages, they mostly maintained their traditional lending standards. Wider private-sector expansion into the GSEs' terrain would surely have brought more of the saturnalia that marked the privates' move into subprime.

Fannie Mae and Freddie Mac never truly recovered from the scandals. Conscious of their political weakness, they deliberately allied themselves with Countrywide, IndyMac, Washington Mutual, Lehman Brothers and other private firms that would find expanded GSE lending and guarantees useful.

This led the GSEs to buy more and more mortgages for resale or their own accounts and eventually to move heavily into lower-grade (Alt-A) mortgages. It appears that the GSEs never really sorted out their accounting issues and, indeed, considered these a distraction from their main mission of sustaining themselves by supporting homeownership (and short-term profits). Critics continued to complain that the firms were undercapitalized, taking on too much debt, and were extravagantly rewarding top management while lining the pockets of politicians and lobbyists. They were right on all counts, even if the claims many also advanced about how private markets had rendered Fannie Mae and Freddie Mac unnecessary were about to be spectacularly shown up.

As private lenders withdrew from the market in 2007, Fannie and Freddie became virtually the sole sources for mortgage refinancing, as Figure 6.2 shows. In the face of mounting deterioration in subprime markets, the Bush administration, with the acquiescence of congressional Democrats, pushed to loosen standards. A new phase of the shadow bail-out began: "Paulson wanted to use the troubled companies to unlock the frozen credit market by allowing Fannie and Freddie to buy more mortgage-backed securities from overburdened banks." Accordingly, "the White House pitched in. James B. Lockhart, the chief regulator of Fannie Mae and Freddie Mac, adjusted the companies' lending standards so they could purchase as much as $40 billion in new subprime loans."[26]

---

26 The first quotation is from J. Becker, S. G. Stolberg and S. Lebaton, "White House Philosophy Stoked Mortgage Bondfire," *New York Times*, December 20, 2008; the second is from Duhigg, "Pressured." This latter adds considerable detail that illustrates the real relationships between the GSEs and private lenders. The article also relates a story according to which Paulson later sent a deputy, Robert K. Steele, to urge restraint on the GSEs. But for reasons unexplained, Steele failed to convey the message. This part of the story has all the earmarks of a precautionary memo for the files. It is unlikely in the extreme that Steele, who worked closely with Paulson, would

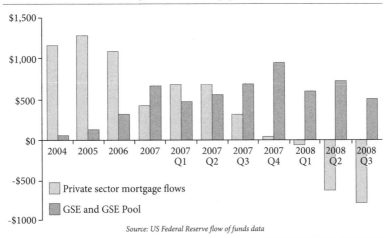

Figure 6.2: The Shadow Bailout 2007–08: Lending and guarantees from GSE's advances as private sector mortgage flows retrench ($ billions)

Private sector mortgage flows

GSE and GSE Pool

Source: US Federal Reserve flow of funds data

The End of the Shadow Bail-out

For Paulson to engineer all this in the midst of a presidential election was quite a feat—as well as an eloquent warning about the state of financial journalism in America. But prodigious as it was, the shadow bail-out was simply not enough. As markets for mortgages and housing collapsed in the late summer of 2007, demand for commercial paper backed by CDOs or mortgages also dried up. Conduits and structured investment vehicles (SIVs) that relied on this "asset-backed commercial paper" market for refinancing now faced a new crisis. They accordingly pressed banks that had sold them the toxic junk to take it back by exercising "liquidity puts" they held on the parent banks. Because this threatened to push some of America's largest banks over the edge, Paulson commenced another search for rescue funds that did not require going hat in hand to Congress.

He located two. For a while, the Treasury and many others on Wall Street excitedly talked up possibilities that Sovereign Wealth Funds (SWFs) might provide the necessary resources. These were investment arms of countries that had accumulated hoards of

have failed to convey a message his boss thought was important. As Becker et al. demonstrate, the priority just then was the shadow bail-out.

dollars, from either selling oil or pegging their currencies and exporting back into the United States. The notion of buying big blocks of shares in leading US banks clearly attracted some of these. Critics, including some skeptical investment bankers, suggested that was because owning banks carried with it the prospect of substantial political power.

Former Treasury secretary Lawrence Summers, a prominent Democrat who had parachuted from the presidency of Harvard University into a large investment fund, advised overseas investors to work with American financiers in evaluating possible acquisitions. Citigroup's Robert Rubin and other American financiers also made strong pitches to various SWFs. Several eventually made substantial investments in Citigroup, Merrill Lynch, UBS, Morgan Stanley and a few other firms. But as the Crisis deepened, and bank stocks sagged, fears of emulating Mitsubishi's legendary purchase of Rockefeller Center at the top of the last great real-estate bubble overcame every other emotion. After investing some $38 billion, the SWFs listened, occasionally talked, but effectively withdrew from the market.[27]

Paulson groped in desperation for another solution that did not put the government visibly on the hook. He proposed that the big banks organize a "super SIV" (or "master liquidity enhancement conduit" as the Treasury styled it) into which they would pour their toxic junk. What was to happen then was murky, but the idea appears to have been to slowly liquidate the mess over time. The proposal, reminiscent of the scheme for a "National Credit Corporation" briefly floated by bankers and President Herbert Hoover in the early stages of the Great Depression, was widely mocked, even by financiers.[28] In principle, however, it contained the germ of a good idea, one of the few with real prospects for helping to resolve the Crisis. If implemented early, on a sufficiently vast scale, the plan would have kept money markets functioning normally, because traders could be confident that the institutions they were dealing with were in fact solvent once the toxic assets were gone. For financial houses, however, the scheme promised less exalted benefits: warehousing toxic assets would stop fire sales that kept driving down asset prices.

27 Estimates of SWF investment differ, at least in part because they count slightly differently. This estimate can be compared with those proffered by Brad Setser on his blog at the Council of Foreign Relations. For our purposes, the differences make no difference.
28 Epstein and Ferguson, "Monetary Policy."

The scheme had obvious drawbacks. It was in effect a "bad bank," a superfund for banks. At what price were bad assets to be transferred to this bad bank? Too low would leave huge holes in bank's balance sheets. Too high would overwhelm the superfund with certain losses. Most urgent of all, however, was the question of where the money would come from, because the whole point of the exercise was to avoid going to Congress in the midst of the election.

The only plausible private sources of new cash were the banks themselves. Not surprisingly, they found this prospect daunting. Institutions with large exposures to conduits, such as Citigroup, JPMorgan Chase, Bank of America and Wachovia, were reported to be intrigued. Other banks, with less exposure, were more skeptical; whereas foreign financial institutions, like the governments that were in several instances bailing them out, wanted no part of what was obviously a US-centered scheme. So the banks dithered, as did Fidelity, Pimco and other investment companies.

Paulson, a former Goldman Sachs CEO, neither could nor would force them to do what they did not want to do. The proposal died when HSBC and a few other institutions made a show of putting their conduits and SIVs on their balance sheets. Citigroup thereupon quickly and visibly reorganized. Rubin's choice to run the bank, Vikram Pandit, was announced on December 11. The next day the Fed quietly opened a new special facility expressly designed for distressed banks and stated its readiness to engage in swap agreements (for dollars) with foreign central banks. Citi then announced it was moving $49 billion of SIV assets onto its balance sheet.

Abandonment of Paulson's superfund proposal left all the toxic waste in place, with more showing up every day. Because no one knew what anyone's balance sheet was really worth, including his or her own, banks hesitated to lend to anyone, including other banks ("counterparty risk"). They also doubted their own ability to refinance in a timely fashion, which encouraged them to hoard resources. As a result, the financial system started locking up. With consumers stressed out and actual costs of credit rising as banks, struggling to digest bad assets, ceased making anything but super-safe loans, Fed rate cuts did not filter down to borrowers. They simply fattened banks' otherwise thinning margins by lowering their cost of funds.

Desperate banks also socked customers with all sorts of new charges and fees. Meanwhile the tide of foreclosures overwhelmed

Fannie Mae and Freddie Mac's efforts while igniting fears about their own financial positions. Anxieties about possible insolvency of bond ("monoline") insurers added to all these pressures because many institutions could legally hold only insured bonds. Such insurance, for example, was critical for the functioning of the market for "floating rate notes" that many institutions, including hospitals and other non-profits, used to raise funds. Repeated Fed rate cuts did little to relieve the situation. Downward pressures on the economy, accordingly, intensified, though at first the rate of growth declined surprisingly slowly. In the midst of all this, a scandal over a call girl abruptly drove from the scene Governor Eliot Spitzer (D–NY), the only public official actively challenging the notion of simply handing out long-dated bills for the bail-out to the public. His dizzying fall triggered a media firestorm.[29]

It was almost at once eclipsed by the even more sensational story that Bear Stearns had suddenly become Bare Stearns. Bear had been a major player in the market for mortgage-backed securities for many years. Two of its hedge funds had been among the first casualties of the break in mortgage markets the previous year. In addition, Bear was a major holder of GSE debt and creditor to an Amsterdam hedge fund that was itself heavily invested in GSE paper. As spreads widened between Treasury notes and GSE paper—an inevitable consequence of the shadow bail-out—holders of that paper suffered losses. For the Amsterdam hedge fund, the shock was too great. When it failed to meet margin calls, its collateral was seized and partially sold, further depressing GSE securities prices and putting yet more pressure on firms that held large blocks of these instruments, such as Bear.

As an investment bank, Bear was not normally eligible to borrow from the Fed or receive cash infusions from Federal Home Loan Banks. But like all investment houses and primary dealers in government securities, the firm had borrowed massively on its own account. It also owed millions of dollars to clients whose money it invested. Perhaps scariest of all, however, was the Bear's ubiquitous status as a "counterparty" in the dense web of credit

29 Some of the many twists in the Spitzer saga are discussed in note 24 of Ferguson and Johnson, "'Paulson Put', Part II". An early effort to explain the significance of the monolines to Congressman Barney Frank, Chair of the House Financial Services Committee, did not fare well. See Ferguson and Johnson, "Britney and the Bear: Who Says You Can't Get Good Help Anymore?" *Huffington Post*, March 27, 2008.

default swaps that radiated out from the principal Wall Street houses.[30]

The specter of chain-bankruptcy, derivative counterparty default, and a consequent run on the dollar plunged the Fed and the Treasury into something very much like a religious crisis. As citadels of market fundamentalism, their leaders clearly found it hard to accept that sticking to the old-time religion and letting Bear go bust would likely bring down the whole system. After Bear's fall, many analysts, including former company executives, also suggested that the Fed and other financial houses, notably Goldman Sachs (which, of course, Paulson had previously headed), may have been out to get the firm. To be sure, resolutions of past financial crises, such as those of the New Deal era, were crucially affected by efforts of stronger rival financial houses to enhance their positions.[31] But, given the fragmentary state of the documentary record, assessments of such claims in Bear's case have to be provisional and tentative.

Our reading of the evidence is thus deliberately cautious. Bear had famously declined to join the syndicate of investment houses that the New York Fed organized in 1998 to save the hedge fund Long Term Capital Management (LTCM). That mockery of the Fed's leadership and refusal to join peers certainly left a legacy of persistent bad feeling. But there is no particular reason the lingering bitterness from that episode should have uniquely affected Paulson, even though he had been involved in the LTCM negotiations. In truth, as even Bear executives admit, the house was widely detested.[32]

The apparent leak to the business-news cable channel CNBC of an email to clients by Goldman's derivatives department indicating that the firm would no longer accept Bear as a counterparty was disastrous to Bear's effort to portray itself as still open for business.[33]

---

30 G. Morgenson, "In the Fed's Crosshairs: Exotic Game," *New York Times*, March 23, 2008. The next few paragraphs cover very controversial ground. Readers are once again referred to our *International Journal of Political Economy* essays, which sift through the claims and counter-claims.

31 See the discussion in T. Ferguson, "From 'Normalcy' To New Deal: Industrial Structure, Party Competition and American Public Policy in the Great Depression," in Ferguson, *Golden Rule*, 113–72.

32 B. Bamber and A. Spencer, *Bear Trap: The Fall of Bear Stearns and the Panic of 2008*, New York: Brick Tower Books, 2008. Bamber was a senior managing director at Bear.

33 Ibid., Chapter 6.

It is also true that throwing wide open the Fed's discount window to primary dealers in government securities before, rather than just after, JPMorgan Chase purchased Bear might well have kept Bear in business, at least for a while. Instead, the announcement by the Fed on March 11, 2008, of another special facility, the $200-billion Term Securities Lending Facilities, was widely taken by markets as a signal that the Fed suspected one or more large investment banks were in trouble.

In the end, however, judged by the standards of past bail-outs, the disposition of Bear itself was unremarkable. Whether run by the FDIC or the Fed, bail-outs and forced mergers of banks normally resulted in total losses to stockholders. By contrast, the fates of bondholders and other creditors were negotiable, but, typically, most were rescued. The wrinkle in Bear's case was its stockholders' success in bidding up the share price they were originally offered from $2 to $10 a share.

What startled the world were the parts of the bail-out that touched JPMorgan Chase and the wider financial world. Paulson and then New York Fed President Timothy Geithner, with broad support from Greenspan's successor at the Fed, Ben Bernanke, brought in the single-payer insurance scheme discussed earlier. Stretching both law and precedent, they decided to extend the Fed's safety net to cover all primary dealers in government securities, even investment banks. Armed with a letter from Paulson agreeing that losses by the New York Fed could be deducted from monies the bank annually remits to the Treasury (thus putting taxpayers directly on the hook for losses), the New York Fed took over $30 billion of the worst junk in Bear's portfolio for its own account. Then the Fed hired BlackRock, a large investment fund, to run these assets. This allowed JPMorgan Chase to buy out Bear and save itself billions of dollars in losses it would have been hit with if Bear had simply declared bankruptcy.[34]

Financial markets celebrated both the rescue and new safety net for investment banks. Stocks rose smartly, led by financials. For the Fed and Treasury, however, the downside was profound. Though the Paulson Put was still alive, the shadow bail-out was over. Henceforth, Paulson, Bernanke and Geithner would have

---

34 The New York Fed lent $29 billion against $30 billion in assets; the loan was formally to a Delaware corporation set up to hold the assets. JPMorgan Chase contributed $1 billion in the form of a note subordinated to the Fed's. For Paulson's letter to Geithner, see http://online.wsj.com.

to work in a glare of publicity, even as they fought to withhold details from the public, whose money was financing the whole enterprise.

The heightened scrutiny emerged very quickly as a towering problem. Squirreled away in custodial accounts at the Federal Reserve were over $900 billion of GSE paper belonging to other central banks. SWFs—funds controlled at least nominally by foreign governments—probably held almost as much for their own accounts outside the Fed. With criticism of the Fed's policy of holding down interest rates running high, foreign holders of the GSE securities needed reassurance about the safety of their holdings—or else both the market for GSE paper and the dollar itself could crumble.

Few foreign holders appreciated the subtleties of the shadow bail-out, if they knew about it at all. But what was happening on the GSEs' balance sheets was easily tracked. In the unlikely event foreign creditors missed the signs of deterioration, the din raised in the US press by domestic critics of Fannie Mae and Freddie Mac, such as William Poole (by then retired from the St. Louis Fed) could hardly escape their attention. *Barron*'s began asking if the two firms were "toast." A run began on both GSE stocks and, especially, their debt. Spreads between the agency debt and Treasury notes ballooned, especially after the FDIC took over giant IndyMac, a major mortgage institution, in July 2008.[35]

Paulson and Bernanke simply could not permit a GSE collapse. By July 2008, private mortgage firms had all but melted away. Fannie Mae and Freddie Mac were virtually the only players left in the US secondary mortgage market. If they went south, no-one would step up to take their place. Primary mortgage markets would soon lock up, bringing housing sales across the United States to a screeching halt. Housing prices, already falling like a runaway elevator, would go into a steeper tailspin, pulling national income—and the dollar—down with them.

Not surprisingly, Paulson and Bernanke lunged once again for single-payer insurance, though it was sure to stir up a hornet's nest. Claiming that "if you've got a bazooka and people know

---

35 For Poole, see D. Kopecki, "Fannie, Freddie 'Insolvent' after Losses Poole Says (Update 1)," *Bloomberg.com*, July 10, 2008; for *Barrons*, see J. Laing, "Is Fannie Mae Toast?" *Barron's*, March 11, 2008, available at http://www.smartmoney.com.

you've got it, you may not have to take it out," Paulson asked Congress for standby authority to inject federal money into the GSEs as capital and, if necessary, to take them over. In effect, he was offering federal guarantees to GSE debt-holders. In return, he agreed to support modest bank-inspired proposals for mortgage relief that congressional Democratic leaders had been elaborating since the late winter. As a precaution, the Federal Reserve also granted Fannie Mae and Freddie Mac the right to borrow from the New York Fed.[36]

Senator Dodd has stated subsequently that when he agreed to support Paulson's quest for new powers, he believed Paulson's assurances that they would never be used. He and the Democrats mostly went along, though coming on the heels of the Bear bail-out, the prospect of nationalization flabbergasted many in both parties.

To many Republicans, the combination of big bail-outs for two more giant financial institutions and even modest government help for ordinary Americans with bad mortgages was too much. Many went ballistic, including some Republican House leaders. The Bush administration had no choice but to stand with Paulson on the GSEs, but it could not stomach some of the housing provisions. The president threatened a veto. Anxious foreign holders thereupon accelerated their selling. GSE paper in Fed custodial accounts started dwindling fast. As spreads widened between GSE debt and Treasury notes, the administration had to back down.

The veto threat was withdrawn when it became clear that the bill would not pass without additional Democratic votes to steamroll the raging opposition of Congressional Republicans. For a few weeks after the passage of the rescue bill, Paulson put on a brave face. He acted as though the Crisis had been surmounted. Few agreed. Critics on the Right called for breaking up the GSEs. Others railed against the notion that the government would actually use the authority it now possessed to take over the firms. In the meantime, a team of analysts from Morgan Stanley that Paulson had engaged poured over the GSEs' books. Foreigners steadily sold GSE securities, while stocks of Fannie Mae and Freddie Mac fell. Chinese spokespersons issued barely

---

36 The "bazooka" quotation comes from A. R. Sorkin, "Paulson's Itchy Finger on the Trigger of a Bazooka," *New York Times Deal Book*, September 8, 2008.

veiled warnings that something had to be done to guarantee the
GSEs.[37]

As *The New York Times* recognized, "the bailout became
inevitable when central banks in Asia and Russia began to
curtail their purchases of the companies' debt, pushing up
mortgage rates and deepening the economic downturn." Even
as delegates to the Republican National Convention dispersed
from their celebration of free markets and the minimal state,
Paulson exercised his authority under the new legislation.
Surprising both managements, he took Fannie Mae and Freddie
Mac into conservatorship. At a stroke, the Federal Government
was now in charge of financial institutions with gross holdings of
securities equivalent to 40 percent of the gross domestic product
(GDP). To guarantee GSE solvency, the Treasury also agreed to
purchase up to $100 billion dollars' worth of additional preferred
stock in each. It also committed to purchasing mortgage-backed
securities from them—effectively circumventing legal restrictions
on their total lending that the bill also contained—and opened
short-term credit lines for both with the Federal Reserve Bank
of New York.[38]

FATAL REVERSAL

Reaction was intense. "Comrade Paulson" jokes punctuated
late-night television and radio and even some newspaper
columns. Yet almost immediately alarm bells started ringing
about an even bigger crisis. The venerable investment banking
firm of Lehman Brothers was on the edge of bankruptcy. Several
firms—US and British press accounts dwelt on Barclays, HSBC,
and Bank of America, though Deutsche Bank and BNP Paribas
were also mentioned—were interested in buying Lehman. But
like JPMorgan Chase earlier, would-be buyers claimed that any
deal would require subsidies or guarantees of some kind from
the Fed.

Paulson, Bernanke, and Geithner began another round of
meetings stretching late into the night with heads of leading
private banks and investment houses. In the end, they decided

---

37 For the Chinese warnings, see for example K. Hamlin, "Freddie, Fannie Failure
Could Be World 'Catastrophe' Yu Says," *Bloomberg.com*, August 22, 2008.
38 The *Times* quotation is from "The Bailout's Big Lessons," *New York Times*,
September 8, 2008.

to do what free-market conservatives had been demanding since the beginning of the Crisis: let a giant financial institution fail. They thereby turned a desperate situation into a world-historical disaster.

Because, as Napoleon famously remarked, victory has many fathers, but defeat is an orphan, pinning down how the trio arrived at their position is even more difficult than in the case of Bear Stearns. At the time, the decision to let the firm go down was presented as a group product in which all three concurred. Both the Fed and the Treasury also claimed that they had a much better feel for the markets than they did in March and expected that the fallout could be contained. As Bernanke related to Congress the following week, "We judged that investors and counterparties had had time to take precautionary measures."[39]

Later, as the debris scattered around the world, however, stories began to appear that the Fed—presumably Bernanke—had wanted since July (about the time the GSE legislation passed) to approach Congress for legislation sanctioning a broader bail-out. The implication was that Paulson's role was critical—an emphasis that Paulson did not dispel in several interviews he gave.

The Treasury Secretary's own rationales for refusing aid to Lehman have been confusing and contradictory. On some occasions, he has claimed that he "never once considered it appropriate to put taxpayer money on the line in resolving Lehman Brothers." The evidence is overwhelmingly against this claim, because some of the private bankers involved in the negotiations talked to the press. Indeed, on at least one occasion, Paulson himself indicated that he was open to government assistance and, according to the reporter, other officials involved corroborated those claims.[40]

On the key question of what made Lehman different from Bear Stearns, Paulson later asserted that existing law made it impossible

---

39   See US Congress, Senate, 2008, Chairman Ben S. Bernanke, Testimony Before the Committee on Banking, Housing, and Urban Affairs, on September 23, 2008. Available at www.federalreserve.gov (accessed on July 29, 2009).

40   The Paulson quotation comes from J. Nocera and E. Andrews, "Struggling To Keep Up As The Crisis Raced On," *New York Times*, October 22, 2008. This article indicates clearly that Paulson in fact considered some form of assistance. K. Guha, "Paulson Rues Lack of Tools As He Stared Into the Abyss," *Financial Times*, December 31, 2008, is a specific and important confirmation.

for the government to help the former. Bear, he claimed, had good collateral, but Lehman did not. Bernanke echoed this line on several occasions. But the story is flimsy indeed. The $30 billion worth of CDOs and similar instruments that JPMorgan Chase persuaded the Fed to absorb were obviously not AAA paper, whatever their ratings. For a long time, the New York Fed fiercely resisted calls for transparency, but it is now clear that Bear's collateral depreciated substantially following agreement to the deal.[41]

The most compelling reasons for regarding the lack of legal justification as a fairy tale, however, are three simple facts. First, just days after Lehman blew up, the Treasury and the Fed collaborated in the de facto nationalization of the giant insurer AIG. The law had not changed, and in this case the collateral was clearly worthless, as AIG's repeated trips back to the well since then attest more eloquently than any accounting statement. Even more devastating was the belated revelation that, in fact, the Fed did make two gigantic loans to Lehman—for $87 billion and then, after the first was repaid, for $51 billion—*after* it went bankrupt, to help wind down its affairs. Even if these were so-called conduit loans formally through another bank (that passed the money through to Lehman), the collateral for them cannot have been any better following bankruptcy than it was before. It is also embarrassingly plain that, in other contexts, Paulson trumpeted his personal willingness to push the limits of the law in emergency situations. Indeed, as discussed below, it appears that only a few days later, as world markets melted down, his preference, in sharp contrast to Bernanke's, was to push on and avoid going to Congress.[42]

41 For Paulson's claims about collateral, see Nocera and Andrews, "Struggling"; for Bernanke's, see for example his speech to the Economic Club of New York in *Wall Street Journal Economics Blog*, "Fedspeak Highlights: Bernanke on House Prices, Lehman, More." *Wall Street Journal Economics Blog* (October 15), available at http://blogs.wsj.com (accessed on July 29, 2009). For the collateral depreciation, see Y. Smith, "The Fed's Bear Stearns Assets: 'No Prospect For A Profit'," *Naked Capitalism*, February 5, 2009.
42 The loans and the AIG case are discussed in Ferguson and Johnson, "'Paulson Put,' Part II"; for Paulson's pride in pushing the limits of the law, see D. Cho, "A Skeptical Outsider Becomes Bush's 'War Time General'," *Washington Post*, November 19, 2008; for the contrast with Bernanke on whether to go to Congress, see J. Hilsenrath, D. Solomon and D. Paletta, "Paulson, Bernanke Strained For Consensus in Bailout," *Wall Street Journal*, November 10, 2008.

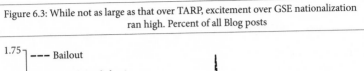

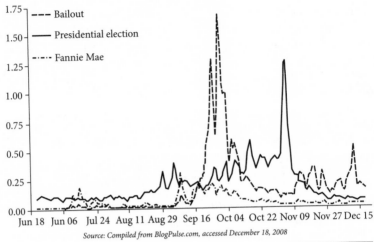

Figure 6.3: While not as large as that over TARP, excitement over GSE nationalization ran high. Percent of all Blog posts

Source: Compiled from BlogPulse.com, accessed December 18, 2008

The most convincing explanation for the decision begins by recognizing that sometimes the order of events matters. And the commanding fact about the Lehman decision is that it happened only days after the GSE bail-outs, as the firestorm triggered by their nationalizations still blazed. Though the GSE controversy pales by comparison with the tumult engendered a few weeks later by Paulson and Bernanke's bail-out proposal to Congress, statistical indicators of media attention confirm our qualitative judgment about the fierceness of the reaction to the earlier decision (Figure 6.3).

Although expressions of dismay erupted across the political spectrum, the most vehement responses came from Republicans, where faith in markets was virtually a litmus test for Party membership but where frustration had been building since the Bear Stearns bail-out. The weathervane most sensitively registering all these tensions was hard to miss: it was Senator John McCain (R–AZ), who had clinched the Republican presidential nomination well before Bear Stearns went down. In March, only days before Paulson & Co. bailed out Bear, McCain had proclaimed: "It is not the government's role to bail out investors who should understand that markets are about both return and risk, or lending institutions who didn't do their job."[43]

For McCain, the sudden embrace of the single-payer idea by Paulson, Bernanke, and Geithner was acutely embarrassing. Nevertheless, he gamely climbed aboard; his rationale throughout the campaign was that allowing Bear to go bankrupt would have had catastrophic consequences.[44] But he obviously found the episode painful and felt the pressure from the Party base. Less than two weeks later he went back to preaching the old-time religion. Rejecting government help for Americans with troubled mortgages, McCain declared that "it is not the duty of government to bail out and reward those who act irresponsibly, whether they are big banks or small borrowers."[45]

Paulson's appeal to Congress for legislation allowing him to take over the GSEs gave McCain a new headache at a moment when he was trailing in the polls and his campaign was sputtering. In the run-up to the convention, he was desperate to court the right wing of his party, which took the hardest line against bail-outs. But an open breach with the Bush administration was a practical impossibility as the administration still controlled the Party machinery. Its assistance remained vital for fundraising (which was increasingly channeled through so-called joint committees with the national party, which the administration also controlled, because McCain had earlier accepted public financing out of desperation).

McCain thus fell in line behind Paulson's request for standby authority to seize the GSEs but took pains to register his distaste for bail-outs. He justified his position by saying that it was too risky to leave the government without authority in case the worst happened. He did express some hope that perhaps the problem would go away. Though, in other contexts, he claimed early familiarity with the GSEs' problems, he doubted that it would be necessary to take them over.

43 For McCain's statement, see J. McCain, "Statement by John McCain on America's Credit Crunch," http://www.johnmccain.com, March 13, 2008.
44 S. L. Myers, "Bush Backs Fed's Actions, But Critics Quickly Find Fault," New York Times, March 18, 2008, for McCain's support for the Bear bail-out; see also his continued defense in "The Times Interviews John McCain," New York Times, July 13, 2008.
45 L. Rohter and E. Andrews, "McCain Rejects Broad US Aid on Mortgages," New York Times, March 26, 2008.

Haunted by continuing dissension, McCain returned to the question less than two weeks later. In late July, he released a new position statement. It began by reassuring doubters yet again that he was really on their side: "Americans should be outraged at the latest sweetheart deal in Washington. Congress will put US taxpayers on the hook for potentially hundreds of billions of dollars to bail out Fannie Mae and Freddie Mac." Then, after reiterating reluctant support for the legislation, he added several sentences whose explosive import was widely missed:

> If a dime of taxpayer money ends up being directly invested, the management and the board should immediately be replaced, multimillion dollar salaries should be cut, and bonuses and other compensation should be eliminated. They should cease all lobbying activities and drop all payments to outside lobbyists. And taxpayers should be first in line for any repayments.[46]

The place of preferred stockholders in a GSE takeover was just then emerging as an issue. It was obvious that common stockholders would suffer if Paulson took over the GSEs. The government's new equity rights would leave little for them, even if they were not formally wiped out. Saving debt-holders, of course, was the point of the whole exercise; they were supposed to emerge whole. Preferred stock, however, lay in a gray zone intermediate between debt and common stock. Its owners had rights to income but no voting rights. Much of the preferred stock was in the hands of financial institutions, which had strong reasons for expecting to be treated like debt-holders: Paulson was actively encouraging banks to buy GSE preferred stock as a way to shore up both the GSEs and themselves because regulators allowed GSE-preferred shares to be counted as part of banks' capital.[47]

In the end Paulson essentially wiped out holders of both common and preferred stock. The decision left many banks' capital-adequacy ratios precariously exposed and engendered a widespread feeling of betrayal. But the step made perfect political sense: by heavily diluting the preference shares, it met the test laid out by his party's nominee.

---

46   J. McCain, "Taxpayers on Hook to Bailout Fannie, Freddie," http://www. johnmccain.com, July 24, 2008.
47   J. Dizard, "This short-term fix creates a long term problem," *Financial Times*, September 16, 2008.

Nevertheless, not only McCain but much of the Party was clearly taken aback by the decision to emulate Mussolini (their usual comparison was Lenin). Although Senator Barack Obama and most Democrats said little beyond signaling general support, McCain and his controversial new running mate, Alaska governor Sarah Palin, felt obliged once again to take a strong stand. They published a high-profile attack on bail-outs in what was virtually a Republican house organ, the *Wall Street Journal*'s op-ed page. Although they again repeated McCain's reluctant support for the takeover, they ratcheted up the vehemence of their language. They also flatly promised to break up and privatize Fannie Mae and Freddie Mac if elected.[48]

Between the lines, it was obvious that McCain was close to being fed up. This is not an inference. Only days later, as the financial world melted down in the wake of the Lehman decision, McCain stood up and denounced Paulson's nationalization of AIG. He also drafted a statement attacking the Bush administration's bail-out policies, although this was not released until later, after it had been watered down beyond recognition and McCain had done another 180-degree turn. Returning to the administration's fold, he now grudgingly supported the nationalization. But the point is clear: as Lehman slid to the brink, Paulson and Bernanke, who both enjoyed solid links to the Bush administration, could hardly expect McCain and an indefinitely large bloc of the rest of their party (including many congressional Republican leaders, who also denounced the AIG rescue), as well as many Democrats, to take yet another giant bail-out lying down.[49]

Bernanke was, in addition, just back from an almost Dickensian encounter of his own with the ghost of bail-outs past. At the annual conclave in Jackson Hole, Wyoming, sponsored by the Federal Reserve Bank of Kansas City, his conduct had been roundly criticized to his face. In front of other Central Bankers, economists, policy-makers and financiers, a raft of critics assailed him for

---

48 J. McCain and S. Palin, "We'll Protect Taxpayers from More Bailouts," *Wall Street Journal*, September 9, 2008.

49 For McCain's somersaults, see for example K. Chipman and H. Nichols, "McCain, Obama Blame Regulators; McCain Shifts on AIG (Update 3)," *Bloomberg.com*, September 17, 2008; and Sam Stein, "McCain Removed Bush Criticism From Wall Street Statement," *Huffington Post*, September 18, 2008. For the GOP leadership, see T. Barrett, Diana Walsh and B. Keilar, "AIG Bailout Upsets Republican Lawmakers," *CNN.com*, September 17, 2008.

betraying free-market principles and capitulating to demands
from the financial sector for bail-out. A paper by Willem Buiter
accused the Fed of falling victim to "cognitive" interest-group
capture and specifically referenced historical studies of similar Fed
behavior in the Great Depression. Some press accounts claim that
Bernanke was exhausted and hint that he was demoralized, but
there is no question that he appreciated the gravity of the charges,
which received wide publicity in the *Financial Times* and other
major media.[50]

THE PUT IS DEAD; LONG LIVE THE PUT

If the extinction of preferred shareholders in the GSE bail-out
was an unheeded warning shot that the days of the Paulson Put
were numbered, the decision to let Lehman go bankrupt marked
the Put's definitive expiration. Thereafter so much happened so
fast that it is easy to lose sight of the disastrous new course
that Paulson was now charting, with Bernanke and Geithner
assisting.

The trio's first problem was simply to try to keep up with
the dizzying scale and pace of devastation. Contrary to claims
recently advanced by revisionists who argue that the real break
in world markets came more than a week later, when Paulson
and Bernanke approached Congress with their broader bail-out
proposal, the evidence that the Lehman bankruptcy sundered
world markets is overwhelming.[51]

Every direct indicator of financial risk we have examined for
this period explodes, in some cases a day or two in advance of the
actual declaration of bankruptcy: prices of credit default swaps on
the four largest American banks, controlling some 40 percent of
all deposits, for example, all rose like rockets before falling back
when Paulson, Bernanke and Geithner reversed course two days

50   Buiter, "Central Banks and Financial Crises," 102, citing Epstein and
Ferguson, "Monetary Policy." There was more irony than Buiter could know: as
Epstein and Ferguson, "Answers to Stock Questions: Fed Targets, Stock Prices,
and the Gold Standard in the Great Depression," *Journal of Economic History*
1991, 51 (March), pp. 190–200, went to press, Bernanke offered collegial advice
and comments. He understood the problem very well.

51   J. Taylor, "The Financial Crisis and the Policy Responses: An Empirical
Analysis of What Went Wrong," Cambridge, MA: National Bureau of Economic
Research, Working Paper 14631, 2009, presses this case; he has repeated it in
numerous forums since.

later and once again embraced single-payer by bailing out AIG. The same holds for credit default swaps of Goldman Sachs and Morgan Stanley, the two most important remaining investment banks. (See Figure 6.4, which shows credit default swap prices for Goldman Sachs and JPMorgan Chase.) Another excellent general indicator of stress, the "option adjusted" spread on broad investment-grade bank debt—what banks had to pay to raise new capital—also shows a sharp rise as Lehman gave up the ghost (Figure 6.5).

Default on Lehman's bonds and subsequent fire sales of assets staggered many firms, including a substantial number of European houses. Hedge funds that used Lehman as their prime broker lost access to their funds, while losses on Lehman's commercial paper caused some money-market funds to "break the buck." In a matter of hours, markets for both regular and asset-backed commercial paper dried up, and an awesome run began out of money-market funds altogether, as panicky depositors recoiled.[52]

Suddenly unable to refinance by issuing commercial paper, banks became fearful both for themselves and their counterparties. They frantically hoarded reserves at central banks instead of lending them out. In the five days after Lehman collapsed, bank reserves held at the Fed more than doubled, while bank borrowing from the Fed surged.[53] Perhaps the most striking indicator of the Crisis, however, was the behavior of the London Inter-Bank Offered Rate (LIBOR), the rates banks in London charge each other. Interest rates charged on the shortest maturities, which should be the safest, doubled, while the LIBOR yield curve inverted, as bank

---

52 Cf. P. T. Larsen, "Shockwaves that took Europe by surprise," *Financial Times*, October 4, 2008; J. Mackintosh and J. Hughes, "New York Steals UK Hedge Fund Business," *Financial Times*, October 17, 2008; and the fine discussion in S. Jones, "Why Letting Lehman Go Did Crush the Financial Markets," *Financial Times*, March 12, 2009.

53 For the refinancing fears, see G. Finch and K.-M. Cutler, "Money Market Rates Double amid Global Credit Squeeze (Update 4)," *Bloomberg.com*, September 16, 2008; for the doubling, see Jones, "Why Letting Lehman go." The Fed's H.4.1 statistical release, available on the Federal Reserve Board website for the seven days ending September 17, 2008, shows that borrowing from the Primary Dealer Credit Facility, which carried a clear stigma, jumped sharply, as indeed did the whole category of "other loans." The former had been zero the week before then jumped all at once to an average of $20.268 billion. The use of weekly averages disguises the dimensions of the explosion that followed Lehman's bankruptcy, because the Wednesday total is $59.78 billion.

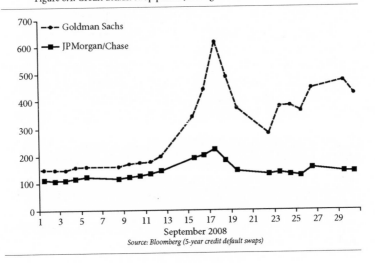

Figure 6.4: Credit default swap prices: JPMorgan Chase and Goldman Sachs

Source: Bloomberg (5-year credit default swaps)

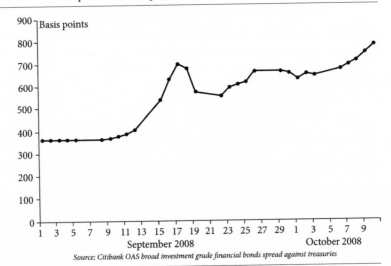

Figure 6.5: Spreads on bank debt blow-out as Lehman
Collapses Bank bond spreads versus US Treasuries: Sept–Oct 2008

Source: Citibank OAS broad investment grade financial bonds spread against treasuries

willingness to lend at longer maturities appears to have withered (Figure 6.6).[54]

Most of the world, however, only dimly appreciated the meaning of the reports in the financial press that interbank lending was grinding to a halt. Instead, for most observers, the most arresting effects of the bankruptcy came in stock markets, as market operators realized that even the greatest Wall Street houses and banks now could not be worth much more than Lehman.

---

54 Taylor relies on the spread between three-month LIBOR and the three-month overnight index swap as his measure of disruption. The latter records the market's guess about what the Fed funds rate will be over the same period, so the difference between the two rates should reflect banks' anxieties about lending to each other. That measure did not move much until roughly the time when Paulson and Bernanke went to Congress. Taylor, accordingly, argues that it must have been the political intervention rather than Lehman's bankruptcy that disrupted world markets.

Economic historians will be familiar with previous economic crises in which published rates failed to reflect market realities. Such appears to be the case here. Let us set aside, for now, suspicions voiced earlier in the year that LIBOR rates had gradually become extensively fictional (cf. C. Mollenkamp, "Bankers Cast Doubt on Key Rate amid Crisis," *Wall Street Journal*, April 16, 2008). Jones, "Why letting Lehman go did crush the financial markets," describes problems in interpreting LIBOR quotations even in normal times. In the Lehman crisis, special force attaches to all his reservations. Our Figure 6.6 indicates a tremendous demand for the shortest-term LIBOR borrowings; it is inconsistent with any notion that money was easily available for longer periods. This conclusion also coheres with the evidence of the Fed's H.4.1 statistical release discussed above, which indicates sharply increasing demand for official short-term credits, even if they carry a stigma, and with Jones's analysis of the behavior of money-market funds and bankers' reserve balances at the Fed. Additional evidence that banks were desperately seeking short-term funds because money for the longer term was unavailable is found in Phillip Swagel, "The Financial Crisis: An Inside View," *Brookings Papers on Economic Activity*, 2009; see especially his remarks on commercial-paper borrowings.

We also think that the "event analysis" approach Taylor uses is more problematic than he allows. He is, of course, aware that, in principle, complex, lagged causal effects could muddy the distinction he wants to draw between market reactions to the bankruptcy as opposed to the government's subsequent interventions. But his paper appears to underestimate the market turmoil. For example, American brokerage houses with operations in London only slowly awoke to the dangers that English bankruptcy laws posed to their ability to gain access to funds they had deposited with Lehman; see for example Mackintosh and Hughes, "New York." The Fed just as clearly misjudged its ability to fund the UK part of Lehman's broker-dealer business (cf. J. Gapper, "We Need to Share the Burden on Bailouts," *Financial Times*, March 25, 2009). Such confusions took some time to sort out, or even to be recognized. They imply that neat distinctions between the periods are likely to be very misleading.

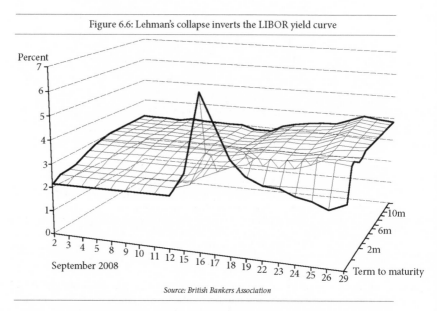

Figure 6.6: Lehman's collapse inverts the LIBOR yield curve

Source: British Bankers Association

They immediately started shorting the stocks, as other investors fled. Within hours, one of the most famous and characteristic features of American financial life—the powerful, indeed often dominant, role of a handful of famous investment banks—came to a sudden, terrifying end. Seeing the handwriting on the wall, Merrill Lynch consented to a shotgun wedding with Bank of America just hours before Lehman became history. Beset by wave after wave of short sellers, Goldman Sachs briefly flirted with buying Wachovia (whose CEO was a former Goldman executive) before emulating Morgan Stanley and transforming itself into a bank holding company, able to tap the Fed forever.

In the meantime, a wave of bankruptcies and defensive mergers rippled through the commercial banking system. Fears of already nervous investors turned to sheer terror, however, when the FDIC's terms became public for JPMorgan Chase's takeover of Washington Mutual (WaMu), the largest savings-and-loan association in the United States. The FDIC insisted that WaMu actually go bankrupt first, then approved sale of the deposits to Morgan for $2 billion. This reduced strain on the FDIC's insurance fund but wiped out both stockholders and unsecured creditors of WaMu. On the heels of Lehman's bankruptcy and the GSE restructurings, the message seemed clear: neither bank debt nor preferred stock in financial institutions was safe; deposits alone were a stable source of bank funds. Investors responded by stampeding out of bank stocks and dumping debt.[55]

The first step to a new, born-again Paulson Put took place as AIG came under attack. AIG was nominally in the insurance business, but the day after Lehman went down the world awoke to discover that the firm had been running a massive, now disastrously money-losing, division that wrote credit default swaps (insurance contracts against defaults on bonds). Though details of the rescue decision remain murky, certain key facts have slipped out. First, AIG had written credit default swaps for a broad cross-section of the leading financial houses of New York and Europe. It had also overextended its securities lending with many of the same firms. Bankruptcy of AIG would leave these firms exposed just as financial companies were going down like ninepins. AIG's biggest domestic counterparty (customer) just happened to be giant Goldman Sachs, the firm Paulson had formerly headed. As officials deliberated on how to respond, only one private bank chief executive was in the room: Goldman CEO Lloyd Blankfein.[56]

Reeling from the Lehman shock, Paulson & Co. made a dramatic about-face back to single-payer: law or no law, they effectively nationalized AIG by taking warrants for the Treasury worth 79.9 percent of AIG's stock in exchange for an $85-billion loan from the Fed.[57] In fact, however, the $85

---

55 H. Sender et al., "WaMu Seized and Sold to JPMorgan," *Financial Times*, September 25, 2008; Lex, "Washington Mutual," *Financial Times*, September 26, 2008.

56 For Blankfein, see G. Morgenson, "Behind Insurer's Crisis, Blind Eye to a Web of Risk," *New York Times*, September 27, 2008, including the "Correction" that ran two days later. For Goldman and AIG, see M. Williams Walsh, "A.I.G. Lists Banks It Paid with US Bailout Funds," *New York Times*, March 15, 2009. AIG also appears to have overextended itself in the repo market. See M. Mackenzie, "Deleveraging Leads Repo Market into Mire," *Financial Times*, April 8, 2009.

57 Had the Treasury taken 80 percent of the stock, AIG would have had to be carried on its books. In August, 2009, incomplete records of Paulson's phone calls during the Crisis leaked into the media (G. Morgenson and D. Van Natta Jr, "Paulson's Calls to Goldman Tested Ethics," *New York Times*, August 9, 2009). These showed the Treasury Secretary making far more calls to the head of his old firm than to other leading figures on Wall Street and raised searching questions about possible conflicts of interest. The article quotes a range of views; some claims put forward are obviously far from the truth. The

billion was just a down payment; AIG soon claimed many billions of dollars more.

The nationalization aroused outrage, not only from McCain but also from many others who could not understand why AIG was being granted what Lehman had been denied. In succeeding weeks, their outrage turned to perplexity, as the Treasury and the Fed kept pouring money into the firm with no real explanation. Eventually, the deal's true nature became dimly visible. It only appeared to be about AIG. In fact, the Treasury and the Fed were subsidizing the giants—including Goldman, Citigroup, Bank of America, Morgan Stanley, and other large European firms—that were its counterparties on credit default swaps and securities lending. At a time when no-one else in the market was getting a hundred cents on the dollar, these fortunate concerns were having their credit default swaps paid off at par by the people of the United States. It was big government corporatism in almost laboratory-pure form, public-private partnership in the tradition of Mussolini's *Istituto per la Ricostruzione Industriale* (Institute for Industrial Reconstruction).[58]

But with world markets raging out of control, Wall Street and the banks now had more problems than just credit default swaps. Short sellers were still having a field day with Goldman and Morgan Stanley, while Citigroup was turning into the Incredible Hulk. There was not a moment to be lost. In a stunning display of money politics in action, Morgan Stanley's John Mack telephoned Senator Charles Schumer (D–NY).

Treasury, for example, had to play a major role in the takeover of AIG; the Fed may have provided the financing, but by law it cannot hold the warrants. The Treasury has control of those, which is surely why it was Paulson himself who informed AIG's chief that he was out, as the story records. The evidence we present in this paper on the price of credit default swaps on Goldman Sachs confirms the implication of the phone records—presented in a web link to the electronic version of the *Times* story at http://www.nytimes.com—that Tuesday and Wednesday, not the weekend before, were crucial decision days for the AIG rescue.

58   G. Morgenson, "At AIG, Good Luck Following the Money," *New York Times*, March 14, 2009. Paulson tapped Edward Liddy to be the new head of AIG. Liddy resigned from the board of Goldman Sachs when he took the job but continued to hold over $3 million worth of stock in Goldman. As of April 2009, he had not divested himself. See T. P. Carney, "AIG Head's $3M in Goldman Stock Raises Apparent Conflict of Interest," *Washington Examiner*, April 10, 2009.

Schumer in turn pressed the Treasury, the Fed and the SEC to temporarily ban short sales. Barely months before, regulators had stonewalled desperate pleas for regulatory relief from consumers as oil prices spiraled upward. This time the SEC unceremoniously tossed free-market ideology overboard and honored Schumer's request.[59]

The Fed and the Treasury had been discussing the limits of their authority for weeks. For the Treasury, the priority was "to avoid Congress." It "maintained that the Fed had broad legal authority and could possibly take on distressed assets from banks directly, without congressional approval." But the hammer blows of Lehman, AIG, and the worldwide market downturn appear to have crystallized the doubts of Bernanke and senior Fed staff. On September 17, after consulting at least some other Fed governors, Bernanke informed Paulson that the time for bazookas was over. It was time to go to Congress and ask for the economic equivalent of nuclear weapons—a gigantic on-budget bail-out fund. Initially noncommittal, Paulson watched world markets plummet. The next morning he agreed.[60]

There is no doubt that the Fed understood how this should be done, at least in broad outline. Economic history is littered with examples of bursting asset bubbles. Best practices for coping are not secret. The government, operating preferably through a specially dedicated, on-budget entity, such as the New Deal's Reconstruction Finance Corporation, rather than the Central Bank (which can be tempted to monetize its way out of problems) or the Treasury (which has other things to do), surveys the condition of the banking system. It closes banks that only St. Jude, the patron of hopeless cases, could love—a step that, although wildly unpopular with financiers, saves vast sums for taxpayers. The government then sweeps all the toxic waste into a "bad bank" and gets it out of circulation. Finally, the state recapitalizes the banking system to a level higher than the minimum capital adequacy requirement after marking down bank assets to realistic levels, not banker fictions. Counterparty risk vanishes, as the new

59 For Schumer, see "Schumer's Stands," *New York Times*, December 12, 2008; and J. Nocera, "As Credit Crisis Spiraled, Alarm Led to Action," *New York Times*, October 1, 2008; for the earlier oil futures case, see David Cho, "Investors' Growing Appetite for Oil Evades Market Limits," *Washington Post*, June 6, 2008. Then Senator Hillary Clinton and others joined in the pleas.
60 Hilsenrath, Solomon, and Paletta, "Paulson," including the quoted passage.

equity gives the banks the cushion they require to take risks and make loans again.[61]

Done properly, as in Sweden or Norway in the early 1990s or the United States during the New Deal, such schemes do not necessarily saddle the public with large losses. They can even show a modest profit in the long run. At least some bad assets can eventually be sold at reasonable prices. The critical step, however, is for the government to take equity (common or preferred stock) or warrants (rights to stock at a set, low price) in banks it recapitalizes. After the banks revive, the shares can be sold, recouping most or all the expense. There is a catch and it is a big one: the new public shares dilute holdings of existing shareholders because the public has first claim on future earnings and the government shares normally also pay a dividend.

The Swedish bail-out of the early 1990s is perhaps the most widely acclaimed contemporary example of a rescue along these lines. In the late spring of 2008, after Bear Stearns failed, Federal Reserve Vice Chair Donald Kohn was reported to be closely studying that experience. But there were no hints of Kohn's advance work in the plan Paulson and Bernanke presented to Congress: their insultingly brief two-and-a-half-page sketch made no mention of inspection or recapitalization. It proposed only a publicly financed version of the superfund that Paulson had unsuccessfully tried to interest the banks in in the fall of 2007. The maximum size of this superfund was set at $700 billion (a so-called balance sheet limit, implying that over time the Treasury could replenish it by selling assets it acquired and recycling the proceeds into new purchases). What and how to buy was left entirely to Paulson: there was to be no review or accountability, with language borrowed from the Gold Reserve Act of 1934 banning even court reviews.

The concept was breathtakingly flimsy. Paulson subsequently admitted that even he no longer believed in it by the time the bill passed. Buying $700 billion worth of assets might have made a difference in the earliest days of the Shadow Bail-out. But the delay arising from the shadow bail-out was fatal: there was already too

---

61 Readable summaries of the traditional approach are J. Stiglitz, "A Bank Bailout That Works," *The Nation*, March 23, 2009; or T. Ferguson and R. Johnson, "Bridge Loan To Nowhere," in K. van den Heuvel, ed., *Meltdown*, New York: Nation Books, 2008. On the RFC, see Todd, "History"; and Epstein and Ferguson, "Monetary Policy."

much junk in the system. After the Lehman bankruptcy, all $700 billion could buy was relief for a few lucky financial houses, not a serious bail-out for the US banking system.

Realizing this point, critics asked how Paulson and Bernanke planned to determine the prices at which the Treasury bought the assets. Despite heady talk of "reverse auctions" in which the Treasury would select the house that offered the lowest price (which would force would-be sellers to offer only assets they urgently needed to get off their books), under questioning Bernanke proved uncharacteristically elusive. Setting aside his prepared text, he indicated a preference for the Treasury to buy at prices "close to the hold-to-maturity price," that is well above anything shattered markets were likely to offer. A leaked Treasury conference-call revealed that the Treasury was clearly hoping to pay above-market prices. And, as the Treasury eventually acknowledged, it opposed diluting existing shareholders and thus wanted to avoid injecting capital into banks. Treasury was also averse to the whole idea of government becoming involved in the running of private businesses.[62]

"Thou shalt not dilute shareholders" was, indeed, the First Commandment enshrined in the new Paulson Put and key to the disaster that engulfed the United States and the world.[63] The new, truncated Put's Second Commandment was equally predictable: "Thou shalt not constrain bankers' compensation." In the face

---

62 For Bernanke, see S. Lanman and C. Torres, "Bernanke Says Normal Markets Needed or Growth to Halt (Update 3)," *Bloomberg.com*, September 23, 2008; for the leaked telephone call, see Y. Smith, "Mussolini-Style Corporatism in Action: Treasury Conference Call on Bailout Bill To Analysts (Updated)," *Naked Capitalism*, September 29, 2008; on Treasury and dilution, see D. Solomon and D. Paletta, "Treasury Hones Next Rescue Tool—Direct Investment in Bank Likely Would Be Designed To Spare Existing Shareholders," *Wall Street Journal*, October 13, 2008; for Treasury's objections to government ownership, cf. K. Guha and J. Politi, "US Shift as UK Takes Path to Recapitalize," *Financial Times*, October 9, 2008.

63 One very special case of the Treasury's adherence to this dictum merits separate notice. In October, after declines in Morgan Stanley's stock value threatened a previously negotiated investment by Mitubishi UFJ Financial Group, the Treasury smoothed agreement to complete the deal by helping to work out an arrangement that protected the Japanese investors from dilution in the event of later capital injections by the Treasury. This deal had obvious foreign-policy implications, but they must wait for another paper. See A. R. Sorkin, "US Said To Offer Mitsubishi Protection on Morgan Deal," *New York Times Dealbook*, October 13, 2008.

of white-hot public indignation, members of Congress called—in public—for restrictions on executive compensation. The Treasury responded with proposals that it privately assured financial houses would be unenforceable.[64]

After his much-ridiculed testimony to Congress about asset prices, Bernanke lowered his profile, whereas Paulson raised his. Under withering criticism from George Soros and many others, the notion of just buying assets lost steam in favor of capital injections. These would support many times their value in new lending, and thus held the promise of halting the deadly process of "deleveraging" that was now shrinking the supply of credit.[65]

But capital injections proved a hard sell. Many Democratic Congressional representatives, labor-, and liberal-interest groups did not understand what was at stake. They had little to say about the bail-out and concentrated on agitating for an economic stimulus program or mortgage relief. The first version of the bail-out legislation contained language authorizing capital injections, though it still afforded pride of place to asset purchases. As the much-amended second incarnation of the bill emerged, Representative Barney Frank, chair of the House Financial Services Committee, insisted on taking out the language authorizing capital injections. Eventually, after Soros spoke to Speaker of the House Nancy Pelosi (D–CA), Frank and the Democratic leadership agreed to accept an "intent of Congress" statement from the House floor by Representative Jim Moran (D–VA) in conjunction with Frank that would provide legal cover for capital injections. By then, Democratic leaders were claiming that the intervention was in accord with the Treasury's program; this is consistent with Paulson's later confession that he changed his mind before the bill

64 The Treasury made a small change in the final bill limiting its application only to firms that actually sold assets to the Treasury—precisely the plan that Paulson has since confessed he did not believe in by the time the bill passed. None of the banks that subsequently received capital injections were affected by this clause, though heads of several leading houses talked about voluntarily foregoing bonuses and, in the end, sometimes did. Note that the bonus pool for six large Wall Street houses for 2007 was estimated to amount to 10 percent of the value of the entire TARP. At some moments in fall 2008, indeed, Morgan Stanley's bonus pool was worth more than the firm's entire value on the stock market.
65 G. Soros, "Paulson Cannot Be Allowed a Blank Check," *Financial Times*, September 25, 2008.

passed.[66] But this backdoor authorization ensured that there were minimal safeguards against frittering the money away.

PATH TO DISASTER

The Worldwide Market Meltdown that greeted passage of the bill and the creation of the Troubled Assets Relief Program (TARP) shocked the American establishment. It should not have. As soon as the bill passed, Paulson and Bernanke should have followed with a series of rapid-fire announcements of actions taken under its auspices. Instead, they lay low, while the Treasury put out word that a thirty-something former Goldman Sachs executive who had previously served as Paulson's special assistant would start figuring out how to implement TARP.

World markets could see clearly what neither the Democrats nor the Republicans, for different reasons, could admit—that even if TARP worked perfectly, it could at best only unclog the arteries of the financial system. Getting blood flowing through the patient's arteries again would not make her healthy; it would just keep her from dying. Private investment and consumption were collapsing in both the United States and the rest of the world; only large and immediate government fiscal-stimulus packages (including major housing relief) held any prospect of checking this. Republicans, in the main, were opposed to stimulus for the usual ideological reasons. Democrats were divided, with even many supporters of a stimulus package preferring to hold off until a new Democratic president took office. The United States and some other countries were also reluctant to negotiate internationally coordinated packages for various reasons, including the prospect that the United States veto over the International Monetary Fund would

---

66 The best existing account of the legislative maneuvering is N. Roubini, "How Authorization to Recapitalize Banks Via Public Capital Injections ('Partial Nationalization') Was Introduced—Indirectly Through the Back Door—Into the TARP Legislation," *RGE Monitor*, October 9, 2008. We had excellent vantage points to observe what happened, and we draw on this experience for other details here. J. Toobin, "Barney's Great Adventure," *New Yorker*, January 9, 2009, portrays Barney Frank as a strong supporter of equity injections; in fact, he came late to that position and remained very friendly to asset buying. Note that Frank represents a Boston area district; the city is a center for money-market funds, which, in sharp contrast to investment houses, have no easy way to permit government equity ownership in the funds themselves.

eventually come up for discussion. As a result, leaders of both parties agreed that the bail-out would not include a fiscal stimulus. Senator Obama also urged Democratic congressional leaders not to try to include provisions in the bill giving bankruptcy judges power to alter mortgage terms.[67]

The TARP, in short, was a failure from its first day. Nothing Paulson did later improved the situation. When, under international pressure, he saw the light and abandoned his emphasis on asset buying, he (and Bernanke) did not insist on rigorous bank examinations to find out who was solvent and who was not. The Fed and Treasury did not try to estimate whether and how much money it would take to get solvent banks to resume normal lending. Instead Paulson conferred with the heads of nine leading financial institutions. He then simply awarded them sizeable sums, on terms that contrasted glaringly with, for example, those that Warren Buffett received for his much-ballyhooed investment in Goldman Sachs.

Although TARP money was formally a capital injection, it soon became clear that much of the money would, practically speaking, offset funds committed to banks' bonus pools, so that taxpayers were in effect financing bonuses for the people who had created the mess.[68] Paulson also pointedly declined to set any targets for lending; indeed, it quickly became clear that the Treasury was deliberately encouraging the lucky banks that received money to consider buying other banks. When no-one was looking, the Treasury also issued a ruling giving massive tax breaks to banks—worth perhaps as much as $140 billion. The FDIC also guaranteed new bank debt, allowing banks to raise funds when almost no-one else could.[69]

Non-banks could see the handwriting on the wall. Not surprisingly, they stampeded to the trough. American Express, many insurers, and even the General Motors Acceptance Corporation (GMAC), started turning themselves into banks or buying banks or thrifts. The Fed also obligingly changed the rules

---

67 For Obama, see T. Edsall, "Obama Says Bailout Bill Should Not Include Bankruptcy Reform," *Huffington Post*, September 26, 2008.

68 S. Bowers, "Wall Street Banks in $70 bn Staff Payout—Pay and Bonus Deals Equivalent to 10 Percent of US Government Bail-Out Package," *Guardian*, October 18, 2008.

69 For the bonuses, see Bowers, "Wall Street"; for buying other banks, see J. Nocera, "So When Will Banks Make Loans?" *New York Times*, October 24, 2008; for the tax breaks, see A. R. Paley, "A Quiet Windfall For US Banks," *Washington Post*, November 10, 2008.

to make it easier for private equity groups—by now desperate for financing—to buy into banks. Other industries began building cases for bail-outs too.

But the financial system showed few signs of returning to normalcy. As a result, the Federal Reserve increasingly moved to fill the vacuum. It cut rates virtually to zero and proliferated special facilities for lending. It lent directly to large corporations. Some of these efforts showed results: with the Federal Reserve buying commercial paper of the fifty largest issuers, that market thawed out. Effectively, however, the Fed was no longer supporting private financial markets. It was extensively replacing them. There seemed little to do but wait for the new US president and hope for the best.

GLOBAL DIMENSIONS

7

STRUCTURED FINANCE FOR FINANCED STRUCTURES

American Economic Power Before and After the Global Financial Crisis

Herman Schwartz

Global financial flows, like power, seem abstract, delocalized and fluid. Housing, by contrast, is reassuringly concrete, local and rooted. Yet, during the past two decades (1991–2010), American power, finance and housing have been tightly connected. Put simply, America's ability to securitize large quantities of mortgage debt and sell it into global markets enabled the US economy to temporarily escape the normal economic constraints, to grow faster than its peer competitors, and to expand its firms' control over global production chains. These three conditions restored US global economic power after the troubling 1970s and 1980s. Yet the financial deregulation and innovation that permitted securitization also created the conditions for the subsequent Financial Crash. Like all economic processes, the economic bust emerged endogenously from the exhaustion of the very factors that initially fueled the boom, throwing the long-term renewal of US economic power into question by undercutting the current basis for above-average rates of growth in the United States.

This chapter thus has four parts. Part One defines power and establishes that US economic power grew during the past two decades when judged by the three criteria noted above. Part Two shows that the structure of the American housing-finance system was the source of the growth differential between the United States and its peer competitors during the long 1990s. Part Three shows how the current Crisis emerged endogenously from the 1990s boom. Part Four looks forward in order to offer some conclusions. It considers how the current Crisis may change relations between the United States and its largest creditor, China, and the United States and its rich-country peer competitors.

American Global Economic Power Over Four Decades

Power is difficult to observe. At best we have proxy measures. Thus I will define US global economic power as differential growth: growth rates of GDP per capita and employment above the average rate for its peer competitors. Like the tracks made by subatomic particles in a cloud chamber, the sources for differential growth reveal the otherwise invisible contours of US economic power. Differential growth is both a cause for and a consequence of US economic power. Related but lesser sources of power are the ability to escape the normal economic constraints because the US dollar is used as an international reserve currency, and increased control over global production as US firms remain relatively more innovative and relatively better at assimilating information technologies than firms from peer competitors. Differential growth both generated large volumes of profit that could be used to take control of critical nodes in production chains, and encouraged and validated investment in new production processes related to those critical nodes. Control assured continued profitability. Differential growth also attracted foreign capital, reinforcing the dollar's international role and removing constraints on the US economy, while making other economies more reliant on US growth for their own growth. Yet these processes were not fully independent, as capital inflows also helped activate US differential growth in a temporarily self-sustaining dynamic. It is impossible and pointless to try to assign causal priority here, particularly because, as we will see, deliberate policy decisions mattered less than the automatic operation of several pre-existing institutional structures. While US state officials sought and acted to revive American power, much of the action occurred behind their backs and not as a consequence of their policy decisions. In addition, the international role of the US dollar is a mixed blessing, as it contributes to the US trade deficit.

Politics is ultimately about power, and, as Jonathan Nitzan argues, economic power ultimately is about *differential rates of growth* and not just absolute growth.[1] In political economy, power flows from differential accumulation, that is, above-average growth rates for output, profitability and capitalization. All other things being equal, relatively faster growth will enable an economy or firm to command more resources of all kinds from a market economy. Faster growth generates a larger mass of profits that can be deployed in the struggle for control over the economy and the struggle to set prices. Control, particularly control over production chains, matters because control affects the distribution of profits and value across actors, and thus their ability to consolidate or expand their control in the future.[2] Any analysis of US power thus has to look first at the sources of differential growth and control rather than specific strategies, like financialization, aimed at attaining differential growth and control.

Over the past two decades, the United States outgrew its peer rivals—Japan and Germany—with respect to GDP per capita and employment growth, reversing the dynamics of the 1970s and 1980s. Table 7.1 presents population-adjusted data on the change in per capita GDP and job creation from 1991 to 2005. We start in 1991, because the collapse of the Soviet Union established economic competition as the primary strategic problem faced by the US state. At the end of the 1980s many feared that the United States was in an irreversible economic decline. Though now a dim memory, 1989 saw serious speculation that the yen or European currencies might replace the dollar.[3] While the dollar comprised nearly 75 percent of official reserves in 1978, by 1989 it had fallen below 50 percent as central banks diversified into deutschmarks

---

1   On differential accumulation as a concept, J. Nitzan, "Differential Accumulation: Towards a New Political Economy of Capital," *Review of International Political Economy*, 1998, 5(2), and J. Nitzan and S. Bichler, "New Imperialism or New Capitalism?" unpublished paper, http://bnarchives.yorku.ca; on the importance of relative gains, see J. M. Grieco, "Anarchy and the Limits of Cooperation: A Realist Critique of the Newest Liberal Institutionalism," *International Organization*, 1988, 42(3).

2   R. Gilpin, *US Power and the Multinational Corporation*, New York: Basic Books, 1975; C. Palloix, "Self-expansion of Capital on a World Scale," *Review of Radical Political Economy*, 1977, 9(2); N. Poulantzas, "Internationalisation of Capitalist Relations and the Nation-State," *Economy and Society*, 1974, 3(2).

3   F. C. Bergsten, ed., *International Adjustment and Financing: The Lessons of 1985–1991*, Washington, DC: Institute for International Economics, 1991.

and yen.[4] Various Euro currencies peaked at 40 percent of reserve holdings in 1990, and the yen at 10 percent. Similarly, Japan's apparent ability to generate new assets made many in the United States fear Japanese firms would embark on a buying spree that would give them control of the commanding heights of the US economy.[5]

Table 7.1:   Relative Economic Performance in the United States, Germany, Japan, and the OECD, 1991–2005

Population-adjusted percentage change	USA	OECD–19 Average	FRG	Japan
GDP (real, local currency)	33.5	28.1	17.3	13.3
Change in the number of employed	1.8	3.0	–2.9	–2.7
Change in the number of unemployed	–24.8	6.8	91.5	109.7
Gross Fixed Capital Formation	79.9	48.2	2.7	–13.5
GFCF, Metals and Machinery	159.8	100.1	19.0	22.8
GFCF, Housing	90.4	62.9	1.9	–28.0
GFCF, Non-residential Construction	–3.2	6.7	–24.8	–34.6
Gross value added	33.5	28.1	19.5	14.4
GVA, Manufacturing	52.0	28.3	6.5	16.1

Source: Author's calculations based on data from OECD, "Main Economic Indicators, volume II, 2008," http://www.sourceoecd.org, accessed June 18, 2008.

Yet, by 2005, all these conditions were reversed. From 1991 to 2005 US per capita GDP, employment, and fixed capital formation

---

4 P. Wooldridge, "The Changing Composition of Official Reserves," *Bank for International Settlements Quarterly Review*, 2006, September.

5 See, for example, the overheated D. Burstein, *Yen! Japan's New Financial Empire and Its Threat to America*, New York: Fawcett Columbine, 1990. Burstein has written similar books about Europe and China.

grew well above OECD averages and thus much faster than below-average Germany or Japan.[6] While housing investment clearly contributed to above-average US growth, especially after 2000, US growth was not only about housing, as manufacturing fixed capital formation and gross value added also increased strongly above the OECD-average level. The United States also generated nearly half the OECD's net new jobs despite having only one-third of the OECD's population.[7]

Above-average growth increased US economic power relative to its rich-country peers while preserving its position relative to developing-country challengers. The United States grew so much faster than its rich-country competitors that between 1991 and 2005 its "market share" in the global economy relative to those countries increased by an astonishing 4.2 percentage points to 42.7 percent.[8] Despite rapid Chinese and Indian growth, the US share of global GDP remained stable at about 21 percent on a purchasing-power parity basis (which biases China's share upwards). Put aside quibbles about outsized American consumption; GDP measures output net of imports. US differential growth in the long 1990s reversed trends in the 1980s, when both Germany and particularly Japan had grown faster than the US. After 1990 and 1992 respectively, each lost ground relative to the US on an aggregate and per capita basis; they also lost ground to the faster-growing developing countries. Meanwhile, faster US growth became a self-reinforcing process that sucked capital out of Europe, Japan and China. Faster US growth produced rising tax receipts and enabled the US federal budget to move into surplus by the end of the 1990s, ameliorating fears of an ever expanding US budget deficit. Faster growth and a falling deficit also restored faith in the US dollar, inducing foreign investors to bid up US-dollar-denominated assets. By 2001 the dollar was back to 70 percent of official holdings, and the euro down to 25 percent; yen

---

6 OECD here refers to the old, rich-country OECD-19: Australia, Austria, Belgium, Canada, Denmark, Finland, France, Germany, Ireland, Italy, Japan, Netherlands, New Zealand, Portugal, Spain, Sweden, Switzerland, the United Kingdom, and the United States.

7 Uwe Becker and Herman Schwartz, eds., *Employment Miracles: A Critical Comparison of the Dutch, Scandinavian, Swiss, Australian and Irish Cases versus Germany and the US*, Amsterdam: University of Amsterdam Press, 2005.

8 Calculated from the EU–KLEMS database at http://www.euklems.net, using purchasing-power parity GDP in constant 1990 Geary–Khamis dollars, which controls for fluctuations in exchange rates and inflation.

holdings were below 5 percent. These trends removed the normal constraints on the US economy, reinforcing differential growth and providing a second indicator of renewed power.

The American economist Benjamin Cohen sees this absence of constraint as the essence of monetary power.[9] The United States was able to operate without constraint and to delay any adjustment to its rising current-account deficit. The US economy avoided the normal trade-offs across domestic consumption, domestic investment, and overseas investment. US consumption and on- and off-shore investment all expanded faster than its GDP. Consumption rose from its average level of 65 percent of GDP to 71 percent in 2004. Despite rising consumption, gross fixed capital formation also grew relative to GDP, from 14 percent to 19 percent. American investors also sent nearly $7 trillion back out into the world from 1997 to 2007. What made this possible? Massive foreign inflows to the US relieved the usual constraints, providing between 10 and 20 percent of total lending in US credit markets annually after 1994. By 2005, US foreign borrowing accounted for 26 percent of total lending in the US economy.[10]

Wily foreigners lent against collateral, or so they thought, by buying, among other things, $1.5 trillion of mortgage-backed securities issued by Fannie Mae and Freddie Mac. With the nominal market value of US houses rising by about $14 trillion, and mortgage debt rising by nearly $7 trillion from 1991 to 2006, there was plenty of new collateral to go around. The connection between the new $7 trillion of mortgage debt and the $7 trillion in US outward capital flows is more than just an accounting identity. In essence, Americans borrowed against their houses and their state, at low interest rates, both to consume more and to invest more in domestic and overseas vehicles they hoped would yield higher returns.

The recycling of US trade deficits into foreign lending to the United States enabled a recycling of that foreign lending into US purchases of foreign assets, just as in the original Bretton Woods arrangement. Back then, European sterilization of US current-account deficits removed constraints on the US economy

9   B. Cohen, "The Macrofoundations of Monetary Power," in D. Andrews, ed., *International Monetary Power*, Ithaca NY: Cornell University Press, 2006.
10   J. D'Arista and S. Griffith-Jones, "The Dilemmas and Dangers of the Build-up of US Debt," in J. J. Teunissen and A. Akerman, eds, *Global Imbalances and the US Debt Problem*, The Hague: Fondad, 2006, p. 64.

and helped fund US MNCs' investments in Europe, as well as US security interests.[11] In the long 1990s, foreign lending and differential growth funded US passive and active acquisitions abroad, expanding the share of global production controlled by US firms and individuals relative to firms from rich-country competitors. From 1994 to 2006, the US-owned share of the Morgan–Stanley MSCI All Country World ex-US Market Index rose from 10 percent to 24 percent of total market capitalization. By contrast, foreign holdings of US equities rose more slowly, from 5.1 percent to 9.7 percent of market capitalization.[12] US firms also grew faster overseas than foreign firms grew in the US market during 1995–2004. Despite a 10 percent increase in the dollar's exchange rate (which diminishes measures of overseas activity), their overseas value added increased by 40 percent, while turnover nearly doubled to 7.8 percent of gross world product.[13] Moreover, despite slower growth in other rich countries, the ratio of US MNCs' overseas sales to sales in the United States by firms engaged in FDI into the United States also rose from 1.3 to 1.5 in 1995–2004. This indicates that US firms increased their control over foreign markets faster than foreigners increased their control in US markets. There is no one-for-one correspondence between the interests of firms and the interests of the US state. Nevertheless, most research on MNCs suggests that they remain firmly rooted in their national economies and political cultures.[14] This is particularly true for high-technology firms, as they rely more on defense contracting

---

11 E. Mandel, *Europe versus America*, London: Verso, 1970; J.-J. Servan-Schreiber, *The American Challenge*, New York: Avon, 1969; H. Zimmermann, *Money and Security: Troops, Monetary Policy and West Germany's Relations with the United States and Britain, 1950–1971*, Cambridge: Cambridge University Press, 2002.
12 L. Heckman, "Insight: Refuge May be Found via New Frontiers," *Financial Times*, February 13, 2008, http://www.ft.com; note that the weight of US equities in the global stock of equities is generally not large enough for the smaller foreign share of US equities to overshadow the US share of foreign equities.
13 United Nations Conference on Trade and Development, *World Investment Report, 2006*, New York: UN, 2006, pp. 332–33; Bureau of Economic Analysis, "An Ownership Based Framework of the US Current Account, 1995–2005," *Survey of Current Business*, January 2007, p. 45; OECD, *Measuring Globalization: Activities of Multinationals, II, 2008*, Paris: OECD, 2008, pp. 378, 382.
14 P. Doremus, W. Keller, L. Pauly and S. Reich, *Myth of the Global Corporation*, Princeton, NJ: Princeton University Press, 1998.

and require government enforcement of intellectual property rights.

There also was no one-for-one correspondence between capital inflows and outflows; these were macroeconomic, not micro-economic flows. Yet in the aggregate, the mismatch between the kinds of inflows into the United States and the kinds of outflows from the United States had huge consequences. These flows constituted a huge system of financial arbitrage, in which the United States (as a macroeconomic entity) exchanged disproportionately low-yielding, short-term and passive assets for higher-yielding, longer-term, active assets. Net, the United States sold Treasury bonds and mortgage backed securities (MBS) to finance purchases of equities and to fund foreign direct investment.

The corresponding flows of international investment income reflect these different investment patterns. America's overseas investments have consistently yielded more income than did foreign investments in the US, even though the United States has been a net foreign debtor for nearly two decades. In 2007, removing six zeros, this was rather like a private investor, who owed $20,082 while holding investments worth only $17,640, somehow managing to pay out only $726 on her debts while earning $818 from her own investments, and thus receiving net income of $92. It is perfectly plausible that a savvy individual investor might be able to borrow money, invest only part, and still net a positive return. But it is implausible that on average every US investor is smarter than every foreign investor. It is even less plausible that every US investor suddenly became even smarter after the US became a net debtor, as data from Pierre-Oliver Gourinchas and Hélène Rey suggest. They calculate that from 1960 to 2001, US overseas assets earned an annualized rate of return 2 percentage points higher than US liabilities to foreigners, at 5.6 percent versus 3.6 percent.[15] Furthermore, the gap expanded after 1973, as US assets yielded 6.8 percent while liabilities cost only 3.5 percent. This is one reason why, despite five years of cumulating trade deficits, US net foreign debt was

---

15 P.-O. Gourinchas and H. Rey, "From World Banker to World Venture Capitalist: US External Adjustment and the Exorbitant Privilege," NBER Working Paper 11563, August 2005, Chicago: NBER, 2005. See also R. Caballero, E. Farhi and P.-O. Gourinchas, "An Equilibrium Model of Global Imbalances and Low Interest Rates," NBER Working Paper 11996, Chicago: NBER, 2006.

the same 20 percent of GDP in 2007 as it had been in 2002. The mismatch in maturity and control between the US and foreign investment positions generates these different returns. Table 7.2 shows that about three-fifths of US outward investment is composed of high-yielding equities and direct investment (columns 1 and 2), while over three-fifths of foreign investment in the United States is composed of bonds and loans (columns 3 and 4), which yield less income.

Table 7.2:   International Investment into and out of the United States, 2007, US$ Billions and Percentage

	1	2	3	4	5
$ billion	FDI[a]	Portfolio Equities	Portfolio Debt[b]	Loans	**Total**
US to World	5,148	5,171	1,478	5,002	16,799
Rest of World to US	3,524	2,833	6,965	4,982	18,304
Of which, Central Banks			2,931	406	3,337
% shares					
US to World	30.6	30.8	8.8	29.8	100
Rest of World to US	19.3	15.5	38.1	27.2	100
Of which, Central Banks			16.0	2.2	18.2

Notes: [a] market valuation
               [b] omits trivial US holdings of currency and foreign holdings
               of US currency totaling $279 billion.

Source: Data from BEA, International Investment Position, http://www.bea.gov, accessed August 1, 2008.

The structure of US housing markets helped make this kind of US arbitrage possible. Possessing an international reserve currency was a necessary condition for US financial arbitrage, because otherwise the risks of buying dollar-denominated debt—and hence also the interest rates on that debt—would have been considerably higher. Leo Panitch and Sam Gindin are precisely correct on this point.[16] But a supply of sellable assets is also a necessary condition. Treasury bonds alone could not supply enough assets on the scale observed in the 1990s, because the underlying fiscal deficit corresponding to that outflow of Treasury bonds would have spooked international investors, just as US fiscal deficits scared foreign (and domestic) investors in the late 1980s and early 1990s. In other words, massive sales of Treasury debt would have undermined the conditions permitting massive sales of Treasury debt, by driving investors away from the dollar. Massive sales of corporate equities to foreigners would also have provoked a political backlash, as in the late 1980s when Japanese investment into the United States surged. Instead housing-related debt filled the gap. Sales of government-agency (i.e. Fannie Mae and Freddie Mac) MBS and privately generated asset-backed securities filled the gap. Foreign holdings of Agency mortgage-backed securities amounted to about $260 billion (or 7 percent of the outstanding amount) by 2000, and about $1.5 trillion (or 21 percent) by 2008. The foreign share of corporate bonds was similar, at $2.8 trillion and 22.6 percent.[17]

As noted above, total US mortgage debt increased by about $7 trillion from 1991 to 2006. This debt corresponded to both an upward valuation of existing housing and a wave of new construction. The United States built 17.7 million units of housing between 1990 and 2000, and an additional 10 million units through mid-2006, which helped the US create half of the OECD's new jobs in the period 1991–2005. What was it about the structure of US housing finance that permitted housing to drive above-OECD-average US growth?

HOUSING FINANCE MARKETS AND GLOBAL CAPITAL FLOWS

US housing finance structures turned US global financial arbitrage into above-OECD-average US economic growth. Two cautions are in order, however. First, it is important to note that the argument here is *not* that housing finance structures alone explain

---

16 L. Panitch and S. Gindin, "Finance and American Empire," *Socialist Register 2005*.

17 *Report on Foreign Portfolio Holdings of US Securities, June 2008*, Washington DC: United States Treasury, 2009, p. 5. Note that much corporate bond debt to "foreigners" is actually holdings by US firms operating through subsidiaries chartered in tax havens.

all growth. The rich OECD countries all experienced many of the same general growth impulses of the 1990s and 2000s: the supply-chain revolution, the internet, mobile telecommunications and deregulation. Differences in housing finance structures explain the difference in GDP growth rates, not the absolute rate of growth. Second, the argument here is *not* that the United States alone possessed the "right" kind of growth-promoting housing finance structures. Rather, many countries possessed elements of the "right" structure. What allows me to claim that housing finance structures mattered is precisely the correlation between above-average growth and what I will call US-style housing finance structures in some but not all countries.[18] How did foreign capital inflows and US housing finance structures interact to create above-average growth?

Four key features characterize US housing finance markets:

1. relatively high levels of private homeownership
2. relatively high levels of mortgage debt in relation to GDP
3. easy and relatively cheap refinance of mortgages as well as "cash out" of home equity
4. securitization of mortgage loans

These four features enabled a relatively straightforward process of Keynesian demand stimulus to operate in the US economy when disinflation and large-scale foreign capital inflows began in the 1990s. After 1979 monetary policy everywhere became less accommodative, reversing three decades of steadily rising inflation. By 1990, policy credibility and the off-shoring of manufacturing to low-wage economies produced a period of profound disinflation (a decline in the rate of inflation). Disinflation in turn permitted a steady decline in long-term nominal interest rates. Euro-area long-term interest rates fell from 11.2 percent in 1990 to 4.7 percent in 1999. US long-term rates similarly fell from 8.7 percent to 4.0 percent in the period 1990–2003, almost halving the average new mortgage interest rate.[19]

---

18   See H. Schwartz, *Subprime Nation: American Power, Global Capital and the Housing Bubble*, Ithaca, NY: Cornell University Press, 2009, Chapter 4 for an extended analysis.
19   Organisation for Economic Co-operation and Development, *OECD Factbook*, Paris: OECD, 2005, at http://www.sourceOECD.org; Harvard University Joint Center for Housing Studies, *The State of the Nation's Housing*, Cambridge, MA: Harvard University JCHS, 2008, p. 36.

Disinflation in the long 1990s could have released additional purchasing power as debtors' interest payments fell with falling nominal interest rates, and as consumers' dollars went farther in goods markets. Yet housing represents most consumers' single biggest debt (and asset). As disinflation filtered through different housing-market finance systems it might produce increased aggregate demand, and thus employment gains. But different housing finance systems translated disinflation into increased aggregate demand differently. Countries with housing finance markets most like those in the United States received the greatest increment to purchasing power, causing rising employment through normal Keynesian multiplier mechanisms. The first two items on the list above affect the potential for a fall in mortgage interest rates to free up consumer cash-flow. The greater the number of people who have mortgages, and the larger those mortgages are in relation to GDP, the more money can be freed up by declining interest rates. Conversely, the more housing is socialized and the more impediments there are to consumer access to housing-related credit, the smaller the aggregate demand "bang" a given economy can get from a "buck" of disinflation. Thus Italy, which had widespread homeownership but very low levels of mortgage debt relative to GDP, did not get a housing-related fillip to growth. Similarly, low levels of homeownership in Germany precluded a housing-related bump despite its high levels of mortgage debt relative to GDP.

While the first two items determine the potential size of the housing-related bump, the second two items determine whether both sides of the mortgage contract will permit that bump to occur. If it is difficult and expensive to refinance a mortgage (to retire the mortgage early by borrowing new money at lower interest rates), then consumers will not do so. In Germany, for example, borrowers are required to compensate their bank for lost interest income if the borrower retires the mortgage early. These pre-payment penalties are largely absent in the United States. One major reason pre-payment penalties are absent is the high level of securitization of mortgages. When banks keep mortgage loans on their books, they are exposed to interest-rate risk. Banks borrow funds on a short-term basis, but commit some of those funds to long-term loans like mortgages. If interest rates on deposits rise, older, lower-interest mortgages may fail to cover the cost of the new-deposit interest rates. The reverse is also true—if deposit rates fall, older higher-interest-rate mortgages are more profitable to banks. But in the absence of pre-payment penalties, consumers will rationally choose to retire those high-interest mortgages (in effect taking their call option), and leaving the bank with only the losing side of bets on interest-rate volatility. Banks can avoid this dilemma by selling mortgages to longer-term investors. This is the essence of securitization, which occurs when banks bundle a set of similar assets—in this case mortgages—into one larger bond and sell it to institutional investors. Securitization makes banks willing to countenance easy refinance.[20]

In the United States, two large government agencies created and facilitated widespread securitization of mortgages.[21] "Fannie Mae"—the Federal National Mortgage Association—essentially invented the mortgage-backed security (MBS) in 1981. "Freddie Mac"—the Federal Home Loan Mortgage Corporation—invented the collateralized mortgage obligation (CMO), a derivative that slices up principal and interest payments so that investors can buy bonds of varying maturities. CMOs and MBSs are thus different, if simpler, flavors of the larger category of CDOs, or collateralized debt obligations, which includes receivables from car loans, student loans, credit cards and other forms of debt. Altogether, Fannie and Freddie (collectively called "the Frannies") owned or guaranteed $5 trillion in MBSs as of 2008. The Frannies were the pipe connecting international credit markets to the domestic US housing market via the sale of securitized mortgages to foreign investors.[22]

Securitization and easy refinance in the United States and similar housing-finance systems abetted a normal process of Keynesian demand stimulus and growth. As nominal interest rates fell, US homeowners refinanced mortgages, shifting considerable purchasing power away from rentier interests and toward individuals with a higher propensity to consume goods, services and more (if not better) housing. This consumption in turn generated new employment through standard Keynesian multiplier effects, sustaining the expansion by helping shift the

---

20 Note that the German *Pfandebrief*—"covered bond"—does not remove interest-rate risk because banks retain them on their books.
21 Both agencies began life as fully government-owned entities (Fannie Mae, 1938; Freddie Mac, 1970), were privatized in 1968 (Fannie Mae) and 1979 (Freddie Mac), and de facto returned to public ownership when the US government took a 79.9 percent ownership stake during the Financial Crisis in fall 2008.
22 See also K. Gotham, "The Secondary Circuit of Capital Reconsidered: Globalization and the US Real Estate Sector," *American Journal of Sociology*, 2006, 112(1).

US federal budget into surplus, and thus enabling the Federal Reserve to continue lowering interest rates. Falling interest rates also ramified through liquid housing markets to create fictitious capital that boosted employment and growth.

Nominal interest rates matter for asset valuation. Falling nominal interest rates meant that the same nominal dollar income could be used to service a larger and larger mortgage. People entering the housing market thus bid up housing prices because they could enjoy more "housing" at the same monthly mortgage price. Much the same happened in equity markets. But retrospective analyses confirm that the release of home equity mattered much more than rising share markets for the net increase in real personal consumption in the OECD from 1996 to 2001, both because the propensity to consume new home equity is much higher than for rising capital gains, and because home equity bulks larger in the average person's portfolio.[23]

Foreign capital inflows accelerated this process by depressing US mortgage interest rates. Fifty-nine percent of foreign investment in US bonds as of December 2005 occurred as purchases of US government and government-guaranteed agency debt. At that time, foreign investors held 51.7 percent of outstanding marketable US Treasury securities and 14.1 percent of outstanding "agency" mortgage-backed securities.[24] Agency debt refers to MBS originated by the Frannies as well as their direct borrowing. Current estimates suggest that these outsized foreign holdings of Treasury and agency debt during the late 1990s and early 2000s depressed yields on ten-year US Treasury debt by about 90 basis points, or almost 1 percentage point, and as much as 150 basis points in 2005.[25] The interest rate on the ten-year Treasury bond serves as the reference rate or benchmark for nearly all US

---

23   A. Ludwig and T. Slok, "Impact of Changes in Stock Prices and House Prices on Consumption in OECD Countries," IMF Working Paper 02/01, Washington DC: International Monetary Fund, 2002; Claudio Borio, "The Structure of Credit to the Non-Government Sector and the Transmission Mechanism of Monetary Policy: A Cross-Country Comparison," BIS Working Papers, 1995, p. 24; K. Case, J. Quigley and Robert Shiller, "Comparing Wealth Effects: The Stock Market Versus the Housing Market," National Bureau of Economic Research Working Paper 8606, http://www.nber.org, 2001.

24   US Department of the Treasury, Report on Foreign Holdings of US Portfolio Securities, Washington DC, 2005, p. 13; US Department of the Treasury, Report on Foreign Holdings of US Portfolio Securities, Washington DC, 2007, pp. 3, 5.

25   F. E. Warnock and V. C. Warnock, "International Capital Flows and US Interest Rates," FRB International Finance Discussion Paper, 2006, 840.

mortgages. Falling interest rates for T-bonds thus immediately affect interest rates on new mortgages and on adjustable (variable, floating) rate mortgages that are resetting.

While the total foreign share of securitized agency debt is *relatively* lower than their share of Treasury debt, the *absolute* amounts are nearly identical because there was usually about twice as much agency debt in circulation as Treasury debt until the vast expansion of the Federal Government deficit after 2008. Indeed, agency debt typically represented a full third of all marketable US debt securities, public and private, until 2008. This reflected an increase in the aggregate value of US personal-mortgage debt from roughly $2.5 trillion in 1990 to about $9.5 trillion in mid-2006.[26] Foreign purchases directly depressed yields on US mortgages by lowering the reference rate for mortgages and by absorbing mortgages in the form of MBSs. US arbitrage in global capital markets thus stimulated its domestic housing market by providing relatively low interest rates to existing homeowners wishing to refinance their mortgages, and to new homebuyers. This is why the US system of global financial arbitrage largely benefited the United States and those economies with similar housing-market institutions. Housing-market financial systems more like those in the United States were better at translating 1990s disinflation into increased demand, and thus employment and GDP growth.

FROM BOOM TO BUST

Like all booms, the housing-bubble burst when the boom used up its fuel. Global disinflation, US financial arbitrage via the recycling of US trade deficits, and a ready supply of new buyers at the bottom of the US housing ladder powered the housing-market bubble in the United States and US differential growth. When these gave out, so did the boom. The boom ultimately was built on three related sets of debt: from the Unites States to its foreign creditors; from homebuyers to their mortgagees; and from the highly leveraged buyers of MBSs and CDOs to the funders of asset-backed commercial paper. These debts could not be validated unless

---

26 US Department of the Treasury, *Report on Foreign Holdings of US Portfolio Securities*, Washington DC, 2007, pp. 3, 5; A. Greenspan and J. Kennedy, "Sources and Uses of Equity Extracted from Homes," Finance and Economics Discussion Series, 2007 (20), Board of Governors of the Federal Reserve System, 2007.

188   HERMAN SCHWARTZ

incomes in the bottom 60 percent of the population continued to rise, because these incomes funded the majority of subprime mortgages inside highly leveraged holdings of MBSs and CDOs. Until roughly 2000, disinflation had income-enhancing effects at the bottom. Yet the same forces that produced income-enhancing disinflation ultimately generated income-sapping inflation, which in turn called into question leveraged strategies for buying MBSs and CDOs built on subprime mortgages. It remains to be seen whether the United States can make good on its promises to foreign creditors. As of summer 2009, the dollar remained the central international reserve currency, and US financial arbitrage continued to yield positive returns for the US economy. The United States continued to enjoy differential growth over its peer competitors, albeit by virtue of having a relatively smaller fall in GDP (but not employment). How did the underlying causes of disinflation eventually generate inflation?

One powerful force causing disinflation was the steady increase in cheap imports from low-wage countries. During the 1990s, US multinational and retail firms off-shored increasing volumes of labor-intense production to low-cost Asia, producing a flood of ever cheaper non-durable goods imports. Disinflationary imports from low-wage China and Hong Kong rose from 5.7 percent to 15 percent of total US imports between 1990 and 2005. By contrast, the share of US imports from high-wage Japan shrank by almost the same 10 percentage points, while imports from medium-income Korea, Taiwan and Singapore fell by 4.5 percentage points.[27] Prices for consumer non-durables fell by 10 percentage points relative to prices for services.[28] This shift initially benefited the bottom 60 percent of the US population by income, as they spend relatively more on consumer non-durables than services, compared to the better paid. Second, cheap imports lowered official inflation rates and thus the corresponding interest rates for mortgages. So at the bottom people had more income and potentially lower housing costs. Unsurprisingly, during the 1990s the real cost of buying a house decreased for most Americans. Housing costs fell from 21 percent of pre-tax

27 Calculated from Bureau of Economic Analysis data at http://www.bea.gov, "Table 2b: US Trade in Goods."
28 C. Broda and J. Romalis, "Inequality and Prices: Does China Benefit the Poor in America?" unpublished paper, University of Chicago, March 2008; C. Broda and D. Weinstein, "Exporting Deflation? Chinese Exports and Japanese Prices," unpublished paper, University of Chicago, 2008.

income and 19.2 percent of post-tax income to 16.9 percent and 15.9 percent respectively, from 1991 to 1998, largely reflecting a steep fall in mortgage interest rates. Housing costs as a share of income did not return to the 1990 level until 2004.[29] Equally unsurprisingly, the homeownership rate rose, from 64 percent to 69 percent from 1994 to 2004, with most of the gains occurring in the 1990s.

Third, just as with disinflationary imports, the shift of millions of aspiring US homebuyers from rentals onto the bottom rungs of the housing ladder initially had beneficial consequences. Incumbent homeowners generally cannot move up the housing ladder unless someone below them buys their house, validating the incumbent's equity in the house and providing them with a down payment (purchase money) on their new one. The combination of millions of new housing-market entrants, falling interest rates and securitization provided this validation and more. New housing-market entrants generated trillions of dollars of fictitious capital gains for incumbent homeowners by driving up housing prices. The structure of the US housing-finance system meant that houses behaved like any other asset; falling interest rates cause the market value of any existing asset value to rise, even if that asset is not for sale at that moment.[30] Because US banks could securitize mortgage debt, they allowed homeowners to tap into this fictitious capital through "home equity lines of credit." These home equity loans increased from roughly $325 billion in 1994 to nearly $1 trillion annually in 2005–07, helping to expand aggregate demand in, and thus differential growth for, the United States.[31]

The constant inflow of foreign capital connected disinflationary imports to cheap mortgage credit. Just as with these forces, this inflow initially had positive effects. Foreign debt grew only marginally in relation to US GDP, despite its marked absolute increase. Foreign investors willingly paid ever increasing prices

---

29 Harvard University Joint Center for Housing Studies, *The State of the Nation's Housing*, Cambridge, MA: Harvard University JCHS, 2008, p. 33.
30 By contrast it is difficult for the occupants of social housing—co-ops, public housing, union-owned housing—to cash out their equity. For one example of the politics of social housing cash-out, see B. S. Tranøy, "Bubble, Bust and More Boom: The Political Economy of Housing in Norway," *Comparative European Politics*, 2008, 6(3).
31 Harvard University Joint Center for Housing Studies, *The State of the Nation's Housing*, Cambridge, MA: Harvard University JCHS, 2008, p. 37.

for US equities and bonds, reinforcing the international role of the dollar and thus US global financial arbitrage.

Why could this cycle not run infinitely? The very success of US differential growth threw the housing growth machine from top gear into reverse gear. The exhaustion of growth was an endogenous feature of growth itself. Net, new homebuyers by definition tended to be lower-income, lower-skilled workers. The more that labor-intense production moved off-shore, the fewer potential housing-market entrants there could be as incomes stagnated at the bottom. Second, the very success of Asian industrialization created inflationary pressures and thus rising interest rates on mortgages. Eventually the two blades of the scissors of falling wages and the rising cost of mortgage debt had to meet, cutting the fuel line to the housing-boom machine.

The subprime mortgage market was nothing new, but until the 2000s was a marginal part of the mortgage market. Total subprime lending in 1995 was a trivial $65 billion (about 10 percent of the $639 billion total market), and only 28 percent of this was securitized. The lack of securitization meant that banks were cautious about extending subprime credit, as they retained the credit risk on these mortgages. Even as late as 2003, subprime lending only amounted to 9 percent of total lending. But what had changed was the degree of securitization, which had risen to 59 percent.[32] More securitization meant that subprime lending changed from a specialized product originated by regulated depository institutions (i.e. "banks") to a more generally available product largely originated by unregulated finance companies drawing capital from banks and the capital market. These finance companies had nothing to lose from extending credit to marginal borrowers because they did not face credit risk. And stagnant nominal wages at the bottom of the market meant that more and more potential homebuyers had to resort to subprime loans to qualify for increasingly expensive houses. Debt–to-income ratios for prime mortgages—the kind that the Frannies securitize—are capped at 28 percent for housing-related debt and 34 percent for all debt. As house-price-to-income ratios rose 60 percent above the average levels in the 1990s, fewer and fewer people qualified for a prime loan.

---

32 S. Chomsisengphet and A. Pennington-Cross, "Evolution of the Subprime Market," *Federal Reserve Bank of St. Louis Review*, 88(1), 2006, pp. 37–8.

The very nature of housing and credit markets meant that the last entrants into the market would be the least credit-worthy, making loans to them a risky proposition. From 1995 to 2005, the US homeownership rate rose by roughly 5 percentage points, pushing the homeownership frontier out into the terra incognita of the uncreditworthy. Indeed, homeownership peaked in 2004, just as subprime loans shot up from about 7 percent of new mortgages to nearly 20 percent, indicating that nearly all creditworthy buyers had been "housed." A near majority of loans made during 2004–06 were of the subprime or "Alt-A" variety, indicating that borrowers were not creditworthy, lacked a down payment (purchase money) or were buying a wildly overpriced house relative to their income.[33] These loans were generally at high and variable interest rates, making debtors vulnerable to any up-tick in the reference rate for mortgages. Everyone understood that these buyers could not survive an increase in their mortgage interest rate. Thus these subprime loans were designed to be refinanced into lower, fixed-rate loans after a few years of house-price appreciation. Yet rising interest rates meant price appreciation would surely slow or reverse. Why did interest rates begin to rise?

Successful off-shoring of low-wage manufacturing to China and other developing countries eventually generated inflation rather than disinflation. Successful industrialization produced multiplier effects in Asia, powering their economic growth but also creating new inflationary pressures. Given Asia's initial low level of development, economic growth necessarily involved greater and greater calls on global raw-material supplies, including, most importantly, oil. Development meant creating an entirely new infrastructure—roads, buildings, power generation, telecommunications—and thus huge energy-intensive inputs of cement, steel, and copper. All told, Chinese imports of oil, soybeans, and copper were about thirty times higher in 2008 than they were in 1995.[34] Developing nations' calls on global resources

33 Harvard University Joint Center for Housing Studies, *The State of the Nation's Housing, 2008*, Cambridge MA: Harvard University, 2008. Alt-A mortgages involve borrowers with a good credit score but with excessive debt, while subprime borrowers have bad credit and typically did not document their income.
34 S. Jen and L. Bindelli, "AXJ as a Source of Global Disinflation and Inflation," Morgan Stanley Global Economic Forum, November 30, 2007, at http://www. morganstanley.com.

reversed the 1990s disinflation, forcing developed-country central banks to raise interest rates in 2005.

China's export surge was particularly problematic, as it caused the US current-account deficit to soar. China's exports rose from around $270 billion in 2001 to over $1,400 billion in 2008, and its surplus with the United States increased from $84 billion to over $200 billion by 2005.[35] The rising deficit in turn caused the US dollar to weaken in world markets, driving up US import prices, particularly for oil, and deterring private investors for accumulating US-dollar-denominated assets. By 2005–07 almost all net inflows of capital to the United States were from official sources such as central banks and sovereign wealth funds. The weakening dollar and rising inflation cut a second fuel line for the housing boom, as the US foreign debt appeared increasingly unsustainable.

In short, by 2006 the housing boom had exhausted its inputs of new homebuyers, disinflation, and low interest rates. The housing-led differential growth machine then began to run backward, slowing the US economy. Why did this produce a Global Financial Crisis? The macroeconomic phenomena above were not disembodied, abstract flows. Instead they were channeled through a relatively small set of financial intermediaries which transformed global capital flows into mortgages and then back out into global financial markets as MBSs and CDOs, derivatives largely based on MBSs. This is the third form of debt that proved unsustainable.

Global financial firms had devised what they thought was a relatively simple system for profiting from the trillion-dollar flows into mortgages.[36] Put as simply as possible, banks used structured investment vehicles (SIVs) to borrow billions of dollars on a short-term (90–180-day), low-interest-rate basis in the form of asset-backed commercial paper (ABCP). Financial firms and banks used SIVs to shift these investments off their books, and thus increase their profits by evading regulation. Foreign capital inflows permitted the Federal Reserve to depress interest rates after the

35 B. Setser, "Not Just Emerging Markets," at http://blogs.cfr.org on June 3, 2009; Bureau of Economic Analysis data at http://www.bea.gov, "Table 2b: US Trade in Goods."

36 See H. Schwartz, "Origins and Global Consequences of the US Subprime Crisis," Chapter 9 in H. Schwartz and L. Seabrooke, eds, *The Politics of Housing Booms and Busts*, Basingstoke: Palgrave, 2009, for a more detailed analysis.

2000 recession. While these low interest rates sparked the final spasm of the housing boom, they also drove financial firms to take greater and greater risks to eke out as much return as possible. So financial firms created a carry trade in which they borrowed billions in short-term money to buy their own apparently long-term CDOs, profiting from the difference in long-term and short-term interest rates. Their SIVs borrowed short-term to invest in long-term CDOs nominally based on thirty-year mortgages and paying higher interest rates. The raw material for most of these CDOs was the $1.6 trillion in subprime and Alt-A mortgages securitized from 2004 to 2007. Issues of ABCP increased $600 billion over those same years.[37]

Though simple, the combination of SIVs, ABCP leverage, and CDOs proved lethal. Borrowing short-term to invest long-term is very risky. Banks thought that they could avoid such risks, as they believed that the maturity mismatch was more apparent than real. They thought that most of the adjustable-rate mortgages behind the MBSs and MBS-based CDOs their SIVs were buying would be refinanced (i.e. retired) after two years, as housing prices continued to rise. This would allow banks' SIVs to repay their borrowed short-term money before the macroeconomic environment turned against them. Financial firms did not believe that defaults would occur across the board rather than being contained to a few localities. But when Chinese growth turned disinflation to inflation and the housing boom absorbed all the creditworthy buyers, housing prices turned down and began a self-sustaining fall mirroring the earlier self-sustaining rise. To banks' surprise, housing prices began falling in 2006, making it impossible for subprime and Alt-A borrowers to refinance their loans. Delinquency on all US mortgages made in 2007 ran at three times the level for 2005 vintage mortgages, with 15 percent of 2007 subprime mortgages and 7 percent of Alt-A mortgages delinquent.[38] Defaults on mortgages then caused the market value of CDOs to plummet. This triggered the financial crisis when the funders of ABCP refused to roll over the debt of financial firms' SIVs. With $1.6 trillion outstanding in MBSs built on subprime and Alt-A mortgages, and 56 percent of the global total of $1.3

---

37   G. Tett and P. Davies, "Out of the shadows: How banking's secret system broke down," *Financial Times,* December 16, 2007, at http://www.ft.com.
38   R. Simon, "Mortgages Made in 2007 go Bad at a Rapid Clip," *Wall Street Journal*, August 9, 2008.

trillion CDOs backed by US residential mortgages, this threw highly leveraged financial firms into a crisis of their own making.[39] Financial firms' unregulated sales of credit default swaps—a kind of insurance—insuring SIVs against mortgage defaults propagated the Crisis to the entire financial sector. The near collapse of the financial sector threw the rich OECD economies into a deep recession.

LOOKING FORWARD: AMERICAN POWER AND GLOBAL CAPITAL

America's economic power revived after 1991 as the US economy experienced differential growth relative to its rich OECD peer competitors. Above-average US economic growth emerged from the interaction of disinflation and foreign capital inflows with the specific structure of the US housing-finance system. That system translated disinflation and foreign capital inflows into extra aggregate demand, stimulating the US economy. Roughly one-third of US growth in the 1990s and virtually all growth in the mid-2000s can be attributed to the translation of increased housing wealth into extra demand. American differential growth attracted foreign investment into US-dollar-denominated assets in a temporarily self-sustaining and self-amplifying cycle. This investment re-established the dollar as the international reserve currency and allowed US investors to consolidate their own outward investment and control over foreign economies.

The Financial Collapse and economic bust after 2007 has destroyed this particular mechanism for growth. American global financial arbitrage remains robust, but mostly because Treasury debt remains a haven during such panics. But the rest is gone. Housing finance is now largely the preserve of the Federal Government through the newly nationalized Frannies and the Federal Home Loan Banks. Banks' willingness to extend credit against home equity and to borrowers with limited documentation or weak credit histories will never return to the levels of 2006. Much hope is pinned on the possibility of a green economy, but there is little to show for this as yet. Can the United States retain its global "market share" versus China or again outgrow its peer OECD rivals?

---

39 F. Salomon, "What's a CDO?" at http://www.portfolio.com.

Nothing here is certain, but two issues stand out. The first is the degree to which America's peer rivals and China are capable of domestically driven growth. This question is as much political as it is economic. Put aside the debate over whether the "unregulated" Anglo model is superior to the "regulated" Rhenish model. This debate largely missed the point, as it focused on labor markets and corporate finance to the exclusion of the housing-finance systems that clearly accounted for most of the growth differentials after 1991. The relevant issue is whether export powerhouses like Japan, Germany and China can shift investment out of manufactured export production and into something else in the face of the worst peacetime drop in global trade since the Great Depression. The first two seem trapped between a reliance on external demand for growth and a slow-moving demographic squeeze on domestic demand. If Japan and Germany cannot export directly or indirectly (via an export-oriented China) to a faster-growing America, then it seems unlikely that they can outgrow the United States. In the medium run, productivity gains will continue to erode manufacturing's share of employment, creating an ever larger group of underemployed people, especially in manufacturing-dominated economies. Shifting resources to more domestically oriented services is politically difficult given the hegemony of export manufacturing firms and unions. Finally, neither Japan nor Euroland is politically willing to accept the trade deficits that necessarily accompany turning their currencies into an effective global reserve currency.[40]

What about China, which (including Hong Kong) increased its share of global GDP from 8.7 percent to 15.2 percent on a purchasing-power basis from 1991 to 2004, and from 2.3 percent to 5.6 percent on an exchange-rate basis, from 1991 to 2005? China's growth obviously had domestic roots, particularly in the 1990s.[41] But exports equaled 40 percent of GDP by 2007 and the trade surplus equaled 7 percent of GDP; neither suggests robust expansion of domestic demand given that much of China's investment was directed toward either export production or infrastructure for export production. Furthermore the profitability of the state-owned sector rested on access to cheap credit, which

---

40   However, countries on the European Union's periphery are likely to continue to join the eurozone when they attain the macroeconomic qualifications.
41   Y. Huang, *Capitalism with Chinese Characteristics*, Cambridge: Cambridge University Press, 2008.

in turn required ferocious domestic financial repression and the continued provision of non-renminbi assets to banks by the central bank.[42] Coupled with the political power of China's export elites—largely Party members and their relatives—a massive shift toward domestically led growth seems unlikely.[43] Yet the gap between China's share of global GDP based on nominal exchange rates and the purchasing-power parity rate indicates the degree to which the renminbi is undervalued. China would have to narrow this gap through revaluation to be able to express its global economic power, but such a move would price many Chinese exports out of world markets.

The foreign-invested firms that generate most of China's exports have plenty of other places to find cheap labor, and many are closer to the United States and Europe. Transport costs from China are low but non-trivial. While a stronger renminbi would make energy costs cheaper for China, it would also increase Chinese demand for oil, driving up transport costs from China to end markets. This would add to the revaluation-driven increase in China's export prices. Transport costs are already greater than wage costs for many Chinese manufactured exports. Given these constraints, it's no surprise that the Chinese state responded to the Global Slowdown in 2009 with *increased* subsidies for exports rather than measures to boost domestic demand. China's reliance on external markets, and particularly the US market, for growth binds the Chinese to continued support for the dollar. Chinese protests about the US fiscal deficit in 2009 seemed mostly to be pleas not to abruptly devalue their holdings of dollar-denominated assets. In short, in the medium term, China could have continued export surpluses and export-driven growth through an under-valued renminbi, or global financial and economic power through a stronger renminbi, but not both.

Where does that leave the United States? Recall that global economic power is built on differential growth, the absence of constraint, and control over production. US MNCs' share of global output remains robust, particularly in the dynamic service sector and high technology. While automobile production will continue its inexorable shift to China, India and other developing

---

42 M. Pettis, "Distortions in the Chinese Lending Environment," at http://mpettis.com.

43 C. Holz, "Have China Scholars All Been Bought?" *Far Eastern Economic Review*, 2007, 170(3).

countries, even a bankrupt General Motors was careful to preserve its ownership of factories there, while partially shedding factories in slow-growth Europe.

The US dollar's role as an international reserve currency continues, although the bulk of foreign capital inflows to the United States now come from official sources, especially from China. Validation of these claims on the United States could come through a struggle for control—purchase of US corporate equities—or through an expansion of US exports. The former course remains politically charged, particularly for Chinese purchases. These politics involve not only US sensitivities to denationalization of productive assets, but also to foreigners' sensitivities to the inevitable losses that sovereign wealth funds or other official investors might incur. Huge losses on investments into US financial firms in 2007–08 made that clear. The latter course of action would be positive for the US economy. Precisely this dynamic helped set off the 1970s and 1990s recoveries after dollar depreciation both cheapened US exports and imposed huge capital losses on holders of US-dollar-denominated assets.

An export-led revival of the US economy would of course reinforce the demographic trends giving the United States differential growth relative to its rich-country peer competitors. While the United States will most likely experience very slow growth over the next few years, its relative lack of reliance on external demand for growth means it will probably grow faster than the more export-reliant Japan and Germany. Similarly, the United States has a backlog of possible reforms, most notably in health-care, that might free up cash for consumption. The problem in the long term for both the United States and its rivals is to find a more stable growth path that does not rely on excessive and speculative finance. Hyman Minsky argued that such a path was impossible, and the record of the 2000s suggests he is right. Still, the severity of this crisis will concentrate minds on the issue. Responses to it will necessarily reduce the potency of housing-driven growth in the US economy. But this does not mean an end to differential growth favoring the United States.

8

A VERY NORTH ATLANTIC CREDIT CRUNCH

Geopolitical Implications of the Global Liquidity Crisis

Anastasia Nesvetailova and Ronen Palan

This chapter explores the geopolitical implications of the Global Credit Crunch. In its methods and subject matter, geopolitics is a field alien to financial economics. While financial economics seeks to derive a theory of economic trends from past experiences, geopolitics is speculative, intuitive, and aimed at anticipating the future. If financial economics treats the financial market as a disembedded category, with no home or address, geopolitics is all about location, interests and power.

This does not mean that economists are unable to explore the latter.[1] Willem Buiter, for instance, persistently alludes to the broader geopolitical implications of the continuing financial turmoil. He has suggested that the Meltdown may spell the end of the supremacy of London and New York as financial centers.[2] John Plender, a *Financial Times* columnist and chairman of Quintain Plc, agrees in part. He believes that from 2002 to 2007, the US and the UK were able to maintain significant balance-of-payment deficits because both economies generated positive investment income, by

1 See, for instance, G. Soros, *The New Paradigm for Financial Markets: The Credit Crisis of 2008 and What it Means*, New York: Public Affairs, 2008; J. Kay, "Same old folly, new spiral of risk," *Financial Times*, August 13, 2007; P. Stephens, "Uncomfortable truths for a new world of them and us," *Financial Times*, May 29, 2008.
2 W. Buiter, "Lessons from the North Atlantic Financial Crisis," NBER Working Paper, http://www.nber.org, 2008.

borrowing short in safe liabilities to invest long in riskier assets.[3] Both observers believe that the two economies will be unable to pull this trick in the future. Therefore—although neither says so openly—the Anglo-Saxon model founded on deregulated credit markets may become unsustainable in the future.

We have considerable sympathy with Buiter's and Plender's lines of thinking. We note, however, that when economists discuss geopolitical issues, the link to financial crisis theory remains somewhat obscure. The question we ask in this article is whether a firmer theoretical connection can be developed between theories of financial fragility and crisis on the one hand, and geopolitical analysis on the other.

We suggest that such a connection can be forged through an important, yet so far missing, aspect in the theoretical analyses of the nature of the current Financial Crisis. Until now, the key issue for financial economists has been the *supply* of new assets and credit facilities. Indeed, the analytical and policy discussion of the origins of the current Crisis has centered on the supply side of liquidity: on the quality, provision and regulation of new financial instruments and the process of financial innovation as a whole—the underlying assumption being that demand will follow suit. In reality, however, newly invented esoteric financial instruments do not find their customers by themselves. As we show below, even during the boom years, markets for these products needed to be created, and "liquidity" relied critically on demand being whipped up. Thus, when economists step outside the frame of finance theory and speculate about the geopolitical implications of the crisis, they are confronted with the messier world that makes up the *demand* side for the products of financial innovation, shaped as it is by the combination of historical, political, social and economic factors operating in a specific context. Demand-side explorations draw upon and yet transcend the theoretical boundaries of financial economics.

In this chapter, we focus on one intriguing aspect of the demand for the complex financial products that are at the heart of the Credit Crunch. Although the "subprime" mortgage was an American invention, and the securitization boom was crucially tied to developments in US housing finance, it is not

---

3 J. Plender, "Insight: Painful lesson for UK banks," *Financial Times*, August 26, 2008.

just American financial institutions that are bearing the brunt of losses from the subprime fiasco. European banks, which during the expansion from 2002 to 2007 had been keen to join their shrewd US competitors in buying up high-risk, high-yield assets, have also suffered severely under the fallout from the Credit Crunch. As we will demonstrate, the process of liquidity build-up and subsequent meltdown and the policy response to the Crisis on both sides of the Atlantic, have a distinct geopolitical dimension to them.

The Crisis is neither simply an American nor a "global" event. Rather, it is a crisis of the North Atlantic economy (a notion that academia has long considered somewhat archaic) and, more specifically, the Atlantic banking community. While the "supply side" of the Crisis was exclusively American, its "demand side" was distinctly North Atlantic.

The specific geographical nature of the demand side was shaped, it appears, by the different regulatory regimes in which banks and other financial institutions operate. The political and regulatory regimes in which the North Atlantic banking community operates are shaped by three important actors: the US, the EU and the UK. Significantly, as we explain below, there are signs that each of the three is reacting to the Credit Crunch in substantially different ways. The diverging paths of regulatory response, we believe, are likely to have a longer-term impact and thus reshape the future development of financial innovation and, possibly, future financial crises. Our analysis of the diverging regulatory responses presented below leads us to a somewhat controversial conclusion. In contrast to many of the experts with whom we share an analysis of the causes of the Crisis, we cautiously suggest that there may be reasons to believe that in the foreseeable future, the US will be unable to produce another meltdown of such magnitude. The current Credit Crisis is, in a sense, the last big throw of a declining US hegemony.

THE THREE PILLARS OF LIQUIDITY ILLUSION

Liquidity, or rather, the lack of it, has been at the epicenter of the continuing financial turmoil since its start in August 2007. Variously described as the fallout from the American subprime-mortgage fiasco, a global Credit Crunch or a crisis of securitization, the Financial Crisis has been underpinned by the rapid evaporation of liquidity—in particular in the markets for complex financial derivatives which had thrived during the securitization boom. Liquidity has also evaporated from the interbank markets, signaling banks' reluctance to lend to one another. As a result, liquidity strains have been a key trigger of many major casualties of the Credit Crunch.

One of the troubling aspects of liquidity is that its meanings and functions as a financial category vary according to the context and level of economic activity, as well as to the phase of the business cycle.[4] Liquidity of a market or a portfolio of assets during "good" times is not the same as liquidity during an economic downturn or a financial crisis. Assets that are easy to sell when economic agents share a sense of optimism about their profitability, liquidity and safety, often turn out to be unwanted and expensive bundles of "illiquid" debt when the sense of optimism evaporates. Hence "liquidity" can dry up literally overnight.

This is exactly what has happened to hundreds of billions of dollars' worth of securitized loans, mortgage-backed securities (MBSs), asset-backed securities (ABSs), collateralized debt obligations (CDOs) and a plethora of other obscure financial instruments since the summer of 2007. During the 2002–07 "liquidity boom," financial strategists could confidently sell highly complex instruments such as synthetic derivatives or "CDOs square" in large quantities to clients across the world. Few buyers bothered to inquire what the obscure labels actually meant. The market for these products appeared highly liquid and profitable. Indeed, only weeks before the Crisis erupted, leading policy-makers were concerned with what they saw as a structural "liquidity glut."[5] In a matter of days, these worries turned into fears of a global "liquidity meltdown." When the boom came to a halt, synthetic financial products became unwanted parcels of debt, and their markets lost liquidity.

In this respect, scholars and market analysts aiming to understand the relationship between liquidity and financial fragility have used several relevant concepts. Keynes wrote about the "fetish" of liquidity—a false sense of security an investor develops about the liquidity of the market as opposed to the liquidity of her own

4 A. Nesvetailova, "Three Facets of Liquidity Illusion: Financial Innovation and the Credit Crunch," *German Policy Studies*, 2008, 4(3).
5 BIS, 76th *Annual Report*, Basel: Bank for International Settlements, 2006, p. 98; R. Rajan, "Investment Restraint, The Liquidity Glut, and Global Imbalances," Remarks At the Conference on Global Imbalances organized by the Bank of Indonesia, Bali, November 16, 2006.

portfolio.[6] Warburton referred to "debt delusion" as an inherent problem which arises from confusing the large volumes and easiness of trade, as well as the popularity of financial instruments, with greater "liquidity" as such.[7] More recently, Claudio Borio of the BIS has used the concept of "artificial liquidity" to describe a fragile pre-crisis condition of the market, typically at the very peak of an investment boom,[8] while Avinash Persaud has used the term "liquidity black holes" to describe "episodes in which the liquidity faced by a buyer or seller of a financial instrument virtually vanishes, reappearing again a few days or weeks later."[9]

From these and other studies of the relationship between liquidity and financial fragility,[10] we have teased out three core elements that, we believe, sustained the liquidity illusion during the boom period, thereby creating a state of artificial liquidity in the market. They are: Ponzi-type finance, which develops in a climate of deregulated credit and rampant financial innovation; the market's underlying faith that the financial innovation will

---

6   J. M. Keynes, *The General Theory of Employment, Interest and Money*, London: Macmillan, 1936.

7   P. Warburton, *Debt and Delusion*, London: Penguin Books, 2000, p. 91.

8   C. Borio, "Market Liquidity and Stress: Selected Issues and Policy Implications," *BIS Quarterly Review*, November 2000; C. Borio, "Market Distress and Vanishing Liquidity: Anatomy and Policy Options," BIS Working Paper no. 158, Basle: Bank for International Settlements, July 2004.

9   A. Persaud, "Liquidity Black Holes," discussion paper no 2002/31, WIDER/UN University, 2002; A. Persaud, *Liquidity Black Holes, Understanding, Quantifying and Managing Financial Liquidity Risk*, London: Risk Books, 2003; A. Persaud, "Liquidity Black Holes: What Are They and How Are They Generated?" in the Singapore Foreign Exchange Market Committee Biennial Report 2001–2002; M. Lagana, M. Perina, I. von Koppen-Mertes and A. Persaud, "Implications for Liquidity from Innovation and Transparency in the European Corporate Bond Market," ECB Occasional Paper Series, No. 57, August 2006.

10   M. Aglietta, "Financial Market Failures and Systemic Risk," *Working Papers* 1996-01, CEPII Research Center, 1996; R. Bookstaber, "Understating and Monitoring the Liquidity Crisis Cycle," *Financial Analysts Journal*, September/October 2000; H. Minsky, "A Theory of Systemic Fragility," in E. Altman and A. Sametz, eds, *Financial Crises: Institutions and Markets in a Fragile Environment*, New York: John Wiley and Sons, 1977; H. Minsky, *Can "It" Happen Again?* New York: M. E. Sharpe, 1982; H. Minsky, *Stabilizing an Unstable Economy*, New Haven, CT: Yale University Press, 1986; A. Nesvetailova, *Fragile Finance: Debt, Speculation and Crisis in the Age of Global Credit*, Basingstoke/New York: Palgrave Macmillan, 2007; M. O'Hara, "Liquidity and Financial Markets Stability," Working Paper no. 55, National Bank of Belgium, May 2004; M. Pettis, *The Volatility Machine: Emerging Economies and the Threat of Financial Collapse*, Oxford: Oxford University Press, 2001.

be rewarded—by political means if necessary (in other words, a type of moral hazard); and finally, a structure of authority which legitimizes the products of financial innovation in the market and hence ensures their liquidity (credit-rating agencies in the case of the current Crisis). As we shall see below, each of the three elements requires a distinct regulatory condition that allows the liquidity illusion to flourish. When combined, the three pillars set up the workings of artificial liquidity (the boom phase) which inevitably ends in a meltdown (the crisis phase). In what follows, we show that the three pillars of the liquidity illusion, or artificial liquidity, have been at the heart of the ongoing Crisis.

Ponzi finance

In his financial instability hypothesis, Hyman Minsky used the notion of "Ponzi finance" to describe a situation of financial fragility, in which an economic agent can pay his debts only through new borrowings.[11] For Minsky, "Ponzi" is a method of financing old debt with new debt. In essence, it is a pyramid scheme, often containing an element of deception or fraud. Many believe that the epicenter of the Credit Crunch was a giant Ponzi scheme.[12]

The subprime industry was Ponzi for several reasons. First, the practice of providing people with uncertain credit histories, no prospects of higher incomes and often no jobs, with 100 percent (or sometimes higher) mortgages, was deception on a very large scale. From the very start it was clear that many of those subprime borrowers would be unable to pay their mortgages if, or rather when, the interest rates on their loans rose. Any Ponzi scheme can thrive only as long as it continues to attract new participants. In the US, subprime lending was fueled by the belief that the rising values of property would suffice to repay the loans, and, as in any Ponzi scheme, this belief operated as a self-fulfilling prophecy.

---

11   Minsky, *Can "It" Happen Again?*
12   M. Fish and B. Steil, "Root out bad debt or more pain will follow," *Financial Times*, December 21, 2007; N. Dorn, "Just where does the locus of corruption lie?" *Financial Times*, July 28, 2008; K. H. Ee and K. R. Xiong, "Asia: A Perspective on the Subprime Crisis," *Finance and Development*, 45(2), 2008; J. Kregel, "Minsky's Cushions of Safety: Systemic Risk and the Crisis in the US Subprime Mortgage Market," Public Policy Brief No. 93, Levy Institute of Bard College, 2008; R. Wray, "Lessons from the Subprime Meltdown," *Challenge*, 2008, 51(2).

According to Kregel, once the bottom layer of properties was inflated through the creation of massive demand, the entire US housing market entered into a bubble phase.[13] Housing markets, however, are notoriously cyclical. It was this fact, along with the actual terms of the subprime loans, that the scores of financial advisers who sold the products omitted to mention to their clients.

Second, the terms of borrowing and the conditions for repayment appear, in retrospect, to be key blocks in the Ponzi pyramid of subprime loans. Ponzi-type methods employed by lending institutions included large prepayment penalties and low "teaser" rates that reset at much higher rates, inducing many to borrow on terms they would not be able to meet.[14]

The reasons the subprime industry flourished for a prolonged period go beyond economics. Subprime lending mushroomed in the US (and to a lesser extent in other Anglo-Saxon countries such as the UK, Australia and New Zealand) due to historically low interest rates in the 1990s and 2000s that presented ample opportunities for borrowers. But low interest rates were available in many other regions—notably in continental Europe and Japan—which avoided the spread of similar Ponzi schemes. This suggests that the Ponzi pyramid of subprime finance and the related securitization boom, were significantly shaped by the political climate in Anglo-Saxon economies and financial authorities' benevolent and ill-informed views on the risks posed by the expanding bubble of artificial liquidity. Indeed, the boom of housing finance and related securitization markets was celebrated by many officials on both sides of the Atlantic, since there were significant political benefits to making housing more affordable.

Financial innovation

Subprime lending was a time bomb waiting to explode. Nevertheless, it would have played a limited (if still important) role in sustaining the boom of 2002–07, had there not been a second pillar to the liquidity illusion. That pillar consists of a series

---

13   Kregel, "Minsky's Cushions of Safety."
14   Wray, "Lessons from the Subprime Meltdown," p. 51. Often, borrowers were lured into taking a mortgage on their new home without being told that they would be unable to prepay it, to change the terms of the mortgage, and that their interest repayments after the initial "teaser" periods would be up to 6 percent higher than the market average. In other words, they were simply trapped in the subprime net (Kregel, "Minsky's Cushions of Safety").

of financial innovations that bestowed on the subprime-related financial markets an appearance of unprecedented and virtually infinite liquidity. Securitization techniques transformed tranches of fundamentally illiquid debts into easily tradable, liquid securities. The two went hand in hand. The CDO market grew in tandem with the subprime boom, and fed upon it. In 2004, the monthly issuance volume of cash and synthetic CDOs stood at just over $20 billion. During the following years, it expanded rapidly, with the synthetic CDOs growing at a higher rate than cash CDOs. By the first quarter of 2007, monthly issuance of CDOs stood at more than $90 billion.[15] By mid-2007, just before the start of the Credit Crunch, the outstanding value of CDOs in the US market was $900 billion. Of this, about 17 percent had been created out of subprime mortgages, with an average credit rating of BBB. Another 30 percent had been created out of leveraged loans in the form of collateralized loan obligations (CLOs).[16]

According to Kregel, at the centre of this process lay a transformation of the US banking system.[17] Institutionally, the spread of securitization is related to the way risk has been modeled, valued and traded by banks and financial houses since liberalization reforms were introduced in the 1980s.[18] These reforms gave rise to a new type of banking, now known as the "originate and distribute" (ORD) model. Under this principle, the bank is no longer an institution focused on taking deposits and giving out loans. Instead, it is a competitive financier seeking to maximize fee and commission income from originating assets, managing those assets in off-balance-sheet affiliate structures (SIVs), underwriting the primary distribution of securities collateralized with those assets, and servicing them. Bankers today pay less attention to credit evaluation since the interest and

---

15 Basel Committee on Banking Supervision (BCBS), "Credit Risk Transfer Developments from 2005 to 2007," Consultative Document, April, Basel: Bank for International Settlements, 2008, p. 32.
16 R. Dodd, "Subprime: Tentacles of a Crisis," *Finance and Development*, 2007, 44(4); J. Lipsky, "The Global Economy and Financial Markets: Where Next?" Speech at the Lowy Institute, Sydney, Australia, July 31, 2007.
17 J. Kregel, "The Natural Instability of Financial Markets," Levy Institute Working Paper no. 523 (December), Levy Institute of Bard College, 2007; Kregel, "Minsky's Cushions of Safety."
18 In this respect, Kregel ("The Natural Instability of Financial Markets," "Minsky's Cushions of Safety") notes, the ongoing financial crisis does differ from the context Minsky identified originally, yet the consequences will still be severe: it may still lead to a process of debt deflation and recession.

principal on the loans originated will be repaid not to the bank itself, but to the final buyers of the collateralized assets.

The adoption of the ORD model of risk trading has underpinned a phenomenal rise in commission fees and income from capital-market-related activities for banks. According to one estimate, between 2004 and 2006 earnings from derivatives trading and capital-market-related activities at the top ten global investment banks rose by almost two-thirds, from $55 billion in 2004 to $90 billion in 2006.[19] As a reflection of these changes, profits from the sales and trading operations had not only been growing, but also assuming a greater share of the investment banks' revenues: over 90 percent for the Americas, over 80 percent for Europe, the Middle East and Africa, and just over 40 percent for Asia Pacific.[20]

In this spiral of financial innovation, driven by the aggressive search for profits and the desire to outperform competitors, the usual trend of a Ponzi scheme prevailed: "old style" prudent banking was derided as boring and conservative, while the risk-takers were considered sophisticated, innovative and shrewd. As long as this market atmosphere was supported by the belief in robust economic "fundamentals," the under-valuation of risks (especially liquidity risk), the aggressive expansion of new borrowings, and the frequent use of quasi-legal investment techniques and outright swindling, it flourished.

Herding, moral hazard and liquidity illusion as a "state of mind"

The broadening of securitization to include new markets and increasingly esoteric financial products meant that origination standards in the newly securitized assets were driven by the

---

19 "The Alchemists of Finance," *The Economist*, May 17, 2007.

20 "Here, There and Everywhere," *The Economist*, May 17, 2007; "Black Boxes," *The Economist*, Special Report on Investment Banking, May 17, 2007; "Investment Banks Post Record 2006 Profit," Fundhouse, http://fundhouses. blogspot.com, 2006. Emblematic of the securitization era, in the fourth quarter of 2006 Bear Stearns' revenue from its institutional equities business rose 7 percent to $397 million, while its money-management and wealth-management revenue jumped 33 percent to $245 million. Lehman Brothers' revenue from equity sales and trading rose 22 percent to $900 million in the fourth quarter of 2006, compared with $2.14 billion in revenue from bond trading. Its money-management and wealth-management revenue grew 26 percent to a record $640 million (Fundhouse, December 14, 2006).

requirements of investors as much as by the credit views of the firms that originated the credits.[21] Here, the illusion of infinite market liquidity became self-fulfilling. As one former risk manager recalled recently: "The possibility that liquidity could suddenly dry up was always a topic high on our list but we could only see more liquidity coming into the market—not going out of it."[22] Therefore it was the continually growing demand for, and turnover of, the newly minted securities—as much as the efforts of brainy financial engineers—that created and sustained the illusion of liquidity. At the same time, artificial liquidity of such magnitude was built not only on the desire and ability of financial institutions to make debts liquid (to innovate and trade), but also on their underlying confidence in the *quality* of liquidity they had supplied.

Confidence in these new instruments was generated, in part, by the notorious moral-hazard factor: the belief on the part of financial institutions that they will be bailed out in the event of a crisis, since their individual collapse could trigger a contagion of defaults by other institutions. They had good reasons to believe so. The recent history of American finance provides abundant examples of such cases of moral hazard—which goes some way in explaining the willingness of US banks to take on inordinate risks. In all major systemic crises of the past twenty years—the fallout from the Tequila Crisis of 1994–95, the Asian Crisis of 1997–98, the Long-Term Capital Management fiasco of 1998 and even the dot-com collapse of 2000–01—Western financial institutions were, directly or indirectly, saved from bankruptcy by the Fed's injections of credit.[23]

In the fallout from the Subprime Crisis, the moral hazard phenomenon was not only validated but propagated further: the nationalization of Northern Rock in the UK, the takeover of Bear Sterns in the US, the Fed-orchestrated support for Fannie Mae and Freddie Mac, as well as the sheer scale of liquidity injections by the world's major central banks since August 2007, confirm the fact that moral hazard has been a major factor contributing to financiers' excesses and exuberance.

---

21 Basel Committee on Banking Supervision (BCBS), "Credit Risk Transfer Developments from 2005 to 2007," Consultative Document, Basel: Bank for International Settlements, April 2008, p. 7.
22 *The Economist*, "Confessions of a Risk Manager," August 9, 2008, p. 68.
23 G. Dymski, "Is Financial Governance Feasible in the Neoliberal Era? Reflections on the Post-War Evolution of Financial Risk," paper to the Conference on the Crisis of Financialization, London: SOAS, May 27, 2008.

Making bad debts liquid:
the role of the credit-rating agencies

Yet no matter how exuberant, canny or short-sighted financial strategists might be, illusions of prosperity, including the liquidity illusion, can only be sustained over periods of time if there is some credibility to the new instruments. In other words, something or someone was needed to sustain the collective belief in the liquidity of what were, in essence, bundles of bad debts and to make the complex structures of IOUs "worth—or seem to be worth—more than the sum of their parts." That something, Roger Lowenstein writes, was the credit rating.[24]

As he explains, the escalation of securitization has given the credit-rating agencies unprecedented power. The tradability (synonymous for many with "liquidity") of mortgage-based securities fundamentally depended on the ratings they acquired. Here, two complex processes have been at work: first, vehicle finance, driven by regulatory avoidance, manipulation of legal ownership of assets, and "creative accounting"; and second, the technique of layering securitization structures. Credit-rating agencies have been pivotal to both.

First, from the very beginning of the securitization boom, a central objective in ensuring the marketability of securitized debt has been to enable the rating agencies to grade the credit risk of the assets in isolation from the credit risk of *the entity* that originated the assets. Rating agencies demanded legal opinions that the securitized assets represented a so-called true sale and were outside the estate of the originator in the event the latter went bankrupt.[25] Such separation was essential for the approval stamp certifying that the risk was redistributed and removed from the originator's books. This role was played by scores of offshore Special Purpose Vehicles (SPVs) set up specifically as sham operations to isolate the originator from the product they sold. Once the assets were isolated from the insolvency risk of the originator, there was no additional credit-risk analysis required on the part of the purchaser.[26]

---

24 R. Lowenstein, "Triple A Failure," *New York Times*, April 26, 2008.
25 N. Baron, "The Role of Rating Agencies in the Securitization Process," in L. Randall and M. Fishman, eds, *A Primer on Securitization*, London/Cambridge, MA: MIT Press, 2000, p. 87.
26 "Securing the Future," *Credit* magazine, Legal Spotlight, May 2008.

Risk analysis, however, was required by credit-rating agencies, and it is in this task that they failed most miserably. Again, as Lowenstein explains, in the euphoric climate of 2006, Moody's analysts had, on average, a day to process the credit data from the bank. The analyst was not evaluating the mortgages but the bonds issued by the SPV. The SPV would purchase the mortgages; thereafter, monthly payments from the homeowners would go to the SPV, which financed itself by selling bonds. The question for Moody's analysts was whether the inflow of mortgage checks would cover the outgoing payments to bondholders. For the bank, the key to the deal was obtaining an AAA rating—without which the deal would not be profitable. The secret to making "subprime" into an AAA asset lay in the innovative technique of layering various types of assets according to their seniority. The highest-rated bonds would have priority on the cash received from mortgage holders until they were fully paid, then the next tier of bonds, then the next, and so on. The bonds at the bottom of the pile—the "equity" tranche—got the highest interest rate, but would absorb the first losses in case of defaults.[27] Amidst the global meltdown, we have not yet heard of any AAA defaults. But these tiers of "super-senior" debt may hide more risks, and thus prove to be as illusory as the liquidity boom that was based on them.[28]

SUSTAINING THE LIQUIDITY ILLUSION: THE DEMAND SIDE

In this way, the shift in the US banking system to the ORD model underpinned the massive expansion of the Ponzi mode of financing. No longer accountable for the quality and creditworthiness of loans they were taking on, banks and other financial houses eagerly took on bundles of bad debts on the assumption that they could pass on the risk to other parties. Yet this risk-dispersing capacity of the new markets for "credit risk transfer" (CRT) proved to be illusory. Much of the debt was, in fact, recycled through the banking system: in the end, the banks ended up not only selling

---

27 Lowenstein, "Triple A Failure"; IMF, *Global Financial Stability Report, Financial Market Turbulence: Causes, Consequences and Policies*, October, Washington, DC: International Monetary Fund, 2007.
28 N. Kochen, "Securitization from the investor view: meeting investor needs with products and price," in *A Primer on Securitization*.

off bad debt, but also buying bad debts from others. In addition, they recycled the bad debts to other institutions such as hedge funds. But when the crisis erupted, they were forced to take some of these bad debts back on their books.

Here, one development was crucial. The expansion of the subprime industry was financed not only by the US domestic market. It appears that American financial institutions managed to convince (primarily) their European counterparts of the value of "sophisticated" debt instruments and the risk-dispersing capacity of securitization. Although the key players of the rapidly growing CRT markets included many non-bank institutions, banks on both sides of the Atlantic began to actively trade in highly complex instruments of credit-risk transfer.

The thriving securitization process, and the wider process known as the financialization of the economy,[29] created an impression of abundant global liquidity.[30] While the financial services industry accounted for only about 16 percent of corporate output in 2007, it claimed more than 40 percent of corporate profits. From 2000 to mid-2007, the value of the American stock market grew at about 6 percent per year, while the value of financial services stocks increased by 78 percent. But while total corporate profits roughly doubled, business investment was almost flat—a clear sign of troubles to come.[31] The US banking system, cheered on by the Fed and the government, played a key role in (a) propagating the liquidity illusion internationally, and (b) expanding the subprime market beyond the considerable capacity of the US banking system.

---

29 For key literature on the subject, see M. Aglietta and R. Breton, "Financial Systems, Corporate Control and Capital Accumulation," *Economy and Society* 30, 2001; R. Blackburn, "Finance and the Fourth Dimension," *New Left Review*, 2006, II/39; T. Cutler and B. Waine, "Social insecurity and the retreat from social democracy: occupational welfare in the long boom and financialization," *Review of International Political Economy* 8, 2001; S. French and A. Leyshon, "The new, new financial system? Towards a conceptualization of financial reintermediation," *Review of International Political Economy* 11, 2004; J. Froud, S. Johal and K. Williams, "Financialisation and the Coupon Pool," *Capital & Class* 78, 2002.

30 B. Bernanke, testimony before the Committee on Financial Services. *Semiannual Monetary Policy Report to the Congress*, US House of Representatives, February 15, 2006; J. Studwell, "Liquidity Glut Bars Market Pricing of Capital," *FT.Com*, March 13, 2006.

31 C. Morris, "Imploding Credit Bubble to Hit $1 Trillion," *The Washington Independent*, February 12, 2008.

Long considered the most innovative and competitive, US banks led the way in securitization techniques, experimenting and financing new customers for debt-based securities. Operating primarily through their London subsidiaries, Wall Street banks eyed the large European market. After 2000, the revenues of the biggest American banks generated from trading in Europe doubled.[32] Not surprisingly, European banks and financial institutions, particularly the so-called universal banks, were keen to emulate the success of their American brethren, and after 2002 they increasingly adopted US financing strategies.[33]

Indeed, European banks not only caught up with the trend, but excelled in it. After 2002, the pace of debt and share issuance in Europe outstripped that in the US. One of the most well known participants in this tendency was the Swiss firm UBS, which traditionally had gained most of its profits from private banking services, selling tax-avoidance schemes worldwide, but now discovered the new opportunities that MBS and ABS trade offered.[34] It is likely that in its search for new lines of business, UBS was reacting to the growing pressure on tax havens from the EU, the OECD and the FATF. By 2006, UBS became one of the top share underwriters in the US.[35]

By the first half of 2006, securities markets overseas overtook the US domestic market; in early 2007 they were expanding three times faster than the American markets.[36] While the debt boom attracted some financial institutions in Asia and other emerging markets, it was fundamentally a North Atlantic phenomenon. This observation is at odds with current characterizations of the crisis as a global phenomenon. However, we believe that the build-up of the artificial liquidity bubble and the fallout from the Crisis center critically on the dynamics of the North Atlantic political economy, where regulatory differentials and local and regional circumstances played a key role in determining how banks would participate in trading in the new esoteric securities.

According to the IMF, within Europe itself, the securitization boom was most pronounced in the UK. The UK securitization

---

32 Data from Bernstein Research, cited in "Here, there and everywhere," *The Economist*, May 17, 2007.
33 In many cases this also meant using their London subsidiaries.
34 R. Palan, R. Murphy and C. Chavagneux, *Tax Havens: At The Heart of Globalization* Ithaca: Cornell University Press, forthcoming.
35 "The Alchemists of Finance," *The Economist*, May 17, 2007.
36 "Here, There and Everywhere," May 17, 2007.

volume accounted for the bulk of the total European (EU-15) level, having reached its peak in late 2006 and early 2007. Only from early 2007 onwards was this trend reversed, and the securitization volume in the EU-15 came to far exceed the UK market.[37] Here we should note that Spanish banks, which had been prohibited from taking risky assets off their books and hiding them in SPV structures, have escaped the Crisis relatively unscathed.

Key buyers of CDOs were hedge funds, banks, asset managers and insurance companies. CDOs assumed great weight in the portfolios of hedge funds (comprising around 47 percent of their portfolios), while for banks the figure stood at about 23 percent. Interestingly, as far as the quality of these securities is concerned, it appears that banks got the worst deal: their share of AAA tranches of assets was smaller than that of the hedge funds, while the bottom layer of these tranches (the "equity" layer, the riskiest) was proportionately much higher than for any of the other types of buyers. In terms of a regional distribution, US financial institutions purchased the bulk of ABS CDOs (around 75 percent), while Europeans purchased around 15 percent and Australians and Asians no more than 10 percent, respectively.[38]

Therefore the CDO trade was critically tied to the US mortgage market, but was internationalized as the North Atlantic boom of securitization. During 2002–07, various types of CDOs became Ponzi parcels that tied the two regions in a web of bad, highly overpriced, debt.

AND NOW TO THE LOSSES

The statistics of the fallout from the Crisis reflect the very North Atlantic character of the preceding boom. It has been American and European banks that have had to sustain dramatic losses. There were, of course, significant write-offs in other regions, but Asian and Middle Eastern banks appear to have been less caught up in the frenzy. In fact, liquidity as such has not disappeared completely; it seems to remain elsewhere in the financial system, primarily in the holdings of the sovereign wealth funds of Asia and the Middle East. The data also shows that European institutions

---

37   IMF, *World Economic Outlook*, April 2008, p. 19.
38   IMF, *World Economic Outlook*, September 2007, p. 15.

have raised only $125.5 billion of capital to compensate for the losses.[39]

Analyzing the risks of financial innovation, Kindleberger argued that it is typically the institutions who are the latest to join in the innovation-led boom that suffer most from the inevitable bust. The fate of UBS is a case in point: the latest kid on the block of investment banking, it became the largest European casualty of the Crisis. As of August 12, 2008, UBS's write-downs of bad debts for the April–June period totaled $42.5 billion.[40] Deutsche Bank warned of a €2.5 billion mark-down, while Credit Suisse, UBS's Swiss rival, announced it is likely to take a loss as well. As of August 2008, only two European banks, HSBC and Santander, still had a market cap of more than $100 billion, compared with five in January 2007.[41]

Admittedly, the concepts of "European" or "American" institutions, or "European" or "American" losses, are difficult to specify. Today the largest banks and financial institutions operate internationally. Irrespective of their nationality, many conduct a good portion of their wholesale banking activities through centers such as London, as well as offshore financial centers such as the Cayman Islands or Jersey, which are considered among the largest financial centers in the world.[42] Existing nationality-based statistics are not sensitive enough to these developments. Nevertheless, even if the statistics must be considered rough, they are indicative of certain trends.

This analysis raises two issues. The first, oddly missing in most current discussions, is the clear sign that the magnitude of the artificial liquidity bubble was made possible by the combined efforts of American and European banks and financial institutions and, to a far lesser degree, by the Asian financial institutions. This observation is highly significant in the context of the debate about the future of the so-called Anglo-Saxon model of capitalism referred to above. There has been a long-running debate about Asian savers subsidizing the US consumer through the massive purchase of US treasuries. What is less known, yet no less important, is that one-tenth of all US mortgages are in

39   G. Tett, "European banks hit harder by the credit crunch," *Financial Times*, June 5, 2008; M. Scott, "Europe Hit Harder than US by Credit Crunch," *BusinessWeek*, June 6, 2008.
40   *International Herald Tribune*, August 12, 2008.
41   *International Herald Tribune*, "UBS posts Q2 Losses, Writedowns of US$5.1B," August 12, 2008.
42   Palan et al., *Tax Havens*.

the hands of institutions and governments outside the country. At the end of March 2008, one-fifth of the securities issued by Fannie May and Freddie Mac and a handful of smaller quasi-government agencies (worth around $1.5 trillion) were held by foreign investors.[43] Between them, China and Japan hold more than $600 billion of these bonds. An additional third tranche of the massive subsidy to US consumers was provided by European savers purchasing CDOs through their banking system. Therefore, the American consumer-led boom of 2002–07 relied not on one, or even two, but on three massive subsidies from overseas. Considering these figures, the sustainability of Anglo-Saxon capitalism, heavily dependent on foreign subsidies, comes into question.

One emerging post-Crisis trend is of relevance here. Several Asian and Middle Eastern funds became investors of last resort for the victims of the securitization experiments. For instance, the Government of Singapore Investment Corporation (GIC) invested $6.8 billion in Citigroup shares and bought a 9 percent stake in UBS, while fellow Singaporean fund Temasek acquired a 10 percent stake in Merrill Lynch. The Abu Dhabi Investment Authority invested $7.5 billion in a stake in Citigroup, while the Kuwait Investment Authority snapped up a $6.6 billion holding in Merrill Lynch. The Gulf state of Qatar, via its Qatar Investment Authority, took a £1.7 billion stake in Barclays. The China Investment Corporation paid $5.5 billion to acquire a near 10 percent stake in Morgan Stanley.[44] Against these signs of growing appetite for corporate business, there are doubts whether Asian and Middle Eastern governments will continue investing in US treasuries. The debate on this issue is well known and needs no rehearsal here.

We are concerned here, instead, with a related and equally exasperating question: whether Europeans will be prepared to continue providing indirect forms of subsidy to US consumers by joining in the (next) bout of financial innovation. As we saw above, Europeans have ended up subsidizing a good portion of the Ponzi pyramid of US finance while bearing a significant share of losses from the Crisis. Will there be any political response from Europe? The answers to these questions are

---

43   H. Timmons and J. Werdigier, "US Bonds Facing Global Test of Faith," *International Herald Tribune*, July 21, 2008.
44   Data from the BBC.

by their very nature speculative, not least because they are based on projections of current trends and attempts to predict a political response in a complex and highly fluid situation.

A New Transatlantic Regime
of Financial Regulation?

Although monetary and financial authorities on both sides of the Atlantic have called for a coordinated international approach to governing risks in the Financial System, European regulators are taking a more radical stance on the lessons from the Meltdown than their Anglo-Saxon counterparts. The US conceptual response to the Financial Meltdown, as well as the Fed's bail-outs of ailing institutions and markets with massive offerings of liquidity (over a trillion dollars just between August 2007 and September 2008),[45] suggested that the architects of the Anglo-Saxon financial system did not recognize any fundamental flaws in the existing models of financial innovation and risk trading. On the contrary, the American regulatory response, as articulated by the US Treasury Secretary in March 2008 in the "Blueprint for a Modernized Financial Regulatory Structure," emphasized that innovation and market competition remain the priority for the US. The chief aim of US regulators throughout the Crisis has been to restore confidence (synonymous in their minds with "liquidity") in the markets and install the conditions for a renewed period of economic growth. Specifically, the so-called objectives-based plan for a new regulatory framework the blueprint advocates[46] is designed to address specific market failures, rather than question the very principles underpinning the functioning of the financial system.

At first glance, the reform proposal launched by the Obama administration in summer 2009 takes a different approach, aiming to build "a new foundation" for financial regulation and supervision that is simpler and more effectively enforced, protects consumers and investors, rewards innovation, and is able to adapt

---

45 This figure does not include the $700 billion bail-out plan finalized by the US Congress in early October 2008. According to the Fed, the amount of loans outstanding through various lending facilities increased from $76 billion in mid-December 2007 to $440 billion at the end of May 2008 (J. Hoefle, "The Banking Crisis Is Back in the Headlines," *European Intelligence Review*, June 13, 2008).
46 As opposed to the "functional" approach that has existed so far.

and evolve with changes in the financial markets.[47] In its calls for a system-wide overhaul of financial supervision, nationally and internationally, it is a much-needed and welcome step toward a public acknowledgement that financial excesses have disastrous consequences for society and the state, and that existing market-friendly standards of governance have been unable to address them.

Yet critics have already pointed out that the apparent comprehensiveness of the plan is illusory. While full of good intentions, the proposal is thin on concrete initiatives and overlooks many important issues.[48] Moreover, the call for more regulatory bodies and extended powers in the American network of financial regulators means that there is a risk that the reforms will only complicate the already cumbersome structure of financial governance. Lack of clarity associated with the division of powers and responsibilities between monetary authorities and financial supervisors has been a major factor in aggravating the Crisis. In this respect, a more effective mechanism of crisis resolution would need to be much more transparent, and simple rather than complex. A more complicated domestic regulatory framework would also undermine the effectiveness of any international coordination in terms of cross-border supervision, which has been a major problem in the Global Crisis.[49] Therefore, notwithstanding its radical tone, the Obama administration's proposals have left many questions unanswered. Moreover, the plan has yet to pass through congressional approval, and it is unclear which, if any, version of the proposals is likely to make it to the finish line.

On the face of it, the EU's regulatory response has echoed the themes of the American Blueprint.[50] Like the US, the EU acknowledges the need for international policy coordination in financial reform, not least because the risk of a cross-border banking crisis is high. However, there are significant divisions,

---

47 *Financial Regulatory Reform: A New Foundation: Rebuilding Financial Supervision and Regulation*, Washington, DC: Department for the Treasury, 2009, p. 2.

48 As Crook ("A Thin Outline of Regulatory Reform," *Financial Times*, June 23, 2009) writes, such loose ends concern technical aspects of regulatory capital and leverage ratios for financial institutions; there is vagueness about how Fannie and Freddie—central to the mortgage-securities bubble—will be regulated under new rules.

49 Ibid.

50 K. Barysch, "A Joint Response to the Credit Crunch," Centre for European Reform, http://centreforeuropeanreform.blogspot.com, March 19, 2008.

both conceptual and policy-related, between the US and Europe (UK excluded) on this issue.

There are important differences between US and European officials on the risks and benefits of financial innovation and liberalization. The European "roadmap" for a new regulatory structure is built around four conceptual areas: qualitative improvement and transparency for investors, upgrading valuation standards, strengthening prudential frameworks and risk management in financial institutions,[51] and reviewing the role and use of credit-rating agencies in the financial markets.[52] Leaving aside the Ponzi dimension of the Subprime Crisis—which the Europeans can do little about—the proposed regulation touches on every aspect of the transmission mechanism of the artificial liquidity boom in Europe.

Specific regulatory norms suggested by the EU include higher and tighter capital and liquidity requirements for all banks operating in Europe, including European units of American banks. These regulations would make it more expensive to package and sell products like MBSs in Europe, and thus create a hurdle for the further evolution of securitization. In the US, banks as a rule do not face capital charges related to assets they securitize, but must set aside capital for assets that remain on their books. There are no proposals that we are aware of to change that state of affairs.[53]

Another crucial issue for Europe's roadmap to better financial governance is the regulation of credit-rating agencies. According to Charles McGreevy, EU Commissioner for internal market and services, it is doubtful that strengthening the voluntary framework established by the International Organization of Securities Commissions' code is an appropriate response to a crisis of this magnitude.[54] McGreevy sought to propose a registration and external-oversight regime for the rating agencies, whereby

---

51 Including, crucially, accounting rules which have been cited as a major factor behind the undervaluation of risks.

52 C. McCreevy, "Regulation and Supervision after the Credit Crunch," Speech to the Public Affairs Ireland Conference, Dublin, July 4, 2008, pp. 4–5.

53 Predictably, banking groups and associations, led by the British Bankers' Association are objecting to the proposed requirements. Among their complaints: the rules would prevent the securitization market from recovering, and would stymie lending (http://remington-work.blogspot.com).

54 McCreevy, "Regulation and Supervision," p. 5. He noted that the IOSCO Code of Conduct to which the rating agencies signed up had not produced the desired effects.

European regulators will supervise the policies and procedures related to the work of credit-rating agencies, and, critically, aim to make the ratings market more open. Reforms to the corporate and internal governance of rating agencies will also be included.[55]

Condemning the regulators for what he felt was their ignorance about the nature of financial innovation, McCreevy called on European authorities to ensure that financial supervisors will have at their disposal sufficient resources and expertise to keep up with financial innovation and to challenge the CRAs in the right areas, on the right issues, at the right time.[56] Overall, McCreevy emphasized the need for Europe to take the lead in designing a regulatory response to the crisis.

The rise of the euro

McCreevy is not alone. In December 2007, Italy's finance minister, Tommaso Padoa-Schioppa argued that the turmoil showed the need for a European rule book for banking and more powers at the EU level to supervise pan-European banks.[57] The idea of Europe taking the lead in setting up a new regime of financial governance may raise a few eyebrows. Europe is riddled with its own problems: high costs associated with enlargement, the risks of higher inflation and unemployment in many states, a stronger euro and thus weaker exports, housing bubbles in countries like the UK and Spain, and, according to recent prognoses, negative growth in 2008–09.

In addition, the European financial architecture is highly fragmented. The EU's post-Crisis initiatives for setting up a pan-European financial regulator have already met with strong opposition from the UK: the City of London is keen to protect its peculiar unregulated position as a global financial centre. Moreover, Europe does not speak with one voice on financial and monetary regulations, and is divided between the highly regulated continental states and their "offshore" finance brethren operating chiefly through London, Luxembourg, Switzerland and Ireland. Indeed, the large European banks tend to buy and sell complex derivatives through subsidiaries in London, and offshore satellite locations that

---

55 Ibid.
56 Ibid.
57 He also pointed out the lack of an EU crisis management mechanism: "Even with signs of a clear risk of contagion, no common analysis of the situation, no sharing of confidential information, no coordinated communication and no emergency meetings appear to have taken place among EU supervisors."

have developed in British dependencies such as the Channel Islands, the Cayman Islands and Bermuda. The UK has always maintained much looser financial regulation and shows no sign of changing its stance. The Irish "No" to the proposed European constitution, ostensibly a vote of no confidence in the so-called European super-state project, in reality ensured the continuing development of Dublin's International Financial Centre, an offshore entity currently home to financial assets worth about ten times the Irish GDP.[58]

There are other important issues to be considered. As Europe tightens up its rules, the more lenient capital regime of the American Financial System (if sustained) may divert a share of European financial operations to the US market, just as the Tax Equalization Act drove American banks into European offshore markets in the 1960s.[59] In addition, achieving a coordinated transatlantic regulatory response in matters of finance is a tall order: this had been shown already by the problematic implementation of the Basel II Accord before the Crisis, and the divergence in regulatory responses to the Financial Crisis by the Anglo-Saxon and European systems has made this even more apparent.[60]

The combination of these factors suggests that the European Commission's ambition to take the lead in guiding the new transatlantic regime of financial governance may bear little fruit. Historically the EU, while economically powerful, has been politically feeble—unable or unwilling to stand up to the Americans. The current conjuncture is no exception. Facing an imminent recession and inflation—or, in the worst case scenario, stagflation—the European Central Bank (ECB) has maintained its traditional monetary stance, taking the lead in raising interest rates, to the displeasure of some key member states such as France. In light of our analysis above, the response seems almost pathetic, ensuring that European taxpayers bear a significant share of the burden brought on by the Crisis. Not only do they shoulder a large share of the costs, they also are likely to end up in a deep recession.

Yet, paradoxically, and perhaps unwittingly, in the long run

58   J. Steward, "Fiscal Incentives, Corporate Structure and Financial Aspects of Treasury Management," *Accounting Forum*, 2005, 29 (27).
59   R. Palan, *The Offshore World*, Ithaca: Cornell University Press, 2004.
60   For an excellent analysis of the history and current agenda of transatlantic approaches to financial regulation see A. Singer, *Regulating Capital: Setting Standards for the International Financial System*, Ithaca and London: Cornell University Press, 2007, Chapter 5.

this position may have considerable geopolitical implications, since the actions of the ECB are likely to strengthen the position of the euro as a global reserve currency. According to a recent ECB report, the global use of euro banknotes has been on the rise. The cumulative net total shipped by banks beyond the eurozone had expanded noticeably—taking the total to more than €70 billion ($110 billion, £56 billion) by the end of 2007. The actual total, counting other ways of shifting cash, was probably significantly higher.[61] (Officially, the ECB does not seek to promote the euro's international use; attempting to downplay the significance of this trend, therefore, the ECB argued that recent rises in the share of euro holdings were almost entirely due to the rising value of the currency.)[62] In the meantime, the policy position of the Federal Reserve, true to tradition, has been to deal with the Crisis by injecting more dollars into the system. This has caused sharp swings in the value of the dollar, which, combined with the crisis within the Fed itself, may further weaken the dollar as a global reserve currency.[63]

CONCLUSION

If our observations are correct, then one likely impact of the current developments stands out. The relative rise of the euro in importance, combined with the likelihood of stricter regulatory regimes in Europe, brings us to a somewhat unexpected conclusion. It suggests that the hidden subsidies to US consumers may—if not dry out entirely—at the very least slow down considerably. This, in turn, implies that the next US-generated financial boom may not be as big as the last one, in proportion to the overall size of the North Atlantic economies, and hence that the eventual and inevitable meltdown may not be as dangerous as this one. This

---

61 Monitoring the use of the euro in official reserves is hard because many countries do not reveal details of their holdings. The ECB's study was based on International Monetary Fund data, which covers only about two-thirds of total foreign-exchange reserves, and excludes China. See R. Atkins, "ECB plays down rise in euro's global status," *Financial Times*, July 10, 2008.

62 At constant exchange rates, the share of the euro in global foreign reserves had fallen by one percentage point between December 2006 and December 2007, the ECB said.

63 Our view is consistent with the analysis of the longer-term structural implications of the current Crisis by George Soros (*The New Paradigm for Financial Markets*, pp. 124–8), although he is more optimistic about the prospects of European recovery.

observation goes against some grim predictions of skeptics who believe that the solution to this Crisis is already sowing the seeds of an even bigger crisis in the next seven to ten years.[64] In our view, the current meltdown is the last big throw of a declining American hegemony; the next—most likely, bigger—crisis will be generated, we believe, somewhere else.

---

64   See, for instance, "Two Fed Bank Presidents Warn About Lending to Securities Firms," *New York Times*, June 6, 2008.

9

THE POLITICS OF
SMOKE AND MIRRORS

The G-20 London Summit and the Restoration of Neoliberal Development

Susanne Soederberg

Since the Global Credit Meltdown of 2008—the worst financial crisis since the 1930s—global policy-makers have been scrambling to deal with its fallout. The monetary and fiscal policy response to the crisis—taken and planned—represents the largest stimulus effort in modern times.[1] Despite these efforts, the Crisis continues to erode wealth across the globe on an unprecedented scale. The International Monetary Fund (IMF) expects that debt resulting from the current Economic Crisis may reach a staggering $4 trillion, of which two-thirds will be incurred by banks.[2] The latter, and other financial institutions, have been the main beneficiaries of the bail-out packages, as opposed to the poor and middle classes, who will be forced to live with the devastating consequences of the crisis.[3] While the advanced industrial countries may be at the center of the storm, they are not the only victims of the crisis.

---

1 Institute of International Finance, Letter issued by Chairman Charles H. Dallara to His Excellency Dr. Youssef Boutros-Ghali, Chairman of the International Monetary and Financial Committee [of the IMF], April 13, 2009, Washington, DC: IIF.
2 IMF, *Global Financial Stability Report: Responding to the Financial Crisis and Measuring Systemic Risks*, Washington, DC: IMF.
3 D. Harvey, *A Brief History of Neoliberalism*, Oxford: Oxford University Press, 2005; S. Soederberg, *Corporate Power and Ownership in Contemporary Capitalism: The Politics of Resistance and Domination*, London: Routledge, 2009.

At the time of writing, the Crisis "has already driven more than 50 million people into extreme poverty, particularly women and children" in the developing world.[4] Unsurprisingly, the Crisis and the manner in which it has been dealt with have elicited anger and frustration from taxpayers and investors, expressed in countless protests across the globe.

Notwithstanding government officials' threats of imposing stronger forms of financial regulation,[5] global solutions to the Crisis have not been commensurate with its devastating effects on humanity and the environment. A case in point is the outcome of the much-anticipated London Summit of the Group of 20 (G-20) in April 2009. The G-20 is composed of the finance ministers and Central Bank governors of the world's most "systematically important" developed and emerging market economies.[6] The members of the G-20 gathered in London to hammer out ways to repair, restore, and strengthen the existing system. Rhetoric aside, the proposals tabled at the London Summit neither introduced rigorous, state-led regulation of global finance nor represented a departure from previous international efforts to steady the world economy, most notably the "New International Financial Architecture" (NIFA) of 1999.[7] The NIFA, it will be recalled, was a global initiative aimed at repairing, strengthening, and restoring growth and stability in the international financial system in the aftermath of the spate of financial crises that swept across emerging market economies during the 1990s. Like its successor at the London Summit, the NIFA was essentially composed of market-based forms of regulation.

Two basic, yet unaddressed, questions emerge: (1) What exactly is being repaired and strengthened, and who benefits from these efforts? Put another way, why restore a system that has not only wreaked high levels of social and economic havoc, but has also largely failed to benefit the majority of the world's population since the early 1980s? And (2) Why have the similarities between the

---

4 Development Committee Communiqué, Joint Ministerial Committee of the Boards of Governors of the Bank and the Fund on the Transfer of Real Resources to Developing Countries, April 26, 2009, Washington, www.imf.org (accessed on April 28, 2009).
5 "Super-Sarko's plans for the world," *Financial Times*, October 20, 2008.
6 S. Soederberg, *The Politics of the New International Financial Architecture: Reimposing Neoliberal Domination in the Global South* London: Zed, 2004.
7 Ibid.

London Summit and its predecessor, the NIFA, been downplayed by policy-makers? Similar to the sleight of hand of magicians who make objects appear and disappear by manipulating mirrors amid a confusing burst of smoke, I argue that the so-called broad, sweeping reforms tabled at the G-20 London Summit were primarily designed to disappear fundamental critiques of the capitalist system and magically restore neoliberal rule, primarily by infusing massive amounts of capital into the financial system in the face of the ongoing and deepening levels of human suffering and economic instability. Moreover, the disappearance of the NIFA from official discourse was a political decision that aimed not only to create the illusion of innovation at the London Summit, but also, and more importantly, to draw attention away from the latter's continuity with its predecessor, which has failed to meet its objectives of curtailing crises and achieving widespread sustainable growth and stability.

By taking the above position, this chapter seeks to provide a more critical understanding of re-regulation than has appeared thus far in the mainstream international political-economy literature.[8] These debates essentially fail to grasp the point that without fundamentally challenging and reorganising the existing relations of domination in the global capitalist system, the re-regulation of the international financial system—including the symbolic attempts of democratic representation by including certain countries and actors from the developing world—amounts to nothing more than bolstering the neoliberal order and its class-based interests.[9]

This chapter is organized into three main sections. The first section supplies an overview of the NIFA and its successor, the G-20 reforms of 2009, or what I refer to as "NIFA-lite." The discussion then identifies two key "illusions" that underpin both initiatives, so as to reveal the continuity of neoliberal rule. Having established the connection between the NIFA and G-20 reforms, the second section examines the state of global capitalism over the span of NIFA's lifetime by focusing on the deepening contradictions

---

8 See for example G. R. D. Underhill, "Global Financial Architecture, Legitimacy, and Representation: Voice for Emerging Markets," GARNET Policy Brief, No. 3, January 2007; R. Hall and T. Biersteker, eds, *The Emergence of Private Authority in Global Governance*, Cambridge: Cambridge University Press, 2002.

9 For a further critique see Soederberg, *Politics of the New International Financial Architecture*.

within neoliberal-led development. The aim of this section is to reveal the neoliberal and capitalist nature of the NIFA, so as to shed critical light on the appeal for "NIFA-lite" by the world's political elite and capitalist classes. The final section concludes by discussing some implications of the argument presented here.

REPOLITICIZING THE PROMISES
OF GLOBAL FINANCIAL STABILITY

The former New International Financial Architecture

Before discussing the main features of the NIFA, it is useful to identify some of its premises, so as to help us understand the ways in which it is connected to the reform initiatives of the London Summit.

According to official accounts, the main cause of the financial crises of the 1990s (e.g. Mexico's Peso Debacle in late 1994–95, the East Asian Crisis in 1997, followed by crises in Brazil and Russia in 1998) was not located in the speculative nature of largely deregulated financial flows, but instead in imprudent policy choices of Third World governments, as well as the lack of transparency and accountability of market actors in the developing world. The NIFA sought to strengthen, as opposed to question, the standard economic assumption that free capital mobility leads to growth. It suggested that while the state should refrain from playing a major role in the market, governments should complement and protect the infrastructure in which markets operate by implementing good governance policies. Specifically, such policies should primarily be aimed at encouraging perfect information between contracting parties in the marketplace.[10] Reflecting the underlying tenets of the post-Washington Consensus, the architects of the NIFA sought to facilitate market transparency without imposing state-led regulations. The creators of the NIFA opted for voluntary principles and market-based rules as opposed to legal reforms restricting capital flows.[11]

The standard economic theory underpinning the above policy assumes that when left to their own devices (read: free capital mobility and low levels of regulation), private capital flows are central to development to the extent that they flow from capital-

10 Ibid.
11 Ibid.

abundant countries to capital-scarce (developing) countries.[12] The
basic assumption is that capital flows will bring about efficiency
gains and lead to growth, which in turn will, through rational
market mechanisms, "trickle down" to the rest of the population.
To attract and retain foreign capital, the onus is on governments
and firms in developing countries ensuring that they adhere to
the "correct" (market-led) policy and institutional frameworks.
Correct policies reflect, among other things, minimal state
intervention in the market. The reason for this position is that the
state is seen as representing not only a direct source of inefficiency
(i.e. rent-seeking behavior), but also as encouraging "wasteful use
of resources to gain essentially corrupt advantage."[13]

Reality appears to contradict economic theory, however.
"Since 1997 developing countries have made increasingly large
transfers to developed countries. In addition, private capital
flows to developing countries have been concentrated in a small
group of large middle-income countries," otherwise known as
"systematically important" emerging markets—as opposed to
those countries in most need of financing.[14] Indeed, financial
liberalization has led to the "privatization" of global development
finance. Private capital flows such as foreign direct investments
(FDI) and foreign portfolio investments (FPI) have overshadowed
official financial flows in the forms of bilateral and multilateral
loans and aid over the past ten years.[15] Capital flows, especially
FPI, have done little to smooth domestic expenditure, however.
Instead, "private capital flows seem to have contributed to making
it more volatile. In many cases they have produced costly currency
and financial crises that have reversed development gains."[16]

Seen from this perspective, it is not surprising that key global
players such as the IMF and countries that benefited greatly from
financial liberalization, most notably the United States, did not call
into question either the short-term and highly speculative nature
of financial markets or the absence of regulatory mechanisms

12 J. A. Ocampo, J. Kregel and S. Griffith-Jones, eds, *International Finance and
Development*, London: Zed, 2007.
13 B. Fine, "The New Development Economics," in K. S. Jomo and B. Fine, eds,
The New Development Economics: After the Washington Consensus, London:
Zed, 2006, p. 5.
14 Ocampo et al., *International Finance and Development*, p. 17.
15 *Global Development Finance: The Globalization of Corporate Finance in
Developing Countries*, Washington, DC: World Bank Group 2007.
16 Ibid.

at the global level as potential sources of the crises in emerging markets during the 1990s.[17] Instead, international policy-makers, led by the general directive of the United States, created the G-20 to help repair, restore and strengthen, as opposed to radically alter (e.g. through the introduction of capital controls and other forms of state-led regulation) the existing financial system. The G-20 was widely celebrated as an inclusive project that comprised the powerful Group of 7 (G-7) industrialized countries, the IMF, and the World Bank, and which, for the first time, brought on board several "systematically important" (read: profitable) emerging market economies such as Brazil, India, Russia and China.

Another major component of the NIFA was the Financial Stability Forum (FSF). The latter was seen as an important venue through which the central banks and finance ministries of select countries within the G-20 could exchange information and work toward financial supervision and surveillance to prevent future crises. To this end, the FSF created twelve voluntary international codes and standards, which are monitored by several key international organizations such as the IMF and World Bank. These standards and codes, which are known as the Reports on the Observances of Standards and Codes (ROSCs), are based on good-governance practices ranging from accounting to corporate governance. It should be underlined that, although these standards and codes are said to reflect international norms, they tend to replicate the Anglo-American version of neoliberalism, which accords a high value to minimal state intervention and high exposure to market forces.[18] Taken together, the institutional and governance innovations that comprised the NIFA were lauded by its supporters as an important policy corrective to the economistic focus of global development finance.[19]

The G-20 reforms or NIFA-lite?

Almost a decade after the construction of the NIFA, the managing director of the IMF, Dominique Strauss-Kahn, stated that the global financial architecture had failed to adapt to the needs of

17 Soederberg, *Politics of the New International Financial Architecture*.
18 Ibid.
19 B. Eichengreen, *Toward a New International Financial Architecture: A Practical Post-Asia Approach*, Washington, DC: Institute for International Economics, 1999.

twenty-first-century globalized markets.[20] Without engaging specifically or directly with the NIFA or its underlying premises, the reforms put forward by the G-20 at the 2009 London Summit revolved around three similar themes: reforming growth and jobs, strengthening financial supervision and regulation, and strengthening global financial institutions. The IMF was granted a central role in crisis management and mitigation largely by trebling resources available to the lending agency to $750 billion.[21] Given the neoliberal orthodoxy within which the IMF operates, it is not surprising that the basic aim of this new infusion of money is to support neoliberal restructuring in the global South. The creation of the IMF's new Flexible Credit Line (FCL) is a case in point. According to the London Summit communiqué, the FCL and the IMF's "reformed lending and conditionality framework . . . will enable the IMF to ensure that its facilities address effectively the underlying causes of countries' balance of payments financing needs, particularly the withdrawal of external capital flows to the banking and corporate sectors."[22]

Another major Summit initiative aimed at strengthening the financial system was the creation of the Financial Stability Board (FSB), the successor to the FSF. Given the fact that the IMF was a major backer of the FSB, it is useful to discuss the Fund's interpretation of the Global Credit Crisis in order to grasp the reasoning for yet another oversight body. According to the IMF, the main cause of the current crisis is market imperfections (lack of sufficient information), which have, in turn, enticed a few bad apples to engage too heavily in high-risk ventures. Put another way, the Crisis was brought about by the failure of existing governance structures to ensure that markets function in a highly transparent manner—that is, in a fashion in which all actors have sufficient information on which to base their decisions to buy or sell. To correct this problem and thereby reduce uncertainty for market actors, the IMF pressed for new disclosure guidelines and frequent asset valuations, which in turn resulted in the creation

---

20 "Quick, Forceful, Cooperative Action Needed on Crisis—IMF," *IMF Survey*, October 9, 2008.
21 IMF, "The G-20 Summit: Outcomes and Next Steps," *IMF and Civil Society*, April 15, 2009, available at www.imf.org (accessed on April 26, 2009).
22 London Summit, "Global Plan for Recovery and Reform: The Communiqué from the London Summit," April 2, 2009, available at www.londonsummit.gov. uk (accessed on April 5, 2009).

of the FSB.[23] According to the G-20 communiqué, the FSB is to have a strengthened mandate that will transcend that of the FSF, although the details of this stronger mandate remain unclear. The FSB will be somewhat more inclusive than the FSF, as it will include all G-20 countries, FSF members, Spain, and the European Commission. It is expected that the FSB will collaborate with the IMF to provide early warning of macroeconomic and financial risks and suggest actions needed to deal with them. The FSB is mandated to reshape the regulatory system by extending oversight to all "*systemically important* financial institutions, instruments and markets," which will include, for the first time, "*systemically important* hedge funds."[24] Finally, the IMF and FSB are to work closely together to create and execute an Early Warning Exercise to help mitigate the economic damage caused by a potential crisis.

Cutting through the smoke and mirrors

Cutting through the smoke and mirrors of the G-20 reforms involves identifying two seemingly conventional assumptions underpinning the official debates. The political nature of these core assumptions, or illusions, as I refer to them below, and their underlying connection to neoliberal-led development, have been distorted by the technical trappings of the predominantly economistic treatment of the Crisis.

The first illusion of the G-20 London Summit has been the frequent use of the word "regulation" without actually committing to a clear definition. The deception is intentional, as the term conjures up ideas of some sort of rule-based system involving legal structures, and thereby states to help enforce these rules. Yet, it is clear from the above discussion that, like the NIFA, the G-20 reforms involve updating, especially with regard to greater oversight, existing voluntary and market-led regulatory schemes, as opposed to creating mandatory, rule-based regimes. It is important to note that recent experiences have revealed that regulation, even rule-based, state-backed regulation, can often be deceiving. As I have argued in detail

23 IMF, *Global Financial Stability Report—Financial Stress and Deleveraging: Macro-Financial Implications and Policy*, Washington, DC: IMF, 2008, p. xiv.
24 Ibid.

elsewhere,[25] the Sarbanes-Oxley Act, which was an attempt by the George W. Bush administration to impose the "most far-sweeping regulatory reforms since the New Deal" in the wake of Enron-style debacles in the US, has had the effect of naturalizing market-led governance in both the corporate and financial sectors. Seen from this perspective, the meaning of "more regulation," as used by international policy-makers at the London Summit, refers largely to a voluntary, market-led regime as opposed to state-led reforms. An open letter by a key lobby group for the world's most powerful financial interests, the Institute of International Finance (IIF), also supports this view. According to the IIF—in keeping with the assumption of market imperfections and the lack of adequate information—regulation should be understood as involving closer and more frequent consultation between private- and public-sector actors to help facilitate new initiatives such as the FSB–IMF Early Warning Exercise.[26] The preference for market-led forms of regulation is further reflected in the neoliberal ethos of the London Summit, which focuses on key measures aimed at building trust for consumers and investors, stability, and economic growth through further market-led reforms. This is clearly articulated in the following quotation furnished by the G-20: "We believe that the only sure foundation for sustainable globalization and rising prosperity for all is an open world economy based on market principles, effective regulation, and strong global institutions."[27]

A second illusion of the London Summit has been the disappearance of history and politics from policy discourse. The convenient disappearance of the NIFA by the summiteers is a case in point. The failure to draw links between the London Summit's 2009 proposals and the NIFA, especially with regard to the latter's limits in monitoring and preventing the 2008 crisis, not to mention Argentina's Sovereign Debt Fiasco in 2001, amounts to more than benign neglect on the part of the G-20. Rather, there are important political and class-based considerations that underpin this selective memory, which serve to augment the apparent novelty of the reforms tabled at the London Summit,

---

25 Soederberg, *Corporate Power and Ownership in Contemporary Capitalism.*
26 Institute of International Finance, letter issued by Chairman Charles H. Dallara.
27 London Summit, "The Global Plan for Recovery and Reform," available at www.G-20.org.

such as the freshly minted FSB, and to distract attention from the ineffectiveness of the NIFA. The latter, like the G-20 reforms, had been carefully designed to restore and thus reproduce the status quo regarding the existing relations of power and free movement of private capital flows, and, more fundamentally, the uneven and exploitative nature of global capital accumulation. By erasing the existence of the NIFA from the discourse around the G-20 reforms, global policy-makers have also been able to downplay the inability of market-led reform, including the central tenet of free capital mobility, to deliver on its promises of stable forms of economic growth and general prosperity across the globe, particularly for the developing world. It has also deflected attention away from the fact that the NIFA has benefited primarily wealthy nations and capitalist interests, from both the global North and global South, at the expense of the majority of the world's population,[28] a point explored in more detail in the next section.

THE DEEPENING PARADOXES OF NEOLIBERAL-LED DEVELOPMENT

Since the G-20 reforms are an extension, both in terms of policy and ideology, of the NIFA, it is useful to explore what the latter has accomplished in terms of its promises of growth and stability via market freedom, especially with regard to the global South. In doing so, we can also begin to identify who benefits from the restoration of neoliberal-led capitalism, especially in terms of market-led forms of financial deregulation. I approach this brief historical overview by drawing on my earlier work, wherein I identify three interrelated components that characterize the paradoxes and social power undergirding the NIFA and, by extension, the reforms tabled at the London Summit:[29] (1) the neoliberal nature of global capitalism, which has taken the form of financialization; (2) the complex and interdependent relationship between the US and free capital mobility; and (3) the growing political and social insecurity caused by free capital mobility in the global South.

---

28 Harvey, *Brief History*.
29 Soederberg, *Politics of the New International Financial Architecture*.

Financialization and the ongoing contradictions of the credit system

According to Gerald Epstein, the term "financialization" can be used to capture the growing influence of financial markets and institutions on economic growth and development since the late 1970s.[30] However, this situation is not, as neoliberal ideologues would have us believe, created by an inevitable or natural set of external forces beyond political control. Nor is it merely a narrative or set of voluntary performances largely devoid of structures and paradoxes rooted in, albeit not determined by, social relations of capitalism and the bourgeois state, as some cultural theorists have argued.[31] Instead, financialization has been socially constructed and reproduced through relations of power within the wider constraints posed by the crisis-prone, uneven, and highly exploitative nature of global capitalism.[32] One chief contradiction of global capitalism is the underlying tendency of capitalism to overaccumulation. Put simply, the latter is a "condition where surpluses of capital lie idle with no profitable outlets in sight."[33] When crises emerge, capitalists and states respond swiftly by increasing levels of economic exploitation over labor and the environment and establishing new forms of political domination to legitimate, discipline, and naturalize their power. One of the key features of capitalism's resiliency, most notably its ability to continue to expand, even in times of crisis, is the credit system. This system, which lies at the heart of financialization, has played a central role in facilitating the expanded reproduction of capitalism, not only in everyday life, but also, and especially in times of crises, when it has historically been marked by strategies of speculation, fraud and predation.[34] The debt-led forms of capital accumulation that have come to shape the economies of many countries, and most notably the US, are a case in point.[35]

30 G. Epstein, *Financialization and the World Economy*, Cheltenham, UK: Edward Elgar, 2005.
31 See, for example, I. Erturk et al., eds, *Financialization at Work: Key Texts and Commentary*, London: Routledge, 2007.
32 K. Marx, *Capital, Volume 3*, London: Penguin Classics, 1991.
33 D. Harvey, *The New Imperialism*, Oxford: Oxford University Press, 2003, p. 149.
34 R. Luxemburg, *The Accumulation of Capital*, London: Routledge, 2003.
35 Soederberg, *Corporate Power and Ownership in Contemporary Capitalism*.

Contrary to what is suggested by the discourses surrounding NIFA, the credit system is not merely a sum of economic transactions. Instead, as Susan Strange notes, it is marked by relations of power: the "power to create credit implies the power to allow or to deny other people the possibility of spending today and paying back tomorrow."[36] It is necessary to go beyond Strange's insight, however, to stress that the credit system and the power relations therein are integral features of capital accumulation. As such, the credit system appears to have the potential to resolve all of the imbalances to which capitalism is prone, such as overaccumulation of capital. The problem is, as Marx noted, that the credit system also internalizes these contradictions and often acts to heighten rather than diminish the paradoxes of capitalism.[37] Moreover, it should be underlined that this power in the credit system is not a natural feature of the market but is both constructed and guaranteed by the capitalist state and by international organizations that comprise neoliberal projects such as the NIFA.[38] For example, the $4 trillion government-sponsored bailout to support banks and restart money markets, primarily in the US and Europe, was an attempt not only to avert a global recession but also, and more generally, to guarantee conditions for the expanded reproduction of capital. As I have argued elsewhere, the power relations within the credit system are, like capitalism itself, highly uneven (who gets credit and on what conditions) and disciplinary (capital flight or strikes, high-risk premiums for poor credit ratings, and so forth) in nature.[39]

Against the backdrop of the highly precarious debt-led accumulation of neoliberal globalization, there have been many features of the predatory and speculative nature of the global credit system that have served to widen and deepen the levels of economic insecurity across the global North and global South over the past decade. Two features are worth noting here. First, pension and mutual funds have played a central role in driving and expanding financialization. These funds are valued at some $24.6 trillion, with a ratio of Organization of Economic Cooperation and Development (OECD) pension fund assets to OECD gross

36 S. Strange, *States and Markets*, London: Pinter, 1994, p. 90.
37 D. Harvey, *Limits to Capital*, London: Verso, 1999.
38 P. Bourdieu, *The Social Structures of the Economy*, Cambridge, UK: Polity Press, 2005.
39 Soederberg, *Politics of the New International Financial Architecture*.

domestic product of nearly 73 percent in 2006, and above 100 percent in a few countries.[40] Due to ongoing privatization strategies, we have seen a shift from more secure, defined-benefit pension plans to market-based, defined-contribution pension schemes, which has meant that an increasing number of people, in both rich and poor countries, have become dependent on the economic performance of financial markets for their old-age security. This phenomenon reflects what Richard Minns refers to as "social-security capital," comprising all deferred wages or salaries that enter the credit system in the form of company stocks and bonds.[41] Social-security capital has become an important source of capital for corporations both in the core and at the periphery.

Seen from the above perspective, there exists a growing interdependency of social-security capital and the global financial system, including publicly traded corporations. This dependency is both asymmetrical and disciplinary in nature. That is to say, international financial markets and actors wield far more power over decision-making processes, and gain more from deregulated markets, than the middle and working classes; but international financial markets and actors also wield enormous discipline over societies, as workers (skilled and unskilled) are socialized into relying on the market to deliver economic security in their old age.[42] With each crisis and subsequent downturn, however, social security capital across the globe has taken a considerable hit, leading to widespread insecurity. The latter is said to occur when individuals and communities are exposed to adverse events, and to arise from their inability to cope with and recover from the downside losses.[43] According to the United Nations (UN) publication *World Economic and Social Survey 2007: Development in an Ageing World*, "Eighty per cent of the world's population do not have sufficient protection in old age to enable them to face health, disability and income risks . . . In developing countries alone, about 342 million older persons currently lack adequate income security."[44] The asymmetrical dependency

---

40 OECD, *Pension Markets in Focus*, Paris: OECD, 2008.
41 R. Minns, *The Cold War: Stock Markets versus Pensions*, London: Verso, 2001.
42 Soederberg, *Corporate Power and Ownership in Contemporary Capitalism.*
43 United Nations, *World Economic and Social Survey 2008: Overcoming Economic Insecurity*, New York: United Nations, 2008.
44 R. Blackburn, "A Global Pension Plan," *New Left Review*, 2007, II/47, p. 71.

between Wall Street and social-security capital expresses itself in many ways: from the high fees charged by money managers to the $700 billion-plus bail-out of investment banks and insurance companies that engaged in predatory and speculative activities with pension savings. At a more fundamental level, asymmetries manifest in the ability of the powerful to define and select risk, while others do the risking.[45]

The asymmetrical dependence between social-security capital and financial markets is aggravated by a second characteristic of financialization, namely the increasing leveraging and speculation that has emerged over the past decade—not from the natural evolution of the market, but instead largely through state design, i.e. the decision to adhere to the principle of minimal state intervention in capital markets. The credit system normally operates with a certain level of fictitious capital—that is, a flow of money capital not backed by any commodity transaction, such as highly leveraged credit derivatives and strategies such as short-selling, which have little to do with the realities of the productive economy and have played an increasingly large role in both the Enron-style debacles at the beginning of the new millennium and the subprime mortgage scandal of 2007. However, reliance on this form of capital has risen to alarming levels.[46] The market for credit-default swaps, described as insurance contracts on bonds and other assets that are intended to pay off if and when those assets default, is one example. Having mushroomed over the past several years, these swaps lie at the centre of the 2008 Credit Crisis. The swaps do not require public disclosure and do not carry any legal requirement to report to the Securities and Exchange Commission (SEC). According to the Chair of the SEC, as of 2008 there was about $55 trillion in credit-default swaps outstanding, which amounts to more than the gross domestic product of all countries combined, and more than twelve times the total amount of official reserves in the developing world.[47] This also pales in comparison to the $750 billion in additional funding for the IMF tabled at the G-20 London Summit. Interestingly, the SEC has not suggested doing away with these swaps or subjecting them to state-led regulation; but instead, and mirroring the above

---

45 S. Žižek, "Don't Just Do Something, Talk," *London Review of Books*, October 9, 2008 available at www.lrb.co.uk.
46 Harvey, *New Imperialism*, p. 265ff.
47 United Nations, *World Economy and Social Survey*.

neoliberal premises of the NIFA, it has recommended measures that promote greater transparency.

The ongoing perils of American empire

The second feature of the NIFA relates to the privileged status of the United States in the global financial system due to the uncontested role of the US dollar as the world's trading and, more significantly, reserve currency.[48] This position has allowed the US state, as well as global capitalist interests linked to it, to maintain structural power through what I have labeled as "imposed leadership"— which involves control not only over other countries, especially the global South and the institutions and policies of the NIFA, but also over international lending institutions such as the IMF, where the US wields veto power over other countries through influencing international monetary and credit arrangements.[49] Structural power allows the US to "exercise purchasing power and thus influence markets for production," and also gives the US "the power to manage or mismanage the currency in which credit is denominated."[50] Since the demise of the Bretton Woods System in 1971—and the shift to freely floating exchange rates, the eradication of capital controls and low levels of financial regulation—the structural power of the US has been underpinned by a deep-seated paradox, or what I have referred to elsewhere as the Frankenstein Factor, as it captures the similar symbiotic yet mutually destructive relationship between Dr. Frankenstein and his monster.[51]

On the one hand, the relationship between the structural power of the United States and free capital mobility is mutually beneficial. As international financial markets grow in size and power, so does the US economy, which, since the 1980s, has absorbed the majority of these flows to feed its debt-driven accumulation strategy. The structural power of the US is buttressed by its ability to capture massive amounts of global capital flows (largely in the form of US Treasury Bills and bonds and corporate securities) from the rest of the world, especially from Asian surplus countries, most

---

48 See Gowan's contribution in this volume.
49 Soederberg, *Politics of the New International Financial Architecture*; Soederberg, *Global Governance in Question*.
50 Strange, *States and Markets*, p. 90.
51 Soederberg, *Politics of the New International Financial Architecture*.

notably China. As Robert Wade argues, this privileged position has allowed the US, over the past ten years, to spend 5 to 7 percent more than it produces and import twice as much as it exports.[52]

In addition, the United States has reaped immense corollary benefits, including fast growth, low unemployment, and easy financing for its military activities in Iraq and elsewhere, even with tax cuts. The developing world has also been contributing to debt-fueled growth in the US. According to the UN, net transfers of financial resources from developing to developed countries from 1997 to 2005 amounted to more than half a trillion dollars. While these transfers were initially the result of primarily debt-related capital outflows from the global South, they have come to reflect increasingly large foreign-exchange reserve accumulation taking place in many developing countries, particularly Asia. Such reserves, for example, have increased "from 2–3 percent of gross domestic product in the 1980s to about 5 percent in the 1990s and about 12 percent in the current decade."[53]

There is also a dark side to the growing reliance of the US economy on the constant inflow of global capital: the viability of US structural power and, by extension, its debt-led accumulation regime, is heavily reliant not only, as Peter Gowan suggests, on the US dollar as the chosen reserve currency, but also, and more fundamentally, on the health and stability of financial markets, including its own.[54] With each crisis, more and more people are dispossessed of their old-age savings, homes, livelihoods, and so forth, which makes it increasingly difficult for free-market ideologues to justify the benefits of free capital mobility. In the wake of the 2008 Global Credit Crisis, for instance, we may see a reversal in the use of the US dollar as the preferred reserve currency in the developing world, which could change the current direction of net capital transfers. According to some observers, "reserve accumulation in several countries in Asia now appears to exceed the requirement for self-insurance, raising questions about the balance of costs and benefits of additional accumulation, especially if such reserves are invested in low-yielding assets and in the US dollar, which has been, and is expected to continue

52 R. Wade, "The First-World Debt Crisis of 2007–2010 in Global Perspective," *Challenge*, 2008, 51 (4), pp. 23–54.
53 United Nations, *World Economy and Social Survey*, p. 12.
54 P. Gowan, *The Global Gamble: Washington's Faustian Bid for World Dominance*, London: Verso, 1999.

to depreciate."[55] Mexico and Brazil, Latin America's biggest economies, have sought to stop the depreciation of their currencies by selling reserves, most of which were denominated in US dollars. The Mexican Central Bank, for instance, moved to auction off its reserves of $2.5 billion after the peso fell to a record low of 14 against the US dollar in October 2008.[56]

Another development closely related to the foreign reserve build-up has been the explosion of internal public debt levels mainly in middle-income countries. Mexico's internal public debt levels, for instance, have been hovering around 50 percent of its gross domestic product, which has been further frustrated by persistent trade deficits.[57] It is thus little wonder that Mexico was first in the queue to request a $47 billion loan from the IMF's newly minted Flexible Credit Line to help deal with the aftershocks of the crisis.[58] According to one observer, "servicing of the internal public debt [in the developing world] in 2007 amounted to $600 billion—in other words, triple the cost of servicing the external debt. Total servicing of external and internal public debt exceeds the astronomical sum of $800 billion—the amount repaid each year by public authorities in developing countries."[59] To put this figure into perspective, it would cost "only $80 billion a year over a period of 10 years—a total of $800 billion—for the entire population of these countries to have access to essential services, such as basic health care, drinking water and primary school education."[60]

The logic underpinning the IMF's proposal that developing countries turn to expansionary fiscal and monetary policies to overcome the effects of the First Word debt crisis is highly questionable on at least two counts. First, the total funding allocated to the FCL pales in comparison to the amount of capital many countries in the global South need in order to stem

55 United Nations, *World Economy and Social Survey*, p. 25.

56 "Mexico Unveils Emergency Spending," *BBC*, October 9, 2008.

57 J. Jonakin, "Contradictions of Neo-Liberal Reforms on Mexico's Balance of Payments and Labour Markets," *International Journal of Development Issues*, 2006, 5(2), pp. 93–118.

58 IMF, "IMF Approves $47 Billion Credit Line for Mexico," *IMF Survey Magazine*, April 17, 2009, available at www.imf.org (accessed on May 3, 2009).

59 E. Toussaint, "Developing Countries: Dangerous Times for the Internal Public Debt," *MRZine*, November 8, 2008, available at http://mrzine.monthlyreview. org (accessed on November 10, 2008).

60 Ibid.

the tide of the global recession. Moreover, these countries have very little wiggle-room in terms of spending their way out of the recession, especially given that Southbound private capital flows have slowed down considerably since 2008.[61] Second, within the prevailing neoliberal order there is a heavy stigma attached to the pursuit of expansionary policies by governments of the developing world, even if sanctioned by the IMF. Such policies will inevitably be interpreted by private lenders, who comprise the bulk of capital flows to the "systematically important" emerging markets, as untenable and thus imprudent, largely owing to the fact that such strategies would lead to higher levels of public indebtedness. While acceptable in the context of the advanced industrial countries, the stigma of pursuing "imprudent" (debt-driven expansionary) policies in the developing world could result in either an investment strike, or, in the best-case scenario, more expensive loans for the debtor countries through the imposition of higher-risk premiums and interest rates by international investors and creditors. Notwithstanding these two negative effects of the FCL, the short-term benefits accrued by those countries dependent on the status quo, such as the United States, is that general economic policies guiding emerging market economies remain entrenched in the market-oriented framework of neoliberalism, especially with regard to liberalized trade and financial flows.

The growing political instability and social insecurity in global finance

The third and final component of the NIFA, which has been tempered by the previous two characteristics and, more fundamentally, by the underlying nature of global capitalism, is the growing political and social insecurity caused by capital account liberalization in the global South. While the effects of allowing financial flows to move freely in and out of countries have been highly uneven across the developing world, there have been two general tendencies—neither of which has brought about the promised efficiency gains and faster growth. First, as governments of emerging markets embrace foreign portfolio investment as an important source of financing, their exposure to risk increases. As the 2008 Global Crisis has made abundantly clear, the global South continues to pay a higher price for risks associated with

---

61 London Summit, www.londonsummit.gov.uk.

US-led strategies of expanded reproduction of capital, which primarily involve the credit system. Second, to attract international creditors, which include institutional investors, governments of emerging markets must continually signal creditworthiness, such as low labor standards, balanced budgets, low taxation, favorable environmental and financial regulation, and trade deregulation— all of which have had harmful effects on the social fabric and environmental sustainability in the developing world. At a more fundamental level, this locks many countries into adherence to market discipline, instead of forging policies that would benefit their productive and social structures. In what follows, I look more closely at these two points.

Some emerging markets have used windfalls from high commodity, oil and gas prices to build up currency reserves to help buffer their economies from the devastating effects of capital flight. This strategy has entailed relatively high opportunity costs, however.[62] Reserve accumulation is associated with a high carry cost of reserves, which, according to the UN, amounts to about $100 billion. This represents a net transfer to reserve-currency countries well above what they provide in terms of Official Development Assistance (ODA). Reserve accumulation also results in forgone domestic consumption, social services and investment in the productive sector.[63] In the era of free capital mobility, many countries with weak growth and balance of payments, for example in Latin America and sub-Saharan Africa, are compelled to absorb net capital inflows into low-yielding reserve assets instead of using them for investment.[64] The fact that developing countries are seeking to amass huge foreign-currency reserves—as opposed to strong current accounts, healthy and productive workers, and a sustainable environment—to shield them from global instability, should give us cause to question the benefits assumed to derive from the unshackling of finance.

Despite the existence of $4.5 trillion in official reserves in the developing world, financial capital flows have remained highly volatile in recent decades, generating high costs for individuals and groups in both developing and developed countries, especially those relying on pension savings.[65] This precariousness of the

---

62 United Nations, *World Economy and Social Survey*, p. 76ff.
63 Ibid., p. 12.
64 Ibid., p. 28.
65 Ocampo et al., *International Finance and Development*.

global financial system was made abundantly clear with the 2008 Credit Crisis, which forced several countries—most of which were believed to possess strong economies, such as Brazil, Turkey, and South Africa—to go cap-in-hand to the IMF.[66] The point is that global capital flows have not led to growth in the productive sectors and thus the generation of secure jobs with living wages, but have rather increased economic insecurity, inequality and the (asymmetrical) dependence on unregulated financial flows. Such asymmetrical dependence is often produced by factors beyond the control of recipient countries, including shifts in monetary and fiscal policies in the core countries (e.g. high-interest-rate policies pursued by the US). Three major waves of international financial flows to (some) developing countries—i.e. the petro-dollar-driven debts of the 1970s; the portfolio and direct investment of the 1990s up to the Asian Crisis; and the subsequent portfolio and direct investment rush from 2003 to 2005—have left little doubt that private capital inflows were highly dependent on "favorable investment conditions," including the ability of foreign investors to engage in arbitrage, or taking advantage of a price differential in two different markets.[67]

In sum, over the past decade the steady expansion of capital flows linked to the predatory and speculative global credit system has not delivered on the promises made by the architects of the NIFA. Financial globalization has led to growing volatility and reversibility of capital flows to emerging market economies. Many of the poorer and smaller developing economies have been particularly affected by the growing role of private capital flows to the developing world, which has been compounded by the continual drop in ODA by wealthy countries over the past decades. Aside from several Scandinavian countries, wealthy countries have refused to provide 0.7 percent of their gross national income in the form of aid flows to the poorest countries.[68] Within the parameters of the G-20 London Summit, assistance for these countries will more than likely come primarily from funds allocated to the IMF through its Poverty Reduction and Growth Facility (PRGF) and Exogenous Shocks Facility (ESF), both of which are predicated upon austerity and structural adjustment

---

66 "Global Economy Talks Call for Greater Role for IMF," *Guardian*, October 25, 2008.
67 Ocampo et al., *International Finance and Development*, p. 2.
68 World Bank, *Global Development Finance*.

policies.[69] It should be noted that the World Bank, independent from the G-20 reforms, has established a Vulnerability Financial Facility, including the Global Food Crisis Response Program and the new Rapid Social Response Program. However, critics argue that while these programs are welcome, the funding levels are too low to adequately protect the most vulnerable in the wake of a crisis.[70] Indeed, the monies allocated to the Vulnerability Fund are far less than the financing reserved for ensuring that the wheels of global trade remain well greased through, for example, the Global Trade Finance Program and the Global Trade Liquidity Programme, both of which fall under the ambit of the World Bank's International Finance Corporation.[71] Reflecting both the NIFA and the G-20 reforms, the World Bank's initiatives once again point to the priority of capital interests over the interests of individuals and groups in the global South. The latter always pay the highest price for "market imperfections," which usually occur beyond the borders of their countries.

CONCLUSION

I have argued that the G-20 reforms introduced at the London Summit in April 2009 represented a reinvention of the NIFA, which was designed by global policy-makers a decade earlier. Underpinning the reproduction of these global regulatory initiatives—which seek to repair, restore and strengthen the international financial system—is the ethos of market rule, centered on free capital mobility and voluntary forms of regulation. By exploring two basic questions concerning what is being restored and why, as well as the political motives behind creating an official separation between the discourses of the NIFA and the G-20 reforms, this chapter has examined more fully the capitalist nature of the reforms. At a more fundamental level, it

69   IMF, "IMF Executive Board Approves Doubling of Borrowing Limits for Poorest Countries," Press Release No. 09/138, April 23, 2009, available at http://www.imf.org (accessed on April 25, 2009).
70   Put People First Alliance, "UK Civil society statement on emergency financing," March 20, 2009, available at http://www.ifiwatchnet.org (accessed on April 3, 2009).
71   IMF, Development Committee Communiqué, Joint Ministerial Committee of the Boards of Governors of the Bank and the Fund on the Transfer of Real Resources to Developing Countries, April 26, 2009, Washington, DC, available at www.imf.org (accessed on May 2, 2009).

has also explored the transformative and adaptive processes of neoliberalization as those in power attempt to re-legitimize the dominant ideology and policy of market rule vis-à-vis global finance and the development project.[72]

Contextualizing the reforms tabled at the G-20 London Summit in April 2009 against the backdrop of the neoliberal solution to the financial crises of the 1990s—the NIFA—I have identified the illusions and paradoxes of global development finance over the past decade. In so doing, I have demonstrated that the neoliberal promises relating to free capital flows, made almost a decade ago, have not been met. It follows that there is a danger in recreating another building that rests on the same foundations as the NIFA. While there are capitalist interests that will no doubt benefit from the status quo of market-led forms of financial regulation and the associated strategy of debt-led forms of capital accumulation and an ever expanding credit system, a much larger segment of the world's population will see a further deterioration of their standard of living. Given the enormous productive and social costs of each financial crisis on the global South, it will be interesting to see how, and to what extent, the free-market ideology of neoliberalism can be legitimated and reproduced in the wake of the current meltdown. According to the UN secretary-general, Ban Ki-moon, "the crisis could strike a 'final blow' to some poor countries."[73] The legitimacy of US-imposed leadership, as well as the position of the IMF and the central role accorded to the predatory and fraudulent credit system under its control, may be called into question as an increasing number of people across the globe become further disenfranchised. As with all social change, however, this will ultimately depend on the configuration of political power in contesting the status quo, as well as the structural nature of global capital accumulation.

---

72 J. Peck and A. Tickell, "Neoliberalizing Space," *Antipode*, 34(3), pp. 380–404. For more information about the neoliberal development project, see P. McMichael, *Development and Social Change: A Global Perspective*, Thousand Oaks, CA: Pine Forge Press, 1996.
73 "Global Economy talks call for greater role for IMF," *Guardian*, October, 25, 2008.

HOW THE NEOLIBERALS
BANKRUPTED "NEW EUROPE"

Latvia in the Global Credit Crisis

Michael Hudson and Jeffrey Sommers

Only a few years ago "New Europe" was hailed as the world's new set of tiger economies, touted as providing Europe's main engine of growth. These post-Soviet economies had the world's fastest-growing real-estate and stock-market bubbles. The World Bank announced that "Eastern Europe had overtaken Asia in ease of doing business"[1]—thanks to their unregulated and anti-labor business environment, lack of workplace protection and labor unionization, and a flat tax that fell almost entirely on wage earners rather than on property. European and American neoliberals joined with international financial institutions in the hope that the rise of Eastern Europe would signal the end of Jacques Delors' Social Europe model. The star performers were the Baltic States. Before the Economic Crisis broke in the fall of 2008, Latvia showed the highest rates of economic growth in Eastern Europe. Many voices proclaimed they were creating Europe's new future, a model for even the West to follow. The Baltics, it was hoped, would bury the idea of state-led development.

---

[1] "News Release Doing Business 2008: Large Emerging Markets Reforming Fast; Egypt the Top Reformer, Eastern Europe Overtakes East Asia on Ease of Doing Business," *International Financial Corporation World Bank Group*, September 26, 2007, http://www.doingbusiness.org. These points are elaborated in "Neo-Liberalism and the Fragmentation of Social Solidarity in the Baltic States: Can the Pieces Be Picked Up?" presentation by Charles Woolfson, REMESO, Institute for Research in Migration, Ethnicity and Society, Linköping University and School of Law, University of Glasgow.

In a relatively short period of time, however, the liberalizers saw their favorite economies implode. Latvia's current-account deficit rose to over 20 percent during the run-up to the crisis. In 2009 the money stopped flowing in and jobs disappeared, while the government slashed spending in an attempt to reduce the trade deficit. The economy will shrink by 15 percent in 2009, with some economists projecting even higher numbers as conditions continue to deteriorate. Baltic labor's already low take-home pay has been reduced further.

This chapter traces how this turn of events transpired so rapidly and inevitably. Long in the making, the crisis resulted from the neoliberal financial model the United States deployed to advance its own interests. The post-1980 Washington consensus turned the post-Soviet economies into economic and financial satellites. It did so in conjunction with Western European countries, which had little interest in helping the post-Soviet economies develop into potential industrial and agricultural rivals and instead viewed them primarily as markets for exports and bank credit.

THE NEOLIBERAL RECONSTRUCTION OF EASTERN EUROPE

Even though the early post–Second World War era is often contrasted with the neoliberal era, the US effort to reshape the global economy during that period is best characterized as a set of proto-neoliberal policies. While the US private sector was in international balance throughout the 1960s, rising overseas military spending after 1951 pushed the national balance of payments into chronic deficit. This could be financed by boosting the export capacity of the "real economy," and financially by attracting foreign capital.[2]

The "real economy" program involved building up US farm exports (the mainstay of the trade balance) and industrial exports in the way that had made America so dominant internationally in the first place: by protectionist policies. Buy-American clauses were inserted everywhere from foreign-aid policies to state and local infrastructure spending programs; quotas were placed on steel; and, crucially, the US intensified its farm protectionism, quadrupling grain prices. This helped the US trade balance but

---

2 M. Hudson, *Super Imperialism*, Sterling, VA: Pluto Press, 2003 [1992].

violated the ostensibly free-trade philosophy that American diplomats had written into the post-war GATT. US economic policy also destabilized the balance of payments of food-dependent Third World countries, making it difficult for them to pay their (mainly American) creditors. Matters came to a head in 1973, when the oil-exporting countries responded to the US quadrupling of grain prices by quadrupling the price of oil to stabilize their own international payments position. From 1973 to 1980, oil prices rose tenfold. Foreign countries began to talk of a New International Economic Order to achieve greater economic justice and parity.[3]

In August 1971 the payments deficit forced the US to end convertibility of the dollar into gold. Viewed initially as a loss of American power, this turned out to pave the way for a new kind of US-centered economic order—one that provided the nation with an unprecedented free lunch in the form of automatic foreign financing for its overseas military spending, foreign investment outflows and rising trade deficit.

American officials told OPEC countries that they could charge as much as they wanted for their oil as long as they recycled the dollars they received for their exports in the form of Central Bank holdings of US Treasury bills. Henry Kissinger was sent to cut a deal with the Saudis to price oil in dollars, making it even more important to hold as a reserve currency. This arrangement spread to other countries even without US threats being needed. Once gold purchases were no longer an option, central banks had little alternative but to recycle their reserves to the US. Other currencies—mainly sterling, yen, Swiss francs and deutschmarks—were used much less widely in international trade, limiting Central Bank demand for non–US government bonds.

---

3 As the second-largest exporter of oil and closest ally of the United States in the Middle East at the time, the Shah of Iran asserted: "Of course [the world price of oil] is going to rise. Certainly! And how . . . You [Western nations] increased the price of wheat you sell us by 300 percent, and the same for sugar and cement . . . You buy our crude oil and sell it back to us, redefined as petrochemicals, at a hundred times the price you've paid to us . . . It's only fair that, from now on, you should pay more for oil. Let's say ten times more." See W. D. Smith, "Price Quadruples for Iranian Oil," *New York Times*, December 12, 1973. For details on the economic maneuverings of the post-1971 period, see M. Hudson, *Global Fracture: The New International Economic Order*, Sterling, VA: [1979] Pluto Press, 2004.

The result of the Treasury-bill standard replacing the gold-exchange standard was that the American balance-of-payments deficit financed a growing proportion of its own government's federal budget deficit. The more dollars the American military, consumers and investors spent abroad, the more were turned over to central banks to invest in Treasury bills. The United States was thus freed from having to do what the IMF demanded other countries running payments deficits do: raise interest rates to attract foreign loans and raise income taxes (i.e. free up domestic output for export by shrinking domestic markets).

As foreigners became the major buyers of new Treasury debt, US investors and savers were free to invest their money abroad, buying up foreign companies and mineral resources. The US government was running up an enormous debt to foreign central banks (reaching $4 trillion by mid-2009), but there were few ways that foreign countries could hope to get any real resources in exchange for their dollars. OPEC countries were permitted to invest their sovereign funds in the US stock market, but not to buy major US firms outright. The same policy limitation was imposed on Japan in the 1980s and on China in the 2000s. US Treasury bonds were becoming much like US paper currency, representing a kind of debt that nobody really expected to be repaid. The United States, of course, had to pay interest on these debts—but it simply added the interest onto the debt and let the sums accumulate. Richard Nixon's Treasury Secretary, John Connally, expressed the policy dilemma for countries confronted with the US balance-of-payments deficit in his folksy Texan way: "We had a problem and we are sharing it with the rest of the world—just like we shared our prosperity. That's what friends are for." Even more to the point was his famously curt assertion to Europe and Asia: "The dollar's our currency, but it's your problem." Having become export-dependent economies requiring the US market to take their goods, foreign economies had to accept dollars as IOUs in exchange for their exports to America and the sale of their companies and resources to US investors.

Other debtor countries had no such easy options. Unable to pay their foreign debts (most of which were denominated in dollars and owed to US institutions), Latin America and other countries were allowed to convert most of these debts into "Brady bonds," on the condition that they finance their future payments deficits by selling off their public enterprises, mineral and land rights and the rest of their public domain to foreigners. US and other investors bought up this infrastructure. In effect, the US economy exchanged paper IOUs yielding low interest for the "commanding heights" of foreign economies—i.e. their higher-income-yielding resources, on which US banks and other financial institutions advanced the funds for foreign buyers to leverage their own investment, turning foreign economies into "cash cows" to pay interest to banks and bondholders and leave earnings in the hands of US direct investors to pay dividends.

This became the context in which neoliberal economics rose to prominence, first as a dress rehearsal at gunpoint by the "Chicago Boys" in General Pinochet's Chile, and then by Margaret Thatcher's Conservative Party in England after 1979, and Ronald Reagan's Republicans in the United States after 1981. The new economic doctrines claimed that all government spending was inherently unproductive, and all private spending, lending and investment productive.

West Germany was the first country to seek an alternative, hoping that the deutschmark might become an alternative reserve currency. But it lacked the size and market depth to accomplish this. France and Germany subsequently joined forces to launch the euro, but it became more a satellite currency than a real alternative to the dollar. Euro "stability" required throwing the EU into recession, as the Maastricht criteria in 1992 imposed tight monetary limits to pull investors and central banks away from the dollar and into the euro.

But the ensuing economic contraction for Western Europe was mitigated by the opening of the Soviet bloc's consumer-goods markets. The collapse of the Soviet Union in 1991 became an opportunity to put neoliberal economic theory into practice. In every post-Soviet economy an identical set of policies was promoted by the US and a few foreign economic advisers, usually working in conjunction with the US State Department under the Agency for International Development and via the World Bank and International Monetary Fund. The first aim was to pry away the most valuable assets from the public domain—oil and mineral rights in Russia, land sites and real estate in other countries, public infrastructure in the form of transportation, power production and communications, and any private industries that appeared viable.

New domestic kleptocracies were promoted in each country and given public resources virtually for free (or for money that the central government provided itself, often by depositing public funds in the banks that were buying natural resources, as in Russia's notorious "shares for loans" sell-off of Norilsk Nickel and other firms to the "Seven Bankers" in 1996). The theoretical premise was that the new owners would be led "automatically" by market forces to act in an economically rational manner to maximize the value of the enterprises being given away.

It was an essential part of the neoliberal program not to tax real estate or other property, but to leave its EBITDA (earnings before interest, taxes, depreciation and amortization) "free" to take the form of capital flight abroad (about $25 billion annually during 1991–2005 from Russia alone) and to be paid out as interest to the private-sector bankers who advanced the credit to buy out these assets. US investors played a leading role, mainly because the money they spent on foreign investment outflows was recycled by foreign central banks into US Treasury bonds. Under these conditions, mutual funds, hedge funds and investors generally made the post-Soviet stock markets the world's fastest-rising markets. Elites in the US and Western Europe reaped the rents, while consumers in those countries benefited from access to cheap imports.

The same happened in real estate. Not only was it free of debt, but it also was almost entirely tax-free (less than a tenth of 1 percent in most post-Soviet countries). An onerous flat tax was, however, imposed on labor—amounting to some 58.09 percent for Latvia,[4] and similarly high rates for its neighboring Baltic countries. This tax system—precisely the opposite of that which had fueled US and Western European industrial and social development—effectively prevented the post-Soviet countries from developing as industrial rivals to the West. The European Community viewed these countries as customers, i.e. as profitable markets for exports and banking services. Loans were extended in euros, sterling and other foreign currencies—mainly to finance the purchase of real estate and the construction boom. In the Baltics and Central Europe the latter rose to greater heights than in any other countries (although Iceland and Spain gave them a good run for their money). However, all this made these countries so dependent on foreign suppliers of consumer goods, capital goods and credit that there was no plausible way for them to become self-sustaining once the inflow of foreign-currency loans dried up.

---

4 Combined income and social taxes on labor paid by employees and employers.

Latvia was the poster child for neoliberal restructuring. It helped carry the ideological freight of neoliberalism into the East, becoming a Trojan Horse through which the New Europe project was unleashed. Latvia played a major role in restoring profitability to the Western economies. Its location enabled it to serve as the transit point for CIS (Commonwealth of Independent States) raw material sales and flight capital en route to the West. It also provided labor to the West through emigration as its domestic economic "recovery" mainly took the form of a boom in real estate construction and sales rather than industrial growth. Along with labor from neighboring Baltic countries and Poland, this emigration helped check wage costs in Western European countries like Britain, Ireland and Sweden.[5]

LATVIA IN THE POST-SOVIET CONTEXT

Latvia's experience reflects the economic and political structures bequeathed by the late Soviet Union. Already in the 1980s the contours of the global economy were shifting in ways that would shape the fate of the Soviet Union in the 1990s. *Nomenklatura* insiders were evolving into "biznezmen," whom neoliberalizers in the West were soon to treat as heroes. US academics and Washington Consensus diplomats soon played a key role in promoting dependency on foreign trade and credit.

Of course, by the 1990s neoliberalism had become fully hegemonic in the United States itself. After taking office in 1981, Ronald Reagan reduced government regulation and slashed taxes on property and the higher income brackets. He financed these tax cuts partly by imposing a highly regressive Social Security withholding tax on labor that transferred much of this money to general government revenues, while the federal debt quadrupled during the next twelve years. The Republican administration viewed unemployment as a means to hold down wages and thereby promote profitable capital investment. But the key economic policy was to flood the economy with credit. The result was a capital-gains economy of rising real estate and stock market

---

5 Sweden did this through an effort at social dumping. The Laval and Partners case was designed to undermine the EU workers' directive and permit low-cost Latvian contractors to operate in Sweden. This is further elaborated in C. Woolfson and J. Sommers, "Labour Mobility in Construction: European Implications of the Laval un Partneri Dispute with Swedish Labour," *European Journal of Industrial Relations*, 2006, 12(1).

prices, applauded by Federal Reserve Chairman Alan Greenspan as "wealth creation."

Thus, when Latvia gained independence from the Soviet Union in 1991, the global environment was one that allowed Western countries to reorganize their economies on the basis of a comparative advantage in finance, led by the US banking system's ability to create virtually limitless amounts of credit.

Latvia's favorable position on the Baltic Sea provided it with unique opportunities to mediate the largely illicit privatization of gains within the Soviet economy during the 1980s. Its ports were the exit points for Soviet natural resource exports, acquired at low cost and resold at global prices. This practice was pioneered most notably by Grigori Loutchansky. Removed from his post as Vice Rector of the University of Latvia in 1982 for corruption, he engineered the sale of Soviet oil and raw materials to global markets through his trading company Nordex, buying Russian aluminum and other commodities at give-away prices that no doubt were false-invoiced in Russia.[6] This marked the beginning of Latvia's offshore economy and helped establish it as a center for tax avoidance and money laundering, working with foreign partners such as Lucy Edwards at the Bank of New York. In due course Loutchansky joined forces with the American Marc Rich to set up what became a vast criminal empire.[7] His success created a path for others to turn Latvia into a platform from which to export Soviet raw materials. Arbitrage fortunes were made from the usually covert differential between Russian and global prices and the value of the ruble in Moscow and Riga. Latvian money managers eventually grew to establish their own offshore shell companies to handle vast sums of Russian money seeking outlets in the West in order to avoid taxation at home.[8]

---

6 S. Tocs, "Loutchansky: Beating the Times," interview with Loutchansky, *The Baltic Course*, http://www.baltic-course.com (accessed on August 4, 2008). Nordex subsequently became a Canadian company. Loutchansky took the opportunity to be photographed with President Clinton, who subsequently returned the campaign contributions he received from Loutchansky, who now lives in Israel and is reported still to be dealing with Soviet oligarchs.

7 Rich, whose spouse became a major donor to President Clinton, was pardoned on the last day of Clinton's administration for his former indictments on tax evasion and trafficking in Iranian oil. See P. K. Semler, "Marc Rich Linked To $9 Billion Money Laundering Investigation," *Washington Times*, June 23, 2002.

8 The authors have interviewed and personally know some of the actors involved in this activity.

Newly independent Latvia neglected industry, opting for easier gains in the form of privatization giveaways. There were few moves to promote economic policies to strengthen Latvia's farmers, promote a viable middle class or raise labor's basic living standards. De-industrialization was facilitated by the Central Bank's tight money policy that meant a lack of credit for manufacturing. Much of Latvian industry was antiquated and needed dismantling, to be sure, but almost no effort was made to implement an industrial policy, inventory Latvia's industrial equipment (including modern machinery imported from the West) and restructure potentially competitive enterprises. Some valuable equipment was appropriated by individuals and sold on global markets, and other machinery was simply sold for scrap.

US advisers and the leading international financial institutions encouraged this combination of industrial neglect and post-industrial financial policy. Presented as "reforms" to make Latvia and other post-Soviet economies more like those of Western Europe and North America, neoliberal policy grounded Latvia's post-independence economy mainly on insider privatizations, quick windfall profits, tax avoidance and currency arbitrage that fostered a culture of corruption and insider dealing, asset stripping and rent seeking. This "transition economy" deformed Latvia's economy and politics from the outset. Political insiders made money by selling off public property to themselves, and funding their consumption of imports by borrowing against their privatized real estate and other holdings.

The guiding idea was for Latvia to finance its growth by attracting foreign investment. This meant selling off assets and borrowing abroad to cover trade shortfalls, not building up industry and agriculture by capital investment. This policy created many fortunes but far more misfortunes, dislocation, misery and poverty, as nearly all social and health indices declined dramatically in the "new economy" of the 1990s.[9] Intellectual support for this model came from a Latvian-American economist from Georgetown University, Juris Viksnins, who prescribed a variant of the monetarist policy first put in place by the Chicago Boys in Chile under Pinochet. Viksnins helped mentor Latvian

---

9 See W. Iwaskiw, ed., *Latvia: A Country Study*, Washington, DC: GPO for the Library of Congress, 1995, http://countrystudies.us (accessed on January 16, 2008) and C. Woolfson, "A 'Social Europe' or a 'Race to the Bottom' in the Enlarged EU?" 2006, http://www.fes-baltic.lv (accessed on August 5, 2008).

policy-makers such as Einars Repse, who headed the Bank of Latvia, became prime minister in 2002 and is now (2009) finance minister.[10]

This model liberated Latvian politicians from the burden of having to develop an active industrial and agricultural policy. They simply sold off the parts and refrained from taxing land and other formerly public assets, leaving property income "free" to be pledged as collateral against loans. Loans were taken out from banks in the neighboring Western countries—and therefore were denominated in euros or other foreign currency (Sweden became a major source of loans to the Baltics). This "solved" the problem of how the post-Soviet countries would finance their trade deficits now that the old USSR production linkages had been uprooted. Asset stripping in this new economic order went hand in hand with the economy living off inflows of capital from its offshore banking, transit revenues and timber exports.

The overall result was the kind of dispossession that in past times had occurred mainly by military conquest. The trade pattern between Western and Eastern/Central Europe took on a lopsided, almost neocolonial relationship. After the dissolution of the Soviet Union, Western Europe turned its traditional deficit with the East into a trade surplus.[11] For example, in 1991 Czechoslovakia experienced a 2 percent rise in exports to France, while its imports from France rose by 180 percent. By 1999 the EU trade surplus with candidate countries was $26 billion. The Soviet bloc's collapse thus proved to be a godsend for Western Europe, particularly for Germany and France, as access to post-Soviet markets helped mitigate the unemployment problem created by the low inflationary and tight credit policies required by the Maastricht Agreement. Built around the euro, this monetary agreement consolidated a European economic zone under a neoliberal financial leadership whose tight credit

---

10 The classic study of US advisers shaping neoliberal policy in the post-Soviet countries is J. Wedel, *Collision and Collusion: The Strange Case of Western Aid to Eastern Europe 1989–1998*, New York: St. Martin's Press, 1998. See also "Rigging the US-Russian Relationship: Harvard, Chubais, and the Transidentity Game," *Demokratizatsiya*, 1999, 7 (4).

11 J. Sommers, "The Entropy of Order: The Contested Terrain of EU Enlargement," in S. Engel-Di Mauro, ed., *The European's Burden: Global Imperialism in EU Expansion*, New York: Peter Lang Press, 2006.

policies threatened to push the EU into recession.[12] Absorbing this region into the EU enabled Western Europe to lock in place this structural imbalance by negotiating a barrier-free trading and financial system.

The combination of American economic advice and the growth-constricting policies of Maastricht meant that the 1990s were a lost decade for the Latvian economy. Many obsolete industries were scrapped for good reason, but little effort was made to retain potentially viable enterprises. The result was emigration of labor, economic shrinkage, and social polarization as the economy de-industrialized. By the late 1990s its commodity trade with Russia and other former Soviet economies had almost dried up, but the Russian ruble crisis of August 1998 nonetheless hit Latvia hard. Politically, the proliferation of "post-industrial" rent-seeking activities meant growing corruption—a legacy that still permeates Latvian life, above all in the real-estate and financial sectors that became the economy's new core.

LATVIA'S DEBT-FINANCED CAPITAL-GAINS ECONOMY: BOOM AND BUST

In the years leading up to 2008, Latvia's economic statistics appeared to leap from Muscovich to Maserati performance. Yet the much-vaunted Latvian growth model still showed few gains in industrial or agricultural production outside of the construction and tourism sectors. Growth occurred mainly in the finance, insurance and real-estate (FIRE) sectors,[13] taking the form of high-powered consumption based on foreign credit inflows, i.e. rising Latvian indebtedness.

Foreign capital inflows grew after NATO and EU accession in 2004, with the latter bringing significant structural aid funds from Brussels. The main beneficiary was the nation's capital city, Riga, which contains a third of its population and two-thirds of its economy. Oil prices also started their dramatic rise in 2004, from about $20 a barrel at the time the US invaded Iraq to nearly $150 by summer 2008. This enriched the oil-producing regions of

---

12   K. Dyson, ed., *Enlarging the Euro Area: External Empowerment and Domestic Transformation in East Central Europe*, Oxford: Oxford University Press, 2007.
13   Globalis Project data under auspices of United Nations University, http://globalis.gvu.unu.edu (accessed on August 4, 2008).

the former USSR, flooding Russia and its "near abroad," including Latvia, with foreign exchange. Real-estate prices soared in response to the inward rush of hot money and foreign bank credit, especially for luxury housing in Riga's city center and seaside resorts. The resulting gentrification boom was entirely free of property taxes, steering money mainly into property development and retail investment for the burgeoning tourist trade. Despite some contribution to the real economy in the form of construction, much of the credit inflow ended up financing luxury consumption.

GDP grew from some LVL5 billion in 2000 to LVL13.9 billion in 2007 (non-inflation adjusted currency). After 2004, Latvia's GDP growth rose to 7.6 percent and continued to increase thereafter, reaching double digits until the crisis hit in 2008.[14] Financialization reached its peak with the global 2002–07 real-estate bubble. Foreign currency inflows from Russia and bank loans from Western Europe (primarily Sweden) permitted Latvians to enjoy a GDP growth that was among the highest in the world.

As much as 90 percent of Latvia's GDP growth was fueled by the services it provided to handle the foreign money pouring in from abroad, along with the real-estate bubble. While GDP grew at a seemingly impressive 10.6 percent in 2007, exports rose only by about 1 percent.[15] Rising consumption was financed largely with international credit, as imports were almost twice as high as exports by 2008.[16] Scandinavian and Latvian banks were eager to make loans and quick returns. Windfall gains were created by the asset bubble that distorted the economy's development path. In the first nine months of 2007, banks in Latvia earned LVL267 million (after tax), up 50 percent from the same period in 2006 when their profits were LVL177.8 million.[17] Latvia's construction boom doubled the amount of new housing from the first quarter of 2005 to 2007.[18]

---

14   CIA, *The World Factbook* (2005–2008), http://www.cia.gov.
15   Central Statistical Bureau of Latvia, *Latvia's Foreign Trade*, http://www.csb. gov (accessed on May 26, 2009).
16   Commission of Finance and Capital Markets, *General Information*, http:// www.fktk.lv (accessed on May 26, 2009). Latvia's Financial and Capital Market Commission shows that most loans were for real-estate mortgages, and to finance consumption.
17   Ibid.
18   For details on how the real-estate bubble and property sell-offs financed the Baltic trade deficit and capital flight, see M. Hudson, "Fading Baltic Miracle," *International Economy*, Winter 2008, pp. 74–78. See also *Uzb v t s dz vojam s kas pa ceturkš iem (Quarterly Dwelling Construction Statistics)*, http://www.csb. gov.lv (accessed on January 16, 2008).

The results of this shallow growth are now apparent. While many Latvians cashed in on the real-estate surge and the patrimony inherited from Soviet times, many others emigrated in the face of scarcely affordable housing or the lack of decent employment. The government was complicit in this process. Many of its members had privileged access to property and were in no hurry to undertake policies that would curb the real-estate surge, increase the tax base, and ensure that apartments would not be withheld from the market for speculation purposes.

Economists and financial officers at Latvia's leading banks forecast that credit would expand at roughly 15–25 percent in 2008. This rosy view was problematic, predicated as it was on the expectation of a 20 percent rise in savings.[19] This was absurd in view of the actual growth of savings in 2007. Indeed, savings decreased, owing in large part to one of the highest inflation rates in the EU. In combination with the degree to which Latvians were already overextended on credit, this left discretionary income to save.[20] Food costs rose almost 20 percent in 2007 and continued their rapid ascent in 2008, along with prices for other essentials, hitting wage earners hard.[21] Autos bought on credit are being repossessed, and new shopping malls are as empty in Riga as they are in much of the West.

Property prices have begun their decline, dropping by 50 percent from their peak in Riga's city center, with outlying beach suburbs falling by 70 percent. Indeed, from the first quarter of 2008, Latvia has represented the world's largest plunge in house prices (as reported by the Knight Frank Global House Price Index).[22] In June 2006 one of the authors asked the head of the real-estate division of one of Latvia's top three banks why they were inflating the real-estate market with credit. "We know it is unsustainable," she responded, "but everyone's annual bonus depends on making more money. We know it will crash, but we are all making too much money now to stop it."[23] More room remains for property

19 J. Sommers, 2008, interviews with economists and financial officers at several of Latvia's leading banks.

20 "Inflation in Latvia Still the Highest in EU," *The Baltic Course*, January 16, 2008, http://www.baltic course.com.

21 "Latvia's Food Prices Poised to Continue Skyward Trajectory," *Baltic Times*, January 16, 2008, http://www.baltictimes.com.

22 N. Kolyako, "Knight Frank: Latvia Registers Most Rapid Reduction in House prices in Q1," *The Baltic Course*, May 26, 2009, http://www.baltic-course.com.

23 J. Sommers, 2006 interview with head of the real-estate division at one of Latvia's largest banks.

prices to fall, as current city-center prices have only receded to 2005 levels.[24] When we reported this to Latvia's then chief banking regulator (who has since made a well-timed exit from the country, just before the Crisis hit), we were told he would refuse to work with us if we insisted on making it public.

Many Latvians have foreign-currency mortgages larger than the foreseeable worth of their property and face ruin if the lat is devalued and euro-denominated loans balloon in local currency. The debt overhang will saddle the nation with debt service to foreign banks for years to come, and Latvians are discovering that they can no longer borrow from Swedish banks against real-estate collateral that is rapidly dropping in value.[25] New inflows from Russia are also abating as oil prices have fallen back and there is little prospect for new capital investment from domestic sources. To cap matters, the Latvian government has announced that it will take IMF advice to deal with the situation. A recent news report found that "the government has chosen what it calls an 'internal devaluation,' in which wages are forced downward to restore the economy's equilibrium."[26] For instance, government wages have been cut by an initial 15 percent. In response to deepening poverty, on January 13, 2009 about 10,000 Latvians took to the streets to protest against the IMF.

WHAT IS TO BE DONE?

Latvia has been independent for almost two decades, but its economic development has hit the same debt wall that most other post-Soviet economies are experiencing. As in its Baltic neighbors Estonia and Lithuania, as well as Hungary and Ukraine, Romania and Bulgaria—along with Western countries from Spain to Ireland and Iceland—

---

24 "Latio: s rijveida dz vok u cenas R g gada laik krituš s par 7.3%," *Delfi*, January 2, 2008, http://www.delfi.lv (accessed on January 16, 2008).

25 Credit still grew in 2008, but is now severely constricting. The second-largest Swedish bank in Latvia, SEB, saw the greatest curtailing of credit growth. It extended only 14.3 percent more in loans in 2007 than in 2006. Other foreign banks, such as the very sizeable Finnish bank, Nordea, poured 64.9 percent more money into Latvia in 2007 than in 2006, and of course has now pulled back. Mid-size Latvian banks showed very aggressive Latvian credit growth through 2008 despite the fact that these banks have relatively few assets, suggesting perhaps an external capital source, such as Russia. (Data from *Association of Latvian Commercial Banks.*)

26 C. Dougherty, "Latvia Races to Cut Deficit To Keep Its Bailout Deal," *New York Times*, May 24, 2009.

the drop-off in foreign mortgage lending has left the economy without a means of covering its chronic trade deficit, except through impoverishing its people by driving down wage levels. It also faces the problem of carrying its heavy foreign-currency debt. Throughout these economies, hopes to join the euro are foundering. In almost every case the underlying problem is the failure to put in place production facilities to export enough to cover the cost of imports.

The immediate problem is where the future foreign exchange will come from to pay the debt service and cover the structural trade deficit now that the global real-estate bubble has burst. Along with most post-Soviet economies, Latvia has become burdened with a debt overhead far beyond its ability to pay. Much of its mortgage debt is denominated in foreign currency, so that it cannot avail itself of the time-honored policy of inflating its way out of debt. Nor will it help for the government to borrow from the IMF and EU to pay debts owed by insolvent real-estate mortgagees to Swedish and other foreign banks. Public borrowing to bail out bad private debts would involve squeezing the money out of the domestic population through even higher taxes on labor. This is the strategy that Latvia's creditors have proposed— to slash its already low living standards.

This logic was reflected in the now infamous official letter that Joaquin Almunia of the European Commission presented to Latvia's prime minister and finance minister in January 2009, spelling out that Latvia must *not* use EC loans to develop export capacities for its economy. It must instead use the funds it is borrowing primarily to pay off debts to its creditors in the West and bail out banks. Indeed, both the specifics and tenor of Almunia's comments are worth noting:

> external assistance is to be used to avoid a balance of payments crisis. ... Also, if the banking sector were to experience adverse events, part of the assistance would be used for targeted capital infusions. ... Worryingly, we have witnessed some recent evidence in Latvian public debate of calls for part of the financial assistance to be used *inter alia* for promoting export industries or to stimulate the economy through increased spending at large. It is important to stem these misperceptions.[27]

This "conditionality" essentially leaves Latvia in the position of a nation defeated in war and having to pay reparations.

---

27 J. Almunia, "Letter B-1049 Brussels," January 26, 2009, http://www.fm.gov.lv.

Latvia's problems are not merely the result of dishonest or incompetent leadership. This interpretation was brought into relief most clearly on November 26, 2008, when Latvia's then Finance Minister Atis Slakteris gave a bumbling "Borat-like" performance (as many Latvians characterized it) on Bloomberg TV. His characterization of the situation as "nothing special" infuriated Latvians and quickly became an iconic phrase defining the public's discontent and gracing merchandise from posters to T-shirts. Subsequent demonstrations saw many Latvians carrying this quote through the streets on placards in mocking contempt of their government.

Yet while providing a centripetal force around which protests could organize, the sentiment that government corruption is the only problem avoids harder questions of whether the neoliberal system itself is responsible for Latvia's hardships. Neighboring Estonia, which has displayed competence and discipline in executing neoliberal policy, is not substantially better off than Latvia.

TOWARD A PRO-GROWTH TAX POLICY?

Starting with Britain and followed by the US, Germany, France and Japan, it has been the historical norm for nations to build up their economies and labor productivity by protecting their domestic markets, subsidizing agriculture and industry, and providing basic infrastructure at cost or at subsidized prices so as to make their economies more competitive. But as Britain gained a head start during the upsweep of the Industrial Revolution, its national interest shifted from mercantilist trade policies to a "free-trade imperialism" designed to prevent other countries from doing what it itself had done to become the world's leading industrial power. Negotiating free-trade agreements with other countries after repealing its Corn Laws in 1846, Britain became the "workshop of the world" and "the world's banker" by opposing protective tariffs and subsidies abroad.

Britain was able to promote free-market policies in most of its former colonies and in less developed countries, but not in the nations that set out to become industrial and financial powers in their own right. After Japan's Meiji Restoration in 1872, for example, the US government sent its own leading protectionist economist to advise the Japanese government on how to implement the kind of protectionist policies that had spurred the US takeoff after it broke away from British free-trade ideology when its Civil War ended.[28] Almost all the leading American economists in the late nineteenth century studied in Germany to refine their understanding of how governments could best steer industrial and financial policy to develop a national economy.

Latvia's independence after the First World War therefore occurred in a world in which its former imperial masters in Germany, Russia and Sweden (as well as the United States and Japan) understood that the key to economic development lay in nurturing agriculture and industry. Taking the lesson of the United States and Germany, Latvia sought to catch up to these lead-nations using policies similar to those which had guided Japan and later other East Asian nations to achieve their own take-offs, and hence meaningful political independence. Latvia's new middle class took bold moves to promote the interests of its farmers and urban members. In 1921, for example, the Latvian Republic introduced a land-reform program that appropriated mostly German-owned manors and redistributed the land to over 200,000 Latvian farmers. This was undertaken despite the howls of protest it elicited from Western European nations.[29] Latvia's reform also leveled hitherto unequal wealth distribution, creating more overall real wealth by unleashing the entrepreneurial energies of its population rather than merely promoting opportunities for asset stripping and rent seeking.

Latvia's second, post-1991 independence has been quite different. US advisers promoted an ideology of economic dependency. Whereas nineteenth-century US economists promoted an economy based on high wages—on the theory that highly paid, highly educated, well-fed and well-housed labor was more productive—the new ideology advocated a tax and legal system oriented toward grinding down wage levels and minimizing expenditures on health-care and workplace safety. Governments were to sell off public infrastructure and natural monopolies to private investors without oversight. The policy prescriptions of the Washington Consensus thus aimed at dismantling government

28 These policies are described in M. Hudson, *America's Protectionist Takeoff, 1815–1914: The Neglected American School of Economics and Technology* (in press; first edn 1965 as *Economics and Technology in 19th-Century American Thought: The Neglected American Economists*, Garland Press).
29 M. Wright, "Land for Everybody: Latvia's Division of Estates of Baltic Barons—State Ownership Rejected," *New York Times*, March 13, 1921, http:// query.nytimes.com.

regulation and forestalling national development outside of the economies that had already achieved a head start. The consequences have been especially pronounced in Latvia's highly regressive tax system, which rewards rent seeking and speculation while discouraging work and industry. The onerous tax on wages makes it almost impossible for it to compete with its Western European neighbors,[30] while the minimal property tax promotes speculation.

The fallout of the Crisis—including large-scale wage cuts and layoffs, a crushing deflationary spiral and renewed mass emigration—can only be contained through significant capital infusions, which the Latvian government is lobbying for with the IMF and the European Commission. The problem is that the factors underlying Latvia's pseudo-prosperity have now ended. The global real-estate bubble has burst and foreign bank credit has dried up. Bail-out time has arrived. From North America to Europe, banks are asking the IMF, EU and national governments to bail them out of the bad loans they have made. The governments of Latvia and other Baltic countries are borrowing to pay private-sector foreign debts. This borrowing is to be repaid by intensifying the tax burden and lowering wage levels, shrinking the domestic market, and thus making it even harder for debtor economies to "earn their way out of debt." It has led many countries in this position (notably Iceland) to take the position that debts that cannot be paid out of current earnings should not have to be repaid—certainly not by making debtor countries increase bad taxes and lower labor's take-home wages yet further. The balance-of-payments and debt problems of the Baltics and other post-Soviet countries call into question the idea of a "New Europe." Almost no post-Soviet country now qualifies for joining the euro.

Tax policy may provide the path of least political resistance to rebuilding the Baltic economies. The kleptocrats took primarily real estate—hotels and other buildings, land sites, public infrastructure and kindred rent-extracting properties, borrowing against them in the hope of reaping windfall profits on their resale. The European

---

30 Latvia's effective flat tax on wages is composed of a straight 25 percent tax on wages, a 24 percent social-service tax paid by employers (which treats Social Security and medical care as user fees rather than as normal parts of the public budget) and another 11 percent paid by wage earners, on top of which Latvia imposes a value-added tax. No Western industrial economy has so devastatingly high a wage tax or lacks a significant property tax.

banks and agencies that encouraged these privatizations and debt-financed asset-price inflation failed to recognize the need to build up industry or other means of production. Their neoliberal approach did not explain how the economy was to survive once rental income was no longer available to be borrowed against.

Neoliberalism is a short-run policy to burn up resources quickly, much like chopping down a forest or exhausting a coal mine. But the income that has been diverted to the neoliberal "economic mining" venture can be recaptured even without fundamental challenges to property relations. A rent tax on the value of land would restore rentier "free lunch" income to the public domain. By shifting the fiscal burden off excessively taxed wages and genuine industrial profit, a rent tax would enable the Baltics to compete with their European neighbors and other potential customers—while holding down real-estate prices and thereby lowering the cost of living and doing business. The aim would not be to raise overall taxes, but rather to unburden the productive side of the economy while leashing the speculative side that has enriched only a small proportion of Latvia's population.

Latvia and other post-Soviet economies obviously need to break their dependence on foreign banks. Instead of financing industrial and agricultural capital formation, foreign credit has been almost entirely extractive, extended against property already in place. Bank credit in today's world is a basic public utility that can be created by a few keyboard strokes. There is no reason why Latvia's Treasury cannot create such credit more productively. It can extend credit to banks organized essentially like savings banks, lending out deposits and government money creation for productive investment rather than for debt-leveraged speculation.

But financial modernization should be accompanied by fiscal modernization. The main vehicle for debt since 1991 has been mortgage debt, which a land tax would minimize. A resource-rent tax would recapture the "free lunch" of favorable site location and so free Latvia's economy from the heavy neoliberal taxes and high debt-service charges that prevent its labor and enterprise from competing in world markets. This is why, for many centuries, classical economists, from Adam Smith through John Stuart Mill and the architects of the Progressive Era reforms, from Europe to North America, explained that the land's rental value is the natural tax base, the basic patrimony of every nation's citizenry.

Failure to tax what nature (plus public infrastructure spending and economic demand) provides leaves this usufruct available to be pledged to banks, obliging government to tax labor, industry and sales. A land tax would not fall on new construction, but would recapture the value of Latvia's natural endowment—the land's site value with which the nation emerged from Soviet times. It would prevent future speculation in property, while permitting income taxes to be lowered.

THE GLOBAL CRISIS
AND LATIN AMERICA

Henry Veltmeyer

This chapter provides a critical perspective on the dynamics of the Global Financial Crisis in Latin America. Dominant interpretations have tended to assume that the Crisis is not systemic or structural in nature but rather a financial phenomenon that can be corrected through more effective financial governance. This chapter, by contrast, argues that the Crisis is but the latest—albeit most virulent—manifestation of the capitalist system's endemic propensity to crisis. While crises tend to unhinge existing systems of institutionalized practices and can release forces of change, so far the main policy response of Latin American governments has been to shift toward a more pragmatic form of neoliberalism. Truly progressive change requires a politics that is driven not by policy-makers and hopes for re-regulation but rather by popular forces in civil society.

RETHINKING THE CRISIS

Walden Bello has argued that the dynamics of the Global Crisis should be traced back to the system-wide crisis of overproduction that in the early 1970s brought an end to the "golden age of capitalism."[1] This involution in the system of global capitalist production unleashed a protracted restructuring process that

---

1 W. Bello, "The Global Collapse: A Non-Orthodox View," *ZNet*, February 22, 2009, available at http://www.zmag.org.

involved a neoconservative revolution which diminished the power of the state and organized labor vis-à-vis capital;[2] major shifts in the geographical organization of economic activity that produced a new international division of labor;[3] and a process of financialization, leading to the emergence of a huge disjunction between the real economy and a financial superstructure.[4]

Neoliberal restructuring took the form of Reaganism and Thatcherism in the North and "structural adjustment" in the South. The aim was to "invigorate capital accumulation" by (a) "removing state constraints on the growth, use and flow of capital and wealth" and (b) "redistributing income from the poor and middle classes to the rich based on the theory that the rich would then be motivated to invest and reignite economic growth." The problem with this formula "was that in redistributing income to the rich . . . the incomes of the poor and middle classes [were gutted], thus restricting demand while not necessarily inducing the rich to invest more in production." As a result, neoliberal restructuring had a poor development record: "Global growth averaged 1.1 percent in the 1990s and 1.4 percent in the 1980s, compared with 3.5 percent in the 1960s and 2.4 percent in the 1970s when state interventionist policies were dominant."

The second escape route was *globalization*—"the rapid integration of semi-capitalist, non-capitalist, or pre-capitalist areas into the global market economy." The aim was for capital to gain access to cheap labor, emerging markets and new sources of cheap agricultural products and raw materials. Integration was effected through trade liberalization, removing barriers to the mobility of capital and abolishing barriers to investment.

The problem with this escape route was that it exacerbated overproduction. For example, "a tremendous amount of manufacturing capacity has been added in China over the last 25 years, with a depressing effect on prices and profits elsewhere in the system."[5] Not surprisingly, Bello notes, by around 1997 the profits of US corporations stopped growing. By one calculation,

---

2   H. Veltmeyer, *Illusion or Opportunity*, Halifax: Fernwood, 2007.

3   F. Fröbel, Jurgen Heinrichs and Otto Kreye, *The New International Division of Labour: Structural Unemployment in Industrialised Countries and Industrialisation in Developing Countries*, Cambridge: Cambridge University Press, 1980.

4   J. B. Foster and F. Magdoff, "Financial Implosion and Stagnation: Back to the Real Economy," *Monthly Review*, 2008, 60(6).

5   Bello, "Global Collapse."

"the profit rate of the *Fortune 500* went from 7.2 in 1960–69 to 5.3 in 1980–90 to 2.3 in 1990–99 to 1.3 in 2000–02." By the end of the 1990s, with excess capacity in almost every industry, the gap between productive capacity and sales was comparable to what it had been at the time of the Great Depression.

Given the limited progress in countering the crisis of over-production through neoliberal restructuring and globalization, the third escape route—*financialization*[6]—became critical for maintaining and raising profitability. With investment in industry and agriculture yielding low profits, large amounts of surplus funds have been circulating in the financial sector. As Bello puts it, "the financial sector . . . turn[ed] on itself,"[7] resulting in the growing divergence of a hyperactive financial economy and a stagnant real economy.

The history of the neoliberal era can be traced out in four stages:[8] (1) the policies engineered in the 1970s under the military regime of Augusto Pinochet; (2) the call for a "new world order" by Thatcher, Reagan and other neoconservatives, and the implementation of a program of "structural" reforms designed by the economists at the World Bank on the model of Pinochet's neoliberal policies; (3) another round of reforms in the 1990s, which were accompanied by a discourse that emphasized the need for a more socially inclusive, sustainable and governable form of neoliberalism;[9] and (4) the emergence in the new millennium of a financial bubble and a global primary commodities boom led by demand in China and India for energy and natural resources.[10]

---

6 For an analysis of its national dynamics in the case of Brazil see F. de Oliviera and L. M. Paulini, "Financialization and Barbarism: A Perspective from Brazil," in P. Bowles et al., eds, *National Perspectives on Globalization: A Critical Reader*, Basingstoke, London: Palgrave Macmillan, 2007.

7 Bello, "Global Collapse."

8 D. Harvey, *A Brief History of Neoliberalism*, Oxford: Oxford University Press, 2005.

9 On this see in particular J. A. Ocampo, "Latin America and the World Economy in the Long Twentieth Century," in K. S. Jomo, ed., *The Great Divergence: Hegemony, Uneven Development, and Global Inequality*, New York: Oxford University Press, 2006; J. Ocampo, J. S. Jomo and S. Khan, eds, *Policy Matters: Economic and Social Policies to Sustain Equitable Development*, London: Orient Longman / New York and Penang: Third World Network, 2007.

10 On these developments see J. Petras and H. Veltmeyer, *What's Left in Latin America*, London: Ashgate, 2009.

THE DYNAMICS OF THE GLOBAL
CRISIS IN LATIN AMERICA

Between 2003 and 2008, more than a few Latin American economies managed to escape the production crisis that had beset many countries around the turn of the new millennium. They did so by riding a short five-year wave produced by a boom in primary commodities, in turn fuelled by the explosive growth of the Asian demand for energy, minerals and other industrial inputs, as well as middle-class consumer goods. Over the course of this period, the rate of economic growth increased from an average regional rate of 0.6 percent in 1996 and a bare 1 percent in 2002 to a regional average of 6.2 percent in 2004, 5.5 percent in 2005 and 5.6 percent in 2006. In the countries that led the boom, the average rate of growth between 2003 and 2007 ranged from 6.3 percent in Peru to 8 percent in Venezuela and 8.3 percent in Argentina.[11]

In 2008, however, this primary commodities boom got caught up in the vortex of the current financial crisis. At the level of government, the first response to the crisis was to deny it—as Mexico's President Felipe Calderón did, arguing (at Davos, to an assembly of world capitalism's most illustrious representatives) that Latin America was more or less insulated from its effects. Ironically, Calderón heads the most vulnerable economy in the region vis-à-vis the epicenter of the Crisis (the US economy). Even at the time of his public statement, Mexican economists were already predicting the loss of at least 500,000 jobs in a contracting economy. By mid-March 2008, the estimate of Mexico's GNP growth for 2009 was revised from -1.5 percent to -3 percent.[12] Even though other Latin American governments were not quite as quick to discount the effects of the crisis on regional and local economies, many of the initial responses contained more than a little wishful thinking, often expressing confidence that their country could ride out the crisis on the basis of relatively high reserves of foreign currency and relatively low levels of short-term debt.[13]

If economists at ECLAC (Economic Commission for Latin America and the Caribbean) are correct, the leaders of countries

---

11 *CEPAL News*, XXIV, no. 2, February 2009, p. 85.
12 *La Jornada*, March 17, 2009.
13 Petras and Veltmeyer, *What's Left in Latin America*.

in the Southern Cone have few reasons to be optimistic. Not even those countries that, in the context of the primary commodities boom, were careful not to over-spend and build up reserves seem to be immune from the effects of the crisis.[14] Latin America as a whole is already experiencing a slowdown in capital inflows, large declines in stock price indexes, significant currency adjustments and an increase in debt spreads.[15] Growth projections for 2009 were adjusted from 3.6 percent (in September 2008) to 1.4 percent (in December 2008).[16] More recent projections are that Latin America's per capita GDP may well begin to shrink. The number of bankruptcies will grow and unemployment will increase, especially in the agro-mineral and export sectors. Latin America's external position will deteriorate significantly owing to the withdrawal of capital by foreign investors and speculators seeking to cover their losses in the US and Europe, with declining remittances from overseas workers reinforcing the effects.

According to the IMF, Latin America lost 40 percent of its financial wealth in 2008 as a consequence of the meltdown of financial markets and currency depreciation. This decline is expected to reduce domestic spending by 5 percent in 2009. Latin America's terms of trade have deteriorated sharply as commodity prices have fallen, making imports more expensive and raising the specter of growing trade deficits.[17] The onset of the recession in Latin America is evident in the 6.2 percent fall in Brazil's industrial output in November 2008 and its accelerating negative momentum.[18] In other words, Latin America is experiencing the beginning of what is likely to be a profound and prolonged recession.

RESPONSES TO THE CRISIS

Latin American governments (especially those that are heavily dependent on the flow of direct investment from abroad) have begun to pursue various "counter-cyclical policies to buffer

14 ECLAC, *The Reactions of Latin American and Caribbean Governments to the International Crisis: An Overview of Policy Measures up to 30 January 2009*, Santiago: United Nations, 2009.
15 I. Bastillo and H. Helloso, *The Global Financial Crisis: What Happened and What's Next*, Washington DC: ECLAC Washington Office, February 2009.
16 *Financial Times*, January 9, 2009.
17 Ibid., p. 7.
18 Ibid., p. 5.

the impact of the crisis."[19] In a survey of counter-crisis policy measures taken by different governments in the region over the past year, ECLAC notes that sixteen out of twenty-one countries in the region have increased infrastructure spending since the start of the Crisis.[20] Five have also promoted job creation and as many as fourteen maintained or even increased their spending on social programs.

Many of these policies look much like those traditionally advocated by the social-democratic Left. But hopes that this will by itself lead to a significant political and social transformation are likely to prove futile. Government responses to the Crisis have remained tied to established capitalist interests and, on an ideological level, to a relatively superficial understanding of the Crisis. Thus, while the demise of neoliberal ideology may be inevitable, its replacement will most likely be a more socially inclusive, pragmatic and "sustainable" form of neoliberalism.

But governments are not the only organizations responding to the Global Crisis. Popular sector organizations that bring together unions, diverse class-based organizations and social movements throughout the region have conducted their own analysis of what the Global Crisis means. As they see it, the Crisis reflects the contradictions of neoliberalism as well as conditions of capitalist development that are endogenous to the region. They also recognize that the Crisis is fundamentally a crisis of the social organization of production that entails a massive loss of jobs, the erosion of incomes and pensions, the cutback of essential government services and the declining affordability of food.

The most radical responses and popular demands, according to Petras,[21] will likely occur in those countries most dependent on primary product exports and world demand, and in those countries integrated into the depressed markets of the US and the EU. This group of countries includes Mexico, Central America, Ecuador, Peru, Venezuela and Bolivia. Countries like Chile, Argentina, Brazil and Colombia, with more diversified exports and a larger internal market, will also be impacted but not as severely or abruptly. A radicalization of the Left could well take hold as the recession deepens and the counter-cyclical economic

---

19   *CEPAL News*, XXIV, no. 2, February 2009.
20   ECLAC, *The Reactions of Latin American and Caribbean Governments to the International Crisis.*
21   Petras and Veltmeyer, *What's Left in Latin America.*

stimulus plans and public works programs fail to stimulate the
economy. Key to the growth of transformative movements is their
organizational ability to link and articulate local discontent to a
national plan of struggle, informed by an anti-imperialist socialist
program.[22]

Present circumstances hold significant prospects for the re-
emergence of mass movements, which in turn would provide
conditions for a revival and renewal of socialist movements.
However, the process of socialist renewal will undoubtedly reflect
the limitations imposed by the Left's fragmentation and the
disconnect between its political organization and its grassroots
presence in communities, neighborhoods and workplaces. This is
by no means to dismiss the relevance of policies aiming to change
the structural organization of national and regional development,
which have been pursued by a number of progressive governments
in the region for some years—most notably by Venezuela, the pivot
of the Latin American Left since 1999. Insofar as such measures
point to the "need for a systemic alternative to capitalism,"[23]
they may well have an important role to play in supporting the
more radical proposals of the popular movements. Yet the point
remains that this will not happen without popular mobilization
and pressure from below that forces national and regional
institutions to disconnect from the global capitalist system.

THE POPULAR MOVEMENTS AND THE STATE

On February 29, 2009, a Bolivia-based regional alliance of
indigenous, peasant and social movements called for a "Minga
of Resistance" in association with "other peoples and processes"
in the region.[24] *Minga* is a Quechua word for "collective action"
that makes cultural and historical references to a shared experience

22 Ibid.
23 L. Panitch and S. Gindin, "From Global Finance to the Nationalization of the
Banks: Eight Theses on the Economic Crisis," *ZNet*, February 25, 2009 available
at http://www.zmag.org.
24 This alliance includes the Coordinadora Andina de Organizaciones Indígenas
(CAOI); the Coordinadora de Organizaciones Indígenas de la Cuenca Amazónica
(COICA); the Consejo Indígena de Centro América (CICA); the Movimiento
Sin Tierra del Brasil (MST); Vía Campesina; the organizations of the Unity Pact
(Pacto de Unidad) of Bolivia; and diverse indigenous organizations of Colombia,
Ecuador and Peru—meeting most recently on February 26, 2009, in the locality
of the Unity Pact in La Paz.

of subjugation. It enjoys wide currency among the poor, both indigenous and mestizo, in the Andes. Thought and action along these lines is underway in the popular sectors of several countries in the region—as could be witnessed, for instance, at the Convocation of the Social Movements of America at the World Social Forum in Belém in 2009. Recognizing that capital and the state will try to "offload" (*descargar*) the effects of the crisis on the population at large, a broad coalition of social movements announced its intention to create a popular form of regional integration from below and to pursue "social solidarity in the face of imperialism."

According to such popular perspectives, the Global Crisis is not just about finance but also about production and social organization, involving questions about sustainable livelihoods, employment and the price of food. ECLAC Executive Secretary José Luis Machinea has noted that the steep and persistent rise in international food prices is hitting the poor in Latin America and the Caribbean particularly hard. Poverty and indigence will rise dramatically unless urgent measures are taken to reduce the effects of these hikes.

Access to food has become a key issue, as prices for the staple tortilla have skyrocketed over the past year or so. An example of popular action to counteract the effects of the production crisis is the peasant-worker alliance, recently formed in Mexico, to make available affordable food to workers.[25] The producers in the alliance aim to deliver goods to workers and their families at cost, or at prices at least 20 percent below those charged by commercial enterprises. In a similar vein, different organizations in Mexico's peasant movement have insisted that the government's anti-crisis plan include a policy to promote the local production of staples such as corn, rice, milk, vegetable oil and pork products. In this way they are seeking to end the policy of free agricultural imports under NAFTA, which, as the Zapatista Movement had predicted, has been the cause of a major production crisis in the agricultural sector.[26]

As indicated earlier, in the wake of the Crisis virtually all governments in the region have adopted counter-cyclical policies designed to pump-prime demand, prevent massive unemployment

---

25 *La Jornada* online, February 24, 2009.
26 As the president of the Senate's Rural Development Commission pointed out, the elimination of import duties on vegetable oil alone has resulted in the loss of up to 40,000 jobs.

and minimize the negative socio-economic effects of the crisis. Yet a major objective of such policies has been to placate and demobilize popular forces, i.e. to contain the forces of social discontent and political opposition. A key element of the Mexican government's anti-Crisis response is *Oportunidades*, a poverty-alleviation program funded in part by a World Bank loan which continues the time-honored tradition of using rural development as a means of demobilizing the social movement and defusing revolutionary ferment.

A key problem here is that few of even the Left governments in Latin America took advantage of the highly favorable economic and political conditions of the pre-Crisis years (2002–08) so as to change policy in a recognizably socialist direction. With the exception of Venezuela, it is difficult to observe any significant difference between the social policies adopted by these Left-leaning regimes and those with a pragmatic or even dogmatic neoliberal orientation (such as Chile, Peru, Colombia and Mexico). The crisis will only tighten the structural constraints on government policies and therefore may well reinforce this trend.

This means that a great deal hinges on the strategies that popular movements adopt in the current conjuncture. Of particular interest here is the fact that the Crisis seems to have given a further boost to the emerging trend for the popular movements to negotiate their programs with Latin America's most explicitly anti-neoliberal governments, like those of Hugo Chávez, Rafael Correa and Evo Morales.[27] This political Left tends to understand socialism in terms of the nationalization of natural resources and capitalist enterprises in strategic economic sectors, the regulation of the market, and a more just or equitable distribution of the social product. Nationalization is understood as central to "socialism of the twenty-first century," according to Chávez.

Within the popular movement a different conception of socialism as an alternative to neoliberalism prevails: socialism is understood in terms of "communalism," political practices rooted in a culture of solidarity and "relations of reciprocity,

---

27 On the political character or ideological orientation of these regimes in the context of what has been termed the post-neoliberal era see Petras and Veltmeyer, *What's Left in Latin America.*

complementarity and equity."[28] A country's natural resources are common property of the people and cannot be privatized: they are to be under the stewardship of "the people" in their communities, governed on the basis of both social solidarity and "respect and harmony with Mother Earth."[29] According to this perspective, socialism should not take the form of state control. Rather, it implies a decentralized state allowing local communities to exercise their collective responsibility in protecting and sustaining the heritage of humankind.

Similarly, social movements understand regional integration as a mechanism that will promote "integration from below." While a relatively "technical" aspect of economic reform, regional integration has become closely connected to conceptions of "to live well" (*vivir bien*) and the way social movements have rethought the basic goals of economic development. This new development paradigm, rooted in a worldview based on localism and regionalism, views integration not just as a matter of trade but rather as a means for the cultural and political integration of the people in the Andes and Amazonia. Similar sentiments inform the movements' demands for land reform and changes in the pattern of agricultural production, i.e. for a shift away from an agro-export model toward small-scale production for local and national markets.

Just as the region's socialist governments owe their election in no small part to the vibrancy and resilience of the popular movements, so their policies in turn have a potentially important role to play in empowering these movements. They have hardly been passive in doing so. Viewing access to water as a "fundamental human right" and a public good, one of the first actions of the government of Evo Morales in Bolivia was to renationalize ownership of natural resources such as oil and gas, and to prevent a commercial encroachment on the global commons.[30] Efforts to strengthen the institutional basis for economic cooperation in the region, led by Chávez's government, have resulted in the launch of ALBA (*Allianza Bolivariana para los Pueblos the Nuestra América*), an alternative regional trade alliance involving Bolivia,

28 A. Yala, "Diálogo de Alternativas y Alianzas de los Movimientos Indígenas, Campesinos y Sociales," *Minga Informativa de Movimientos Sociales*, La Paz, February 26, 2009.

29 Ibid.

30 Ibid.

Ecuador, Cuba, Nicaragua and Honduras. And while Chávez's proposal to form the Bank of the South has had to overcome many political hurdles, the Global Crisis has revived the project, allowing companies and governments in the region access to an alternative source of capital.

Such measures, however, represent little more than a small step toward the kind of political program that would be capable of providing a systematic alternative to the imperatives of global capitalism. Over the next years, external pressure on all Latin American governments to adopt pro-capitalist policies will increase significantly. Only those governments that are allied to a vibrant civil society and organically linked to the discontent of a radicalizing populace will be capable of resisting the effects of such external constraints.

CONCLUSION

The present Crisis represents a crisis of the operating system governing global capitalist production. So far, however, the predominant response of governments in Latin America on both the Centre-Left and the Right has reflected little awareness of this. While the Crisis has hastened the demise of neoliberalism as both an ideology and as an economic model, governments' responses have not pointed beyond a muted and more pragmatic form of neoliberalism that emphasizes the need for a more socially inclusive and sustainable form of capitalist development. The diverse "solutions" to the Crisis proposed by the political Left are generally framed within the institutional forms of capitalism, seeking only to mitigate the effects of the crisis and to ensure a more sustainable and humane form of capitalist development.

To ensure that the usual victims—i.e. people in what Sub-comandante Marcos termed the *bolsillos de olvido* (forgotten pockets)—are able to resist, adjust to or otherwise cope with the forces released in capitalism's restructuring process, it is essential that the forces of resistance and change be actively mobilized and to some extent unified. The analysis of the regional dynamics of the global crisis that has been presented in this chapter leads to the conclusion that the popular movements should resist proposals for solutions to the Crisis framed within the institutional forms of capitalist society. For such reforms are unlikely to alter the system's fundamental dependence on the exploitation of labor and the unequal distribution of productive resources. Genuinely progressive change and truly alternative development requires the supersession of capitalist principles of production, which in turn is predicated on the mobilization of the diverse forces of change in the popular sector.

12

WILL CHINA SAVE THE WORLD FROM DEPRESSION?

Walden Bello

This chapter examines China's international economic role in the current conjuncture. In the wake of the current Economic Crisis, many have argued that America's massive debts and China's credit are just different sides of the same coin: while Americans could be criticized for taking on too much debt, it was only fair that the Chinese should take the blame for facilitating it. If such reasoning seems a little contorted, this did not prevent it from gaining widespread adherence in policy circles or from being taken seriously by the Western media.

The real objective of such statements was subtly different from their official message: the US hardly has an interest in China withdrawing its financing of American debts. Rather, they were part of an attempt to get China to take seriously not only its role as a global producer but equally its role as a global consumer. Western commentators realized that an economic revival would take a sustained increase in the capacity of Chinese markets to absorb global production. This chapter examines the likelihood that China will consume the world out of its current recession and set it on a path of new growth.

A Crisis of Overproduction

The root causes of the current global recession have little to do with the lack of regulation of finance capital. The unrestrained mobility of speculative capital that many orthodox analysts view as the central factor is in reality a symptom of a more fundamental and comprehensive crisis: one of overproduction.

Overproduction or overaccumulation is the tendency of capital to amass tremendous productive capacity that outstrips the population's capacity to consume—owing to, among other things, persistent economic inequality. As Marx put it, "The real barrier of capitalist production is capital itself ... The means—unconditional development of the productive forces—comes continually into conflict with the limited purpose, the self-expansion of existing capital."[1] This contradiction between productive capacity and effective demand (to put it in Keynesian terms) leads to the erosion of profitability, recession, and, at certain junctures, even depression.

One cannot understand the current crisis without harking back to the stagflation of the late seventies, when something that orthodox macroeconomic doctrine (as expressed in the "Philips Curve," which depicts an inverse relationship between employment and inflation) said could not happen, did happen: stagflation, i.e. simultaneous economic stagnation and rising inflation. This was followed by the recession during the first years of the Reagan presidency in the early eighties. These years saw the end of the post-war boom that had been triggered by the pent-up demand from the Second World War and the reconstruction of Japan and Europe. That boom had added significant new industrial capacity, while persistent inequality eventually restrained the growth of effective demand.

There were three escape routes available to capital in its attempt to surmount the profitability crisis of the seventies. The first was neoliberal restructuring, which sought to liberate capital from state regulation and roll back wages by tearing up the capital-labor compromise that had served as the social basis of the Keynesian social-democratic growth regime during the post-war boom. The second was financialization, or the redirection of investment from the low-growth, low-profit real economy to speculative activity in the financial economy. The third was globalization, or the integration of semi-capitalist, pre-capitalist, and non-capitalist areas into the capitalist system; as Rosa Luxemburg argued in the early twentieth century, such strategies serve to raise the rate of profit by allowing capital to exploit new markets, super-exploit labor,

---

1 K. Marx, *Capital*, Vol. 3, London: Penguin, 1981, p. 250.

gain control of natural resources, and access new investment outlets.[2]

While temporarily alleviating the erosion of profitability, these three escape routes ended up in dead ends. Neoliberal restructuring (also known as "structural adjustment"), while rolling back wages and raising profits in the short run, had the effect of gutting the effective demand needed to sustain profits over the long term. Financialization, dependent on squeezing value out of already created value, created asset bubbles whose explosions periodically unhinged the real economy. Finally, globalization might have opened up new markets and access to cheap labor, but it also added significant new productive capacity that exacerbated the crisis of overproduction.

CHINA AND GLOBALIZATION

China was the most significant market added to the capitalist world economy during the last twenty-five years. This momentous development stemmed from two complementary interests: the desire of China's ruling Communist Party to develop China's productive forces through capitalist mechanisms, and global capital's desperate need for profitable self-expansion and accumulation. The result of this process has been double-edged.

On the one hand, China's 8–10 percent annual growth rates have probably been the principal stimulus of growth in the world economy over the last two decades. In the case of Japan, for instance, a decade-long stagnation was broken in 2003 by a recovery fueled by exports to slake China's thirst for capital and technology-intensive goods; exports shot up by a record 44 percent, or $60 billion.[3] Indeed, China became the main destination for Asia's exports, accounting for 31 percent, while Japan's share dropped from 20 to 10 percent. Chinese demand pulled East Asia from the doldrums following the Asian Financial Crisis: "In country-by-country profiles, China is now the overwhelming driver of export growth in Taiwan and the Philippines, and the majority buyer of products from Japan, South Korea, Malaysia, and Australia."[4]

---

2 R. Luxemburg, *The Accumulation of Capital*, New York: Monthly Review Press, 1951.
3 "Riding China's Coattails," *Business Week*, p. 50.
4 "China the Locomotive," *Straits Times*, February 23, 2004, p. 12.

On the other hand, China became a central contributor to the growing crisis of global overcapacity. Even as investment in many economies (particularly Japan and other East Asian countries) declined sharply in response to the crisis of excess capacity,[5] in China it continued to increase at breakneck pace. Investment in China was not just the obverse of disinvestment elsewhere—even if the shutting down of facilities and sloughing off of labor was significant not only in Japan and the United States but in the countries on China's periphery like the Philippines, Thailand and Malaysia. China was not simply absorbing capacity eliminated elsewhere: it was significantly beefing up the productive capacity of its industrial base. At the same time, however, the ability of the Chinese market to absorb its own industrial output was limited.

A major actor in such overinvestment was transnational capital. Originally, when transnational corporations moved to China in the late 1980s and 1990s, they saw it as the last frontier, the unlimited market that could endlessly absorb investment and deliver profitable returns. However, investment, in many cases, turned into excess investment because of China's restrictive rules on trade and investment, which forced transnationals to locate most of their production processes in the country instead of outsourcing only a select number of them. Analysts termed this the "excessive internalization" of production activities by transnationals.[6]

By the turn of the millennium, the dream of exploiting a limitless market had vanished. Foreign companies no longer headed for China in hopes of selling to millions of newly prosperous Chinese customers, but rather in order to take advantage of its seemingly inexhaustible supply of cheap labor, in the process transforming the country into a manufacturing base for global markets. Typical of companies that found themselves in this situation was Philips, the Dutch electronics manufacturer. While Philips operates twenty-three factories in China and produces about $5 billion worth of goods, two-thirds of its production is not consumed in China but exported to other countries.[7]

The other set of actors promoting overcapacity were local governments which invested in and built up key industries.

5   R. Rajan, "Global Imbalances," International Monetary Fund, Washington, DC, October 2005, available at http://www.imf.org.
6   United Nations, *World Investment Report 2003*, New York: United Nations, 2003, p. 45.
7   "Burying the Competition," *Far Eastern Economic Review*, October 17, 2002, p. 30.

While these efforts are often "well planned and executed at the local level," notes Ho-fung Hung, "the totality of these efforts combined ... entail[ed] anarchic competition among localities, resulting in uncoordinated construction of redundant production capacity and infrastructure."[8]

The result is that idle capacity in such key sectors as steel, automobile, cement, aluminum, and real estate has been soaring since the mid-1990s—with estimates that, even before the Global Financial Crisis, over 75 percent of China's industries were plagued by overcapacity, and fixed-asset investments in industries experiencing overinvestment accounted for 40–50 percent of China's GDP growth in 2005.[9] The State Development and Reform Commission projected that by 2010 automobile production would grow to more than double what the market can absorb.[10] The impact on profitability is not to be underestimated if we are to believe government statistics: at the end of 2005, the average annual profit growth rate of all major enterprises had plunged by half and the total deficit of losing enterprises had increased sharply by 57.6 percent.[11]

Excess capacity could have been overcome had the Chinese government focused on expanding people's purchasing power through a policy of income and asset redistribution. Doing so would have meant a slower but more stable process of growth. China's authorities, however, opted for a strategy aimed at the domination of global markets through the exploitation of the country's cheap labor. More than half of China's population of 1.3 billion lives in the countryside, earning an average of just $285 a year and thus serving as an almost inexhaustible source of cheap labor. Because of this reserve army of rural poor, manufacturers (both foreign and local) have been able to keep wages down. The negative social and economic effects of this strategy are well described by Ho-fung Hung:

> [U]nder the post-Tiananmen consensus among the ruling elite, the Communist Party single-mindedly pursues rapid economic growth without directing much attention to the alleviation of social

---

8 H. Hung, "Rise of China and the Global Overaccumulation Crisis," paper presented at the Global Division of the Annual Meeting of the Society for the Study of Social Problems, Montreal, August 10–12, 2006.
9 Ibid.
10 Ibid.
11 Ibid.

polarization. Class, urban-rural, and inter-regional inequalities expanded hand in hand with the economic miracle. Poverty spreads and intensifies in the rural inland area and the old bastions of state industry are besieged by extensive unemployment. The peasants-turned-workers in the coastal boom towns are not doing much better. Owing to the colossal size of the pool of surplus labor and the "despotic factory regime" under the auspices of the party-state, industrial wage growth amid China's economic miracle is dismal in comparison with the growth of manufacturing wages in other East Asian NICs during their miraculous moment. During the most explosive phase of takeoff, South Korea and Taiwan remained modestly egalitarian societies . . . In contrast, China's gini-coefficient has ascended from 0.33 in 1980 to more than 0.45 today. The pattern of income distribution in China's development is more reminiscent of the Latin American experiences than the East Asian ones, so much so that some begin to forewarn of the "Latin Americanization of China."[12]

In addition to its potentially destabilizing political consequences, the concentration of wealth and the relative pauperization of the vast majority "impedes the growth of consumption relative to the phenomenal economic expansion and great leap of investment."[13] This meant, among other things, an exacerbation of the crisis of global overproduction and the dumping of much of China's industrial production in markets constrained by slow growth. It meant as well that, instead of becoming a rival growth center to the US for East and Southeast Asian economies, China served mainly as an assembly point for goods from these economies that were then incorporated into final products for the US market. There was never much substance to the hypothesis—which has enjoyed particular popularity since the onset of the current crisis—that China had become "decoupled" from the US and served as an independent engine of global demand.

CHAIN-GANG ECONOMICS

By the late 1990s, the world was, in the words of the International Monetary Fund's chief economist, "investing too little."[14] And too little investment was responsible for stagnation. In the last few years, for instance, Europe's GDP has grown by only 1.45

12 Ibid.
13 Ibid.
14 R. Rajan, "Global imbalances—an assessment," available at http://www.imf.org.

percent per annum, while growth in Latin America, Africa, and the Middle East has been equally lackluster.

China and the United States, however, appeared to buck the trend. But rather than a sign of health, the growth in these two economies reflected a special relationship that was fraught with danger. Chinese production and American consumption were like the proverbial prisoners who sought to break free from one another but could not because they were chained together. This relationship increasingly took the form of a vicious cycle. On the one hand, China's breakneck growth increasingly depended on the ability of American consumers to continue their consumption of much of China's output. On the other hand, America's high consumption rate depended on Beijing lending the US private and public sectors a significant portion of the trillion-plus dollars it has accumulated over the last decade owing to its yawning trade surplus with Washington.

By 2006, China's bilateral trade surplus with the US was $235 billion. This represented over a third of the US trade deficit, making China by far the biggest country component of the deficit. This translated into a massive accumulation of dollar reserves: between December 2000 and December 2003, foreign exchange holdings of China's central bank more than doubled—from $166 billion to $403 billion. In 2006, this figure had exceeded $1.2 trillion, of which $600 billion was denominated in the US currency, and it had reached $1.7 trillion in 2008.[15]

As noted above, a large share of these enormous reserves was simply recycled back to the US through the purchase of US bonds and securities or reinvested in dollar-denominated assets. These funds were a significant factor in fueling the speculative mania that rocked the US economy in the last few years—first the technology bubble that burst in 2001, then the even more dangerous subprime bubble that collapsed in 2007, bringing the real economy, both in the US and globally, into deep recession.

In short, Chinese funds were central to the financialization of investment that has been responsible for the current crisis; financialization, in turn, was a response to the crisis of overcapacity that had gripped the global economy, partly as a consequence of the globalization of production, of which China had been the

---

15 B. Lucarelli, "The United States Empire of Debt: The Roots of the Current Financial Crisis," *Journal of Australian Political Economy* 62, 2008, p. 18.

principal beneficiary. The chain-gang relationship was ultimately unsustainable.

CHINA: THE COMING ENGINE OF CONSUMPTION?

With the spread of the global recession, a new role is being fashioned for China by many analysts: it is now increasingly touted not as the driver of global production but rather as the engine of global consumption. Whether China will be the new "growth pole" and snatch the world from the jaws of depression has become a widely discussed question as the heroic American middle-class consumer, weighed down by massive debt, ceases to be the key stimulus for global production.

Despite the fact that China's GDP annual growth rate fell to 6.1 percent in the first quarter of 2009—the lowest in almost a decade—optimists see "shoots of recovery" in a 30 percent surge in urban fixed-asset investment and a jump in industrial output in March. These indicators are proof, they say, that China's stimulus program—which, in relation to GDP, is much larger than the American program—is working.

CHINA'S COUNTRYSIDE:
A LAUNCHING PAD FOR RECOVERY?

With China's export-oriented urban coastal areas suffering from the collapse of global demand, many inside and outside China are pinning their hopes for global recovery on the Chinese countryside. A significant portion of Beijing's stimulus package is destined for infrastructure and social spending in rural areas. 20 billion yuan ($3 billion) worth of subsidies is being allocated to help rural residents buy televisions, refrigerators, and other electrical appliances. The great question is: will this strategy—i.e. propping up rural demand in the hope that it will come to serve as an alternative to export demand and so sustain the country's massive industrial machine—actually work?

There are grounds for skepticism. For one thing, even when export demand was high, many of China's industries were already plagued by overcapacity.[16] Before the crisis, for instance, it was projected that by 2010, the automobile industry's installed capacity could turn out 100 percent more vehicles than could be

---

16 Hung, "Rise of China and the Global Overaccumulation Crisis."

absorbed by a growing market. In the last few years, overcapacity problems have resulted in the annual profit growth rate for all major enterprises being halved.

The greater problem with the strategy of making rural demand a substitute for export markets is that even if another hundred billion dollars were thrown in, it is unlikely that the stimulus package would significantly counteract the depressive impacts of a twenty-five-year policy of sacrificing the countryside for export-oriented urban-based industrial growth.

SUBORDINATING AGRICULTURE TO INDUSTRY

Ironically, China's ascent during the last thirty years began with the rural reforms initiated by Deng Xiaoping in 1978. The peasants wanted an end to the Mao-era communes, and Deng and his reformers obliged them by introducing the "household-contract responsibility system." Under this scheme, each household was given a piece of land to farm. Of what it produced, the household was allowed to retain what was left over after selling to the state a fixed proportion at a state-determined price, or by simply paying a tax in cash. The rest it could consume or sell on the market. There is consensus among China specialists that these were the halcyon years of the peasantry, when rural income grew by over 15 percent a year on average, while rural poverty declined from 33 percent to 11 percent of the population.

This "golden age" of the peasantry came to an end, however, with the adoption of a strategy of coast-based, export-oriented industrialization premised on rapid integration into the global capitalist economy. This strategy, which was launched in 1984 at the Twelfth National Party Congress, was essentially one that built the urban industrial economy on "the shoulders of peasants," as rural specialists Chen Guidi and Wu Chantao put it.[17] Thus, primitive accumulation was achieved mainly by policies that cut heavily into the peasant surplus.

The consequences of this urban-oriented industrial development strategy were stark. Peasant income, which had grown by 15.2 percent a year from 1978 to 1984, dropped to 2.8 percent a year from 1986 to 1991. Some recovery occurred in the early 1990s, but stagnation of rural income marked the latter part of the

---

17 C. Guidi and W. Chantao, *Will the Boat Sink the Water?* New York: Public Affairs, 2006.

decade. In contrast, urban income, already higher than that of peasants in the mid-1980s, was, on average, six times the income of peasants by 2000.

The stagnation of rural income was caused by policies that resulted in rising costs of the agricultural sector's industrial inputs, falling prices for agricultural products and increased taxes—all of which operated to transfer income from the countryside to the city. The main mechanism for the extraction of surplus from the peasantry was taxation. By 1991, taxes on 149 agricultural products were levied on the peasants by central state agencies, which was but part of a much bigger bite, as the lower levels of government began to levy their own taxes, fees and charges. Currently, the various tiers of rural government impose a total of 269 types of tax, along with all sorts of (often arbitrarily imposed) administrative charges. Taxes and fees are not supposed to exceed 5 percent of a farmer's income, but the actual amount is often much greater; some Ministry of Agriculture surveys have reported that the peasant tax burden is 15 percent—three times the official national limit.

Expanded taxation would perhaps have been bearable had peasants experienced returns such as improved public health and education and more agricultural infrastructure. In the absence of such tangible benefits, peasants' taxes essentially served to subsidize what Chen and Wu describe as the "monstrous growth of the bureaucracy and the metastasizing number of officials"— who seemed to have no other function than to extract more and more from the peasantry.

Aside from being subjected to higher input prices, lower prices for their goods, and more intensive taxation, peasants have borne the brunt of the urban-industrial focus of economic strategy in other ways. According to one report, "40 million peasants have been forced off their land to make way for roads, airports, dams, factories, and other public and private investments, with an additional two million to be displaced each year."[18] Other researchers cite a much higher figure of 70 million households, implying that (calculating 4.5 persons per household) by 2004 as many as 315 million people may have been displaced by land grabs.

---

18 C. F. Bergsten, B. Gill, N. Lardy and D. Mitchell, *China: the Balance Sheet*, New York: Public Affairs, 2006.

THE IMPACT OF TRADE LIBERALIZATION

But the impact of all these forces may yet be dwarfed by that of China's commitment to eliminate agricultural quotas and reduce tariffs, made when it joined the World Trade Organization in 2001. The cost of admission for China is proving to be huge and disproportionate. The government slashed the average agricultural tariff from 54 percent to 15.3 percent, compared with the world average of 62 percent, prompting the commerce minister to boast (or complain): "Not a single member in the WTO history has made such a huge cut [in tariffs] in such a short period of time."

The WTO deal reflects China's current priorities. If the government has chosen to put at risk large sections of its agriculture, such as soybeans and cotton, this is because the Party wants to open up or keep open global markets for its industrial exports. The social consequences of this trade-off are still to be fully felt, but the immediate effects were alarming enough. In 2004, after years of being a net food exporter, China registered a deficit in its agricultural trade. Cotton imports had skyrocketed from 11,300 tons in 2001 to 1.98 million tons in 2004, a 175-fold increase. Chinese cotton farmers were devastated, as were sugarcane and soybean farmers. In 2005, according to Oxfam Hong Kong, imports of cheap US cotton resulted in a loss of $208 million in income for Chinese peasants, along with 720,000 jobs. Trade liberalization is also likely to have contributed to the dramatic slowdown in poverty reduction in the period between 2000 and 2004.

LOOSENING THE PROPERTY REGIME

In the past few years, the priority placed on a capitalist transformation of the countryside to support export-oriented industrialization has moved the Party to promote not only agricultural trade liberalization but a loosening of a semi-socialist property regime that favored peasants and small farmers. The process has involved easing public controls over land in order to move toward a full-fledged private property regime. The idea is to allow the sale of land rights (the creation of a land market) so that the most "efficient" producers can expand their holdings. In the euphemistic words of a US Department of Agriculture publication, "China is strengthening farmers' rights—although stopping short of allowing full ownership of land—so farmers can rent land, consolidate their holdings, and achieve efficiencies in size and scale."[19]

The liberalization of land rights included the passage of the Agricultural Lease Law in 2003, which curtailed the village authorities' ability to reallocate land and gave farmers the right to inherit and sell leaseholds for arable land for thirty years. With the buying and selling of rights to use land, private property in land was essentially re-established in China. In talking about "family farms" and "large-scale farmers," the Chinese Communist Party was, in effect, endorsing a capitalist development path to supplant one that had previously been based on small-scale peasant agriculture. As one proponent of the new policy argued, "The reform would create both an economy of scale—raising efficiency and lowering agricultural production costs—but also resolve the problem of idle land left by migrants to the cities."[20]

Despite the Party's assurances that it was institutionalizing the peasants' rights to land, many feared that the new policy would legalize the process of illegal land-grabbing that had been occurring on a wide scale. This would, they warned, "create a few landlords and many landless farmers who will have no means of living."[21] Given the turbulent transformation of the countryside through the full-scale unleashing of capitalist relations of production in other countries, these fears were not misplaced.

In sum, simply allocating money to boost rural demand is unlikely to counteract the economic and social effects of the structural subordination of the development of the countryside to export-oriented industrialization: growing inequality between urban and rural incomes, the stagnation of poverty reduction in rural areas, and the Chinese farmer's structural lack of purchasing power. To enable the rural areas of China to serve as the launching pad for national and global recovery would require a fundamental policy shift, and the government would have to go against the interests, both local and foreign, that have congealed around the strategy of foreign-capital-dependent, export-oriented industrialization.

---

19 B. Lohmar and F. Gale, "Who Will China Feed?" *Amber Waves*, June 2008, available at http://www.ers.usda.gov.
20 Lu Zixiu, an expert on rural affairs, quoted in A. Bezlova, "Flirting with Land Tenure Reforms," Inter-Press Service, October 13, 2008.
21 "China Liberalizes Farmers' Land Use Right to Boost Rural Development," *Xinhua*, October 19, 2008, available at http://news.xinhuanet.com.

Beijing has talked a lot about a "New Deal" for the countryside over the last few years, but there are few signs that it has the political will to adopt policies that would translate its rhetoric into reality. Given this, while Chinese rural demand might help mitigate the impact of the global recession in China, it is unlikely that the Chinese peasant will supplant the now bankrupt American consumer as the engine of global consumption.

CONCLUSION

The non-coincidence of Western and Chinese economic interests has become a topic for the Western media only over the past few years. Until well into the current decade, China was in fact portrayed as a major example of the beneficial effects of capitalist globalization. While it might occasionally have been resented by American workers, whose lives and communities were destroyed by factory closings and relocations, such sentiments remained too localized to have much political impact. On the contrary, China supplied the low-cost goods on the shelves of Walmart, and so gave American workers more consumer bang for their borrowed buck. China's willingness to recycle its export earnings into American debt was widely appreciated, as it served to perpetuate this felicitous situation.

The current crisis and the dim prospects for a new phase of sustained economic growth have reminded Western commentators of the downside of this one-sided arrangement, prompting them to urge China to take seriously its role as a global consumer. As this chapter has argued, hopes that China will transform itself into a major absorber of global (over)production are highly fanciful. There are few signs that the Chinese government is interested in enhancing the purchasing power of its peasant population. Moreover, even if it were prepared to do so, it would only temporarily attenuate the fundamental conflict between the exploitation of the Chinese population and its ability to function as responsible citizen-consumers. As Marx argued, capital's exploitative methods constitute the ultimate barrier to its objective of self-expansion.

13

THE CRISIS OF GLOBAL CAPITALISM

Cyclical, Structural, or Systemic?

William I. Robinson

The crisis that exploded in 2008 with the collapse of the global financial system has been in the making since at least the late 1990s. How we understand it is not just an academic but a burning political question. I want to suggest in this essay that the global capitalism perspective I have put forth in recent years offers a powerful explanatory framework for making sense of this crisis.[1] Following Marx, we should focus on the internal dynamics of capitalism to understand the Crisis; and following the global capitalism perspective, we should look for how capitalism has qualitatively evolved in recent decades. This system-wide crisis will not be a repeat of earlier such episodes in the 1930s or the 1970s precisely because world capitalism is fundamentally different in the early twenty-first century.

Globalization constitutes a new epoch in the ongoing evolution of world capitalism, marked by a number of fundamental shifts in the capitalist system. These shifts include: (1) the transition from a *world economy*, or national circuits of accumulation in an integrated international market, to a *global economy*,

---

1 For my theory of global capitalism and also a more detailed exposition of my ideas on the multidimensional crisis of the system, see, inter-alia, W. I. Robinson, *A Theory of Global Capitalism: Production, Class, and State in a Transnational World*, Baltimore: Johns Hopkins University Press, 2004; and Robinson, *Global Capitalism and Latin America: A Critical Globalization Perspective*, Baltimore: Johns Hopkins University Press, 2008. I would like to thank my research assistant, Brandon Roberts, for his assistance in preparing the three graphs included in this essay.

or globalized circuits of accumulation; (2) the *rise of truly transnational capital* and the integration of every country into a new global production and financial system; (3) the appearance of a new *transnational capitalist class*, a class group grounded in new global circuits of accumulation rather than national circuits; (4) the rise of a *transnational state*, a loose network composed of supranational political and economic institutions and of national state apparatuses that have been penetrated and transformed by transnational forces, and; (5) the appearance of *novel relations of inequality and domination* in global society.

Since the 1970s, the emergence of globally mobile transnational capital increasingly divorced from specific countries has facilitated the *globalization of production*. This involves the fragmentation and decentralization of complex production processes, the worldwide dispersal of the different segments and phases in these processes, and their functional integration into vast chains of production and distribution that span the globe. Values cross borders seamlessly as they move swiftly— often instantaneously—through these new transnational or global circuits of accumulation. This new system is driven, at the strictly technical level, by new information technologies and organizational innovations in capitalist production that have modified how value is created, circulated, and appropriated around the world. National economies have been dismantled and then reconstituted as component elements of this new global production and financial system, which is a qualitatively distinct world economic structure from that of previous epochs, when each country had a distinct national economy linked externally to one another through trade and financial flows. This is a shift from international market integration to global productive integration. At the same time an integrated global financial system has replaced the national bank-dominated financial systems of the earlier period. Global financial flows since the 1980s are qualitatively different from the international financial flows of the earlier period.

The globally integrated production and financial system underscores the increasing interpenetration on multiple levels of capital in all parts of the world, organized around transnational capital and the giant transnational corporations (TNCs). It is increasingly difficult to separate local circuits of production and distribution from the globalized circuits that dictate the terms and patterns of accumulation worldwide. There are still local and national capitalists, and there will be for a long time to come. But they face ongoing pressures to "de-localize" and link to transnational capital if they are to survive. Territorially restricted capital cannot compete with its transnationally mobile counterpart. Transnational capital is the *hegemonic fraction* of capital on a world scale: it imposes its direction on the global economy and shapes the character of production and social life everywhere.

Some of the empirical indicators of the increasing transnational interpenetration of national capitals are: the sharp rise in foreign direct investment; the spread of TNC affiliates; the phenomenal increase in cross-border mergers and acquisitions; the increasing transnational interlocking of boards of directorates; the increasingly transnational ownership of capital shares; the spread of cross-border strategic alliances of all sorts; vast global outsourcing and subcontracting networks; and the increasing salience of transnational peak business associations. There are important new mechanisms that facilitate the transnationalization of capital. The spread of stock markets, for instance, from the principal centers of the world economy to many if not most capital cities around the world, combined with twenty-four-hour trading, facilitates an ever greater global trading and hence transnational ownership of shares. The global integration of national financial systems and new forms of money capital, including secondary derivative markets (as I will discuss later), has also made it easier for capital ownership to transnationalize.

An emergent transnational capitalist class, or TCC, the manifest agent of the system, has attempted to exercise its domination through dense and expanding transnational networks of national states and inter- and supranational institutions that form an incipient transnational state (TNS) apparatus. Globalization does not bring about the "end of the nation-state" but rather a transnationalization of national state apparatuses that are penetrated and transformed by the TCC and allied transnationally oriented bureaucratic and other strata. Once captured by such forces, national states tend to serve the interests of global over national or local accumulation processes. The TNS has attempted in recent years to construct a supranational legal and regulatory system for the global economy and to synchronize the policies of national states around structural adjustment and integration into the global economy, including the imposition of the neoliberal model on the old Third World.

It is through a TNS apparatus that global elites attempt to convert the structural power of the global economy into supranational political authority. Indeed, as capitalism globalizes, the twenty-first century is witness to new forms of poverty and wealth, and new configurations of power and domination. Global capitalism has generated new social dependencies around the world. Billions of people have been brought squarely into the system, whereas before they may have been at the margins or entirely outside of it. The system is very much a life-and-death matter for billions of people who, willing or otherwise, have developed a stake in its maintenance. Global capitalism achieved a certain hegemony in recent years not just because its ideology became dominant but *also*, and perhaps primarily, because it has had the ability to provide material rewards and to impose sanctions.

However, the struggle for hegemony in the global system should not be seen in terms of a dispute *among* nation-states but in terms of transnational social and class groups and their struggles to develop hegemonic and counterhegemonic projects. The class relations of global capitalism are now so deeply internalized *within* every nation-state that the classical image of imperialism as a relation of external domination is outdated. Nation-state-centric analyses of inter- and transnational relations fail to appreciate the integrative character of global capitalism. The TCC has been attempting to position itself as a new ruling-class group worldwide since the 1980s and to bring some coherence and stability to its rule through an emergent TNS apparatus. The world politics of this would-be global ruling class is not driven, as they were for national ruling classes, by the flux of shifting rivalries and alliances played out through the interstate system, but by the new global social structure of accumulation.

Many have mistakenly interpreted militarization and renewed US interventionism through theories of a "new imperialism," according to which the United States set about to renew a US empire and offset the decline in its hegemony amidst heightened inter-imperialist rivalry.[2] The hallmark of "new imperialism"

2 See for example D. Harvey, *The New Imperialism*, New York: Oxford University Press, 2003; E. Meiksins Wood, *Empire of Capital*, London: Verso, 2003; J. B. Foster, *Naked Imperialism: US Pursuit of Global Dominance*, New York: Monthly Review, 2006; P. Gowan, *The Global Gamble: Washington's Bid for World Dominance*, London: Verso, 1999.

theories is the assumption that world capitalism in the twenty-first century is made up of "domestic capitals" and distinct national economies that interact with one another, and a concomitant "realist" analysis of world politics as driven by the pursuit by governments of their "national interest." But these interpretations ignore the changes that have taken place in world capitalism. These changes have vast implications for how we analyze world political and social dynamics as well as the responses by distinct agents to the current crisis. Interpreting the US state as playing a leadership role on behalf of transnational capitalist interests is a more satisfactory explanation than that of advancing "US" interests. The US state has taken the lead in imposing a reorganization of world capitalism. But this does not mean that US militarism and interventionism seek to defend "US" interests. As the most powerful component of the TNS, the US state apparatus attempts to defend the interests of transnational investors and the overall system.

Neither the emergent transnational stage in world capitalism nor the current crisis can be understood through the lens of nation-state-centric thinking. This is not to say that the nation-state is no longer important but that the system of nation-states as discrete interacting units, the inter-state system, is no longer the principal institutional framework that shapes social forces and political dynamics. The nation-state-centric perspective has become a blinder that limits and increasingly distorts our understanding. The global-capitalism perspective summarized here provides much greater explanatory power in making sense of the crisis.

SITUATING THE GLOBAL CRISIS: FROM NATION-STATE TO TRANSNATIONAL CAPITALISM

This globalization stage of world capitalism itself evolved out the response of distinct agents to previous episodes of crisis, in particular to the 1970s crisis of Fordism-Keynesianism, or of redistributive capitalism. In the wake of that crisis, capital went global as a strategy of the emergent transnational capitalist class and its political representatives to reconstitute its class power by breaking free of nation-state constraints to accumulation. These constraints—the so-called class compromise—had been imposed on capital through decades of mass struggles around the world by nationally contained popular and working classes. During the

1980s and 1990s, however, globally oriented elites captured state power in most countries around the world and utilized that power to push capitalist globalization.

Global mobility gave transnational capital newfound structural power over nationally based working classes. Globalization and neoliberal policies opened up vast new opportunities for transnational accumulation in the 1980s and 1990s. What took place, in broad strokes, in these decades? Privatizations facilitated a new round of primitive accumulation as public and community spheres were commodified and turned over to capital. Deregulation, liberalization, and free trade agreements allowed for a wave of foreign direct investment, for a sharp increase in cross-border mergers and acquisitions, and for a heightened concentration and centralization of capital on a global scale. The incorporation of the former Soviet bloc and Third World revolutionary countries into global capitalism provided vast new markets and investment outlets. The revolution in computer and information technology and other technological advances helped emergent transnational capital to achieve major gains in productivity and to restructure, "flexibilize," and shed labor worldwide. This, in turn, undercut wages and the social wage and facilitated a transfer of income to capital and to high-consumption sectors around the world that provided new market segments fueling growth. In sum, globalization made possible a major extensive and intensive expansion of the system and unleashed a frenzied new round of accumulation worldwide that offset the 1970s crisis of declining profits and investment opportunities.

But crises of overaccumulation follow periods of hyper-accumulation. At the structural level, the current global crisis is above all one of overaccumulation, or the lack of outlets for the profitable absorption of surpluses. Global elites giddily declared "the end of History" in the heyday of global capitalism's hegemony in the early 1990s, but by the end of that decade the limits to expansion became clear as global markets became saturated. As privatization programs ran their course, the well of assets to privatize dried up. The initial boom in investment opportunities in the former socialist and revolutionary countries began to taper, after they were brought into global markets. Once plants and infrastructures made the switch to computer and information technology the remarkable rate of fixed-capital turnover that the initial system-wide introduction of these technologies generated could not be sustained. Investment in high-tech slowed greatly in the twenty-first century, and in 2008 telecommunication and computer orders were down 50 percent from their high in the late 1990s.[3] By the turn of the century, it became apparent that the world was headed for a structural crisis. The system was generating ever more massive surpluses, yet opportunities diminished for the profitable absorption of those surpluses after the boom of the 1980s and 1990s. Global economic expansion and global market contraction reflect a— perhaps *the*—fundamental contradiction of capitalism: *over-accumulation*.

Crisis theory suggests that overaccumulation may be manifested in different ways.[4] How is it manifested in the current crisis? In the last major crisis, that of the 1970s, it took the form of a falling rate of profit, as "profit squeeze" theorists writing in that decade demonstrated. But a "profit squeeze" does not explain the current situation, as profits have soared in the period leading up to crisis (see Figure 13.1). In the 1970s, overaccumulation also took the form of stagflation, or inflation together with stagnation. Working and popular classes in the early and mid-1970s fiercely resisted a transfer of the costs of the crisis to themselves. Neither these classes nor capital were willing to shoulder the costs of crisis; this stand-off is what generated stagflation. But working and popular classes were able to put up resistance precisely because they faced capital within the confines of the nation-state. The gains these classes had made within nation-state capitalism and their ability to resist capital's impositions is precisely what led capital to go global in the first place, that is, to undertake a restructuring of the system through globalization. But stagflation and stand-off does not characterize the current crisis, at least not as I write in mid-2009. As has been amply documented, the portion of value going to workers has dropped sharply and living standards have plummeted since the late 1970s. Instead, it seems clear that overaccumulation is now expressed, as it was in the 1930s crisis, as overproduction/underconsumption. The world press, for instance, has been full of images of car lots overflowing with vehicles that cannot be marketed as factories shut down and

3 P. G. Gosselin, "US Economy May Sputter for Years," *Los Angeles Times*, January 19, 2009, p. A1.

4 See, inter alia, David Harvey's discussion in *Limits to Capital*, London: Verso, 2006.

Figure 13.1: Corporate profits, 1993–2008

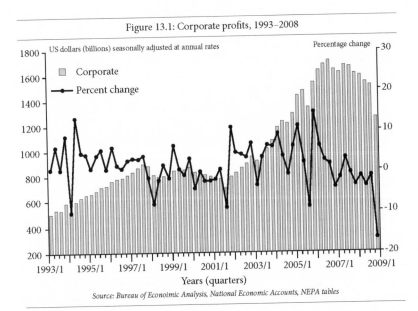

Years (quarters)

Source: Bureau of Econoimic Analysis, National Economic Accounts, NEPA tables

production plummets. And if there is a "Credit Crunch" it is not because bankers and investors do not have money to lend but because they cannot do so profitably due to consumer insolvency.

The capitalist system, in sum, is again facing the recurrent challenge of how to profitably unload surpluses. The system had been stumbling from one lesser crisis to another since the mid-1990s. First was the Mexican Peso Crisis of 1995, and its "tequila effect" elsewhere. This was followed by the Asian Financial Meltdown of 1997–98 that also spread to other parts of the world. Then came the recession of 2001. Between the Asian Meltdown of 1997–98 and the recession of 2001, global elites began to sound alarm bells. Billionaire financier George Soros warned of the need to save the system from itself.[5] These elites became wracked by divisions and infighting as the more politically astute among them clamored for a "post-Washington Consensus" project of reform—a so-called globalization with a human face.[6] The neoliberal monolith began to crack, although

5 G. Soros, The Crisis of Global Capitalism: Open Society Endangered, New York: PublicAffairs, 1998.
6 See, inter alia, J. Stiglitz, Globalization and its Discontents, New York: W.W. Norton, 2003.

it would take several more years before its downfall. By the new century, two major mechanisms for unloading surplus would provide a perverse lifeline to the system: financial speculation and militarized accumulation.

FINANCIAL SPECULATION AND MILITARIZED ACCUMULATION

Globalization has, in large part, been a finance-led process. Deregulation of the financial industry together with the introduction of computer and information technology made possible the creation of a globally integrated financial system. Transnational finance capital is the most mobile fraction of capital and became the hegemonic fraction on a world scale in the late twentieth century. The "revolution in finance" over the past few decades included all sorts of financial innovations— a vast and bewildering array of derivatives, including swaps, futures markets, hedge funds, institutional investment funds, mortgage-backed securities, collateralized debt obligations, Ponzi schemes, pyramiding of assets, and many more. These innovations make possible a global casino, or transnational financial circuits based on speculation and the ongoing expansion of fictitious capital. Securitization made every pile of money, such as pensions, as well as debt itself ("negative money"), a "tradable" and therefore a source of speculation and accumulation. These innovations allowed global speculators to appropriate values through new circuits that were in many ways irrespective of space and irrespective of "real" value or material production.

Transnational finance capital proved to be utterly predatory, seeking out one outlet after another for frenzied speculation. The sequence of speculative waves in the global casino since the 1980s included real-estate investments in the emerging global property market that inflated property values in one locality after another, wild stock-market speculation leading to periodic booms and busts, most notably the bursting of the dot-com bubble in 2001, the phenomenal escalation of hedge-fund flows and pyramiding of assets (see Figure 13.2), currency speculation, one Ponzi scheme after another, and later on frantic speculation in global commodities markets, especially energy and food markets, which provoked a spike in world prices in 2007 and 2008 and sparked "food riots" around the world.

Figure 13.2: Global hedge funds

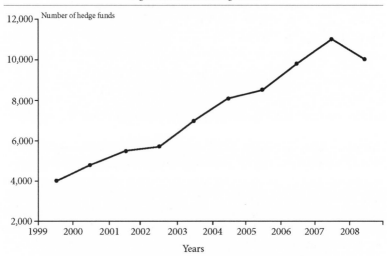

Source: International Financial Services London report—Hedge funds 2009, April 7, 2009.
Estimates of the size of the hedge fund industry vary due to restrictions imposed on advertising
and reporting of performance by hedge funds. As there are no authoritative estimates we have
relied in this report on commercial databases and index providers which rely on information
provided voluntarily

As speculation in the global financial casino reached fever pitch following recovery from the 2001 recession, the gap grew ever greater between fictitious capital in this casino and the productive economy, or what the media popularly called the "real economy." This "real economy" was kept afloat momentarily by a massive increase in consumer debt (largely credit cards and mortgages) and Federal deficit spending in the United States, which converted that country into the world's "market of last resort" and temporarily postponed the crash. US consumer debt climbed from $355 billion in 1980 to $1 trillion in 1994, $2 trillion in 2004, and $2.6 trillion in 2008, while the US current account went from a surplus in 1992 to deficits of $100 billion in 1998, $700 billion in 2004, and $1.2 trillion in 2008, according to Federal Reserve data. The Federal Reserve decision to reduce interest rates to about 1 percent in 2003 as a mechanism to overcome the recession also triggered a wave of speculation in the US mortgage market and prompted investors to begin subprime lending, including the infamous loans with "teaser" interest rates aggressively sold to millions of people who would later be unable to meet their mortgage payments once the rates were increased. Consumption driven by US consumer credit-card and mortgage debt and state deficit financing sustained accumulation worldwide and momentarily displaced the crisis. In the perverse world of predatory transnational finance capital, debt and deficits themselves became new sources of financial speculation.

It was *transnational*—not "US"—capital that relied on US debt and deficits to sustain profit-making around the world. The subprime mortgage market, for example, attracted trillions of dollars from individual, institutional, and corporate investors from all continents. It is a mistake to see things in terms of "US capitalism" rather than global capitalism. The US state has acted as an instrument of global capitalism and the United States as a major axis or nodal point for globalized accumulation. The funds from the US Treasury bail-outs of the Wall Street banks in late 2008 and early 2009, for instance, went to individual and institutional investors from around the world, while the US debt was itself financed by these same investors.

Global casino capitalism produced an ever greater expansion of fictitious capital—that is, money thrown into circulation without any base in commodities or in productive activity. Financial speculation fueled industrial production in part, so that the global casino kept the global factory running for a while. But large amounts of credit served not to expand production but to inflate the prices of assets already in place. The gap between the worldwide speculative economy and the productive economy grew to an unfathomable chasm. In 2000, for instance, the worldwide trade in goods and services was less than $10 trillion for the entire year, according to IMF data, while *daily* movements in currency speculation stood at $3.5 trillion, so that in just a few days more currency circulated as speculation than the international circulation of goods and services in an entire year. By the early years of the twenty-first century, these massive concentrations of transnational finance capital were destabilizing the system and global capitalism ran up against the limits of financial fixes. The bottoming out in 2007 of the subprime mortgage market that triggered the collapse a year later of the global financial system headquartered in Wall Street was merely the "straw that broke the camel's back."

Alongside frenzied financial speculation, the US state militarized the global economy. The cutting edge of accumulation in the "real economy" worldwide shifted from computer and information technology before the dot-com bust to a military-security-industrial-construction-engineering-petroleum complex

Figure 13. 3: US Military Expenditure since 1996

Source: US Government Printing Office

that also accrued enormous influence in the halls of power in Washington. Military spending skyrocketed into the trillions of dollars through the "War on Terror" and the invasions and occupations of Iraq and Afghanistan (Figure 13.3), acting to throw fresh fuel on the smoldering embers of the global economy. Spin-off effects of this spending flowed through the open veins of the global economy—that is, the integrated network structures of the global production, services, and financial system. In this way, the US state has mobilized vast resources and political pressures, taking advantage of the dollar's role as the global currency and therefore of the extraordinary power of the US Treasury to absorb surpluses and sustain global accumulation by militarizing that accumulation and creating a global war economy. But the "War on Terror" also has collateral political and ideological functions. It legitimates new transnational social-control systems and the creation of a police state to repress political dissent in the name of security. It allows states to criminalize social movements and "undesirable" populations, such as undocumented immigrants in the United States.

Many interpreted militarization and renewed US interventionism under the Bush administration through "new imperialism" theories. These theories were quite popular during the Bush years because

THE CRISIS OF GLOBAL CAPITALISM

they allowed critics to identify a visible enemy—a state and its direct agents—responsible for the horrors of global intervention and domination. According to these theories, the United States set about to renew a US empire and offset the decline in its hegemony amidst heightened inter-imperialist rivalry. But this was a fundamentally flawed interpretation of militarized accumulation, as I have argued at length elsewhere.[7] We would do better to see the US state as the most powerful institution in advancing global capitalism, in organizing and sustaining global accumulation. "New imperialism" theories confused capitalist competition with state competition and conflated the disarray, factionalism, and parochial and sectoral interests among transnational capitalist groups and global elites with nation-state rivalries. The US state has attempted to play a leadership role *on behalf of* transnational capitalist interests, taking the lead in imposing a reorganization of world capitalism.

The beneficiaries of US military action around the world have not been "US" but transnational capitalist groups. This is the underlying class relation between the transnational capitalist class and the US national state. Despite the rhetoric of neoliberalism, the US state undertook an unprecedented role in creating profit-making opportunities for transnational capital and pushing forward an accumulation process that, left to its own devices (the "free market"), would have ground to a halt much sooner than 2008. The "creative destruction" of war (and natural and humanitarian disasters) generated new cycles of accumulation through "reconstruction." The trillions of dollars invested by the US state in war and "reconstruction" in Iraq and elsewhere has gone to a vast array of investors and subcontractors spanning the globe. For instance, Kuwaiti Trading and Contracting, Alargan Trading of Kuwait, Gulf Catering and Saudi Trading and Construction Company were just some of the companies based in the Middle East that entered into multiple subcontracting relationships with Halliburton and Bechtel, and shared in the bonanza along with companies and investor groups as far away as South Africa, Bosnia, the Philippines, and India.[8] The picture that emerged was one in which the US state mobilized the resources

---

7 For a review of the "new imperialism" literature and my critique, see W. I. Robinson, "Beyond the Theory of Imperialism: Global Capitalism and the Transnational State," *Sociology Without Borders*, No. 2, 2007.
8 Ibid.

to feed a vast transnational network of profit-making that passed through countless layers of outsourcing, subcontracting, alliances and collaborative relations, benefiting transnationally oriented capitalists from many parts of the globe as the class relations of global capitalism became deeply internalized *within* every nation-state. The crisis then hit the global system as a whole and is as much political—a crisis of legitimacy—as it is economic.

RESPONSES TO THE CRISIS AND ALTERNATIVE FUTURES

Is the current Crisis cyclical, structural, or systemic? *Cyclical crises* are recurrent to capitalism about once every ten years and involve recessions that act as self-correcting mechanisms without any major restructuring of the system. The recessions of the early 1980s, the early 1990s, and 2001 were cyclical crises. In contrast, we are now in a deep structural crisis. *Structural crises* reflect deeper contradictions that can only be resolved by a major restructuring of the system. The crisis of the 1970s was a structural crisis that was resolved through capitalist globalization. Before that, the 1930s was a structural crisis that was resolved through the creation of a new model of Fordist-Keynesian or redistributive capitalism. A *systemic crisis* involves the replacement of a system by an entirely new system or by an outright collapse. A structural crisis opens up the *possibility* for a systemic crisis. But whether it actually snowballs into a systemic crisis—in this case, if it gives way either to capitalism being superseded or to a breakdown of global civilization—is not predetermined and depends entirely on the response of social and political forces to the crisis and on historical contingencies that are not easy to forecast. This is an historic moment of extreme uncertainty, in which collective responses to the crisis from distinct social and class forces are in great flux.

Many global elites have responded to the current Crisis by pushing for a global reformism or neo-Keynesianism from above, aimed at saving capitalism from itself and from contending radical challenges. The Obama administration articulates such a project, involving a shift from neoclassical to institutionalist economics, a limited re-regulation of global market forces, and multi-trillion-dollar state intervention programs to bail out transnational capital. Global reformism appeared to be the dominant response from elites in 2009 but there was no global-elite consensus. It is entirely premature to predict or describe a new model of global capitalism, as social forces will continue to be in conflict for a long time to come. Moreover such a project must contend with the fundamental contradiction of a globalizing economy within a nation-state-based system of political authority and legal enforcement. "We now have global financial markets, global corporations, global financial flows," stated British Prime Minister Gordon Brown, speaking at a late 2008 emergency summit of the G-20 countries. "But what we do not have is anything other than national and regional regulation and supervision. We need a global way of supervising our financial system . . . we need very large and very radical [political, institutional] changes."[9] In fact, it is since the Asian Crisis of 1997–98 that global elites have been scrambling to develop more effective transnational state apparatuses, or institutions and mechanisms that allow for transnational coordination and supervision. These efforts have intensified since the collapse of 2008. In March 2009, for instance, the Chinese government called for the creation of a new global reserve currency to replace the dominant dollar—a super-currency made up of a basket of national currencies and controlled by the IMF.[10]

What are the prospects of a "new New Deal"? At the time of writing (mid-2009) there were few signs that capitalist states could foment a shift back from financial to productive accumulation. Global capital has become a leviathan in which capitals from around the world are so deeply inter-penetrated not only across borders but through the overlap of productive and financial circuits that it is not clear how meaningful it is to continue to make a distinction, in the classical way, between the two. The giant global financial conglomerates draw in individual and institutional investors from around the world and in turn circulate unfathomable amounts of capital into productive, commercial and service circuits. There did not appear to be the political will or even the notion among global elites and capitalist state managers in early 2009 to restructure the system in any way that would re-establish some boundaries between financial and productive circuits or that would modify the role transnational finance capital has played as the regulator

---

9   Gordon Brown, as cited in J. Brecher, T. Costello and B. Smith, "The G-20 vs. the G-6 Billion," *ZNet*, November 20, 2008, http://www.zmag.org (accessed on November 21, 2008).
10   D. Lee, "China Pushes for Bigger Role in Reshaping the World Economy," *Los Angeles Times*, April 2, 2009, p. A1.

of the circuit of accumulation and the causal agent in the Crisis. While some state officials called for a re-regulation of the global financial system, none appeared to challenge in any fundamental way the very structure in which transnational finance capital exercises such utter domination over the world.

In the 1930s reformist forces from above were able to re-structure capitalism by curtailing capital's prerogatives without challenging its fundamental interests. Today, by contrast, I do not see any way a reformism from above could adequately address the current crisis without a head-on collision with the interests of global capital—the transnational banks, the oil/energy sector, the military-industrial-reconstruction complex, and so forth. This is to say that the capitalist state, in order to salvage the system from its own self-destruction, would have to exercise a remarkable degree of autonomy not just from individual capitalists and investor groups but from the leviathan that is the inextricably entangled mass of global capital. Such a role could only come about under a change in the worldwide correlation of class and social forces in favor of popular and working classes. The principle underlying difference between the 1930s New Deal project of reform and restructuring and the twenty-first-century conjuncture is this correlation of class and social forces worldwide. There is no socialist-oriented bloc of countries currently that could exercise a critical counterweight to capitalist elites in response to the current crisis, while mass socialist and worker movements, although they are burgeoning, are weak compared to the 1930s.

On the other hand, although these forces are weaker in a comparative historical sense, they are also more coordinated across borders and regions in the new global age, and reinvigorated by the crisis. To speak of a global justice movement is not mere rhetoric, because resistance and counterhegemonic forces around the world are acutely aware, in a way that we have not previously experienced, that local resistance struggles and alternative projects acquire their meaning in the context of and in relation to transnational struggles and projects. In the late 1990s, popular resistance forces in different parts of the world calling for transformative projects formed a critical mass, coalescing around an agenda for global social justice. Resurgent Left, radical, and anti-capitalist forces worldwide have again placed socialism on the world political agenda. Latin America appears to be the "weakest link" at this time in the global capitalist leviathan. The Venezuelan revolution is attempting to construct a twenty-first-century socialism and to stake out a radical anti-capitalist pole in South America. Everywhere, popular forces are in ferment and mass struggles escalating. The organized Left has a renewed presence in many countries.

These counterhegemonic forces call for the resolution of the crisis through a more far-reaching transformation of the global social order. But severe fragmentation of the popular classes brought about by decades of global informalization and flexible accumulation continues to challenge counter-hegemonic forces to find new ways to aggregate dispersed groups into collective projects of transformation. Anarchist-inspired aversions to struggling for state power and the illusion of being able to "change the world without taking power"[11] are under heightened challenge. A radical response to the crisis from below lacks at this time a "postmodern prince" or political vehicles and concrete projects for reordering the world, a deficiency that the global justice movement seems to be more acutely aware of than before. At the close of a 120,000-strong meeting of the World Social Forum in Belem, Brazil, in January 2009, representatives from social movements from around the world declared:

> We are facing a global crisis which is a direct consequence of the capitalist system and therefore cannot find a solution within the system. . . . In order to overcome the crisis we have to grapple with the root of the problem and progress as fast as possible towards the construction of a radical alternative that would do away with the capitalist system and patriarchal domination. We, the social movements, are faced with an historic opportunity to develop emancipatory initiatives on a global scale. Only through the social struggle of the masses can populations overcome the crisis. . . . The challenge of social movements is to achieve a convergence of global mobilization.[12]

The initiative seemed to pass in early 2009 from global elites to oppositional forces from below. Global elites meeting in January 2009 for the annual summit of the World Economic Form in Davos, Switzerland, appeared to be rudderless—confused and divided, unable to come up with coherent solutions to the crisis, and on the defensive. In contrast, the 120,000 participants from the

---

11 J. Holloway, *Change the World Without Taking Power*, London: Pluto, 2005.
12 Declaration of the Assembly of Social Movements at the World Social Forum 2009, February 5, 2009, available at http://www.globalresearch.ca (accessed on April 5, 2009).

Belem World Social Forum meeting were clearly on the offensive. Could such a global mobilization from below push reformist-minded elites further to the Left, or even push beyond reformism? Popular forces from below need to convert counterhegemony into a hegemony within the gamut of social and political responses to the unfolding crisis. This hegemony must involve a radical critique of the crisis. Now is the time to move from opposition to neoliberalism to opposition to the mildly reformist proposals that do not challenge the power of the transnational capitalist class.

THE DANGERS OF NEO-FASCISM AND COLLAPSE

Nation-states will remain for the foreseeable future a fundamental terrain of battle amongst contending social forces. National states face spiraling fiscal and legitimacy crises. Managers of the capitalist state need to generate conditions for a reactivation of transnational accumulation, yet they also must respond to mass popular pressures from below. Many governments will likely collapse, as happened in Iceland in January 2009, as states find no way to manage the explosive pressures generated by the crisis. Global elites clearly were unable to counter the erosion of the system's authority. Might states turn to national protectionism in response to pressure from national constituencies to address the crisis? The integrated nature of the global production and financial system makes it difficult for it to be disassembled into national systems. Moreover, it is not in the interests of transnational capital to seal off any national territory, which would undermine the transnational circuits of accumulation that are based on vast and overlapping chains of suppliers and subcontractors across the globe and thoroughly transnational ownership and cross-investment of what appear in name alone as "national" corporations.

Apparently protectionist measures in late 2008 and early 2009 sought not to shield national capitals in rivalry with one another, as in the 1930s, but to bail out *transnational* capital within particular nation-states. National constituencies pressing for protectionism were not capitalist groups, which are transnational in character even when headquartered in one nation or another, but popular and working classes. US trade unions, for instance, called for a "buy American" provision to be included in the early 2009 US government bail-out of auto firms, while the US Chamber of Commerce and other business groups railed against such provisions.[13] Such labor protectionism may be progressive in some cases, but in others it is clearly chauvinist, such as in the United States and England, where it has been directed by privileged, largely white, sectors of the working class against immigrants. And it is this constituency that could form the social base for far-Right responses to the crisis. Crises of state legitimacy and vacuums in institutional power, in this regard, open up space not just for popular forces from below but also for the far-Right forces that compete with reformist and radical responses to crisis.

This proto-fascist Right seeks to fuse reactionary political power with transnational capital, to organize a mass base among historically privileged sectors of the global working class, such as white workers in the North and middle layers in the South, that are now experiencing heightened insecurity and the specter of downward mobility. The proto-fascist response to the crisis involves militarism, extreme masculinization, racism, the search for scapegoats (such as immigrant workers in the United States and Europe), and mystifying ideologies. The need for dominant groups around the world to assure widespread, organized mass social control of the world's surplus population and of rebellious forces from below gives a powerful impulse to a project of twenty-first-century global fascism. A twenty-first-century fascism could develop police states drawing on new sophisticated systems of surveillance and coercive and ideological control, and the mechanisms they make possible for controlling space and exercising more selective repression than we traditionally associate with early-twentieth-century fascism. Images of what such a political project would involve spanned from the late-2008-to-early-2009 Israeli invasion of Gaza and "ethnic cleansing" of the Palestinians, to the scapegoating and criminalization of immigrant workers in the United States, genocide in the Congo, the spread of neo-Nazis and skinheads in Europe, and the incipient breakdown of constitutional order under the George W. Bush administration.

Could global civilization collapse if one or another project is unable to impose its hegemony and stabilize the system? There are many historical episodes of collapse when civilizations are unable to resolve the contradictions that tear them apart.[14] When no social

13 See P. Wallsten, "Liberals Watch Obama, and Worry," *Los Angeles Times*, February 16, 2009, p. A1.
14 See, for example, J. Diamond, *Collapse: How Societies Choose to Fail or Succeed*, New York: Penguin, 2005.

or political force is able to prevail and impose a stable system of domination, collapse has been the outcome. This was the case, for instance, with the collapse of the Roman and Mayan empires, several Chinese dynasties, and the Easter Island civilization. The current moment is distinct in that this time the collapse would be of global civilization. Ecological constraints also played a role in previous collapses. However, we face the prospects of a more far-reaching systemic implosion in the twenty-first century through ecological crisis—as suggested in peak oil and other resource-depletion scenarios, the spiral of species extinctions, and scientific predictions of a collapse of central agricultural systems in China, Australia, the US Midwest and other global bread-baskets in the coming decades. The ecological constraints to a resolution of the Global Crisis circumscribe the political possibilities for its resolution. Even if global capitalism could manage to stabilize in the next few years, a recovery would be ephemeral without a more fundamental resolution of the fundamentally unsustainable nature of the system. Sociologist Sing Chew has studied "recurrent dark ages" in world history, including mass dying, political chaos and a regression in levels of social organization and productive forces. He has warned that we face the possibility now of a "new dark age" on a planetary scale.[15]

CONCLUSIONS: WHO WILL PAY?

A crisis of overaccumulation means that the system's capacity for surplus absorption is exhausted and that a phase of the devaluation or destruction of capital surpluses has begun. In 2008 alone close to $7 trillion was wiped out on Wall Street through such devaluation.[16] The neo-Keynesian bail-outs and stimulus packages totaling trillions of dollars are financed by printing money. The resolution of one crisis will thus likely generate another—hyperinflation not unlike what Latin America experienced in the late 1970s and 1980s. This in turn is part of a more fundamental historical process, the "Thirdworldization" of the "First World," in which the wealth concentrated at some poles of accumulation in the world is no longer redistributed downward locally towards

---

15 S. C. Chew, *The Recurring Dark Ages: Ecological Stress, Climate Changes, and System Transformation*, Lanham: AltaMira Press, 2006.
16 R. Merle, "Wall Street's Final '08 Toll: $6.9 Trillion Wiped Out," *Washington Post*, January 1, 2009, p. A1.

First World labor aristocracies. The Crisis is already resulting in a further concentration and centralization of capital worldwide, in hothouse fashion in the hands of the transnational capitalist class. This process was one of the great untold stories of the 1990s boom in the global economy.[17] It has accelerated since the Financial Collapse; for instance, in 2008 alone, the eight great Wall Street financial houses became only four.

Historically, dominant groups attempt to transfer the cost of crisis onto the mass of popular and working classes, and in turn these classes resist such attempts. This is the global political moment. Unemployment, foreclosures, the further erosion of social wages, wage cuts, furloughs, reduced work hours, and mounting debt peonage are some of capital's transfer mechanisms. Unless there is effective resistance, global capital is likely to make permanent the further flexibilization of labor and other concessions it is wringing out of workers through the crisis. The bail-outs of transnational capital, particularly transnational finance capital, come at the expense of taxation on working classes and therefore represent in themselves a transfer of the devaluation of capital onto labor. Will popular sectors manage to forge a social solidarity of the oppressed, the exploited, and the subordinate majorities across ethnic and national lines? Dominant groups, especially in the heartlands of global capitalism, will try to aggravate existing national and ethnic hierarchies of labor, to scapegoat immigrants, unemployed black people, and so forth. Gary Dymski has shown how mortgage lenders in the United States shifted from redlining African-American communities to engaging in predatory lending to them; that is, a move from racial exclusion to racial exploitation.[18] Since the subprime collapse the dominant discourse attempts to shift blame to these African-American families as "irresponsible borrowers." Similarly, anti-immigrant forces in the United States have shifted from a blatant racialist anti-Latino discourse to an economistic discourse of "protecting citizens' employment." These discursive shifts underscore that a major dimension of the battles to come is *whose* interpretation of the Crisis will prevail. How majorities in global society understand the threats to their security and survival will shape their social and political agency.

It is at times of crisis rather than equilibrium that space opens up for new ideas and for collective agency to influence the course

---

17 Robinson, *Theory of Global Capitalism.*
18 See Chapter 4 of this volume.

of structural change. We are entering a period of turbulence, upheavals, collapse of states, political vacuums and prolonged conflict. In my view, resolution of the Crisis must involve a radical redistribution of wealth and power downward to poor majorities. Social justice requires, at the minimum, reintroducing a redistributive component into the global accumulation process. This raises the question of what forces in favor of social justice can hope to achieve if and when poor people and popular sectors are able to win state power in particular countries, or at least to place into state agencies people who are responsive to their plight, aware of their needs, and willing to challenge the prerogatives of transnational capital.

Yet this brings us full circle—back to the issue of globalization and the question of what makes the early twenty-first century distinct from previous moments in the history of world capitalism. In this qualitatively new stage of global capitalism, there are clear limitations to reintroduction of a redistributive project at the nation-state level. It is not clear how effective national alternatives alone can be in transforming social structures and resolving the crisis. If the (capitalist) state as a class relation is becoming transnationalized then any challenge to (global) capitalist state power must involve a major transnational component. Struggles at the nation-state level are far from futile. They remain central to the prospects for social justice, to progressive social change, and to any resolution of the Crisis. But any such struggles must be part of a more expansive transnational counterhegemonic project, including transnational trade unionism, transnational social movements, transnational political organizations, and so on. They must strive to establish sets of transnational institutions and practices that can place controls on the global market and rein in the power of global capital as the first step in a resolution of the Crisis. An alternative to global capitalism must be a *transnational* popular project. The popular mass of humanity in its struggle for social justice must develop a *transnational* class consciousness and concomitant global political protagonism involving strategies, programs, organizations and institutions that link the local to the national, and the national to the global.

POLITICS

14

THE GREAT SILENCE

Their Gilded Age and Ours

Steve Fraser

Google "second Gilded Age" and you will get ferried to 7,000 possible sites where you can learn more about what you already instinctively know. That we are living through a Gilded Age has become a journalistic commonplace. The unmistakable drift of all the talk about it is a Yogi Berra-ism: it's a matter of *déjà vu* all over again. But is it? Is turn-of-the-century America a replica of the world Mark Twain first christened "gilded" in his debut bestseller back in the 1870s?

Certainly, Twain would feel right at home today. Crony capitalism, the main object of his satirical wit in *The Gilded Age*, is thriving. Incestuous plots as outsized as the one in which the Union Pacific Railroad's chief investors conspired with a wagon-load of government officials, including Ulysses S. Grant's vice president, to loot the federal treasury once again lubricate the machinery of public policy-making. A cronyism that would have been familiar to Twain made the wheels go round during the years of the Bush administration. Even the invasion and decimation of Iraq was conceived and carried out as an exercise in grand strategic cronyism; call it cronyism with a vengeance. All of this has been going on since Ronald Reagan brought back morning to America.

Reagan's America was gilded by design. In 1981, when the New Rich and the New Right paraded in their sumptuous threads in Washington to celebrate at the new president's inaugural ball, it was called a "bacchanalia of the haves." Diana Vreeland, style guru (as well as Nancy Reagan confidante), was stylishly blunt:

"Everything is power and money and how to use them both . . . We mustn't be afraid of snobbism and luxury."

That's when the division of wealth and income began polarizing so that, by every measure, the country has now exceeded the extremes of inequality achieved during the first Gilded Age; nor are our elites any more embarrassed by their Mammon-worship than were members of the "leisure class" excoriated a century ago by that take-no-prisoners social critic of American capitalism Thorstein Veblen.

Back then, it was about masquerading as European nobility at lavish balls in elegant hotels like New York's Waldorf-Astoria, locked down to forestall any unpleasantness from the street (where ordinary folk were in a surly mood, trying to survive the savage depression of the 1890s). Today's "leisure class" is holed up in gated communities or houseoleums as gargantuan as the imported castles of their Gilded Age forerunners, ready to fly off—should the natives grow restless—to private islands aboard their private jets.

THE FREE MARKET AS MELODRAMA

At the height of the first Gilded Age, William Graham Sumner, a Yale sociologist and the most famous exponent of Herbert Spencer's theory of dog-eat-dog Social Darwinism, asked a good question: What do the social classes owe each other? Virtually nothing was the professor's answer.

As in those days, there is today no end to ideological justifications for an inequality so pervasive that no one can really ignore it entirely. In 1890, reformer Jacob Riis published his book *How the Other Half Lives*. Some were moved by his vivid descriptions of destitution. In the late nineteenth century, however, the preferred way of dismissing that discomfiting reality was to put the blame on a culture of dependency supposedly prevalent among "the lower orders," particularly, of course, among those of certain complexions and ethnic origins; and the logical way to cure that dependency, so the claim went, was to eliminate publicly funded "outdoor relief."

How reminiscent of the "welfare to work" policies cooked up by the Clinton administration, an exchange of one form of dependency—welfare—for another—low-wage labor. Poverty, once turned into the cultural and moral problem of the impoverished, exculpated Gilded Age economics in both the nineteenth and twenty-first centuries (and proved profitable besides).

Even now, there remains a trace of the old Social Darwinian rationale—that the ascendancy of "the fittest" benefits the whole species—and the accompanying innuendo that those consigned to the bottom of the heap are fated by nature to end up there. To that must be added a reinvigorated belief in the free market as the fairest (not to mention the most efficient) way to allocate wealth. Then, season it all with a bravura elevation of risk-taking to the status of spiritual, as well as economic, tonic. What you end up with is an intellectual elixir as self-congratulatory as the conscience-cleansing purgative that made Professor Sumner so sure in his cold-bloodedness.

Then, as now, hypocrisy and self-delusion were the final ingredients in this ideological brew. When it came to practical matters, neither the business elites of the first Gilded Age, nor our own "liquidators," "terminators," and merger and acquisition Machiavellians ever *really* believed in the free market or the enterprising individual. Then, as now, when push came to shove (and often much earlier), they relied on the government: for political favors, for contracts, for tax advantages, for franchises, for tariffs and subsidies, for public grants of land and natural resources, for financial bail-outs when times were tough, and for muscular protection, including the use of armed force, against all those who might interfere with the rights of private property.

So too, while industrial and financial tycoons liked to imagine themselves as stand-alone heroes, daring cowboys on the urban-industrial-financial frontier, as a matter of fact the first Gilded Age gave birth to the modern, bureaucratic corporation—and did so at the expense of the lone entrepreneur. To this day, that big-business behemoth remains the defining institution of commercial life. The reigning melodrama may still be about the free market and the audacious individual, but backstage, directing the players, stands the state and the corporation.

Crony capitalism, inequality, extravagance, Social Darwinian self-justification, blame-the-victim callousness, free-market hypocrisy: thus it was, thus it is again!

At the end of the Reagan years, public intellectuals Kevin Phillips and Gary Wills prophesied that this state of affairs was insupportable and would soon end. Phillips, in particular, anticipated a populist rising. It did not happen. Instead, nearly twenty years later, the second Gilded Age is alive, if not so well. Why such longevity? The answer tells us something about how these two epochs, for all their striking similarities, are also profoundly unalike.

MISSING UTOPIAS AND DYSTOPIAS

As a title, *Apocalypse Now* could easily have been applied to a movie made about late-nineteenth-century America. Whichever side you happened to be on, there was an overwhelming dread that the nation was dividing in two and verging on a second civil war, that a final confrontation between the haves and have-nots was unavoidable.

Irate farmers mobilized in cooperative alliances and in the Populist Party. Farmer-labor parties in states and cities from coast to coast challenged the dominion of the two-party system. Rolling waves of strikes, captained by warriors from the Knights of Labor, enveloped whole communities as new allegiances extended across previously unbridgeable barriers of craft, ethnicity, even race and gender.

Legions of small businessmen, trade unionists, urban consumers, and local politicians raged against monopoly and "the trusts." Armed workers' militias paraded in the streets of many American cities. Business and political elites built massive urban fortresses, public armories equipped with Gatling guns (the machine guns of their day), preparing to crush the insurrections they saw headed their way.

Even today the names of Haymarket (the square in Chicago where, in 1886, a bombing at a rally of rebellious workers led to the legal lynching of anarchist leaders at the most infamous trial of the nineteenth century), Homestead (where, in 1892, the Monongahela River ran red with the blood of Pinkerton thugs sent by Andrew Carnegie and Henry Clay Frick to crush the strike of their steelmaking employees), and Pullman (the company town in Illinois where, in 1894, President Grover Cleveland ordered Federal troops to put down the strike of the American Railway Union against the Pullman Palace Car Company) evoke memories of a whole society living on the edge.

The first Gilded Age was a moment of Great Fears, but also of Great Expectations—a period infatuated with a literature of utopias as well as dystopias. The two most successful novels of the nineteenth century, after *Uncle Tom's Cabin*, were Edward Bellamy's utopian *Looking Backward* and the horrific dystopia

Caesar's Column by Populist tribune Ignatius Donnelly. The latter reached its denouement when Donnelly's fictional proletarian underground movement, the "Brotherhood of Destruction," marked its "triumph" with the erection of a giant pyramid composed of a quarter of a million corpses of its enemy, "the Oligarchy" and its minions, cemented together and laced with explosives so that no one would dare risk removing them and destroying this permanent memorial to the barbarism of American industrial capitalism.

This end-of-days foreboding *and* the thirst for utopian release were not, moreover, confined to the ranks of agrarian or industrial troublemakers. Before "Pullman" became a word for industrial serfdom and the federal government's bloody-mindedness, it was built by its owner, George Pullman, as a model industrial city, a kind of capitalist utopia of paternal benevolence and confected social harmony.

Everyone was seeking a way out, something wholly new to replace the rancor and incipient violence of Gilded Age capitalism. The Knights of Labor, the Populist Party, the anti-trust movement, the cooperative movements of town and country, the nation-wide Eight-Hour Day uprisings of 1886 which culminated in the infamy of the Haymarket hangings, all expressed a deep yearning to abolish the prevailing industrial order.

Such groups weren't just angry; they weren't merely resentful—although they were that, too. They were disturbed enough, naïve enough, desperate enough, inventive enough, desiring enough, deluded enough—some still drawing cultural nourishment from the fading homesteads and workshops of pre-industrial America—to believe that out of all this could come a new way of life, a cooperative commonwealth. No one really knew what exactly that might be. Still, the great expectation of a future no longer subservient to the calculus of the marketplace and the capitalist workshop lent the first Gilded Age its special fission, its high (tragic) drama.

Fast-forward to our second Gilded Age and the stage seems bare indeed. No Great Fears, no Great Expectations, no looming social apocalypses, no utopias or dystopias—just a kind of flatline sense of the end of history. Where are all the roiling insurgencies, the break-away political parties, the waves of strikes and boycotts, the infectious communal upheavals, the chronic sense of enough is enough? Where are the earnest efforts to invoke a new order which, no matter how sketchy and full of unanswered questions, now seem as minutely detailed as the blueprints for a Boeing 747 compared to "Yes we can"?

What is left of mainstream populism exists on life-support in some attic of the Democratic Party. Even the language of our second Gilded Age is hollowed out. In a society saturated in Christian sanctimony, would anyone today describe "mankind crucified on a cross of gold" as William Jennings Bryan once did, or let loose against "Mammon worship," condemn aristocratic "parasites," or excommunicate "vampire speculators" and the "devilfish" of Wall Street? If nineteenth-century evangelical preachers once pronounced anathema on capitalist greed, twenty-first-century televangelists deify it. Tempers have cooled, leaving God, like many Americans, with only part-time employment.

THE GREAT SILENCE

I exaggerate, of course. Movements do exist today to confront the inequities and iniquities of our own Gilded Age. Wall Street bandits are, once in a while, arrested by a sheriff. Some ministers, even born-again ones, do still preach the Social Gospel. But all this seems a pale shadow of what was. Something fundamental about the metabolism of capitalism has changed.

Perhaps the answer is simple and basic: the first Gilded Age rested on industrialization; the second on de-industrialization. In our time, a new system of dis-accumulation looted American industry, liquidating its assets to reward speculation in "fictitious capital." After all, the rate of investment in new plant, technology, and research and development all declined during the 1980s. For a quarter of a century, the fastest-growing part of the economy has been the finance, insurance, and real estate (FIRE) sector.

De-industrialization has set off an avalanche the impact of which is still being felt in the economy, in the country's political culture, and in everyday life. It laid the industrial working class and the labor movement low, killing it twice over. This, more than anything else, may account for the great silence of the second Gilded Age, when measured, at least, against the raucous noise of the first. Labor was mortally wounded by direct assault, beginning with President Reagan's decision in 1981 to fire all the striking air traffic controllers. His draconian act licensed American business to launch its own all-out attack on the right to organize, which continues to this day.

In itself, however, resorting to coercion to deal with the opposition hardly distinguishes our own gilded elite from the first one. If anything, we live in less savage times, at least here at home. More fatal by far was the arrival of a new mode of capital accumulation, starkly different from the one that had prevailed a century ago. It eviscerated towns, cities, regions, and whole ways of life. It demoralized people, hollowed out popular institutions that had once offered resistance, and stoked the fires of resentment, racism, and national revanchism. Here was the raw material for mean-spirited division, not solidarity.

Dis-accumulation transformed the working class into a disaggregated pool of contingent labor, contract labor, temporary labor, and part-time labor, all in the interests of a new "flexible capitalism." Ideologues gussied-up this floating workforce by anointing it "free agent" labor, a euphemism designed to flatter the free-market homunculus in each of us—and, for a time, it worked. But the resulting reality has proved a bitter pill to swallow. To be a "free agent" today is to be free of health-care, pensions, secure jobs, security in every sense. In our gilded era, downward mobility, lasting a quarter-century and still counting, has marked the social trajectory of millions of people living in the American heartland.

Dis-accumulating capitalism also undermined the political gravitas of poverty. In the first Gilded Age, poverty was a function of exploitation; in the second, of exclusion or marginalization. When we think about poverty, what comes to mind is welfare and race. The first Gilded Age visualized instead coal miners, child labor, tenement workshops, and the shanty towns that clustered around the steel mills of Aliquippa and Homestead.

Poverty arising out of exploitation ignited widespread moral revulsion and a robust political assault on the power of the exploiters. The perpetrators of the poverty of exclusion of our own time have been trickier to identify. In his 1962 book *The Other America*, Michael Harrington noted the invisibility of poverty. That was half a century ago and misery still lives in the shadows. Helped along by an ingrained racism, poverty in the second Gilded Age was politically neutered . . . or worse.

Decline, dispossession, and marginalization: a grim scenario. Yet the new political economy of finance-based dis-accumulation also announced itself as the Second Coming of democratic capitalism. And in the realm of the collective imaginary, if not in reality, it convinced millions.

The Myth of Democratic Capitalism

Aristocrats don't exist anymore, but it is remarkable how long they lasted as major actors in the country's political dramaturgy. Franklin Delano Roosevelt was still denouncing "economic royalists" and "Tories of industry" at the height of the New Deal. The struggle against the counter-revolutionary aristocrat, seen to be subverting the institutions of democratic life, piling up unearned riches, supplied the energy powering American reform for generations. In real life, the robber-baron industrialists and financiers of Wall Street were no more aristocrats than my grandma from the *shtetl*. They were parvenus.

For their own good reasons, however, they actively conspired in this popular misperception by playing the aristocratic role for all it was worth. In hindsight, what looks like one of the silliest utopias of the first Gilded Age was enacted by these *nouveaux riches*, performing in *tableaux vivants* at gala balls dressed in aristocratic drag, or cavorting in the castles and villas they had transported stone by stone from France and Italy, or showing off at the weddings of their daughters to the offspring of bankrupt European nobility, or parading to New York's Metropolitan Opera in coaches driven by liveried servants and embossed with their family's "coat of arms," complete with hijacked insignia and faked genealogies that concealed their owners' homelier origins.

We may laugh at all this now. Back then, for millions, these aristocratic pretensions confirmed an ancient Jeffersonian suspicion: capitalists were nothing more or less than camouflaged aristocrats. And mobilizing to rescue the republic and democracy from such a danger was practically an indigenous instinct. However, pushing beyond this horizon of political democracy in the direction of social democracy is a different matter entirely, arousing anxiety about threatening the understructure of private property which is, after all, also part of the American dream. Having an aristocracy to kick around, even an ersatz one, can be politically empowering.

Minus the oddball exception or two, the new tycoonery of the second Gilded Age does not fancy itself an aristocracy. It does not dress up like one or marry off its daughters to fortune-hunting European dukes and earls. On the contrary, its major figures regularly dress down in blue jeans and cowboy hats, affecting a down-home populism or nerdy dishevelment. However addicted to the paraphernalia of flamboyant excess they may be, the new capitalist elite does not pretend these are the insignia of ruling-class entitlement.

Once upon a gilded time, the lower orders aped the fashions and manners of their putative betters; today it's the other way around. Indeed, it is no longer even apt to talk of a "leisure class," since our moguls of the moment are workaholics, Olympians of the merger-and-acquisition all-nighter.

Although the economic and political throw-weight of our gilded elite is at least as great as that of its predecessors in the days of J. P. Morgan and John D. Rockefeller, an American fear of a moneyed aristocracy has subsided accordingly. Instead, from the Reagan era on, Americans have been captivated by businessmen who took on the rebel role against a sclerotic corporate order and an ossified government bureaucracy that, together, were said to be blocking access to a democracy of the bold.

Often men from the middling classes, lacking in social pedigree, the overnight elevation of people like Michael Milken, Carl Ichan, or "greed is healthy" Ivan Boesky, flattered and confirmed a popular faith in the American dream. These irreverent new "revolutionaries," intent on overthrowing capitalism in the interests of capitalism, made fun of the men in pin-striped suits.

When the captains of industry and finance lorded it over the country in the late nineteenth century, no one dreamed of calling them rebels against an overweening government bureaucracy or an entrenched set of "interests." There was then no government bureaucracy, and tycoons like Russell Sage and Jay Gould were "the interests." They worried about being overthrown, not overthrowing someone else.

Our corporate elite are much more adept than their Gilded Age predecessors were at playing the democracy game. The old "leisure class" was distinctly averse to politics. If they needed a tariff or tax break, they called up their kept senator. When mortally challenged by the Populists and William Jennings Bryan in 1896, they did get involved; but, by and large, they didn't muck about in mass party politics, which they saw as too full of uncontrollable ethnic machines, angry farmers, and the like. They relied instead on the federal judiciary, business-friendly presidents, constitutional lawyers, and public and private militias to protect their interests.

Beginning in the 1970s, our age's business elite became acutely politically minded and impressively well organized, penetrating deeply all the pores of party and electoral democracy. They've gone so far as to craft strategic alliances with elements of what

their nineteenth-century predecessors—who might have blanched
at the prospect—would have termed the hoi polloi. Calls to
dismantle the federal bureaucracy now carry a certain populist
panache, while huffing and puffing about family values has—so
far—proven a cheap date for a gilded elite that otherwise generally
couldn't care less.

Moreover, the ascendancy of our *faux* revolutionaries has
been accompanied by media hosannas to the stock market as
an everyman's Oz. America's long infatuation with its own
democratic-egalitarian ethos lent traction to this illusion.

Horace Greely's inspirational admonition to "Go West young
man" echoed through all the channels of popular culture in the
1990s—from cable TV shows and mass-circulation magazines to
baseball stadium scoreboards and internet chat rooms. Only now
Greeley's frontier of limitless opportunity had migrated back East
to the stock exchange and into the ether of virtual or dot.com
reality. The culture of money released from all ancient inhibitions
enveloped the commons.

"Shareholder democracy" and the "ownership society" are
admittedly more public-relations slogans than anything tangible.
Nonetheless, you can't ignore the fact that, during the second
Gilded Age, half of all American families became investors in the
stock market. Dentists and engineers, mid-level bureaucrats and
college professors, storekeepers and medical technicians—people,
that is, from the broad spectrum of middle-class life who once
would have viewed the New York Stock Exchange with a mixture
of awe, trepidation, and genuine distaste, and warily kept their
distance—now jumped head-first into the marketplace carrying
with them all their febrile hopes for social elevation.

As Wall Street suddenly seemed more welcoming, fears about
strangulating monopolies died. Dwindling middle-class resistance
to big business accounts for the withering away of the old anti-
trust movement, a telling development in the evolution of our age's
particular form of "big-box" capitalism. Once, that movement
had not only expressed the frustrated ambitions of smaller
businessmen, but of all those who felt victimized by monopoly
power. It embodied not just the idea of breaking up the trusts,
but of competing with or replacing them with public enterprises.

Long before the Reagan counter-revolution defanged the whole
regulatory apparatus, however, the "anti-trust" movement was
over and done with. Its absence from the political landscape during
the second Gilded Age marks the demise of an older middle-class

world of local producers, merchants, and their customers who were once bound together by the ties of commerce and the folk truths of small-town Protestantism.

Big-box capitalism, the capitalism of Wal-Mart, still incites local uproars that carry a hint of that anti-trust past, but oppositional forces are divided. The capitalism of which Wal-Mart is emblematic generates a dissonant universe of political and cultural desires. It appeals, first of all, to instincts of individual and family material wellbeing which may run up against calls for a wider social solidarity. Moreover, in its own everyday way consumer culture—more far-reaching than anything imaginable a century ago—channels desire into forms of expressive self-liberation. Grand narratives that tell a story of collective destiny—Redemption, Enlightenment, and Progress, the Cooperative Commonwealth, Proletarian Revolution—don't play well in this refashioned political theater.

THE END OF THE AGE OF ACQUIESCENCE?

However, the wheel turns. The capitalism of the second Gilded Age now faces a systemic crisis and, under the pressure of impending disaster, may be headed back to the future. Old-fashioned poverty is making a comeback. Arguably, the global economy, including its American branch, is increasingly a sweatshop economy. There is no denying that brute fact in Thailand, China, Vietnam, Central America, Bangladesh, and dozens of other countries and regions that serve as platforms for primitive accumulation. Hundreds of millions of peasants have become proletarians virtually overnight.

Here at home, something analogous has been happening, but with an ironic difference and bearing within it a new historic opportunity. One might call it the unhorsing of the middle class.

During the first Gilded Age, the sweatshop seemed a noxious aberration. It lawlessly offered irregular employment at substandard wages for interminable hours. It was ordinarily housed helter-skelter in a makeshift workshop that would be here today, gone tomorrow. It was an underground enterprise that regularly absconded with its workers' paychecks and made chiseling them out of their due into an art form.

Today, what once seemed abnormal no longer does. The planet's peak corporations depend on this system. They have thrived on it. True enough, it has also encouraged the proliferation of petty enterprises—subcontractors, consulting firms, domestic service companies—fertilizing the soil in which our age of democratic capitalism is rooted. But the ubiquity of the sweated economy promises to alter the nation's political chemistry.

Many of the newly flexible proletarians working for Wal-Mart, for auto parts or construction company subcontractors, on the phones at direct-mail call centers, behind the counters at mass-market retailers, earn a dwindling percentage of what they used to. Even new hires at the Big Three automobile manufacturers will now make a smaller hourly wage than their grandfathers did in 1948. So too, the relative job security such employees once enjoyed is gone, leaving them vulnerable to the "lean and mean" dictates of the new capitalism: double or triple workloads; or, even worse, part-time work, always shadowed by indignity and fear; or, worse yet, no work at all.

Meanwhile, the white collar Tomorrowland of "free agent" techies, software engineers, and the like—not to mention a whole endangered species of middle management—lives a precarious existence, under intense stress, chronically anticipating the next round of lay-offs. Yet many of them were once upon a time members in good standing of the "middle class." Now, they find themselves on the down escalator, descending into a despised state no one could mistake for middle-class life.

"Flexible accumulation" joins this dispossession of the middle class to the super-exploitation of millions who never laid claim to that status. Many of these sweated workers are women, laboring away as home health-care aides, in the food services industry, in meat processing plants, at hotels and restaurants and hospitals, because the arithmetic of "flexible accumulation" demands two workers to add up to the livable family wage not so long ago brought home by a single wage earner.

Millions more are immigrants, legal as well as undocumented, from all over the world. They live, virtually defenseless, in a twilight underworld of illegality and prejudice. Thanks to all this, the category of the "working poor" has re-entered our public vocabulary. Once again, as during the first Gilded Age, poverty seems a function of exploitation at work, not only the lot of those excluded from work.

Might these developments augur the end of our second Gilded Age; or rather the end of the age of acquiescence? No one can know. Yet anger and resentment over insecurity, downward mobility, exploitation, second-class citizenship, and the ill-gotten gains of our Gilded Age mercenaries and their political enablers already rippled the political waters during the mid-term elections of 2006. And during the run-up to the presidential elections of 2008, popular anger provoked by the subprime mortgage collapse and the subsequent bail-outs, with public money, of the very elites who had caused it (and garnered tremendous riches in the process) created enough political pressure to produce a discernable leftward shift of the center of gravity within even the cowed leadership ranks of the Democratic Party.

Anger and resentment, however, do not by themselves comprise a visionary alternative. Nor is the Democratic Party, however restive, a likely vehicle of social-democratic aspirations. Much more will have to happen outside the precincts of electoral politics by way of mass-movement building to translate these smoke signals of resistance into something more muscular and enduring. Moreover, nasty competition over diminishing economic opportunities can just as easily inflame simmering racial and ethnic antagonisms.

Nonetheless, the current breakdown of the financial system is portentous. It threatens a general economic implosion more serious than anyone has witnessed for many decades. Depression, if that is what it turns out to be, together with the agonies of a misbegotten and lost war no one believes in any longer, could undermine whatever is left of the threadbare credibility of our Gilded Age elite.

Legitimacy is a precious possession; once lost it's not easily retrieved. Today, the myth of the "ownership society" confronts the reality of the "foreclosure society." The great silence of the second Gilded Age may give way to the great noise of the first.

15

FACING THE ECONOMIC CRISIS

Stanley Aronowitz

The main news since the Summer of 2008 has been the Global Economic Crisis, an event described by economists and most pundits as a "financial meltdown" caused by the irresponsibility of US lending institutions and consumers alike in offering—and accepting—"subprime" mortgages, interest-only loans and a series of complex derivative financial instruments. Many of the variable mortgages, which were initiated during the credit-driven bubble of the 1990s (and welcomed by the Clinton administration) and whose growth accelerated in the first years of the new century, require homebuyers to put no money down. Interest rates on these kinds of mortgages, which begin at 5–9 percent, are slated to rise within a few years, when they can double, triple, or balloon even more. In September 2008 we began to hear of massive foreclosures in almost all sections of the country. The projections for 2008 and 2009 were for 2 million homes (6 percent of the US total) to go into serious default. New home construction came to a screeching halt and commercial building suffered only slightly less pain. A few weeks into October, several major banks, bloated with bad loans, had failed, prompting the Federal Reserve to inject billions of dollars into the financial markets; others, like Merrill Lynch, merged with more stable partners. But the venerable old-line investment banking house Lehman Brothers was fated to fail when the Treasury Secretary and the Fed chair refused to extend bail-out funds. Of course, goliaths like Citibank, Bear Stearns, the insurance giant AIG and a few others were deemed "too big to fail" by the Treasury Secretary, Henry Paulson. By the end of the month the banking system, which held trillions of dollars in unredeemable mortgages, business and credit-card loans, was teetering on the brink of disaster, and the crisis was widely described as a "financial meltdown." Many leading investment banks disappeared and those that remained were reconstituted and converted into bank holding companies.

By October 2008, mobilized by Paulson and backed by the Fed Chair, Ben Bernanke, Congress quickly passed a massive $700 billion bail-out to financial institutions without scrutinizing the fine print. For different reasons, only a band of arch-conservative Republicans and a few liberal Democrats were prepared to let the system collapse, respectively hoping that the market would self-correct or that it would force a more radical program of extensive re-regulation (of the kind that had last been mooted—and rescinded—by the Carter administration and a Democratic Congress in 1978). The purpose of the bail-out legislation was, initially, to permit the government to purchase vast quantities of the bad securities at, or near, nominal value; in effect, this was a major infusion of cash into the banking and insurance systems without imposing stringent conditions on how the banks and insurance companies could spend the money. However, within weeks of President Bush's signing the bill into law and in the wake of the banks' refusal to loosen consumer and business credit, Paulson announced that this strategy was being replaced by a policy of purchasing bank shares. This entailed a direct infusion of cash in return for which the government would assume a measure of temporary and partial ownership, but not outright ownership and management of the system. Nor, as it turned out, did the federal government closely supervise the use of the funds they had so generously given. Within weeks, complaints resounded throughout the economy that the banks, instead of loosening their lending policies, were holding the money close to their chests. Of course business loans were tightened, but many would-be buyers of homes, cars and other durable goods, not to mention borrowers of much-needed cash to pay their bills, were turned away on one pretext or another, often because their credit rating was not top-of-the-line.

Meanwhile, jobless rates began their steep ascent. In reporting the spectacular job losses, the *New York Times* ran an investigative story that argued the official figures were only a fraction of the true extent of joblessness. According to the *Times* the number of discouraged job seekers who left the labor market, premature retirees who had no prospects but to accept inadequate pensions, and recent high-school and college graduates who simply did not look for work, might swell the actual figure by 4 or 5 percent. By early December, the National Bureau of Economic Research (NBER) reported that the economy had been in recession since December 2007, a year before they declared the recession "official." This revelation prompted no leading politician or economist to ask why the information had taken so long to be determined and revealed. The conservative NBER explained that it often takes that long to check their calculations and come up with a definitive judgment. That they felt obliged to offer an explanation at all was no doubt in response to the unspoken suspicion that the delay had something to do with the presidential election. Many believe that if the recession had been declared in the midst of an election season, candidate Obama could have prepared to vacation in Hawaii for more than just a few days.

The NBER's admission that the economy was in recession at least ten months before the financial meltdown poked a huge hole in the initial view that excessive and wanton lending was at the core of the troubles and that the crisis was exclusively financial in nature. Since 2002 the emerging recessionary signs were assiduously ignored by virtually all mainstream quarters. Fall 2006 witnessed the beginning of sagging economic growth, falling housing prices that prompted a severe slowing of new housing starts and sales, and gradual increases in unemployment figures. The fact that throughout the first decade of the new century plants continued to close and reduce workforces (not only in the Midwest but in the South as well) was not registered as a sign of a slowdown.

Indeed, the erosion of US manufacturing was barely noticed in official circles. According to the conventional wisdom, the US economy had become "post-industrial"—well on the way to realizing the belief that the American economy is a service economy and that it is better to let others, such as the Chinese and Koreans, produce material goods. If the US remained a major producer of food, armaments (for national security reasons), aircraft, heavy machinery such as machine tools, trucks and specialty steels, these were necessary to maintain our trade balances, but were not otherwise fundamental for insuring economic health. According to postmodern economics, our future lay in specializing in various forms of "immaterial" production. So, the US could afford to lose the remnants of once-huge garment and textile production industries, even when it was already certain that the US was no longer the center of basic steel and car production. Software, research, and the growth of higher education (both as the center of innovation and, in terms of employment and capital formation, a major industry), pharmaceuticals and other activities linked to the health-care industry, and entertainment, would surely fill the gap left by the demise of the "rust belt" industries. Even if the past thirty years had been times of wage stagnation and decline, the US had perfected a magnificent credit system that spurred consumption and seemed to know no limits. Or so the story went.

The truth is that what has been taken as economic expansion since the early 1970s was a symptom that the US (as well as the UK and other European countries) has survived a genuine period of economic decline by means of a dramatic increase in the creation of *fictitious* capital—credit that speculates on future economic performance. To be sure, fictitious capital is an ordinary function of the credit system: manufacturers borrow and lend money from and to each other and from banks to finance purchases of raw materials and labor on the promise of a future repayment when the value of their products is realized through sales, either within the production sector or through wholesale and retail purchases. But when such loans are extended by banks to businesses and non-commercial consumers and when they become the basis of wide swathes of economic activity, an element of systemic instability emerges. And when consumers or business owners default on their payments on a large scale, the system enters on a course toward collapse.

This is exactly what happened. Small producers, retailers and building contractors routinely borrowed money from banks or other lending institutions with which to purchase raw materials, rent stores or industrial facilities, and hire labor—on the premise that consumers would in turn receive loans from lending institutions and have sufficient income to pay their credit debts on time. But as the edifice of debts collapsed and credit flows froze, what Marx termed a "realization" crisis ensued: commodities cannot be sold at profit rates that are sufficient to stimulate further investment in plant, equipment, construction and labor. In order to alleviate their inventory glut business is obliged to reduce prices, but this tactic may take years before capital investment on a grand scale resumes. What follows is a period of lay-offs, downsizing, and falling prices.

For thirty-five years, the private sector has not produced a net increase in stable jobs. The work it has offered is increasingly low-wage, temporary and contingent; it usually carries no benefits and is often of a casual nature. The growth of jobs in computer-mediated services and software production was counterbalanced by losses in manufacturing; job losses due to mergers and acquisitions in the retail industry were barely matched by growth in fast-food employment. Over the past decade, as the private sector has failed to create new jobs and instead relied increasingly on contingent and temporary labor to meet short-term labor requirements, the public sector (especially education and health-care), became the main source of new, decent paying jobs. As the federal government abdicated responsibility for a variety of services, state and local bureaucracies added jobs. Of course, besotted with the conventional neoliberal ideology that only the private sector is a job creator, economists and politicians conveniently ignored this fact and continued to insist that the private sector can do anything better and more efficiently. What net increases in private sector employment occurred were largely, if not exclusively, the result of contracts awarded by federal, state and local governments who adopted both the mantra and practice of privatizing public goods. Although industrial production held steady, factory jobs stagnated during the boom because computer-mediated production began to dominate key industries. Eventually the technology sector, of which the bubble in software and communications (dot-com) companies was the leading edge, burst; as early as 2000, this sector began to experience mass layoffs, the effects of which were briefly noticed but quickly relegated to the back burner.

A New "New Deal"?

Five prior administrations, beginning with Carter's, relied on monetary policy to address economic problems (interest rates were their major tool) and had strenuously avoided using the tool of fiscal stimulus—that is, increasing spending on public goods and consequent job creation and income support—to address economic grief. After flirting with the possibility of a job-creation program, the Obama administration opted for the historic model, exemplified by the federal government's solution to the Savings and Loan Crisis during the 1980s: bail-out at the top. Given the depth of the present crisis, the Obama administration proposed a stimulus plan of nearly $750 billion. Some jobs were saved, but few were created. We should not expect miracles because job creation is far down the priorities list of the stimulus package: the emphasis remains on a bank and insurance bail-out, intended, ostensibly, to loosen credit. The economic policy of the Obama administration focuses on finance, and indirectly on re-stimulating the debt-based consumption that led to the crisis in the first place. It is clear that beyond the creation of more fictitious capital, the Obama team have few alternative ideas.

Nevertheless, as he took office, the new president promised to save or create 2.5 million jobs in his first term. To begin with, Obama has warned that the 2.5 million job figure is a long-term projection. How much money would it take to create 1 million jobs, about 7 percent of current unemployment? This is a tricky calculation. Would the program(s) be contracted out to private employers or would the government be the direct employer? If contracts are let at 30 percent gross profits, fewer jobs would be created. Moreover, what average wage would be offered? Would the government insist on "prevailing wages" as in the construction industry? If the new jobs paid 50 percent above the poverty level, for example, they would match the current national average of about $20 an hour. The sum required to create a million jobs at prevailing wages would range from 60 to 75 billion dollars annually, depending on whether the Obama administration replicated the New Deal practice of government as direct employer or continued the extant policy of privatization.

There is also the problem of contracting out these activities. During the Great Depression, the Works Projects Administration, a government agency, was the direct employer; today, in the era of privatization, federal and state governments often contract to private companies to perform these tasks. This means that profits must be factored into all expenditures; like the privatized US health-care system, it is more expensive than socialized production and the job pay-off is less. Moreover, under this contracting regime, there are fewer controls over hiring practices; people of color tend to be short-changed. This means that the level of oversight would need to be much more stringent than any administration has been willing to implement. What is the warrant for believing that the Clinton-era appointees who dominate Obama's economic-policy team will be willing to reverse past practices of relaxing government controls, especially if the Obama administration persists in advocating the politics of compromise with a Republican Party dedicated to scuttling any program that would increase government intervention in areas not related to war and national security.

Progressives hope that Obama will usher in a "new" New Deal. But this rests on a misunderstanding of the dynamics of that first New Deal. Even though it employed more than a million workers in government projects, as late as 1940, unemployment still hovered around 20 percent of the labor force. In 1937, four years after Roosevelt took office, the United States was plunged into a new recession from which it did not recover until the advent of the war economy. In contrast to Herbert Hoover and the first New Deal's focus on stimulating economic activity by pouring capital into business corporations, controlling prices and wages in order to foster profits and limiting its direct aid to the unemployed to feeding the hungry, it was the so-called second New Deal that put money in the pockets of the jobless through public works and service programs, promised to save small farms from foreclosure through government purchases of crops and paying farmers to retire part of their growing capacity in a land bank. But it was the farmers themselves who, through direct action and mass organizing, sometimes prevented evictions, created cooperative enterprises to oppose the big processing corporations and, even before the Depression became official, created their own political vehicles. After the mass strikes of 1933 and 1934, conducted without a legal framework for union recognition, in 1935 the National Labor Relations Act guaranteed workers the right to organize unions of their own choosing, established a procedure for official union recognition and collective bargaining, and outlawed company unions and competitive unionism within the same bargaining unit. In short, the second New Deal was a consequence of a popular upsurge, not only the brainchild of FDR and his advisers.

It remains an open question whether the organizations at the base of the Obama administration will match or even exceed the achievements of the movements that forced the second New Deal into existence. There is little or no prospect that the deepening economic crisis can be significantly reversed within the current framework of neoliberal capitalism—at least not when unemployment, wage stagnation and declining living conditions are taken as the relevant indicators. The stock market may rise for a time and prospects for certain professional and technical employment categories may improve, but the situation remains grave for youth, women (whose jobless rate exceeds that of men for the first time since the Second World War), blacks and Latinos, the elderly and semi-skilled workers.

THE POLITICS OF THE CRISIS

The Obama administration has demonstrated, to the disappointment of even some of its fervent supporters, that it has virtually no plan to address the growing jobs crisis except through a program of "trickle down." The most it has done is to extend unemployment benefits beyond the statutory twenty-six week limit, and supplement the food stamps program. Either the Obama administration actually believes that the huge sums handed over to financial institutions and the car industry will, over time, pull us out of the recession or, lacking a genuine protest movement from below, it simply experiences little pressure to do anything different. I suggest that the latter is the case and even some of Obama's supporters (for instance, New York Times columnists Paul Krugman and Bob Herbert) are beginning to come to that realization. The administration obviously believes it has enough breathing room to await an economic turnaround without sacrificing its political standing or directly confronting the large financial corporations with proposals to shift funds in order to directly assist the unemployed and those facing foreclosure. Under these circumstances, its economic advisors have accepted the conventional wisdom that we are in the midst of an ordinary recession which will peak at eighteen months to two years. Skeptics, notably Nobel Prize winners Joseph Stiglitz and Paul Krugman and NYU professor Nouriel Roubini, have cast some doubt on this prognostication—but to little effect since all of them generally support the administration's economic strategy and merely fault it for not being bold enough. On August 21, 2009, Fed Chairman Ben Bernanke looked into his crystal ball and opined that the recession was bottoming out—about the fifth time he made such a statement that year. The statement appeared to be geared to the stock market and intended to assuage popular fears that the recession was dampening home sales and creating more uncertainty in the labor market. Few in the public debate and certainly nobody in the ranks of policy-makers have heeded the warnings that persistent job loss and lackluster consumption were weighing heavily on the prospects for economic recovery. In fact, in numerous statements, the president himself have warned that unemployment could grow well beyond the declaration of official recovery, a tacit acknowledgement that substantial federal jobs and income support are not on the horizon.

Obama's poll numbers declined in summer 2009, a reflection of growing disappointment with the performance of his administration on the economic crisis, health-care reform, and the accelerated war in Afghanistan. But polling is only an indicator of public sentiment. As "progressives" fret, the organized opposition to Obama's programs still comes mainly from the Right. Liberals are divided between those who, in fear of Right-wing putschism (which recently displayed its strength in a plethora of town meetings on health-care reform), are clinging to the administration and those who wring their hands and voice their disappointment more loudly. But neither the labor movement nor the mainstream of the Civil Rights, feminist and environmental movements are prepared to openly oppose a Democratic administration on a broad range of economic issues.

The seriously divided labor movement regularly issues statements calling for a jobs program but has, until now, shown no political will to mobilize its own still vast membership (16 million)—as it did during the 2008 elections when it handed $250 million to the Democrats—to demand a share of the trillions that the Bush and Obama administrations have given or lent to a few key Wall Street banks and insurance companies. Progressives in the main liberal organizations, intellectuals, and the AFL-CIO and Change to Win leaderships have replied to criticism that they are willing to give Obama "the benefit of the doubt" and have stood idly by as joblessness spreads. Until spring 2009, organized labor's main legislative priority was Congressional passage of the Employees Free Choice Act (EFCA), which would have required employers to recognize unions on the basis of card checks rather than a mandatory secret-ballot election. When the administration and the Democratic Congressional leadership pronounced the bill "dead," the unions—notwithstanding brave words to the contrary—folded their tents and followed the administration's call for rapid passage of health-care reform. But at no time in the first year of the Obama administration did they put the dire economic situation facing workers at or near the top of their agenda.

The reasons for the unions' passivity, even as their membership and economic power continues to wane, should not be sought in conspiratorial theories of perfidy or complacency. According to such views, union leaders have simply lost their edge. That is, they sit on top of a bureaucracy that tends to inure them to rank-

and-file suffering: while workers are straining under the burden of job losses, stagnant wages, employer demands for "furloughs" and wage reductions, and rising food and health costs, their leaders seem to have other fish to fry. While there is some truth to such perspectives, they fail to address the deeper causes of labor's organized passivity in the economic crisis. Perhaps the least noticed amongst these is the degree to which the unions— and the social movements that arose during and after the sixties— have become what C. Wright Mills once termed a "dependent variable" in the political and economic "setups." The unions— and the movements—lack autonomy from either the state or the corporations with which they bargain; they experience themselves as subordinate to and dependent on these institutions. While these relationships can easily be characterized as instances of "class collaboration," what often remains unexplained are the origins of this situation and the forces that maintain it. In what follows I would like to venture an informed speculation on this matter.

Historical Transformations

Since the 1950s, organized labor has hitched its fate to capital. During the Cold War it shed all of its socialist ideas and a good number of its militant socialist and communist activists as well. In fact, union leaders have come to believe that capitalism is in both their own and their members' best interests and that full-blown systemic opposition is tantamount to political and economic suicide. This attitude was already encouraged during the heyday of the New Deal, but reached its apogee during the Cold War— when the permanent war economy and US global economic power enabled key sections of the American working class to achieve an unprecedented degree of job and income security. Of course, a major element in the new perception that workers were an integral part of the corporate capitalist order was the initiation by the state and its financial partners of an extensive credit system that permitted working-class people to borrow money with which to own their homes, send children to college, go on vacations and regularly update their cars. After the defeat of Congressional legislation that would have established a National Health Service and the stagnation of the social security (pension) system, unions in key industries (such as steel, auto, coal, electrical, communications, oil and transportation) negotiated a "private" welfare state with their employers, thereby taking the air out of

efforts to enact a publicly financed universal health-care program
and extend the welfare state. After the passage of the Wage-Hour
law of 1938, the only major extension of the welfare state was
Medicare, passed in 1966. While the unions can take considerable
credit for its passage, they were moved to apply the necessary
pressure only after they found that "their" corporations refused
to insure retirees.

These deals were of a tripartite nature. In most cases, the
health and pension contributions were paid in lieu of wages
and to private insurance companies, even where the union
administered the services. Since 1955 many major unions have
become "partners" with some of the leading insurers who
provided benefits in return for fairly substantial fees. Moreover,
the provision of benefits under the union contract rather than
under public authority allows union leaders to claim credit for
health and pension improvements, and so gave them a political
base (needed for re-election to union office) that would not have
been available under socialized medicine. In some instances, the
traffic between unions' health and welfare staff and these private
insurers was fairly heavy. Many unions hired consultants from
Wall Street firms to advise them on how to handle their benefits
programs. During the fiscal crisis of 1976–77 these consultants
actually acted as intermediaries between the union leadership and
city officials in New York, Detroit, Chicago and elsewhere who
successfully persuaded the unions to grant concessions, most of
which are still in effect.

In 1975, union membership was about a quarter of the labor
force. This was down from 35 percent in 1953, but organized
labor was still driving wages and benefits levels for all workers.
Having organized millions of public sector employees, the AFL-
CIO was not only a powerful fraction of the national Democratic
Party, but was also able to name many of the party's candidates at
the state and local level. But the "rational" basis of labor's close
alliance with capital began to vanish in the 1970s. The last thirty
years have witnessed the massive de-industrialization of America
and a profound decomposition and recomposition of the working
and salaried middle classes. Except in the public and health-
care sectors, union organizing slowed to a crawl. By 2009 union
membership was only 7 percent of the private sector labor force
and slightly less than 12 percent of the entire labor force. Today,
what was once an industrial union base of 7 million members
has been reduced to less than 2 million. And the composition of

that membership has radically changed: public- and private-sector service and transportation employees are now, overwhelmingly, the majority of union members.

In the main, having bowed to the view that globalization and technological innovation are engines of "progress" and that workers' pain was temporary, the unions accepted the inevitability of these losses. After conducting a fairly vigorous campaign to defeat the North American Free Trade Agreement in 1993, the bulk of organized labor has settled for crumbs at the table of capital. When some auto, meat-packing and steel-worker locals protested capital flight or refused to accept concessionary bargaining, the national leaderships ruthlessly suppressed these movements, sometimes by agreeing to plant migrations used by corporations to thwart militants. For example, the UAW leadership looked benignly on as the Big Three auto companies removed plants from the Detroit area and Flint—the heart of the union's traditional strength—to the American South and to rural areas. Belatedly, they took something of a stand against outsourcing auto parts production to Mexico, China and other developing countries—but they presented their objections in the form of crude "Buy American" slogans.

The union leadership—and a considerable portion of its members—are suffused with fear that if they conduct a determined struggle against wage freezes, pension and health-care reductions and plant closures, they will lose everything. They are facing capital without weapons that they believe can win. The past thirty years of steady retreat is a tale of collective worker *anxiety* as much as corporate boldness in testing workers' resolve to protect their hard-won gains. The so-called Treaty of Detroit, whereby the auto union all but ceased its shop-floor militancy in return for regular wage rises, early retirement with a substantial pension, and a reasonably good health-benefits program, has been dead for almost thirty years now. It is clear that the UAW and other unions have no strategy that takes into account the fact that the post-war era's capital-labor treaty has been abrogated by management and that capital has no interest in a new accord that would constrain its room to maneuver. In the face of a situation where they have no place to turn except to their families and their communities, workers have beat a steady retreat, forever setting up new rearguard positions until the ground appears to have completely shifted under them. It is no exaggeration to claim that the United States working class has become invisible in the public sphere and to itself as a class. Nowadays, workers often seem caught in a sadomasochistic relationship not only with capital but also with their own union leaders.

We have witnessed several generations of labor's dependence and at least a generation of workers that has never experienced a victory over capital. The political defeat of the unions has reverberated throughout the entire society. The basis of this broader effect of labor's decline should be fairly clear: apart from the churches, the unions remain the largest, most resource-blessed and visible force in the modern liberal camp. Their demise has reduced the prospects for the less organized sectors of society that remain relatively unprotected from the vicissitudes of the Economic Crisis. In the absence of meaningful struggle at the level of civil society and the workplace, millions have turned to electoralism in the hope that government can solve their problems, i.e. to a Democratic Party taken over by neoliberal interests and ideology. The 2008 Obama victory was based on these hopes but is already in the process of producing widespread disillusion.

The Politics of Distraction

Labor's reliance on Congress and the Democratic Party may be interpreted as a strategic shift from the relative autonomy unions enjoyed until the late 1940s. Although some of the "progressive" unions joined the Roosevelt coalition during the 1930s, most of this alliance was forged at the national level. At the local level, most unions still relied on their own shop-floor forms of direct action. One of the Treaty's main provisions was union agreement to observe a "rational" process of adjudicating the thousands of grievances that regularly glutted the channels of contract enforcement. Most of the grievances resulted from management's willful abrogation of the provisions of the bargaining agreement. Where once most of these grievances were settled on the shop floor, by the early 1950s their resolution became subject to a complex bureaucratic process that ordinarily favored management. The move to political action within the framework of the two-party system was a sign that some quarters of the labor movement had given up its weapons of economic independence.

Despite growing skepticism about its policies, the Obama administration does have a well-articulated strategy to keep its labor, social-movement and liberal-intellectual bases quite busy: it has successfully shifted the ground of the debate from the economy to health-care reform. The decision arguably reflects the orientation of the administration toward the Crisis: it has adopted a program that implicitly views rising unemployment as a symptom that can only be addressed by alleviating the Financial Crisis. To be sure, the provision of universal health-care has long been on the progressive agenda. During the New Deal, and again during the fight for a National Health Service in the late 1940s, the proposals, as in Europe, were to finance universal health-care through the federal tax system. As was the wont of the Roosevelt administration, health-care would be subject to a separate tax from income levies. Such is the case for social security, including Medicare. But the Obama administration has chosen a piecemeal approach to the issue. In the first place its program is to address the needs of the 50 million uninsured by offering a "public option" to enable all citizens to buy low-cost insurance, in addition to which it would increase social-security taxes. So employer-based and personal insurances would not be replaced under the Obama/ Democratic Congressional plan. The plan supplements existing health insurance programs and is intended as much to regulate costs as to extend benefits. As many observers have pointed out, the Obama plan amounts to a bonanza for health insurers and, more generally, the health and pharmaceutical industries.

By mid-2009 the unions and liberal organizations had, in effect, turned their backs on the effects of the Economic Crisis and were primarily concerned to defend the Obama administration's health program—which included a publicly financed health insurance option. They were quickly forced to defend it not only against relentless conservative opposition but also against suggestions by members of Obama's own administration that the public option could be dropped if it stood in the way of passing a bill. Despite the threat issued by the next presumptive AFL-CIO president, Richard Trumka—i.e. that organized labor might sit out the next election if the Democrats do not pass a public option in their health legislation—there is little doubt that he would have great difficulty putting this challenge into practice. Labor is so intertwined with the Democratic Party that any actions that might result in its distancing would surely generate significant internal opposition.

The Left's relation to the economic crisis, to health-care debates and to the Obama administration tends to reflect the actual relations of power in American politics. That is, none of the existing forces to the left of the administration have either the credibility or the political will to intervene on the basis of an anti-corporate capitalist approach to the crisis. Perhaps its most effective intervention over the last two years is to have launched a national campaign for single-payer—i.e. socialized—medical care. More than 500 union locals, state and local labor bodies have endorsed the campaign; thousands of physicians, the 60,000-member California Nurses Association and some important national unions (such as the United Steelworkers, United Auto Workers and the American Federation of Teachers) have formally endorsed the single-payer option. And it is a growing movement. Even as the Obama plan remains stalled in a series of compromises which will cripple the effectiveness of the version that Congress will ultimately pass, it may be that the fight for single-payer will constitute the best option for Left intervention in the near future. Compared to the monumental task of reversing neoliberal economic policies across the board, health-care is a manageable fight.

But on the fundamental politics of the economic crisis, on the class nature of the Obama administration's program, for instance, the Left has been unable either to mount a counter-movement or to propose an alternative that can gain some public traction. At the local level, there are some attempts, initiated by community organizations, to organize the unemployed and stage small protest demonstrations against the banks' takeover of the stimulus package. Yet the Left has been unable to forge an independent position in the debate. It remains reactive, on the one hand, to the retreats by the Obama administration and, on the other, to the expressions of disappointment by progressive and liberal public intellectuals. With some exceptions, the Left shared an expectation that Obama, who ran on a centrist platform, was *really* somebody else. However, the fault is hardly his: Obama never pretended to be more or less than he is. As one commentator has stated: illusion leads to disillusion.

In the main, the Left has become a dependent variable of the progressives, the liberals and the movements that provide their social and political base. Lacking a "party" of its own (by which I mean not a third electoral vehicle, but an independent radical political formation), the diverse individuals and institutions of the Left remain buffeted and uncertain where to take their stand. Some are tied to the same electoralism that has afflicted the once vibrant movements. Against all evidence to the contrary, they harbor vain hopes that the progressives can push the Democratic

Party to the left and so loosen its ties with financial capital and force the Democrats to move on pressing economic and social issues. Others, imprisoned by "third party" electoralism, are confident that disillusioned progressives and a section of labor and other movements will become the political base of a new national party. Still others contemplate their retirement from politics and a peaceful return to private life.

Perhaps the most interesting are those who are engaged on two quite distinct fronts: labor and community activists who fight, chiefly at the local levels, for a politics of resistance and alternative. Their ranks are relatively thin, but in some places they have enjoyed some success in opposing gentrification, creating significant environmental initiatives, and building unions that are not of the bureaucratic mold. Others are exploring the concept of new radical political formations, some from anarchist and others from non-dogmatic Marxist perspectives. In this camp are more than a few black and Latino intellectuals and a smattering of whites who refused the blandishments offered by the progressives within the Democratic Party and on the sectarian Left.

The real problem for the Left is that it has no firm moorings on which to build new radical political formations. Postmodern politics has effectively undermined the concept of the totality, mislabeling it "authoritarian." Many hesitate to develop theories of practically anything and have instead resigned themselves to either identity politics or single-issue struggles without making an effort to link them together. Notions of the supersession of class and political economy make it impossible for them to confront the economic crisis or engage in a politics that links issues together and transcends local struggles. But theory should clearly be at the top of our list. While this is not the place to elaborate such a theory, I will conclude with a set of questions that urgently need answers if the Left is to have a chance of making practical interventions that will affect the crises of our time.

- As a starting point the Left must call into question many of its own presuppositions and the unstated theoretical basis of its own politics. For example, should the Left ask whether the working class—and the trade unions—have the ideological capacity and the political will to remain at the heart of radical hope? And if we are still socialists, what does this mean in the light of the failures of the Communist and Social Democratic versions of socialism?

- What is the significance and content of the race question in the United States? Has the Left made an adequate contemporary class analysis of black and other subaltern formations in order to discern the patterns that have conditioned the black and Latino freedom movements? Do we have an adequate understanding of the race/class articulation?
- Although the state remains the primary scene of politics, in view of the global character of capital, what are the relevant global forms of class organization and struggle?
- What is the role of political intellectuals in the struggle for a new society?
- Is reform still possible in contemporary capitalist societies? Or have we reached the point where we should expect struggles for reform to almost inevitably be frustrated? Then what? In this connection, note I have not outlined an alternative program of economic policy. If state and capital have become so tied together that the demand for "government action" is likely to mean strengthening those ties rather than transferring power and resources to the people, what are the new targets of struggle?
- What is radicalism's conception of democracy? To what extent can liberal representative political institutions be incorporated into a radical democratic society? Or must they be replaced, root and branch?
- How does the rise of the new immigration of the past quarter of a century bear on Left political perspectives everywhere?

16

DISMANTLING THE TEMPLE

William Greider

The Financial Crisis has propelled the Federal Reserve into an excruciating political dilemma. The Fed is at the zenith of its influence, using its extraordinary powers to rescue the economy. Yet the extreme irregularity of its behavior is producing a legitimacy crisis for the Central Bank. The remote technocrats at the Fed who decide money and credit policy for the nation are deliberately opaque and little understood by most Americans. For the first time in generations, they are now threatened with popular rebellion.

Since the onset of the present crisis, the Fed has flooded the streets with money—distributing trillions of dollars to banks, financial markets and commercial interests—in an attempt to revive the credit system and get the economy growing again. As a result, the awesome authority of this cloistered institution is visible to many ordinary Americans for the first time. People and politicians are shocked and confused, and also angered, by what they see. They are beginning to ask some hard questions for which Federal Reserve governors do not have satisfactory answers.

Where did the Central Bank get all the money it is handing out? Basically, the Fed printed it. That is what central banks do. Who told the Fed governors they could do this? Nobody, really—not Congress or the president. The Federal Reserve Board, alone among government agencies, does not submit its budgets to Congress for authorization and appropriation. It raises its own money and sets its own priorities.

Representative Wright Patman, the Texas populist who was a scourge of central bankers, once described the Federal Reserve as "a pretty queer duck." Congress created the Fed in 1913 with the presumption that it would be "independent" from the rest of government, aloof from regular politics and deliberately shielded from the hot breath of voters and the grasping appetites of private interests—with one powerful exception: the bankers.

The Fed was designed as a unique hybrid in which government would share its powers with the private banking industry. Bankers collaborate closely on Fed policy. Banks are the "shareholders" who ostensibly own the twelve regional Federal Reserve banks. Bankers sit on the boards of directors, proposing interest-rate changes for Fed governors in Washington to decide. Bankers also have a special advisory council that meets privately with governors to critique monetary policy and management of the economy. Sometimes, the Fed pretends to be a private organization. Other times, it admits to being part of the government.

The antiquated quality of this institution is reflected in the map of the Fed's twelve regional banks. Five of them are located in the Midwest (better known today as the industrial Rust Belt). Missouri has two Federal Reserve banks (St. Louis and Kansas City), while the entire West Coast has only one (located in San Francisco, not Los Angeles or Seattle). Virginia has one; Florida does not. Among its functions, the Federal Reserve directly regulates the largest banks, but it also looks out for their wellbeing—providing regular liquidity loans for those caught short and bailing out endangered banks it deems "too big to fail." Critics look askance at these peculiar arrangements and see "conspiracy." But it's not really secret. This duck was created by an act of Congress. The Fed's favoritism toward bankers is embedded in its DNA.

This awkward reality explains the dilemma facing the Fed. It cannot stand too much visibility, nor can it easily explain or justify its peculiar status. The Federal Reserve is the black hole of American democracy—the crucial contradiction that keeps the people and their representatives from having any voice in regard to these most important public policies. That's why the Central Bankers have always operated in secrecy, avoiding public controversy and the inevitable accusations of special deal making. The current crisis has blown the Central Bank's cover. Many in Congress are alarmed, demanding greater transparency. More than 250 House members are seeking an independent audit of Fed accounts. House Speaker Nancy Pelosi observed that the Fed seems to be poaching on Congressional functions—handing out public money without the bother of public decision-making.

"Many of us were . . . if not surprised, taken aback, when the Fed had $80 billion to invest in AIG just out of the blue," Pelosi said. "All of a sudden, we wake up one morning and AIG was receiving $80 billion from the Fed. So of course we're saying, 'Where is this money coming from?' 'Oh, we have it. And not only that, we have more.'" So who needs Congress? Pelosi sounded guileless, but she knows very well where the Fed gets its money. She was slyly tweaking the Central Bankers on their vulnerability.

Fed chair Ben Bernanke responded with the usual aloofness. An audit, he insisted, would amount to "a takeover of monetary policy by the Congress." He did not appear to recognize how arrogant that sounded. Congress created the Fed, but it must not look too deeply into the Fed's private business. The mystique intimidates many politicians. The Fed's power depends crucially upon the people not knowing exactly what it does.

Basically, what the Central Bank is trying to do with its aggressive distribution of trillions is avoid repeating the great mistake the Fed made after the 1929 Stock Market Crash. The Central Bankers responded hesitantly then and allowed the money supply to collapse, which led to the ultimate catastrophe of full-blown monetary deflation and created the Great Depression. Bernanke has not yet won this struggle against falling prices and production—deflationary symptoms remain visible around the world—but he has not lost either. He might get more public sympathy if Fed officials explained this dilemma in plain English. Instead, they are shielding people from understanding the full dimensions of our predicament.

President Obama inadvertently made the political problem worse for the Fed in June 2009, when he proposed to make the Central Bank the supercop to guard against "systemic risk" and decide the terms for regulating the largest commercial banks and some heavyweight industrial corporations engaged in finance. The House Financial Services Committee intended to draft the legislation quickly, but many members want to learn more first. Obama's proposal gives the Central Bank even greater authority, including broad powers to pick winners and losers in the private economy, behind closed doors. Yet Obama did not propose any changes to the Fed's privileged status. Instead, he asked Fed governors to consider the matter. But perhaps it is the Federal Reserve itself that needs to be reformed.

Some time ago, I ran into a retired Fed official who had been a good source twenty years ago when I was writing my book about the Central Bank, *Secrets of the Temple: How the Federal Reserve Runs the Country*. He is a Fed loyalist and did not leak damaging secrets. But he helped me understand how the supposedly nonpolitical Fed does its politics, behind the veil of disinterested expertise. When we met recently, he said the Central Bank is already making preparations to celebrate its approaching centennial. Some of us, I responded, have a different idea for 2013.

"We think that would be a good time to dismantle the temple," I playfully told my old friend. "Democratize the Fed. Or tear it down. Create something new in its place that's accountable to the public."

The Fed man did not react well to my teasing. He got a stricken look. His voice tightened. Please, he pleaded, do not go down that road. The Fed has made mistakes, he agreed, but the country needs its Central Bank. His nervous reaction told me this venerable institution is feeling insecure about its future.

There are six reasons granting the Fed even more power is a really bad idea:

1. It would reward failure. Like the largest banks that have been bailed out, the Fed was a co-author of the destruction. During the past twenty-five years, it failed to protect Americans against reckless banking and finance adventures. It also failed in its most basic function—moderating the expansion of credit to keep it in balance with economic growth. The Fed instead allowed, even encouraged, the explosion of debt and inflation of financial assets that have now collapsed. The Central Bank was derelict in enforcing regulations and led cheers for dismantling them. Above all, the Fed did not see this disaster coming, or so it claims. It certainly did nothing to warn people.

2. Cumulatively, Fed policy was a central force in destabilizing the US economy. Its extreme swings in monetary policy, combined with utter disregard for timely regulatory enforcement, steadily shifted economic rewards away from the real economy of production, work and wages and toward the financial realm, where profits and incomes were wildly inflated by false valuations. Abandoning its role as neutral arbitrator, the Fed tilted in favor of capital over labor. The institution was remolded to conform to the right-wing market doctrine of its

chairman, Alan Greenspan, and it was blinded to reality by his ideology.

3. The Fed cannot possibly examine "systemic risk" objectively because it helped to create the very structural flaws that led to breakdown. The Fed served as midwife to Citigroup, the failed conglomerate now on government life support. Greenspan unilaterally authorized this new financial/banking combine in the 1990s—even before Congress had repealed the Glass-Steagall Act, which prohibited such mergers. The Central Bank, in other words, is deeply invested in protecting the banking behemoths that it promoted, if only to cover its own mistakes.

4. The Fed cannot be trusted to defend the public in its private deal-making with bank executives. The numerous revelations of collusion have shocked the public, and more scandals are certain if Congress conducts a thorough investigation. When Treasury Secretary Timothy Geithner was president of the New York Fed, he supervised the demise of Bear Stearns with a sweet deal for JP Morgan Chase, which took over the failed brokerage—$30 billion to cover any losses. Geithner was negotiating with Morgan Chase CEO and New York Fed board member Jamie Dimon. Goldman Sachs CEO Lloyd Blankfein got similar solicitude when the Fed bailed out insurance giant AIG, a Goldman counterparty: a side-door payout of $13 billion. The new president at the New York Fed, William Dudley, is another Goldman man.

5. Instead of disowning the notorious policy of "too big to fail," the Fed will be bound to embrace the doctrine more explicitly as "systemic risk" regulator. A new superclass of forty or fifty financial giants will emerge as the born-again "money trust" that citizens railed against 100 years ago. But this time, it will be armed with a permanent line of credit from Washington. The Fed, having restored and consolidated the battered Wall Street club, will doubtless also shield a few of the largest industrial-financial corporations, like General Electric (whose CEO also sits on the New York Fed board). Whatever officials may claim, financial-market investors will understand that these mammoth institutions are insured against failure. Everyone else gets to experience capitalism in the raw.

6. This road leads to the corporate state—a fusion of private and public power, a privileged club that dominates everything else from the top down. This will likely foster even greater

concentration of financial power, since any large company left out of the protected class will want to join by growing larger and acquiring the banking elements needed to qualify. Most enterprises in banking and commerce will compete with the big boys at greater disadvantage, vulnerable to predatory power plays the Fed has implicitly blessed.

Whatever good intentions the Central Bank enunciates, it will be deeply conflicted in its actions, always pulled in opposite directions. If the Fed tries to curb the growth of the megabanks or prohibit their reckless practices, it will be accused of damaging profitability and thus threatening the stability of the system. If it allows overconfident bankers to wander again into dangerous territory, it will be blamed for creating the mess and stuck with cleaning it up. Obama's reform might prevail in the short run. The biggest banks, after all, will be lobbying alongside him in favor of the Fed, and Congress may not have the backbone to resist. The Fed, however, is sure to remain in the cross-hairs. Too many different interests will be damaged—thousands of smaller banks, all the companies left out of the club, organized labor, consumers and other sectors, not to mention libertarian conservatives like Texas Representative Ron Paul. They will recognize that the "money trust" once again has its boot on their neck, and that this time the government arranged it.

The obstacles to democratizing the Fed are obviously formidable. Tampering with the temple is politically taboo. But this crisis has demonstrated that the present arrangement no longer works for the public interest. The society of 1913 no longer exists, nor does the New Deal economic order that carried us to twentieth-century prosperity. Americans thus have a rare opportunity to reconstitute the Federal Reserve as a normal government agency, shorn of the bankers' preferential trappings and the fallacious claim to "independent" status as well as the claustrophobic demand for secrecy.

Progressives in the early twentieth century, drawn from the growing ranks of managerial professionals, believed "good government" required technocratic experts who would be shielded from the unruly populace and especially from radical voices of organized labor, populism, socialism and other upstart movements. The pretensions of "scientific" decision-making by remote governing elites—both the mysterious wisdom of Central Bankers and the inventive wizardry of financial titans—failed spectacularly in our current catastrophe. The Fed was never independent in any real sense. Its power depended on taking care of its one true constituency in banking and finance.

A reconstituted Central Bank might keep the famous name and presidentially appointed governors, confirmed by Congress, but it would forfeit the mystique and submit to the usual standards of transparency and public scrutiny. The institution would be directed to concentrate on the Fed's one great purpose—making monetary policy and controlling credit expansion to produce balanced economic growth and stable money. Most regulatory functions would be located elsewhere, in a new enforcement agency that would oversee regulated commercial banks as well as the "shadow banking" of hedge funds, private equity firms and others.

The Fed would thus be relieved of its conflicted objectives. Bank examiners would be free of the insider pressures that inevitably emanate from the Fed's cozy relations with major banks. All of the private-public ambiguities concocted in 1913 would be swept away, including bank ownership of the twelve Federal Reserve banks, which could be reorganized as branch offices with a focus on regional economies.

Altering the Central Bank would also give Congress an opening to reclaim its primacy in this most important matter. That sounds far-fetched to modern sensibilities, and traditionalists will scream that it is a recipe for inflationary disaster. But this is what the Constitution prescribes: "The Congress shall have the power to coin money [and] regulate the value thereof." It does not grant the president or the treasury secretary this power. Nor does it envision a secretive Central Bank that interacts murkily with the executive branch.

Given Congress's weakened condition and its weak grasp of the complexities of monetary policy, these changes cannot take place overnight. But the gradual realignment of power can start with Congress and an internal reorganization aimed at building its expertise and educating members on how to develop a critical perspective. Congress has already created models for how to do this. The Congressional Budget Office is a respected authority on fiscal policy, reliably nonpartisan. Congress needs to create something similar for monetary policy.

Instead of consigning monetary policy to backwater sub-committees, each chamber should create a major new committee to supervise money and credit, limited in size to members willing to concentrate on becoming responsible stewards for the long run. The monetary committees, working in tandem with the Fed's board of governors, would occasionally recommend (and sometimes command) new policy directions at the federal agency and also review its spending.

Setting monetary policy is a very different process from enacting laws. The Fed operates through a continuum of decisions and rolling adjustments spread over months, even years. Congress would have to learn how to respond to deeper economic conditions that may not become clear until after the next election. This education could help the institution mature.

Congress also needs a "council of public elders"—a rotating board of outside advisers drawn from diverse interests and empowered to speak their minds in public. They could second-guess the makers of monetary policy, but also Congress. These might include retired politicians, labor leaders, academics and state governors—preferably people whose thinking is no longer defined by party politics or personal ambitions. The public could nominate representatives too. No financial wizards need apply.

A revived Congress armed with this kind of experience would be better equipped to enact substantive law—rather than simply turning problems over to regulatory agencies with hollow laws that are merely hortatory suggestions. Reordering the financial system and the economy will require hard rules—classic laws of "Thou shalt" and "Thou shalt not" that command different behavior from certain private interests and prohibit what has proved reckless and destructive. If "too big to fail" is the problem, don't leave it to private negotiations between banks and the Federal Reserve. Restore anti-monopoly laws and make big banks get smaller. If the financial system's risky innovations are too complicated for bank examiners to understand, then those innovations should probably be illegal.

Many in Congress will be afraid to take on the temple and reluctant to violate the taboo surrounding the Fed. It will probably require popular rebellion to make this happen, and that requires citizens who see through the temple's secrets. But the present crisis has not only exposed the Fed's worst failures and structural flaws; it has also introduced citizens to the vast potential of monetary policy to serve the common good. If Ben Bernanke can create trillions of dollars at will and spread them around the financial system, could government do the same thing to finance important public projects the people want and need? Daring as it sounds, the answer is yes.

The Central Bank's most mysterious power—to create money with a few computer keystrokes—is dauntingly complicated, and the mechanics are not widely understood. But the essential thing to understand is that this power ultimately relies on democratic consent—the people's trust, their willingness to accept the currency and use it in exchange. This is not entirely voluntary, since the government also requires people to pay their taxes in dollars, not euros or yen. But citizens conferred the power on government through their elected representatives. Newly created money is often called the "pure credit" of the nation. In principle, it exists for the benefit of all.

In this emergency, Bernanke essentially used the Fed's money-creation power in a way that resembles the "greenbacks" Abraham Lincoln printed to fight the Civil War. Lincoln was faced with rising costs and shrinking revenues (because the Confederate states had left the Union). The president authorized issuance of a novel national currency—the "greenback"—that had no backing in gold reserves and therefore outraged orthodox thinking. But the greenbacks worked. The expanded money supply helped pay for war mobilization and kept the economy booming. In a sense, Lincoln won the war by relying on the "full faith and credit" of the people, much as Bernanke is printing money freely to fight off financial collapse and deflation.

If Congress chooses to take charge of its constitutional duty, it could similarly use greenback currency created by the Federal Reserve as a legitimate channel for financing important public projects—like sorely needed improvements to the nation's infrastructure. Obviously, this has to be done carefully and responsibly, limited to normal expansion of the money supply and used only for projects that truly benefit the entire nation (lest it lead to inflation). But here is an example of how it would work.

President Obama has announced the goal of building a high-speed rail system. The US is the only advanced industrial society that does not have one (ride the modern trains in France or Japan to see what our society is missing). The trouble is that Obama has only budgeted a pittance ($8 billion) for this project. Spain, by comparison, has committed more than $100 billion to its fifteen-year railroad-building project. Given the vast shortcomings in US infrastructure, the country will never catch up with the backlog through the regular financing of taxing and borrowing.

Instead, Congress should create a stand-alone development fund for long-term capital investment projects (this would require the long-sought reform of the federal budget, which makes no distinction between current operating spending and long-term investment). The Fed would continue to create money only as needed by the economy; but instead of injecting this money into the banking system, a portion of it would go directly to the capital investment fund, earmarked by Congress for specific projects of great urgency. The idea of direct financing for infrastructure has been proposed periodically for many years by groups from right and left. Transportation Secretary Ray LaHood co-sponsored legislation along these lines a decade ago when he was a Republican Congressman from Illinois.

This approach speaks to the contradiction House Speaker Pelosi pointed out when she asked why the Fed has limitless money to spend however it sees fit. Instead of borrowing the money to pay for the new rail system, the government financing would draw on the public's money-creation process—just as Lincoln did and Bernanke is now doing.

The bankers would howl, for good reason. They profit enormously from the present system and share in the money-creation process. When the Fed injects more reserves into the banking system, it automatically multiplies the banks' capacity to create money by increasing their lending (and banks, in turn, collect interest on their new loans). The direct-financing approach would not halt the banking industry's role in allocating new credit, since the newly created money would still wind up in the banks as deposits. But the government would now decide how to allocate new credit to preferred public projects rather than let private banks make all the decisions for us.

The reform of monetary policy, in other words, has promising possibilities for revitalizing democracy. Congress is a human institution and therefore fallible. Mistakes will be made, for sure. But we might ask ourselves: If Congress were empowered to manage monetary policy, could it do any worse than those experts who brought us to ruin?

17

THE GLOBAL FINANCIAL CRISIS

Foreclosing or Leveraging Labor's Future?

Dick Bryan, Michael Rafferty
and Scott MacWilliam

The Global Financial Crisis and its associated recession have been widely described as the biggest economic slump since the Great Depression.[1] Yet despite the huge ramifications of poverty and unemployment that would follow from any comparable downturn, there has been surprisingly little conspicuous protest from organized labor or social movements. In addition, that protest which has arisen has focused on reprehensible behavior by financial institutions and corporate executives, the incompetence of public and private regulators, and governments' double standards (above all their willingness to bail out the big end of town while neglecting the plight of individual workers and homeowners)—but it has done little to clarify and render politically salient the systemic dimensions of the crisis.

How do we explain this, in view of the catastrophic scenarios and (patently justified) moral outrage? The issue is not a lack of fear (for there is widespread anxiety about the future) or a lack of anger. It has more to do, we believe, with confusion: in a complex financial system it is difficult to know exactly what to be angry about and where to direct the anger. As a result, there seems to

---

1 The most frequently cited contributions are B. Eichengreen and K. H. O'Rourke, "A tale of two depressions," *VoxEU*, June 4, 2009, http://www. voxeu.org; and N. Roubini, "The Worst Financial Crisis Since the Great Depression," Nouriel Roubini's Global EconoMonitor, September 16, 2008, http://www.rgemonitor.com.

be no distinct agenda for turning rightful anger into creative and long-term responses and strategies.

As time passes, we begin to see a further dimension to the political passivity. Virtually all statements of moral outrage have turned into lamentations of regulatory failure: failure of central banks to moderate expansion, failure of credit-rating agencies, and failure of state regulators to ensure prudence of corporations and appropriate market structures. What follows from a focus on regulatory failure is the promulgation of regulatory solutions, presented as both technical and morally affirming reprisals. The regulatory proposals which now flood forth, from across the political spectrum, have advocated a range of initiatives from bank nationalization to financial taxes, to restrictions on executive bonuses, to specific recommendations on the regulatory capacity of this or that branch of the state.

But once we enter the domain of regulatory reform, protest becomes diluted in the sea of political promises and mediation. Political leaders assure us that the excesses of the past are now acknowledged and will no longer be permitted: corrupt financiers are being jailed and financial-sector reforms are being planned and implemented. The rejoinder, predictably, is that too little reform is happening too slowly. But such criticism of slow and insufficient policy change markedly shifts the debate and the focus of anger from the underlying significance of the crisis itself.

Policy debate is, in important respects, a diversion, and especially so when it is presented as a substantial political response to the crisis. The policy debate fashions solutions but without a clear understanding of problems. It seeks to contain excess, but without certainty that the solution lies in moderation. It moves debate into specific details, when the "big picture" is still contested. It construes policy errors rather than social contradictions. Moreover, it focuses attention on the state—its past "errors" and the prospect of their rectification—but leaves aside an understanding of the practices of institutions and markets. Conceiving of the financial crisis in terms of a policy debate means participating in finding "quick fix" solutions. This does not embody an ongoing politics for labor.

Accordingly, the objective of this paper is to critically appreciate the distinctive dimensions of the Global Financial Crisis in a way that points to new strategic directions for labor and unions. The agenda is as follows. First, we identify how particular financial processes have created a new dimension to the role of labor in accumulation: the absorber of transferable risk. Second, we consider the strategic responses that might follow from an understanding of this role. We contrast this with an agenda focused on regulatory reform. The latter is not merely state-centered in its politics; it is backward-looking, seeking to re-establish a lost state command over finance, but without a clear agenda of how that command should now be exercised. Our vision of an alternative seeks to build on the progressive developments in finance, and to address ways in which Left strategies can engage that progressive element.

CLEARING A SPACE FOR CLASS

Moving beyond a discourse of state lapses (and the prospect of redemption) involves positioning finance within wider economic and social relations and analyzing the way in which financial calculation has transformed social relations, and how the Crisis expresses the contradictions of this transformation. To build this analysis in a way that foregrounds the particularities of the current crisis and political possibilities that arise, it is necessary to challenge some propositions of Marxist (but by no means exclusively Marxist) analysis of finance.

The first argument in Marxist orthodoxy is that finance is discrete from the "real" economy. We are told that finance is about speculation, and that its growth has become unrelated and disproportional to the world of production of goods and services. This proposition, it can be noted, shares a common foundation with monetarist theory (i.e. that money is a veil). It neglects the way in which different forms of capital (money, production, commodities) combine in their relation to labor, and can do little to ground progressive politics. Once we isolate finance from something called the "real" economy and identify profound problems within finance, we have constituted an idealized "real" capitalism, somehow devoid of "finance," which can only "distort." The Financial Crisis is thus cast as a crisis *against* the "real" economy, and the politics becomes one of defending the "real" against the "financial." The focus turns to processes within finance that are anathema to the operation of the real economy, and hence to an agenda of re-regulation—of returning finance to its appropriate, subordinate, functional role.

Yet what is "financial" and what is "real" cannot be disentangled. In one dimension they cannot be disentangled because corporations undertake both financial and industrial operations. For some, this is about having banking and industrial divisions dedicated to advancing consumer credit as well as to "production." But in any circuit of industrial capital there is a competitive engagement with finance involving calls on money capital and subsequent repayments. In another dimension what is "financial" and what is "real" cannot be disentangled because finance itself must be "produced": it cannot be understood simply via a cargo cult of "the state," for finance itself is now created through private processes, whether as bank credit or as more complex financial products like collateralized debt obligations.[2]

Moreover, if we ask why financial aggregates have grown so rapidly, part of the answer may be loose monetary policy, especially in the United States, but another part of the answer lies in the so-called real economy: the growth of loanable funds derived from the growth of massive surpluses in the advanced capitalist countries and Asia. These surpluses have been generated by labor on a global scale, and one of the contributions of globalized finance has been to convert them into a fluid, investible mass: a mass that, in a different social order, would have the potential to create for labor the conditions for abundance, but in capitalism is used *against* labor.

A second, and related, argument is that finance is driven by speculation. For those drawn to images of "casino capitalism," this is almost a definitional proposition. Even when moving beyond such simplistic labeling, we encounter an identification of finance with speculation whenever finance is not attached to either "real" processes (e.g. buying wheat) or involved in hedging "real" positions (e.g. futures contracts on an actual wheat shipment).[3]

But the criterion of whether there is a "real" position underlying the financial position misses a key dimension of financial evolution. We can convey the importance of this dimension through a simple explanation of finance and the monetary function of storing value.

In the current world, there are no formal anchors to the money system, either national or global. We are using the word "anchor" loosely to include directly material anchors like gold or the Bretton Woods Agreement, or proxy anchors like a US

---

2 We have made the argument elsewhere that highly liquid financial products have money-like attributes and can, in critical respects, be seen as money. See D. Bryan and M. Rafferty, "Financial derivatives and the theory of money," *Economy & Society* 36(1), February 2007.
3   D. McNally, "From Financial Crisis to World-Slump: Accumulation, Financialisation, and the Global Slowdown," *Historical Materialism* 17, 2009.

dollar backed by "fundamentals" such as high US productivity, capital investment or trade surpluses. Gold, of course, is now long gone as a formal anchor, and the material basis of a strong US dollar is now contested. It remains the dominant currency, but it is not a safe way to store value. The consequence is that we cannot identify a consensual unit of account on a global scale. Nation-states may be able to guarantee the value of money within their political borders, but they cannot guarantee "their" money's value relative to other monies (currencies).

So how does anyone store value? You don't simply hold US dollars as you once might have, for the exchange rate on the US dollar bounces around. Instead, you hold a bundle of currencies. But you don't just hold currencies in the form of cash, for currencies as a whole (an asset class) are not stable compared with other asset classes like equities or property. So you diversify into other asset types. But as these various asset types become more popular, and financial products are introduced that do the diversification for you, everything starts to cycle together. The effect is that there may be spreading of risks across different forms of assets, but there is little spreading of risk across different forms of risk. So you go looking for different asset types that will cycle differently and hence embody different risks. You start holding weather derivatives or credit derivatives or commodity derivatives, until these too are incorporated into the standard hedging products, and there is a need to further diversify.

If this trading were motivated simply by taking a gamble on the commodity or weather markets, we might call it "speculation," but if it is driven by an agenda of diversification to preserve wealth, it looks rather different. It looks like a never-ending search for safe ways to store value. To attribute the label "speculation" may not be categorically false (and there is no denying a gambling component in these markets) but, in the absence of a monetary anchor, all asset prices are merely relative and so all asset forms are inherently "speculative." So the label of "speculation"—or, in a similar vein, "fictitious capital"—fails to recognize key processes at work in financial markets—indeed, in capital itself.

Diversification of financial exposures is, at least in part, an organic and integral part of accumulation, in which diverse asset forms denominated in diverse currencies and locations become integrated into a single global capital market. The growth of financial transactions shows how difficult and costly it is for global capital markets to create an edifice of monetary stability in the absence of a formal or agreed unit of account.

There is a direct challenge here to the re-regulation agenda. How can we tell if regulations to contain finance and limit "speculation" will not also restrict the process of risk spreading, leading asset holders to be exposed to unwanted and volatility-inducing risk-holding? This is, of course, the conventional financial economist's response to regulation. But the argument is nonetheless valid: in a world with no anchor, it does not follow that stopping some *forms* of "speculation" leads to a net reduction in speculation overall, even if that were the goal.[4]

RISK

The reason for focusing on the store of value issue is not just to confront the ahistorical and simplistic branding of finance through the label of "speculation." It is to set up a framework that focuses on risk and its management as the emergent framework of analysis of social and economic relations in the current era. It is in this framework—one that engages the internal logic of financial growth—that a more promising politics may be sought.

The process of diversification of asset holdings and management of exposures to financial volatility is fundamentally about the management of risk. The discourse of financial risk and risk management has become pervasive in the current era, and the miscalculations of risk that materialized in the Global Financial Crisis are a direct expression of its relevance.

Risk is clearly an issue for capital, and financial derivatives (including securities) have been integral to capital's risk-management practices. Strategically important here is that financial growth has changed the reach and shape of capital: it has served to integrate different forms of capital and give them greater global liquidity. Specifically in relation to household mortgages and other income-generating assets such as credit-card debt, it is the process of securitization (selling securities based on the performance of loans, but not selling the loan itself) that has

---

4 J. Grahl and P. Lysandrou ("Sand in the Wheels or Spanner in the Works? The Tobin Tax and Global Finance," *Cambridge Journal of Economics* 27, 2003) make a similar argument very effectively in relation to the so-called "Tobin tax."

permitted the issuance of massive amounts of debt and has served to transmit the losses around the world.

Beyond the securitization process, there are other derivative markets for currencies and interest rates and a raft of other risk-defined products, including the risk of counterparty default (credit derivatives). These derivative markets are at the centre of the growth of financial aggregates, and their essential role is to commodify and trade risk. Derivatives on interest rate and currency instruments alone turned over more than $10 trillion per day when last subject to comprehensive measurement,[5] and they had been growing exponentially over the past two decades. In part, these products are being traded by parties who face a particular immediate risk they are seeking to cover; in part they are traded by gamblers; but in significant part, they are traded by parties looking to manage their overall risk exposures in a volatile world.

If we consider the aggregation of these derivative trades as a "system of derivatives" we can see that they also form a system of commensuration, where asset exposures are priced relative to each other.[6] We have also seen that it is a crisis-prone system of commensuration, where perceptions of the future, not embodied labor, are central to the unit of measurement. While its propensity to crisis does not deny its centrality in capitalist calculation, it does have limitations, even within its own framework.

One of the key fallacies of this framework is the belief that risks can be comprehensively measured and priced. Individual positioning in risk markets can never account for systemic risks; nor for uncertainty (what Donald Rumsfeld once termed "unknown unknowns"). We saw the masters of risk calculation, who won the Nobel Prize for the formula of options pricing and the recipe for dynamic hedging, Myron Scholes and Robert Merton, got it disastrously wrong and losing billions of dollars when they ran the hedge fund Long Term Capital Management. It was all about the "intrusion" of uncalculated and incalculable "risks."[7]

---

5 Bank for International Settlements (BIS), *Triennial Central Bank Survey of Foreign Exchange and Derivatives Market Activity in 2007—Final results*, December 19, 2007, table C1, http://www.bis.org.

6 D. Bryan and M. Rafferty, *Capitalism with Derivatives: A Political Economy of Financial Derivatives, Capital and Class*, London: Palgrave Macmillan, 2006, Chapter 2.

7 R. Lowenstein, *When Genius Failed: The Rise and Fall of Long-Term Capital Management*, New York: Random House, 2000. Although incalculable risks are perhaps more precisely cast as uncertainties, the critical point is that the limitations on actuarial calculation are endemic within finance.

Combined, these attributes of derivative markets have two important implications. First, the surpluses created by labor, in disparate processes of production around the globe, have been made liquid, mobile, and hence globally integrated. These markets have thereby unified the creations of labor, and permitted us to see the shared potential of global labor. Yet capital's inability to reliably value this surplus labor means that it does not effectively operate as value.

Second, derivative markets show that finance and the (so-called) real economy cannot be thought of discretely: all sorts of risks in accumulation are being defrayed through and expressed in financial markets. Financial markets integrate capital across space and time and give disparate forms and sites of capital a singular form of calculation. And because derivative markets are intensifying com-petition in the valuing of diverse asset types, there are pressures on workers to deliver profitability in the labor process. Accordingly, the growth of finance is integral to capitalist accumulation. This centrality is not appreciated by functionalist approaches to finance, which emphasize its dysfunctionality to the "real" economy.

This system of calculation is integral to accumulation, yet prone to profound crisis. If we are to engage the language of functionalism, the dysfunctionality pertains not to the "real" economy, but to accumulation itself, and hence to the role of labor within accumulation. This is not merely labor's burden—to receive the effects and demands of failing accumulation—it is also the space where labor's new opportunities might be sought. We therefore need to explore the role of labor within the discourse of risk: labor's role as the absorber of risk.

Risk shifting

Risk is not just an issue for capital: it impacts on labor too.[8] Many people will have read books like Jacob Hacker's excellent *The Great Risk Shift*, which explains the process by which the state has progressively offloaded risks onto individuals and families.[9] But we need to extend this argument in new directions.

---

8   D. Bryan, R. Martin and M. Rafferty, "Financialization and Marx: Giving labor and capital a financial makeover," *Review of Radical Political Economics* 41(3), 2009.

9   J. Hacker, *The Great Risk Shift*, Oxford: Oxford University Press, 2006.

In the post-war period, and up to the 1970s, it could be said that in advanced capitalist countries the state covered or mediated a vast range of risks. They were differently framed in different countries, but essentially the welfare state covered the risks of being sick via public health-care; of being poorly educated by free and reasonable-quality public education; of being unemployed or aged by full employment policies and pensions. The state had guarantees for many agricultural prices, for utilities such as water and electricity and telephone services. And in finance, there were fixed exchange rates, capital controls and tightly regulated banking, such that the range of products which financial institutions could "offer" were simple and straightforward.

But that changed from the 1970s. Progressively, we have seen the withdrawal of the state from the management of a variety of risks, and the agenda and the language of economists—and more specifically the language of finance—have come to rule. In this agenda, individuals are cast as having to take responsibility for managing their own risks.

The agenda has taken a range of rhetorical forms, with many governments promoting "shareholder democracies." In the United States, President George W. Bush promoted the conception of an "ownership society" that was central to his campaign for re-election in 2004.[10] In this framework, individuals come to be understood as small businesses. The key ingredients of this discourse are ownership and choice. Both are, at least on the surface, highly desirable: we would, of course, prefer ownership to dispossession and choice to compulsion. But the new agenda meant a change in the way society is organized and how individuals think about each other and society at large.

Calculations and decisions must now be made about a range of issues. Some such issues have emerged because the management of certain exposures is no longer undertaken by the state: there is now a need for private calculation and decisions about such things as health insurance, education investment, and investment in an asset portfolio for retirement. Increasingly, labor law facilitates employment contracts that build in "flexibility," so that the labor market becomes a site of corporate risk management. Other questions stem from increasing competitiveness within the

---

10   George W. Bush, President's Remarks at the National Federation of Independent Businesses, the J. W. Marriott Hotel, Washington, DC, June 17, 2004, http://georgewbush-whitehouse.archives.gov.

financial sector: decisions about the proportion of (expected) income to dedicate to consumer credit and home-loan interest payments; the time profile of loans; fixed or floating-rate loans; the management of consumer credit options; the preferred pension scheme. Finally, there is an emerging set of choices to be made in the face of new financial products—in particular the emergence of derivative or insurance products that permit people to hedge exposure to risks relating to their employment and the value of their home.[11] In each one of these calculations there are (retrospectively, at least) right and wrong choices, requiring the household to be financially savvy, not just in the sense of exercising prudence, but also in identifying the range of financial risk exposures and knowing how to manage them. There occurs, in short, a "financialization of daily life."[12]

These sorts of changes may readily be subsumed under the ideological banner of "neoliberalism." But the central issue is not the state: we need to go beyond labels like "neoliberalism" and beyond Hacker's identification of risk shifting with the diminished role of the state. From the perspective of capital, new opportunities for accumulation have arisen though the "ownership society" culture. In particular, the fact that workers are increasingly also borrowing to acquire assets and long-term consumption goods constitutes a new form of what Marx called primitive accumulation, i.e. capitalist accumulation in sites not formally organized according to a capitalist logic.[13] Over the past decades, the conversion of homes into leveraged capital assets and workers' pension contributions into personalized investment portfolios has become central to capital accumulation. In other words, through payments to finance out of wages as well as via development in production workers' households are now at the frontier of capitalist expansion. Fundamentally, such developments are also about the systematic shifting of risk from capital to labor.

---

11 R. J. Shiller, *The New Financial Order: Financial Risk in the 21st Century*, Princeton: Princeton University Press, 2004.

12 R. Martin, *The Financialization of Daily Life*, Philadelphia: Temple University Press, 2002.

13 In a similar vein, R. Bellofiore and J. Halevi ("Deconstructing Labor: What is 'New' in Contemporary Capitalism and Economic Policies: A Marxian-Kaleckian Perspective," in C. Gnos and L. P. Rochon, eds, *Employment, Growth and Development: A Post-Keynesian Approach*, Cheltenham: Elgar, 2009) uses the term "the real subsumption of labour to finance."

Risk shifting and surplus value

Risk transfer from capital to labor occurs through a range of practices, governed by a logic that is every bit as systematic as the surplus transfer from labor to capital depicted by Marx. Indeed, the parallels are striking.

Central to Marx's explanation of surplus value is the particular characteristic of the labor market that makes it different from other market transactions. The critical point is that the worker cannot be separated from her/his labor-power, and herein lies the capacity of the capitalist to appropriate surplus labor. In Chapter 6 of Volume I of *Capital*, Marx identifies two conditions of this particularity of labor.[14] First:

> The individual whose labour-power it is . . . sells it as a commodity. In order that its possessor may sell it as a commodity, he must have it at his disposal, he must be the free proprietor of his own labour capacity, hence of his person.

Second:

> The possessor of labour-power, instead of being able to sell commodities in which his labour has been objectified, must rather be compelled to offer for sale as a commodity that very labour-power, which exists only in his living body.

This makes labor different from other forms of capital: capital purchases the capacity for labor (labor-power) but acquires "labor." The difference between the value of labor-power (the costs of reproducing the worker) and the value created by labor is surplus value.

Moreover, in this context Marx emphasizes that this sale of labor-power has two attributes. First, it is a voluntary process:

> [The owner of labor-power] and the owner of money meet in the market, and enter into relations with each other on a footing of equality as owners of commodities, with the sole difference that one is buyer, the other seller; both are therefore equal in the eyes of the law.

Second, it is distinct from slavery:

> For this relation to continue, the proprietor of labour-power must always sell it for a limited period only, for if he were to sell it in a

---

14 K. Marx, *Capital* Volume I, Harmondsworth: Penguin, 1867, pp. 271–2.

lump, once and for all, he would be selling himself, converting himself from a free man into a slave, from an owner of a commodity into a commodity.

This same issue of the distinctiveness of labor is apparent in the market for risk. Labor has become a "player" in the market for risk, but the inseparability of labor and labor-power creates an asymmetry between labor and capital in the trading of risk. John Campbell, in his 2006 Presidential Address to the American Finance Association, emphasizes the distinctiveness of labor-power (albeit framed as human capital):

> Models in the Merton tradition assume that all wealth is held in a liquid, easily tradable form. However, the largest component of wealth for most households is human capital, which is nontradable. Put differently, households receive labor income but cannot sell claims to that income . . . In practice . . . much of the risk in labor income is idiosyncratic and therefore unhedgeable.[15]

Workers are players in the market for risk, just as they are players in the labor market. To adopt Marx's phrasing and apply it to the market for risk: there is trading "on a footing of equality," where labor and capital are "equal in the eyes of the law." But the owner of labor-power is limited by himself being the embodiment as well as the owner of his asset risks. The owner of labor-power therefore cannot sell off the risk, "which exists only in his living body." He must absorb the costs of unemployment, increasingly insecure employment and wage flexibility. For the owner of labor-power to trade his risk would involve selling claims to his income "in a lump" (that is, the worker would have to securitize himself). Hence to sell his risk in the Merton tradition involves "converting himself from a free man into a slave."

Formally equal exchange therefore embodies a systematic process of risk shifting. Individual workers can win in the market for risk, just as they can win in the labor market, but the aggregate class process is different. Like capital, labor faces risks but, unlike capital, labor cannot sell on its key risks. Labor therefore systematically absorbs risk.

---

15 J. Y. Campbell, "Household Finance," *Journal of Finance* 61(4), 2006, p. 1559. "Merton emphasizes that long-term investors must consider not only risks to their wealth, but also risks to the productivity of their wealth, that is, the rate of return at which wealth can be reinvested" (p. 1558).

In (interim) summary, we can observe that the market for risk creates winners and losers. Part of that can no doubt be understood within a discourse of gambling. Many might, therefore, advocate state regulations to restrict gambling. But winning and losing in the market for risk fundamentally relates to the different risk-shifting capacities of labor and capital. And this is not something that agendas of re-regulation can hope to address in a meaningful way.

TURNING LABOR'S MEANS OF SUBSISTENCE INTO CAPITAL: THE CATALYST OF CRISIS

It is not, however, just the commodity "labor-power" that is illiquid. Means of subsistence generally are, by definition, not liquid assets, and so the same risk-shifting structure that characterizes labor-power is likely to occur more generally across the range of subsistence goods and services.

The critical change in patterns of accumulation over the past decades has been the conversion of subsistence goods and services into liquid assets through either derivative instruments (converting their price changes into tradable assets) or securitization (converting their income streams into tradable assets). Labor's means of subsistence—housing, health, etc.—become liquid assets for capital at the same time as they are "locked in" as labor's consumption items. The trick for capital is to work out how to trade on the discrepancy between the way in which labor understands subsistence goods and the way capital has now transformed them.

The growth of the subprime mortgage market was driven by the duality of housing as both an illiquid subsistence good for labor and a liquid capital asset. The ingenuity of the subprime innovators was to segment the capital asset risk (i.e. the risk of house price appreciation/depreciation) from the subsistence risk (i.e. the risk of workers defaulting on repayments), and to sell off the latter while retaining the former. The structure of a subprime loan, with its teaser rates and inevitable loan rescheduling, ensured that the risks of non-repayment would be borne by bond holders who purchased exposure to the performance of the loans, while those who retained ownership of the mortgages retained the deeds to the house and fees derived from loan rescheduling. Loan rescheduling was a means to liquidify and so appropriate the capital appreciation of house prices.

How did this work? A worker who wanted to retain her/his house as a place in which to live, but could not keep up with mortgage repayments, would keep rescheduling the loan so long as the value of the house was greater than the value of the loan.[16] Within the subprime contract, there are high fees for rescheduling, but the persistent likelihood of loan default ensured continual rescheduling, and so continual payment of rescheduling fees. The latter enabled lenders to capture much of the asset price appreciation, while securitization permitted them to pass on the risks associated with the growing precariousness of repayment. It was an extraordinary way to trade on the disparity between housing as a subsistence good and housing as a capital asset.

As it turned out, the subprime market became dramatically overextended. The capital risk and the subsistence risk are differentiable only so long as defaults do not result in loan foreclosures on a mass scale, depreciating house prices generally. Once house prices stopped rising, the rationale for rescheduling evaporated. Repayment of loans dried up and mortgage-backed securities tumbled in value and, via the same process, mortgage holders foreclosed and flooded the market with houses for sale.

In the drama of a crash we should not lose sight of the logic that initiated and fueled subprime growth. At the centre of the financial crisis was an asset characterized by a duality of liquidity and illiquidity. Housing, in its illiquid guise, plays a central role in labor's subsistence. But in a context that increasingly treats the household as a small business, housing has also become a means for labor's reattachment to capital; developments in capital markets over the past decades have served to bestow on "labor's capital" more and more attributes of liquidity. In the process, the household has become a site of risk absorption.

While Marx emphasized the separation of labor from capital as the key to surplus value, we here identify this reattachment to capital as the source of a new process of risk transfer. In both cases, the relationship between labor and capital is organized through voluntary exchange, yet this formal equality is underlain by a systematic transfer process. It is this process of risk shifting that ties together many of the changes that have been commented on so frequently by critics of neoliberalism like Hacker.

---

16 This calculation would also include the costs of rental, so that the optimal decision involves rescheduling to maintain a loan in excess of the value of the house, so long as the additional repayments are no more than the cost of renting.

Over the past thirty years, we have seen a growth in labor productivity; in the number of hours that constitute full-time work; in the number of years that constitute a working life; in the number of family members needed to secure the family wage; and in the proportion of a family's income that must be allocated to reproducing the next generation of workers via childcare, health-care and education expenditures. Concurrently, we have seen stagnating wages; the decline of access to publicly funded health-care; the necessity for private insurance; volatile house prices and interest rates; the increasing need to fund education from private sources; and growing charges for access to public utilities. As workers increasingly resorted to borrowing to maintain living standards,[17] they entered further onto the terrain of risk-shifting. With the demands of wage work intensifying but capital markets booming, the structure of labor's aspirations began, formally at least, to resemble those of capital, i.e. to acquire assets. Capital was all too willing to fund these aspirations. As households have had to become lifetime financial risk managers, some have done well for themselves. But this does not negate the fact that this development is inextricably tied up with an overall process whereby risk was systematically redistributed from capital to labor. The new logic of risk management left the majority of workers to manage as best they could: if you lose your job, you will be increasingly likely to lose your home, and, to avoid that, you will probably first stop paying for insurance on things like health and the car; you postpone one risk by loading up others. Those who unsuccessfully manage their labor market, housing, health, pension and education calculations, or find themselves accidental victims of sickness or unemployment, face household insolvency.

STRATEGIC RESPONSES: ABSORBING, RESISTING AND LEVERAGING RISK

In its 2005 *Financial Stability Report*, the International Monetary Fund described households as the global financial market's "shock absorber of last resort."[18] For the IMF this was a lead-in to proposals for promoting financial literacy, but in this chapter we have presented the significance of the mechanism rather differently.

---

17 See the contribution by Leo Panitch and Sam Gindin to this volume.
18 International Monetary Fund, *Global Financial Stability Report*, April 2005, p. 89, http://www.imf.org.

We have framed the issue not in terms of workers' financial illiteracy but as part of a systemic process based on the nature of labor and its class position within capital accumulation.

What sort of strategic response follows? The aspirations for re-regulation that currently abound are based fundamentally on the anticipation that the state can somehow reabsorb and neutralize risks. Yet such proposals ignore the new liquidity of capital, and the relative illiquidity inherent in labor. Perhaps, then, a more fruitful strategy for labor is about resisting the role of risk-absorber of last resort. This means that working-class housing, pensions, education, health-care and basic savings, as well as terms of employment, need to be isolated from the logic and vicissitudes of capital. This may sound like a familiar proposal. However, we identify this strategy not merely as a claim to consumption rights but as a *challenge to capital's new frontier of accumulation*.

It is here that we find the material difference with the re-regulation agenda, which fails to appreciate how consistent its objectives are with the logic of risk-shifting. For drawing labor into capital's world of risk-transfer, for all its flexibility, has the long-term effect of "cannibalizing" labor: labor's financial insolvency undermines capital's own long-term requirements. Capital *needs* labor, so it needs the reproduction of labor as a class. A regulatory agenda for capital follows quite naturally from this imperative: the regulation of households *as a legitimate site of accumulation* will predictably be reformed and given order in the wake of the current Crisis, to ensure its long-term sustainability.

Here, too, we note a parallel with Marx's explanation of surplus value. In volume I of *Capital* Marx depicted the European factory acts of the mid-nineteenth century as a progressive development for labor, securing its physical subsistence by restricting working hours and child labor. But he also identified the factory acts as an intervention on behalf of capital, which capitalists could not implement on an individual basis without losing competitiveness. In other words, they were interventions aiming to set laws of capitalist competition that were consistent with the reproduction of a working class. This development, far from slowing down accumulation in the long run, laid the foundations for a shift toward a more intense form of capitalist exploitation—based not on longer and longer working hours ("absolute surplus value") but on technology and productivity increases ("relative surplus value").

In the current context, the excesses of risk shifting may well be contained through regulatory reform to make it sustainable for both labor and capital. We refer here not to populist demands for "financial re-regulation" aspiring to make financial institutions more prudent, modest and transparent. No doubt worthy outcomes, these are not labor's issues. We refer specifically to reforms aimed to resist extant forms of risk shifting and protect labor's living standards. Such reforms warrant labor's support as a progressive development. But whether the labor movement should seek to present this regulatory agenda as its own is debatable. The historical analogy with the factory acts suggests that, once capital's frontier of primitive accumulation in households is curtailed or restricted, it will swiftly move into new areas and develop new forms of accumulation. Moreover, its ability to do so will be greatly enhanced by the wealth of opportunities that the financialization of social life has opened up over the past decades.

Labor therefore needs to look beyond state regulatory agendas designed to protect workers' living standards, and toward these potential new forms of accumulation, and the opportunities that arise therein. Just as financial innovation has drawn capital into a single web of calculation, so labor's direct absorption into that system, as both subject and object of accumulation, opens new potentials to subvert the process of calculation. That was exactly the unintended effect of labor, as subprime borrowers, in the recent crisis, but it manifested as a destruction of value, not the generation of access to a world of abundance. The experience has made stark that, in a world of risk shifting, labor has a capacity to "leverage off" the liquidity now presumed by capital. Somewhere in that liquidity, both fantastic in its reach and fragile in its form, lies a transformative potential that the backward-looking defensiveness of calls for the re-regulation and rectification of finance no longer possess.

18

THE CURRENT CRISIS

A *Socialist Perspective*

Leo Panitch and Sam Gindin

"They say they won't intervene. But they will." This is how Robert Rubin, Bill Clinton's Treasury Secretary, responded to Paul O'Neill, the first Treasury Secretary under George W. Bush, who openly criticized his predecessor's interventions in the face of what Rubin called "the messy reality of global financial crises."[1] The current dramatic conjuncture of financial crisis and state intervention has proven Rubin more correct than he could have imagined. But it also demonstrates why those, whether from the Right or the Left, who have only understood the era of neoliberalism ideologically—i.e. in terms of a hegemonic ideological determination to free markets from states—have had such a weak handle on discerning what has really been going on over the past quarter of a century. Clinging to this type of understanding will also get in the way of the thinking necessary to advance a socialist strategy in the wake of this crisis.[2]

The fundamental relationship between capitalist states and financial markets cannot be understood in terms of how much or little regulation the former puts upon the latter. It needs to be understood in terms of the guarantee the state provides to

---

1   R. Rubin, *In an Uncertain World: Tough Choices from Washington to Wall Street*, New York: Thomson-Texere, 2003, p. 297.
2   Some of the central ideas in this paper are also taken up in M. Konings and L. Panitch, "US Financial Power in Crisis," *Historical Materialism* 16(4), 2008, esp. pp. 31–2, and even more fully in many of the chapters in L. Panitch and M. Konings, eds, *American Empire and the Political Economy of International Finance*, London: Palgrave, 2009, second edn.

property, above all in the form of the promise not to default on its bonds—which are themselves the foundation of financial markets' role in capital accumulation. But not all states are equally able, or trusted as willing (especially since the Russian Revolution), to honor this guarantee. The American state emerged in the twentieth century as an entirely new kind of imperial state precisely because it took utmost responsibility for honoring this guarantee itself, while promoting a world order of independent nation-states which the new empire would expect to behave as capitalist states. Since the Second World War the American state has been not just the dominant state in the capitalist world but the state responsible for overseeing the expansion of capitalism to its current global dimensions and for organizing the management of its economic contradictions. It has done this not through the displacement but through the penetration and integration of other states. This included their internationalization in the sense of their cooperation in taking responsibility for global accumulation within their borders and their cooperation in setting the international rules for trade and investment.

It was the credibility of the American state's guarantee to property which insured that, even amidst the Great Depression and business hostility to the New Deal's union and welfare reforms, private funds were readily available as loans to all the new public agencies created in that era. This was also why whatever liquid foreign funds could escape the capital controls of other states in that decade made their way to New York, and so much of the world's gold filled the vaults of Fort Knox. And it is this which helps explain why it fell to the American state to take responsibility for making international capitalism viable again after 1945, with the fixed exchange rate for its dollar established at Bretton Woods providing the sole global currency intermediary for gold. When it became apparent by the 1960s that those who held US dollars would have to suffer a devaluation of their funds through inflation, the fiction of a continuing gold standard was abandoned. The world's financial system was now explicitly based on the dollar as American-made "fiat money," backed by an ironclad guarantee against default of US Treasury bonds which were now treated as being as "good as gold." Today's Global Financial Order has been founded on this; and this is why US Treasury bonds are the fundamental basis from which calculations of value of all forms of financial instruments begin.

To be sure, the end of fixed exchange rates and a dollar nominally tied to gold now meant that it had to be accepted internationally that the returns to those who held US assets would reflect the fluctuating value of US dollars in currency markets. But the commitment by the Federal Reserve and Treasury to an anti-inflation priority via the founding act of neoliberalism—the "Volcker Shock" of 1979—assuaged that problem. (This defining moment of US state intervention, like the current one, came in the run-up to a presidential election—i.e. *before* Reagan's election, and with bipartisan support and the support of industrial as well as financial capital in the US and abroad.) As the American state took the lead, by its example and its pressure on other states around the world, in giving priority to low inflation, this bolstered finance capital's confidence in the substantive value of lending; and after the initial astronomical interest rates produced by the Volcker Shock, this soon made an era of low interest rates possible. Throughout the neoliberal era, the enormous demand for US bonds and the low interest paid on them has rested on this foundation. This was reinforced by the defeat of American trade unionism; by the intense competition in financial markets domestically and internationally; by financial capital's pressures on firms to lower costs through restructuring if they are to justify more capital investment; by the reallocation of capital across sectors, and especially the provision of venture capital to support new technologies in new leading sectors of capital accumulation; and by the "Americanization of finance" in other states and the consequent access this provided the American state to global savings.

Deregulation was more a consequence than the main cause of the intense competition in financial markets and its attendant effects. By 1990, this competition had already led to banks scheming to escape the reserve requirements of the Basel bank regulations by creating "Structured Investment Vehicles" to hold these and other risky derivative assets. It also led to the increased blurring of the lines between commercial and investment banking, insurance and real estate. Competition in the financial sector fostered all kinds of innovations in financial instruments which allowed for higher degrees of leverage. This meant that there was an explosion in the effective money supply (this was highly ironic in terms of the monetarist theories that are usually thought to have founded neoliberalism). The competition to purchase assets with these funds replaced price inflation with the asset inflation that characterized the whole era. This was reinforced by the American state's readiness to throw further liquidity into the financial system whenever a specific asset bubble burst (while imposing austerity on economies in the South as the condition for the liquidity the IMF and the World Bank provided to their financial markets at moments of crisis). All this was central to the uneven and often chaotic making of global capitalism over the past quarter of a century, to the crises that have punctuated it, and to the active role of the US state in containing them.

Meanwhile, the world beat a path to US financial markets not only because of the demand for Treasury bills, and not only because of Wall Street's linkages to US capital more generally, but also because of the depth and breadth of its financial markets—which had much to do with US financial capital's relation to the popular classes. The American Dream has always materially entailed promoting their integration into the circuits of financial capital, whether as independent commodity farmers, as workers whose paychecks were deposited with banks and whose pension savings were invested in the stock market, as consumers reliant on credit, or, not least, as heavily mortgaged homeowners. It is the form that this incorporation of the mass of the American population took in the neoliberal context of competition, inequality and capital mobility, much more than the degree of supposed "deregulation" of financial markets, that helps explain the dynamism and longevity of the finance-led neoliberal era.

But it also helped trigger the current crisis—and the massive state intervention in response to it. The scale of the current crisis, which significantly has its roots in housing finance, cannot be understood apart from how the defeat of American trade unionism played out by the first years of the twenty-first century. Constrained in what they could get from their labor for two decades, workers were drawn into the logic of asset inflation in the age of neoliberal finance not only via the institutional investment of their pensions, but also via the one major asset they held in their own hands (or could aspire to hold)—their family home. It is significant that this went so far as the attempted integration via financial markets of poor African-American communities, so long the Achilles heel of working-class integration into the American Dream. The roots of the subprime mortgage crisis, triggering the collapse of the mountain of repackaged and resold securitized derivative assets to hedge the risk involved in lending to poor people, lay in the way the anti-inflation commitment had since the 1970s ruled out the massive public expenditures that would have been required to even begin to address the crisis of inadequate housing in US cities.

As the "Great Society" public expenditure programs of the 1960s ran up against the need to redeem the imperial state's anti-inflationary commitments, the financial market became the mechanism for doing this. In 1977, the government-sponsored mortgage companies, Freddie Mac and Fannie Mae (the New Deal public housing corporation privatized by Lyndon Johnson in 1968 before the word neoliberalism was invented), were required by the Community Reinvestment Act to sustain home loans by banks in poor communities. This effectively gave a boost to the market in mortgage-backed securities associated with private financing for housing for low-income families. From modest beginnings, this only really took off with the inflation of residential real-estate values after the recession of the early 1990s and the Clinton Administration's embrace of neoliberalism leading to its reinforcement of a reliance on financial markets rather than public expenditures as the primary means of integrating working-class, Black and Hispanic communities. The Bush Republicans' determination to open up competition to sell and trade mortgages and mortgage-backed securities to all comers was in turn reinforced by the Greenspan Fed's dramatic lowering of real interest rates to almost zero in response to the bursting of the dot-com bubble and to 9/11. But this was a policy that was only sustainable via the flow of global savings to the US, not least to the apparent Treasury-plated safety of Fannie Mae and Freddie Mac securities as government-sponsored enterprises.

It was this long chain of events that led to the massive funding of mortgages, the hedging and default derivatives based on this, the rating agencies' AAA rating of them, and their spread onto the books of many foreign institutions. This included the world's biggest insurance company, AIG, and the great New York investment banks, whose own traditional business of corporate and government finance around the globe was now itself heavily mortgaged to the mortgages that had been sold in poor communities in the US and then resold many times over. The global attraction and strength of American finance was seen to be rooted in its depth and breadth at home, and this meant that when the crisis hit in the subprime security market at the heart of the empire, it immediately had implications for the banking systems of many other countries. The scale of the American government's intervention has certainly been a function of the consequent unraveling of the crisis throughout its integrated domestic financial system, yet it is also important to understand this in terms of its imperial responsibilities as the state of global capital.

This is why it fell to the Fed to repeatedly pump billions of dollars via foreign central banks into interbank markets abroad, where banks balance their books through the overnight borrowing of dollars from other banks. And an important factor in the nationalizations of Fannie Mae and Freddie Mac was the need to redeem the expectations of foreign investors (including the Japanese and Chinese central banks) that the US government would never default on its debt obligations. It is for this reason that even those foreign leaders who have opportunistically pronounced the end of American "financial superpower status" have credited the US Treasury for "acting not just in the US interests but also in the interests of other nations."[3] The US was not being altruistic in doing this, since not to do it would have risked a run on the dollar. But this is precisely the point. The American state cannot act in the interests of American capitalism without also reflecting the logic of American capitalism's integration with global capitalism both economically and politically. This is why it is misleading to portray the American state as merely representing its "national interest" while ignoring the structural role it plays in the making and reproduction of global capitalism.

A Century of Crises

It might be thought that the exposure of the state's role in the present financial crisis would once and for all rid people of the illusion that capitalists don't want their states involved in their markets, or that capitalist states could ever be neutral and benign regulators in the public interest of markets. Unfortunately, the widespread call today for the American state to "go back" to playing the role of such a regulator reveals that this illusion remains deeply engrained, and obscures an understanding of both the past and present history of the relationship between the state and finance in the US.

In October 1907, near the beginning of the "American Century," and exactly a hundred years before the onset of the current Financial Crisis, the US experienced a financial crisis that for anyone living through it would have seemed as great as today's.

---

3 German Finance Minister Peer Steinbrück, in Bertrand Benoit, "US 'will lose financial superpower status'," *Financial Times*, September 25, 2008.

Indeed, there were far more suicides in that crisis than in the current one, as "Wall Street spent a cliff-hanging year" enduring a stock-market crash, an 11 percent decline in GDP, and a series of bank runs.[4] At the core of the crisis was the practice of trust companies drawing money from banks at exorbitant interest rates and, without the protection of sufficient cash reserves, lending out so much of it against stock and bond speculation that almost half of the bank loans in New York had questionable securities as their only collateral. When the trust companies were forced to call in some of their loans to stock-market speculators, even interest rates which zoomed to well over 100 percent on margin loans could not attract funds. European investors started withdrawing funds from the US.

Whereas European central banking had its roots in "haute finance" far removed from the popular classes, US small farmers' dependence on credit had made them hostile to a Central Bank that they recognized would serve bankers' interests. In the absence of a Central Bank, both the US Treasury and Wall Street relied on J. P. Morgan to organize the bail-out of 1907. As Henry Paulson did with Lehman's a century later, Morgan let the giant Knickerbocker Trust go under in spite of its holding $50 million of deposits for 17,000 depositors ("I've got to stop somewhere," Morgan said). This only fuelled the panic and triggered runs on other financial firms including the Trust Company of America (leading Morgan to pronounce that "this is the place to stop the trouble"). Using $25 million put at his disposal by the Treasury, and calling together Wall Street's bank presidents to demand they put up another $25 million "within ten or twelve minutes" (which they did), Morgan dispensed the liquidity that began to calm the markets.[5]

When the Federal Reserve was finally established in 1913, this was seen as Wilson's great Progressive victory over the unaccountable big financiers. (As Chernow's monumental biography of Morgan put it, "From the ashes of 1907 arose the Federal Reserve System: everyone saw that thrilling rescues

---

4   R. Chernow, *The House of Morgan*, New York: Simon & Schuster, 1990, p. 121; C. A. E. Goodhart, *The New York Money Market and the Finance of Trade*, Cambridge, MA: Harvard University Press, 1969, p. 116; P. Studenski and H. E. Krooss, *Financial History of the United States,* New York: McGraw-Hill, 1965, p. 252; and M. Friedman and A. J. Schwartz, *A Monetary History of the United States, 1867–1960*, Princeton: Princeton University Press, p. 159.
5   Chernow, *House of Morgan*, pp. 123–5.

by corpulent old tycoons were a tenuous prop for the banking system."[6]) Yet the main elements of the Federal Reserve Bill had already been drafted by the Morgan and Rockefeller interests during the previous Taft administration; and although the Fed's corporatist and decentralized structure of regional Federal Reserve boards reflected the compromise the final Act made with populist pressures, its immediate effect was actually to cement the "fusion of financial and government power."[7] This was so both in the sense of the Fed's remit as the "banker's bank" (that is, a largely passive regulator of bank credit and a lender of last resort) and also by virtue of the close ties between the Federal Reserve Bank of New York and the House of Morgan. William McAdoo, Wilson's Treasury Secretary, saw the Federal Reserve Act's provisions allowing US banks to establish foreign branches in terms of laying the basis for the US "to become the dominant financial power of the world and to extend our trade to every part of the world."[8]

In fact, in its early decades, the Fed actually was "a loose and inexperienced body with minimal effectiveness even in its domestic functions."[9] This was an important factor in the Crash of 1929 and in the Fed's perverse role in contributing to the Great Depression. It was class pressures from below that produced FDR's union and welfare reforms, but the New Deal is misunderstood if it is simply seen in terms of a dichotomy of purpose and function between state and capitalist actors. The strongest evidence of this was in the area of financial regulation, which established a corporatist "network of public and semi-public bodies, individual firms and professional groups" that existed in a symbiotic relationship distanced from democratic pressures.[10] While the Morgan empire was brought down by an alliance of new financial competitors and the state, the New Deal's financial reforms, which were introduced before the

---

6 Ibid, p. 128.
7 M. N. Rothbard, "The Origins of the Federal Reserve," *Quarterly Journal of Austrian Economics*, 1999, 2(3). See also J. Livingston, *Origins of the Federal Reserve System: Money, Class and Corporate Capitalism, 1890–1913*, Ithaca: Cornell University Press, 1986.
8 Cited in J. J. Broesamle, *William Gibbs McAdoo: A Passion for Change, 1863–1917*, Port Washington, NY: Kennikat Press, 1973, p. 129.
9 G. Arrighi, *The Long Twentieth Century*, London: Verso, 1994, p. 272.
10 M. Moran, *The Politics of the Financial Services Revolution*, New York: Macmillan, 1991, p. 29.

union and welfare ones, protected the banks as a whole from hostile popular sentiments. They restrained competition and excesses of speculation not so much by curbing the power of finance but rather through the fortification of key financial institutions, especially the New York investment banks that were to grow ever more powerful through the remainder of the century. Despite the hostility of capitalists to FDR's union and welfare reforms, by the time the Second World War began, the New Dealers had struck what they themselves called their "grand truce" with business.[11] And even though the Treasury's Keynesian economists took the lead in rewriting the rules of international finance during the Second World War (producing no little tension with Wall Street), a resilient US financial capital was not external to the constitution of the Bretton Woods order: it was embedded within it and determined its particular character.

In the post-war period, the New Deal regulatory structure acted as an incubator for the growth and development of financial capital. The strong position of Wall Street was institutionally crystallized via the 1951 Accord between the Federal Reserve and the Treasury. Whereas during the war the Fed "had run the market for government securities with an iron fist," it now took up the position long advocated by University of Chicago economists and set to work successfully organizing Wall Street's bond dealers into a self-governing association that would ensure they had "sufficient depth and breadth" to make "a free market in government securities," and thus allow market forces to determine bond prices.[12] The Fed's Open Market Committee would then only intervene by "leaning against the wind" to correct "a disorderly situation" through its buying and selling of Treasury bills. Lingering concerns that Keynesian commitments to the priority of full employment and fiscal deficits might prevail in the Treasury were thus allayed: the Accord was designed to ensure that "forces seen as more radical" within any administration would

---

11   A. Brinkley, *The End of Reform: New Deal Liberalism in Recession and War*, New York: Alfred A. Knopf, 1995, pp. 89–90.

12   This and the following quotation are from R. Herzel and R. F. Leach, "After the Accord: Reminiscences on the Birth of the Modern Fed," *Federal Reserve Bank of Richmond Economic Quarterly* 87(1), 2001, pp. 57–63. Leach, who later became a leading J.P. Morgan executive, was at the time of the Accord the Chief of the Government Planning Section at the Board of Governors of the Federal Reserve System.

find it difficult, at least without creating a crisis, to implement inflationary monetary policies.[13]

Already in the 1950s profits in the financial sector were growing faster than in industry. By the early 1960s, the securitization of commercial banking (selling saving certificates rather than relying on deposits) and the enormous expansion of investment banking (including Morgan Stanley's creation of the first viable computer model for analyzing financial risk) were already in train. With the development of the unregulated Euromarket in dollars and the international expansion of US multinational corporations, the playing field for American finance was far larger than New Deal regulations could contain. Both domestically and internationally, the baby had outgrown the incubator, which was in any case being buffeted by inflationary pressures stemming from union militancy and public expenditures on the Great Society programs and the Vietnam War. The Bank Crisis of 1966, the complaints by pension funds that fixed brokerage fees discriminated against workers' savings, the series of scandals that beset Wall Street, all foretold the end of the corporatist structure of brokers, investment banks and corporate managers that had dominated domestic capital markets since the New Deal, culminating in Wall Street's "Big Bang" of 1975. Meanwhile, the collapse of the Bretton Woods fixed exchange-rate system, due to inflationary pressures on the dollar as well as the massive growth in international trade and investment, laid the foundation for the derivatives revolution by leading to an enormous demand for hedging risk by trading futures and options in exchange and interest rates. The newly created Commodity Futures Trading Commission was quickly created less to regulate this new market than to facilitate its development.[14] It was not so much neoliberal ideology that broke the old system of financial regulations as it was the contradictions that had emerged within that system.

---

13 G. A. Epstein and J. B. Shor, "The Federal Reserve-Treasury Accord and the Construction of the Postwar Monetary Regime in the United States," *Social Concept*, 1995, p. 27. See also E. Dickens "US Monetary Policy in the 1950s: A Radical Political Economy Approach," *Review of Radical Political Economics*, 1995, 27(4), and his "Bank Influence and the Failure of US Monetary Policy during the 1953–54 Recession," *International Review of Applied Economics* 12(2), 1998.

14 D. Bryan and M. Rafferty, *Capitalism with Derivatives: A Political Economy of Financial Derivatives, Capital and Class*, London: Palgrave, 2006. See also *Leo Melamed on the Markets: Twenty Years of Financial History as Seen by the Man who Revolutionized the Markets*, New York: Wiley, 1992, esp. pp. 43, 77–8.

If there was going to be any serious alternative to giving financial capital its head by the 1970s, this would have required going well beyond the old regulations and capital controls, and introducing qualitatively new policies to undermine the social power of finance. This was recognized by those pushing for the more radical aspects of the 1977 Community Reinvestment Act, and who could have never foretold where the compromises struck with the banks to secure their loans would lead. Where the socialist politics were stronger, the nationalization of the financial system was being forcefully advanced as a demand by the mid-1970s. The left of the British Labour Party were able to secure the passage of a conference resolution to nationalize the big banks and insurance companies in the City of London, albeit with no effect on a Labour government that embraced one of the IMF's first structural adjustment programs. In France, the *Programme Commun* of the late 1970s led to the Mitterand government's bank nationalizations, but this was carried through in a way that ensured that the structure and function of the banks were not changed in the process. In Canada, the directly elected local planning boards we proposed, which would draw on the surplus from a nationalized financial system to create jobs, were seen as the first step in a new strategy to get labour movements to think in ways that were not so cramped and defensive.[15] Such alternatives—strongly opposed by social-democratic politicians who soon accommodated themselves to the dynamics of finance-led neoliberalism and the ideology of efficient free markets—were soon forgotten amidst the general defeat of labor movements and socialist politics that characterized the new era.

Financial capitalists took the lead as a social force in demanding the defeat of those domestic social forces they blamed for creating the inflationary pressures which undermined the value of their assets. The further growth of financial markets, increasingly characterized by competition, innovation and flexibility, was central to the resolution of the crisis of the 1970s. Perhaps the most important aspect of the new age of finance was the central role it played in disciplining and integrating labor. The industrial and political pressures from below that characterized the crisis of the 1970s could not have been countered and defeated without the discipline that a financial order built upon the mobility of

---

15 "A Socialist Alternative to Unemployment," *Canadian Dimension*, 20(1), March 1986.

capital placed upon firms. "Shareholder value" was, in many respects, a euphemism for how the discipline imposed by the competition for global investment funds was transferred to the high-wage proletariat of the advanced capitalist countries. New York and London's access to global savings simultaneously came to depend on the surplus extracted through the high rates of exploitation of the new working classes in "emerging markets." At the same time, the very constraints that the mobility of capital had on working-class incomes in the rich countries had the effect of further integrating these workers into the realm of finance. This was most obvious in terms of their increasing debt-loads amidst the universalization of the credit card. But it also pertained to how workers grew more attuned to financial markets, as they followed the stock exchanges and mutual funds in which their pension funds were invested, often cheered by rising stocks as firms were restructured without much thought to the lay-offs involved in this.

Both the explosion of finance and the disciplining of labor were necessary conditions for the dramatic productive transformations that took place in the "real economy" in this era. The leading role that finance came to play over the past quarter of a century, including the financialization of industrial corporations and the greatest growth in profits taking place in the financial sector, has often been viewed as undermining production and representing little else than speculation and a source of unsustainable bubbles. But this fails to account for why this era—a period that was longer than the "Golden Age"—lasted so long. It also ignores the fact that this has been a period of remarkable capitalist dynamism, involving the deepening and expansion of capital, capitalist social relations and capitalist culture in general, including significant technological revolutions. This was especially the case for the US itself, where financial competition, innovation, flexibility *and* volatility accompanied the reconstitution of the American material base at home and its expansion abroad. Overall, the era of finance-led neoliberalism experienced a rate of growth of global GDP that compares favorably with most earlier periods over the last two centuries.[16]

It is, in any case, impossible to imagine the globalization of production without the type of financial intermediation in the circuits of capital that provides the means for hedging the

---

16 A. Maddison, *The World Economy: A Millennial Perspective*, Paris: OECD, 2001, p. 265.

kinds of risks associated with flexible exchange rates, interest-rate variations across borders, uncertain transportation and commodity costs, and so on. Moreover, as competition for access to mobile finance intensified, this imposed discipline on firms (and states) which forced restructuring within firms and reallocated capital across sectors, including via the provision of venture capital to the new information and bio-medical sectors which have become leading arenas of accumulation. At the same time, the very investment banks that have been undone by the current crisis spread their tentacles abroad for three decades through their global role in M&A and IPO activity, during the course of which relationships between finance and production, including their legal and accounting frameworks, were radically changed around the world in ways that increasingly resembled American patterns. This was reinforced by the bilateral and multilateral international trade and investment treaties which were increasingly concerned with opening other societies up to New York's and London's financial, legal and accounting services.

THE AMERICAN STATE IN CRISIS

The era of neoliberalism has been one long history of financial volatility, with the American state leading the world's states in intervening in a series of financial crises. Almost as soon as he was appointed to succeed Volcker as head of the Fed, Greenspan immediately dropped buckets of liquidity on Wall Street in response to the 1987 Stock Market Crash. In the wake of the Savings and Loan Crisis, the public Resolution Trust Corporation was established to buy up bad real-estate debt (the model also used for bail-outs during the current Crisis). In Clinton's first term, Wall Street was saved from the consequences of bond defaults during the Mexican Financial Crisis in 1995 by Rubin's use of the Stabilization Exchange Fund (this Treasury kitty, established during the New Deal, has once again been called into service in today's Crisis). During the Asian Crisis two years later, Rubin and his Under-Secretary Summers flew to Seoul to dictate the terms of the IMF loan. And in 1998 (not long after the Japanese government nationalized one of the world's biggest banks), the head of the New York Federal Reserve summoned the CEOs of Wall Street's leading financial firms and told them they would not be allowed to leave the room (reminiscent of Morgan in 1907) until they agreed to take over the insolvent hedge fund Long-

Term Capital Management. These quick interventions by the Fed and Treasury, most of them without waiting upon Congressional pressures or approval, showed they were aware of the disastrous consequences which the failure to act quickly to contain each crisis could have both domestically and on the global financial system.

When the current Financial Crisis broke out in the summer of 2007, the newly appointed Chairman of the Fed, Ben Bernanke, could draw on his academic work as an economist at Princeton University on how the 1929 Crash could have been prevented,[17] and Treasury Secretary Henry Paulson could draw on his own illustrious career (like Rubin's) as a senior executive at Goldman Sachs. Both the Treasury and Federal Reserve staff worked closely with the Securities and Exchange Commission and Commodity Futures Trading Commission under the rubric of the President's Working Group on Financial Markets that had been set up in 1988, and known on Wall Street as the "Plunge Protection Team." Through the fall of 2007 and into 2008, the US Treasury would organize, first, a consortium of international banks and investment funds, and then an overlapping consortium of mortgage companies, financial securitizers and investment funds, to try to get them to take concrete measures to calm the markets. The Federal Reserve acted as the world's Central Bank by repeatedly supplying other central banks with dollars to provide liquidity to their banking systems, while doing the same for Wall Street. In March 2008 the Treasury—after guaranteeing JPMorgan Chase's takeover of Bear Stearns—issued its *Blueprint for a Modernized Financial Regulatory Structure* especially designed to extend the Fed's oversight powers over investment banks.

At this point, most analysts thought the worst was over, but by the summer of 2008, Fannie Mae and Freddie Mac, whose reserve requirements had been lowered in the previous years to a quarter of that of the banks, were also being undone by the crisis. And, by September, so were the great New York investment banks. The problem they all faced was that there was no market for a great proportion of the mortgage-backed assets on their books. When the subprime mortgage phenomenon was reaching its peak in 2005 Greenspan was claiming that "where once more-marginal applicants would simply have been denied credit, lenders are now able to quite efficiently judge the risk posed by individual

---

17   See B. Bernanke, *Essays on the Great Depression*, Princeton, NJ: Princeton University Press, 2000.

applicants and to price that risk appropriately."[18] But financial
capital's risk-evaluation equations unraveled in the Crisis. And
as they did, so did financial markets' ability to judge the worth of
financial institutions' balance sheets. Banks became very reluctant
to give each other even the shortest-term credits. Without
such interbank credit, any financial system will collapse. The
unprecedented scale of interventions in September 2008 can only
be understood in this context. They involved pumping additional
hundreds of billions of dollars into the world's interbank markets;
the nationalizations of Fannie Mae, Freddie Mac and AIG (the
world's largest insurance company); the seizure and fire sale of
Washington Mutual (to prevent the largest bank failure in US
history); a blanket guarantee on the $3.4 trillion in mutual funds
deposits; a ban on short-selling of financial stocks; *and* Paulson's
$700 billion TARP ("troubled asset relief program") bail-out to
take on toxic mortgage assets.

Amidst the transformation of New York's investment banks in
the course of a week through a dramatic series of bankruptcies and
takeovers, the Treasury undertook to buy virtually all the illiquid
assets on the balance sheets of financial institutions in the US,
including those of foreign-owned firms. We now know that Bernanke
had warned Paulson a year before that this might be necessary, and
Paulson had agreed: "I knew he was right theoretically," he said.
"But I also had, and we both did, some hope that, with all the
liquidity out there from investors, that after a certain decline that
we would reach a bottom."[19] Yet the private market has no secure
bottom without the state. The Fed and Treasury needed to act not
only as lender of last resort, but also, by taking responsibility for
buying and trying to sell all those securities that couldn't find a value
or market in the current Crisis, as *market maker of last resort.*[20]

Is it over? This is the question on most people's minds today.
But what does this question mean? The way this question is
posed, especially on the Left, usually conflates three distinct
questions. First, can the kind of firefighting that began with
the Paulson program, alongside Obama's fiscal stimulus, end
the Crisis? Second, does this Crisis, and both the state and the

18 Speech by Alan Greenspan at the Federal Reserve System's Fourth Annual
Community Affairs Research Conference, Washington, DC, April 8, 2005.
19 "A Professor and a Banker Bury Old Dogma on Markets," *New York Times,*
September 20, 2008.
20 W. Buiter, "The Fed as the Market Maker of Last Resort: better late than
never," *Financial Times,* March 12, 2008.

popular reaction to it, spell the end of neoliberalism? Third, are
we witnessing the end of US hegemony?

There is no way of knowing how far this most severe financial
crisis since the Great Depression might still have to go. On the one
hand, despite the condition of the (no longer) "Big Three" in the
US auto sector, the overall health of US non-financial corporations
going into the Crisis—as seen in their relatively strong profits,
cash flow and low debt—has been an important stabilizing factor,
not least in limiting the fall in the stock market. The growth of US
exports at close to double-digit levels annually over the past five
years reflects not only the decline in the dollar but the capacity of
American corporations to take advantage of this. That said, the
seizing up of interbank and commercial paper markets even after
Paulson's program was announced leaves big questions about
whether it will work. And even if it does, unwinding such a deep
financial *and* housing crisis is going to take a long time.

The immediate problem in this respect is where consumer
demand will come from. Credit is obviously going to be harder
to obtain, especially for low-income groups, and with the end of
housing-price inflation closing off the possibility of secondary
mortgages, and with the devaluation of pension assets and
company cutbacks of benefits, most workers will be not only
less able to spend, but also inclined to try to save rather than
spend. To the extent that a great deal of US consumption in the
neoliberal era was also spurred on by the enormous appetites of
the rich, this is obviously also going to now be restrained. Fiscal
stimulus programs are unlikely to be enough to compensate for
this, especially given the nervousness over the impact of the bail-
outs on the fiscal deficit, the size of the US public debt and the
value of the dollar, and hence over whether low interest rates
can be maintained. To the extent that global growth through the
neoliberal era was dependent on credit-based mass consumption
in the US, the impact of this being cut back will have global
implications, including on US exports. This is why the current
recession is likely to be deeper and longer than the last significant
one in the early 1990s, and maybe even than the severe recession
with which neoliberalism was launched in the early 1980s.

Yet, when it comes to the question of whether this Crisis
spells the end of neoliberalism, it is more important than ever
to distinguish between the understanding of neoliberalism as an
ideologically driven strategy to free markets from states on the
one hand, and on the other a materially driven form of social

rule which has involved the liberalization of markets through state intervention and management. While it will now be hard for politicians and even economists to uncritically defend free markets and further deregulation, it is not obvious that the essence of neoliberal ideology has been decisively undermined—as it was not by the Savings and Loan Crisis at the end of the 1980s, the Asian and LCTM Crises at the end of the 1990s, or after the dot-com bust, Enron and other scandals at the beginning of the century. On the more substantive definition of neoliberalism as a form of social rule, there clearly is going to be more regulation. But it is by no means yet clear how different it will be from the Sarbanes-Oxley type of corporate regulation passed at the beginning of the century to deal with "Enronitis."[21] Nevertheless, it is possible that a new form of social rule within capitalism may emerge to succeed neoliberalism. But given how far subordinate social forces need to go to reorganize effectively, it is most likely that the proximate alternatives to neoliberalism will either be a form of authoritarian capitalism or a new form of reformist social rule that would reflect only a minimal class realignment.

But whatever the answers to questions concerning the extent of the Crisis or the future of neoliberalism, this does not resolve the question of "Is it over?" as it pertains to the end of US hegemony. Just how deeply integrated global capitalism has become by the twenty-first century has been obvious from the way the Crisis in the heartland of empire has affected the rest of the globe, quickly putting facile notions of decoupling to rest. The financial ministries, central banks and regulatory bodies of the advanced capitalist states at the center of the system have cooperated very closely in the current Crisis. That said, the tensions that earlier existed in this decade over Iraq have obviously been brought back to mind by this Crisis. European criticisms of the Bush administration's inadequate supervision of finance, including that US leaders ignored their pleas for more regulation during the last G8 meetings, may seem hypocritical in light of how far they opened their economies to the Americanization of their financial systems, but they are nevertheless significant in terms of their expectation that the US play its imperial role in a less irresponsible or incompetent manner.

---

21 See S. Soederberg, "A Critique of the Diagnosis and Cure for 'Enronitis': The Sarbanes-Oxley Act and Neoliberal Governance of Coporate America," *Critical Sociology* 34(5), 2008.

This is reminiscent of the criticisms that were raised during the 1970s, which were an important factor in producing the policy turn in Washington that led to the Volcker Shock as the founding moment of neoliberalism. US hegemony was not really challenged then; the US was being asked to act responsibly to defeat inflation and validate the dollar as the global currency and thus live up to its role as global leader. With the economic integration and expansion of the EU and the emergence of the euro, many would like to think that Europe has the capacity to replace the US in this respect. But, as Peter Gowan insightfully put it:

> this is not realistic. Much of the European financial system is itself in a mess, having followed the Wall Street lead toward the cliff of insolvency. The Eurozone government bond markets remain fragmented and there is no cohesive financial or political direction for the Eurozone, leave alone a consensus for rebuilding the Eurozone as a challenger to the dollar through a political confrontation with the United States.[22]

If and when the Chinese state will develop such capacities to assume the mantle of hegemonic leadership of the capitalist world remains to be seen. But for the interim, a sober article in China's business newspaper, the *Oriental Morning Post*, reflects a better understanding of the real world than some of those amongst the Western Left who look to China as an alternative hegemon:

> Bad news keeps coming from Wall Street. Again, the decline of US hegemony became a hot topic of debate. Complaining or even cursing a world of hegemony brings excitement to us. However, faced with a decline of US hegemony, the power vacuum could also be painful. We do not like hegemony, but have we ever thought about this problem when we mocked its decline ... at present the world's financial system does not exist in isolation. It is the result of long-term historical evolution, closely associated with a country's strength, its openness, the development of globalization, and the existing global economic, political patterns. The relationship can be described as "the whole body moving when pulling one hair" ... The subprime crisis has affected many foreign enterprises, banks, and individuals which in itself is again a true portrayal of the power of the United States ... Therefore, the world's problems are not merely whether or not the United States are declining, but whether any other country, including those seemingly solid allies of the United States, will help bear the load the US would lighten.[23]

---

22 P. Gowan, in this volume, Chapter 3.
23 D. Gang, "Who Is to Carry the Burden of the US?" (translated by Warren Wang), *Oriental Morning Post*, September 19, 2008.

For the time being, what is clear is that no other state in the world—not only today, but perhaps ever—could have experienced such a profound financial crisis, and such an enormous increase in the public debt without an immediate outflow of capital, a run on its currency and the collapse of its stock market. That this has not happened reflects the widespread appreciation amongst capitalists that they sink or swim with Wall Street and Washington. But it also reflects the continuing material underpinnings of the empire. Those who dwell on the fact that the American share of global GDP has been halved since the Second World War not only underplay the continuing global weight of the American economy in the world economy, but (much like American policy-makers at the time) fail to understand that the diffusion of capitalism was an essential condition for the health of the American economy itself. Had the US tried to hold on to its post-war share of global GNP, this would have stopped capitalism's globalizing tendencies in its tracks. This remains the case today. Not only is the US economy still the largest by far, it also hosts the most important new high-tech arenas of capital accumulation, and leads the world by far in research and development, while American multinational corporations directly and indirectly account for a large proportion of worldwide employment, production and trade.

Moreover, in spite of the New York investment banks having come undone in this Crisis, the functions of American investment banking are going to continue. Philip Augar (the author of the perceptive inside account of the investment banking industry, *The Greed Merchants*), while affirming that "the eight days between Sunday September 14 and Sunday September 21, 2008 [were] part of the most catastrophic shift among investment banks since the event that created them, the Glass Steagall Act of 1933," goes on to argue that

> it is likely that investment banks will exist as recognisable entities within their new organisations and investment banking as an industry will emerge with enhanced validity . . . While they are licking their wounds, the investment banks may well eschew some of the more esoteric structured finance products that have caused them such problems and refocus on what they used to regard as their core business. While we may have seen the death of the investment bank I would be very surprised if we have seen the death of investment banking as an industry.[24]

---

24 P. Augar, "Do not exaggerate investment banking's death," *Financial Times*, September 22, 2008. See also *The Greed Merchants: How the Investment Banks Played the Free Market Game*, London: Penguin, 2006.

Indeed, the financial restructuring and re-regulation that is already going on as a result of the Crisis is in good part a matter of establishing the institutional conditions for this, above all through the further concentration of financial capital via completing the integration of commercial and investment banking. The repeal of Glass-Steagall at the end of the last century was more a recognition of how far this had already gone than an initiation of it; and the Treasury's *Blueprint for a Modernized Financial Regulatory Structure*, announced in March 2008 but two years in preparation, was designed to create the regulatory framework for seeing that integration through. There is no little irony in the fact that, whereas the crisis of the 1930s led to the distancing of investment banking from access to common bank deposits, the long-term solutions being advanced to the insolvencies of investment bankers today is to give them exactly this access.

It Ain't Over Until It's Made Over

The massive outrage over the Wall Street bail-outs is rooted in a tradition of populist resentment against New York bankers which has persisted alongside the ever increasing integration of the "common man" into capitalist financial relationships. American political and economic elites have had to accommodate to—and at the same time overcome—this populist political culture. This could be seen at work in September 2008 when Henry Paulson declared before the House Financial Services Committee, as he tried to get his TARP plan through Congress, that "the American people are angry about executive compensation and rightfully so."[25] This was rather rich given that he had been Wall Street's highest-paid CEO, receiving $38.3 million in salary, stock and options in the year before joining the Treasury, plus a mid-year $18.7 million bonus on his departure, as well as an estimated $200 million tax break against the sale of his almost $500 million share holding in Goldman Sachs (as was required to avoid conflict of interest in his new job).[26] The accommodation to the culture of populism was also seen at work in both McCain's and Obama's campaign rhetoric against greed and speculation, while Wall Street

25 "Paulson Gives Way on CEO Pay," *New York Times*, September 24, 2008.
26 "Wall Street Man," *Guardian*, September 26, 2008.

investment banks were among their largest campaign contributors and supplied some of their key advisers.

This should not be reduced to hypocrisy. In the absence of a traditional bureaucracy in the American state, leading corporate lawyers and financiers have moved between Wall Street and Washington ever since the age of the "robber barons" in the late ninteenth century. Taking time off from the private firm to engage in public service has been called the "institutional schizophrenia" that links these Wall Street figures as "double agents" to the state. While acting in one sphere to squeeze through every regulatory loophole, they act in the other to introduce new regulations as "a tool for the efficient management of the social order in the public interest."[27] It is partly for this reason that the long history of popular protest and discontent triggered by financial scandals and crises in the US, far from undermining the institutional and regulatory basis of financial expansion, has repeatedly been pacified through processes of further "codification, institutionalization and juridification."[28] And, far from buckling under the pressure of popular disapproval, financial elites have proved very adept at not only responding to these pressures but also using them to create new regulatory frameworks that have laid the foundations for the further growth of financial capital as a class fraction and as a lucrative business.

This is not a matter of simple manipulation of the masses. Most people have a (however contradictory) interest in the daily functioning and reproduction of financial capitalism because of their current dependence on it: from access to their wages and salaries via their bank accounts, to buying goods and services on credit, to paying their bills, to realizing their savings—and even to keeping the roofs over their heads. This is why, in acknowledging before the Congressional hearings on his TARP plan to save the Financial System that Wall Street's exorbitant compensation schemes are "a serious problem," Paulson also appealed to people's sense of their own immediate interests when he added that "we must find a way to address this in legislation *without undermining the effectiveness of the program.*"[29] Significantly, both the criticisms

27 R. G. Gordon, "'The Ideal and the Actual in the Law': Fantasies and Practices of New York City Lawyers, 1870–1910," in G. W. Gawalt, ed., *The New High Priests: Lawyers in Post-Civil War America*, Westport, CT: Greenwood Press, 1984, esp. pp. 53, 58, 65–6.
28 Moran, *Politics of the Financial Services Revolution*, p. 13.
29 "Paulson Gives Way on CEO Pay," *New York Times*, September 24, 2008; italics added.

and the reform proposals now coming from outside the Wall Street-Washington elite reflect this contradiction. The attacks on the Fed's irresponsibility in allowing subprime mortgages to flourish pose the question of what should have been said to those who wanted access to the homeownership dream given that the possibility of adequate public housing was (and remains) nowhere on the political agenda. No less problematic, especially in terms of the kind of funding that would be required for this, is the opposition to Paulson's TARP program in terms of protecting the taxpayer, presented in a pervasive populist language with neoliberal overtones. It was this definition of the problem in the wake of Enron's collapse that led to the shaming and convictions of the usual suspects, while Bush and Republican congressmen were elected and re-elected.

At the same time, many of the criticisms and proposed reforms today display an astonishing naiveté about the systemic nature of the relationship between state and capital. This was seen when an otherwise excellent and informative article in the *New Labor Forum* founded its case for reform on the claim that "Government is necessary to make business act responsibly. Without it, capitalism becomes anarchy. In the case of the financial industry, government failed to do its job, for two reasons—ideology and influence-peddling."[30] It is this perspective that also perhaps explains why most of the reform proposals being advanced are so modest, in spite of the extent of the Crisis and the popular outrage. This is exemplified by those proposals advanced by one of the US Left's leading analysts of financial markets:

> The first target for reform should be the outrageous salaries drawn by the top executives at financial firms . . . While we don't want a chain reaction of banking collapses on Wall Street, the public should get something in exchange for Bernanke's generosity. Specifically, he can demand a cap on executive compensation (all compensation) of $2 million a year, in exchange for getting bailed out . . . The financial sector performs an incredibly important function in allocating savings to those who want to invest in businesses, buy homes or borrow money for other purposes . . . The best way to bring the sector into line is with a modest financial transactions tax [on] options, futures, credit default swaps, etc . . .[31]

30 J. Atlas, P. Dreier and G. Squires, "Foreclosing on the Free Market: How to Remedy the Subprime Catastrophe," *New Labour Forum*, Fall 2008.
31 D. Baker, "Big Banks Go Bust: Time to Reform Wall Street," *truthout*, September 15, 2008, available at http://www.truthout.org.

This is a perfect example of thinking inside the box: explicitly endorsing two-million-dollar salaries and the practices of deriving state revenues from the very things that are identified as the problem. Indeed, even proposals for stringent regulations to prohibit financial imprudence mostly fail to identify the problem as systemic within capitalism. At best, the problem is reduced to the system of neoliberal *thought*, as though it was nothing but Hayek or Friedman, rather than a long history of contradictory, uneven and contested capitalist development that led the world to twenty-first-century Wall Street.

The scale of the Crisis and the popular outrage today provide a historic opening for a renewal of the kind of radical politics that advances a systemic alternative to capitalism. It would be a tragedy if a far more ambitious goal than making financial capital more prudent did not now come back on the agenda. In terms of immediate reforms and the mobilizations needed to win them—and given that we are in a situation when public debt is the only safe debt—this should start with demands for vast programs to provide for collective services and infrastructures that not only compensate for those that have atrophied but meet new definitions of basic human needs and come to terms with contemporary ecological challenges.

Such reforms would soon come up against the limits posed by the reproduction of capitalism. This is why it is so important to raise not merely the regulation of finance but the transformation and democratization of the whole system. This would have to involve not only capital controls in relation to international finance but also controls over domestic investment, since the point of taking control over finance is to transform the uses to which it is now put. It would also require much more than this in terms of the democratization of both the broader economy and the state. It is highly significant that the last time nationalization of the financial system was seriously raised, at least in the advanced capitalist countries, was in response to the 1970s crisis by those elements on the Left who recognized that the only way to overcome the contradictions of the Keynesian welfare state in a positive manner was to take the financial system into public control.[32] Their proposals were derided as Neanderthal not only by neoliberals but also by social democrats.

---

32   The best popularly written example of this, and still worth reading today, is R. Minns, *Take Over the City: The Case for Public Ownership of Financial Institutions*, London: Pluto, 1982.

We are still paying for their defeat. It is now necessary to build on their proposals and make them relevant in the current conjuncture. Of course, without rebuilding popular class forces through new movements and parties this will fall on empty ground. Crucial to this rebuilding is to get people to think ambitiously again. However deep the Crisis and however widespread the outrage, this will require hard and committed work by a great many activists. The type of facile analysis that focuses on "it's all over"—whether in terms of the end of neoliberalism, the decline of the American empire, or even the next great crisis of capitalism—is not much use here insofar as it is offered without any clear socialist strategic implications. It ain't over till it's made over.

CONTRIBUTORS

Stanley Aronowitz is Distinguished Professor of Sociology and Urban Education at the Graduate Center of the City University of New York. His publications include *False Promises: The Shaping of American Working Class Consciousness* (Duke University Press, 1991) and *Left Turn: Forging a New Political Future* (Paradigm, 2006).

Walden Bello is a member of the Philippine House of Representatives, president of the Freedom from Debt Coalition, and senior analyst of the Bangkok-based Focus on the Global South. He is the author of numerous articles and fifteen books, the latest of which are *The Food Wars* (Verso, 2009), *Walden Bello Introduces Ho Chi Minh* (Verso, 2007), and *Dilemmas of Domination* (Henry Holt, 2005).

Dick Bryan is Professor in the Department of Political Economy at the University of Sydney. His publications include *The Chase Across the Globe* (HarperCollins, 1995), *The Global Economy in Australia* (Allen & Unwin, 1999, with Michael Rafferty) and *Capitalism With Derivatives* (Palgrave Macmillan, 2006, with Michael Rafferty).

Gary Dymski is Professor of Economics at the University of California, Riverside and Director of the University of California Center, Sacramento. His publications include *The Bank Merger Wave: The Economic Causes and Social Consequences of*

Financial Consolidation in the United States (M. E. Sharpe, Inc., 1999) and *Transforming the US Financial System: An Equitable and Efficient Structure for the 21st Century* (M. E. Sharpe, Inc., 1993, co-edited with Gerald Epstein and Robert Pollin).

Thomas Ferguson is Professor of Political Science at the University of Massachusetts, Boston. He is the author of *Golden Rule: The Investment Theory of Party Competition and the Logic of Money-Driven Political Systems* (University of Chicago Press, 1995).

Steve Fraser is a Visiting Professor at New York University. He is the author of *Every Man a Speculator: A History of Wall Street in American Life* (Harper Perennial, 2006) and *Wall Street: America's Dream Palace* (Yale University Press, 2009).

Sam Gindin was for many years Research Director of the Canadian Auto Workers Union and currently holds the Packer Chair in Social Justice at York University, Toronto. He is the author of *The Canadian Autoworkers: The Birth and Transformation of a Union* (Lorimer, 1995) and *Global Capitalism and American Empire* (Merlin, 2004, with Leo Panitch).

Peter Gowan was Professor of International Relations at London Metropolitan University. He was the author of *The Global Gamble* (Verso, 1999) and a frequent contributor to *New Left Review*.

William Greider is the National Affairs correspondent for *The Nation*. His books include *Secrets of the Temple: How the Federal Reserve Runs the Country* (Simon & Schuster, 1987) and *Come Home, America: The Rise and Fall (and Redeeming Promise) of Our Country* (Rodale, 2009).

Michael Hudson is Distinguished Research Professor at the University of Missouri, Kansas City (UMKC), and was also Director of Economic Research at the Riga Graduate School of Law in 2006. A former bank economist, he has advised governments around the world, and the United Nations. His publications include *Super Imperialism: The Origin and Fundamentals of US World Dominance* (second edn, Pluto, 2003) and *Global Fracture: The New International Economic Order* (second edn, University of Michigan Press, 2005).

Robert Johnson was formerly Managing Director at Soros Funds Management and Chief Economist of the United States Senate Banking Committee.

Martijn Konings is a Lecturer in the Department of Political Economy at the University of Sydney.

James Livingston is Professor of History at Rutgers University. He is the author of *Origins of the Federal Reserve System: Money, Class, and Corporate Capitalism, 1890–1913* (Cornell University Press, 1986), *Pragmatism and the Political Economy of Cultural Revolution, 1850–1940* (University of North Carolina Press, 1994) and *Pragmatism, Feminism, and Democracy: Rethinking the Politics of American History* (Routledge, 2001).

Scott MacWilliam is a Lecturer at the Crawford School of Economics and Government at the Australian National University.

Johnna Montgomerie is a Research Fellow at the Centre for Research on Socio-Cultural Change at the University of Manchester.

Anastasia Nesvetailova is Senior Lecturer in the Department of International Politics, City University, London. She is the author of *Fragile Finance: Debt, Speculation and Crisis in the Age of Global Credit* (Palgrave Macmillan, 2007).

Ronen Palan is Professor of International Political Economy in the Department of Politics and International Relations at the University of Birmingham. He is the author of *The Offshore World: Sovereign Markets, Virtual Places, and Nomad Millionaires* (Cornell University Press, 2003) and *The Imagined Economies of Globalisation* (Sage, 2004, with Angus Cameron).

Leo Panitch is Distinguished Research Professor of Political Science and Canada Research Chair in Comparative Political Economy at York University, Toronto. His publications include *Working Class Politics in Crisis* (Verso, 1986), *The End of Parliamentary Socialism* (Verso, 1997, with Colin Leys), *Renewing Socialism* (Westview, 2001), *Global Capitalism and American Empire* (Merlin, 2004, with Sam Gindin) and *American Empire and the Political Economy of Global Finance* (Palgrave, 2008, co-edited with Martijn Konings). He is the Editor of *Socialist Register*.

Michael Rafferty is a Senior Research Analyst at the Workplace Research Centre of the University of Sydney. His publications include *The Global Economy in Australia* (Allen & Unwin, 1999, with Dick Bryan) and *Capitalism With Derivatives* (Palgrave Macmillan, 2006, with Dick Bryan).

Herman Schwartz is Professor of Political Science at the University of Virginia. His publications include *States versus Markets* (Palgrave, 2000) and *Subprime Nation: American Power, Global Finance and the Housing Bubble* (Cornell University Press, 2009).

Susanne Soederberg is Associate Professor and Canada Research Chair in the Department of Global Development Studies at Queen's University. Her publications include *Corporations, Power and Ownership in Contemporary Capitalism: The Politics of Governance, Activism, and Social Responsibility* (Routledge, 2009), *Global Governance in Question: Empire, Class, and the New Common Sense in Managing North-South Relations* (Pluto Press, 2006) and *The Politics of the New International Financial Architecture: Reimposing Neoliberal Dominance in the Global South* (Zed Books/Palgrave, 2004.)

Jeffrey Sommers is a visiting faculty member at the Stockholm School of Economics in Riga and Associate Professor at Raritan Valley College.

Henry Veltmeyer is Professor of Sociology at Saint Mary's University. His publications include *Globalization Unmasked: Imperialism in the 21st Century* (Zed Books, 1991, with James Petras), *A System in Crisis: The Dynamics of Free Market Capitalism* (Zed, 2004, with James Petras) and *On the Move: The Politics of Social Change in Latin America* (Broadview, 2007).